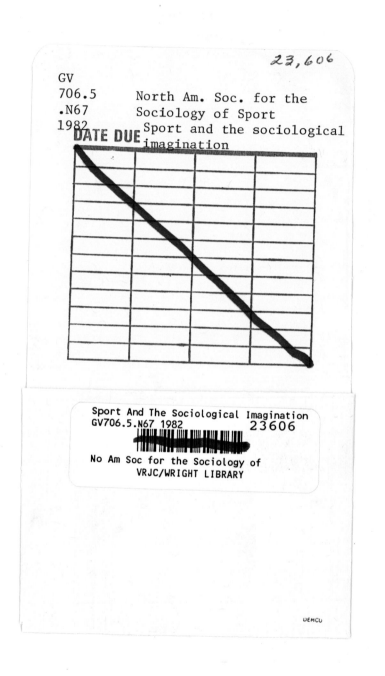

SPORT
AND THE
SOCIOLOGICAL IMAGINATION

SPORT

AND THE
SOCIOLOGICAL
IMAGINATION

Edited by
Nancy Theberge and Peter Donnelly

Refereed Proceedings of the
3rd Annual Conference of the
North American Society for the Sociology of Sport
Toronto, Ontario, Canada, November 1982

TEXAS CHRISTIAN UNIVERSITY PRESS
FORT WORTH

North American Society for the Sociology of Sport.
   Conference (3rd : 1982 : Toronto, Ont.)
   Sport and the sociological imagination.

   Includes bibliographical references.
   1. Sports—Social aspects—Congresses. I. Theberge,
Nancy. II. Donnelly, Peter.
GV706.5.N67 1982   306'.483   83-18123
   ISBN 0-912646-83-7

Cover photograh by Susan Camp, courtesy of The University of Texas
Intercollegiate Athletics for Women.

CONTENTS

SPORT
AND THE
SOCIOLOGICAL IMAGINATION

INTRODUCTION

SPORT AND THE SOCIOLOGICAL IMAGINATION

IN SELECTING THE THEME of "Sport and the Sociological Imagination" for the 1982 NASSS Conference, conference organizers were acknowledging the legacy of C. Wright Mills to sociology and, by extension, to the sociology of sport. The *Sociological Imagination* was perhaps Mills' most celebrated work. In that volume, he outlined his vision of the promise of sociology. That promise "enables us to grasp history and biography and the relations between the two within society." It enables men and women to understand the course of their lives in terms of the broader social structural forces that define and shape the world around them.

In Mills' view, the realization of the promise of the sociological imagination is the mark of the "classic social analyst." He was disturbed by the abdication of the classical tradition in sociology and its replacement by the "habitual distortions" of the tradition prominent in the field in the 1950's. Foremost among these distortions were the tendencies toward "grand theorizing" and "abstracted empiricism." Mills argued that these tendencies diverted sociologists from the promise of the sociological imagination. He exhorted his colleagues to turn away from these practices and devote their energies to examining the significant public issues of their time.

The *Sociological Imagination* rekindled concern in sociology over the cultural and political role of the social scientist. From Marx and Weber to Lynd, Myrdal, Gouldner and others, we have periodically been reminded in forceful terms of the moral dimensions of our work and our responsibility to address the major issues of our time—to be *engaged*. Indeed, one of the enduring features of the sociological enterprise has been periodic reflection upon the proper role of the social scientist in public affairs.

Concern over this issue has also played a prominent role in the sociology of sport. Prompted largely by early writings by Kenyon and Loy,[1] debate about the political dimensions of this emerging field was a significant feature of the literature from the mid-1960's through the 1970's.[2] Unfortunately, this discussion was sometimes marred by inconsistent interpretations of the meanings of 'objectivity,' 'value-neutrality' and 'value-relevance'—concepts which lie at the heart of any analysis of the union of science and politics. Nevertheless, the debate served to force writers and researchers in the field to examine and evaluate the political and social dimensions of their work. The debate prompted many to reflect upon the promise of the sociological imagination as it applies to the sociology of sport.

In the past few years, literature in the sociology of sport has been marked by less introspection and self-analysis. There has also been some movement toward realization of the vision of the sociological imagination that Mills held. That is, while literature in the field remains extremely varied in both substance and quality, there is clear evidence of a growing understanding and appreciation of Mills' conception of the challenge of sociology.

The goal of conference organizers was to assemble a program that reflects this developing maturity. The pieces contained in this volume are a selection of those presented at the conference. The manner in which the volume's contents reflect the theme of "Sport and the Sociological Imagination" is varied. In some cases, selections are concerned with explaining the meaning and relevance of the sociological imagination to the sociology of sport. More often, the theme is illustrated by the authors' choice of topics or theoretical and methodological orientations. We believe that this selection of articles clearly indicates the promise of the sociological imagination in the sociology of sport.

Several persons have helped us to assemble these proceedings. We would like to thank Rhonda Love and Rob Beamish for advice on the volume's contents, Barb Brown and Rena Theberge for editorial assistance, and Ruth Gooding for secretarial and administrative assistance. A special word of thanks goes to Andy Miracle and Roger Rees for his support for our work and for serving as our liaison with Texas Christian University Press.

NOTES

1. Their writings on this topic include Kenyon and Loy (1965); Kenyon (1969) and Loy and Kenyon (1969).
2. Among the contributions to the debate are Hoch (1972); Melnick (1975); Gruneau (1976, 1978); Ingham (1979); and Beamish (1981).

REFERENCES

Beamish, Rob
1981 "The Materialist Approach to Sport Sociology: An Alternative Prescription to the Discipline's Methodological Malaise." Quest, 33(1):55-71.
Gruneau, Richard
1976 "Sport as an Area of Sociological Study: An Introduction to Major Themes and Perspectives" In Richard S. Gruneau and John G. Albinson (eds.), Canadian Sport: Sociological Perspectives. Don Mills: Addison-Wesley.
1978 "Conflicting Standards and Problems of Personal Action in the Sociology of Sport." Quest, 30:80-90.
Hoch, Paul
1972 Rip Off the Big Game. New York: Doubleday.
Ingham, Alan
1979 "Methodology in the Sociology of Sport: From Symptoms of Malaise to Weber for a Cure." Quest, 31:187-215.
Kenyon, Gerald S.
1969 "A Sociology of Sport: On Becoming a Subdiscipline" In Roscoe C. Brown and Bryant J. Cratty (eds.), New Perspectives of Man in Action. Englewood Cliffs, New Jersey: Prentice Hall.
Kenyon, Gerald S. and John W. Loy
1965 "Toward a Sociology of Sport." Journal of Health, Physical Education and Recreation, 36:24-25, 68-69.
Loy, John W. and Gerald S. Kenyon
1969 "Frames of Reference." Introduction to Part 2 in John W. Loy and Gerald S. Kenyon (eds.), Sport, Culture and Society. New York: Macmillan.
Melnick, Merrill
1975 "A Critical Look at the Sociology of Sport." Quest, 24:34-47.

SECTION I
SOCIOLOGY, SPORT
AND POPULAR LITERATURE

ONE OF THE MAIN CHALLENGES posed in the *Sociological Imagination* concerns the range and scope of sociological analysis. Mills wrote that when properly practiced, social science is a craft. The practice of that craft requires creativity and a commitment to stretching our visions—and imaginations—in order to gather observations about the social world. The essays in this section demonstrate the rich analytical possibilities presented by data that are unconventional by the standards of "bureaucratic social science." These data are the contents of literature, both fiction and non-fiction. While the literary works discussed by Allen Guttmann, Alan Tomlinson and Robert Hollands are diverse, their articles share a common concern with explicating the meaning of the sociological imagination through the analysis of cultural forms.

Guttmann's "The Sociological Imagination and the Imaginative Sociologist" was presented as the keynote address to the conference. In this piece, Guttmann offers his own interpretation of the meaning of imagination as the capacity to understand "otherness" or "to adopt another person's perspective." Noting a general absence of concern for otherness in North American sport sociology, he offers some suggestions as to how this quality may better be realized. Guttmann urges his audience to pay greater attention to European sport sociology (particularly to the French and German Marxists and neo-Marxists), to sport history, and to the appearance of sport as a theme in literature. He argues that greater attention to work in each of these areas is needed to broaden the scope and imagination of the sociology of sport and enable a fuller appreciation of the quality of otherness.

Of these three suggestions, Guttmann devotes most extensive discussion to sport as a theme in literature. To illustrate his argument of the relevance of literature to sociological analysis, he pro-

1

vides a review and discussion of Ernest Hemingway's *The Sun Also Rises*. Guttmann shows how Hemingway used sport as a means of characterization and dramatization of important social forms and processes. Sport, Guttmann shows, is much more than a setting for the novel's development; it is a means by which we can explore the quality of otherness.

Tomlinson's article is concerned with illustrating the scope of the sociological imagination. After citing several examples of its development beyond academic sociology, Tomlinson turns to an analysis of the relevance to the sociological imagination of the genre of writing which has come to be called the "New Journalism." Illustrated by the work of Norman Mailer, Gay Talese and Hunter S. Thompson, the new journalism is characterized by an emphasis on probing and identifying the connections between events and the cultural and political contexts in which they occur. Many examples of the new journalism are related to sport; Tomlinson shows how the insights offered by some of these writings display a sensitive appreciation of the sociological imagination.

The final piece in this section is Hollands' analysis of images of women in Canadian sports novels. The article begins with a discussion of similarities between Marxist and feminist literary criticism. Recognizing the continuing debates within and between Marxism and feminism, Hollands argues that there is nevertheless the "possibility of compromise between these two perspectives." With respect to literary criticism, this possibility arises from the emphasis common to both perspectives on locating critiques of cultural forms within the context of social structure and forms of domination in society. Hollands demonstrates his argument that Marxist and feminist literary criticism may profitably be joined through the analysis of the characterization of women in three novels that center on sport. His review indicates how the portrayal and development of women characters is a manifestation and product of women's subordination under capitalist patriarchy. More generally, Hollands shows how the critical analysis of cultural production can provide important insights into the nature and form of power relations.

Because of both its focus on literary analysis and its relationship to the discussions provided by Guttmann and Tomlinson, Hollands' article is included in this introductory section on Sociology, Sport and Popular Literature. It could as well, however, be included in the next section on Feminist Analysis and the Study of Gender in Sport. Hollands' discussion of the possibility of compromise between Marxism and feminism and his illustrations of how such a compromise might provide the theoretical basis for an investigation of cultural forms provide a bridge to the contents of the second section of the volume. In that section, the debate between Marxism and feminism, as well as other issues central to the understanding of gender inequality under capitalism, are developed more fully.

THE SOCIOLOGICAL IMAGINATION AND THE IMAGINATIVE SOCIOLOGIST

Allen Guttmann, Amherst College

THE PHRASE, "THE SOCIOLOGICAL IMAGINATION," was popularized if not invented by C. Wright Mills. By it, Mills meant that faculty which "enables us to grasp history and biography and the relations between the two within society." The sociological imagination enables its possessor to understand that private troubles are related to public issues. Mills did not dwell on the word "imagination," but literary scholars of his generation seized upon the term and used it as the key to literary studies. The word itself goes back, in the English language, to the 14th century, but its importance as a philosophical category dates from the Romantic period, when Samuel Taylor Coleridge suddenly announced, in his *Biographia Literaria*, that the human imagination was an almost divinely creative faculty. It was, in Coleridge's own charged poetic language, "the Living Power and prime Agent of all human Perception. . . ." It is the faculty, said Coleridge, which enabled Shakespeare to create the countless, amazingly various characters who people his works. The imagination, in this Romantic sense of the concept, enables all of us, and not just the great poets, to understand otherness, or, in the homely verse of Robert Burns, "to see ourselves as others see us." The imagination is the equivalent of a transformational framework which suddenly, almost magically, puts us in a position to see things from a new perspective, to see the world and even ourselves as others see us.

Whether or not this particular conception of the term "imagination" is what Mills had in mind, I don't know, but I am convinced that imagination in this precise sense—the ability to understand otherness, to adopt another person's perceptions—is enormously important to any sociologist who wants to move beyond what Mills rather acidly referred to as "abstracted empiricism." To see our apparently private selves as members of a social system is, *ipso facto*, to begin to imagine ourselves as the other, which is part of what George Herbert Mead meant in *Mind, Self, and Society*.

But how does one do it? How does the imaginative sociologist become imaginative? How, in Alvin Gouldner's terms, do we learn to practice reflexive sociology? There's obviously no easy answer, but I have some practical suggestions about what to do. I can recommend certain operations which give practice in that strange feat of intellectual acrobatics, getting out of ourselves. In fact, there are three kinds of investigation that sport sociologists should undertake more often than they now do. They should pay serious attention to European sport sociology, to sport history, and to the appearance of sport as a theme in literature. I acknowledge immediately that I have just urged sport sociologists to become more like me, which is what most pedagogues do most of the time. I acknowledge also that most sport sociologists presently do things—especially with numbers—that I should do more of. I acknowledge finally, that some enlightened scholars already do things I urge them to do. It is they, doubtless, who will be most receptive to my argument while the abstracted empiricists continue to revel in the possibilities of SPSS.

Cross-cultural work has been done and is undoubtedly underway. There are, for instance, studies of the amount of time spent on physical activity in various countries. There are, almost routinely, comparative sections in anthologies—James Riordan on the Soviet Union, Clifford Geertz on Bali. But I have in mind something more intense. I have in mind not merely the examination of data gathered from other cultures but also the serious consideration of social theory developed by European and other foreign sport sociologists. I trust that no one who pretends to be serious about the larger discipline of sociology can shirk an intellectual encounter—what the Germans call an *"Auseinandersetzung"*—with the works of Tocqueville, Marx, Durkheim, Weber, Simmel, Mannheim, Freud. I contend that the subdiscipline of sport sociology has had its founders too and that few American sport sociologists have taken the trouble to confront their theories. Heinz Risse, Michel Bouet, and Bero Rigauer are scarcely known in North America. Of course, language is a problem, but it is not enough to hope that European *magna opera* will be translated. Waiting for translations is like having your scholarly journals lost in the mail or delivered ten years late.

I offer an example of the importance of European theory. The criticism of North American sport from a Marxist or neo-Marxist perspective has been seriously weakened by the refusal, or the inability, of most American and Canadian sport scholars to make use of the intricate and profound analyses of French and German neo-Marxists. If my own work has any special merit, it is in large part the result of my efforts to understand and to answer the criticisms that I encountered in Bero Rigauer's *Sport und Arbeit* and in other neo-Marxist critiques which extended, deepened, modified, and—sometimes—vulgarized his argument about the structural identities of modern sport and modern industrial labor. Rigauer and others of his persuasion made me realize how superficial are the usual criticisms of racism and sexism in North American sport. Admittedly, racism and sexism are at odds with the ethos of modern sport, but most North American critics assume that sport is a goal from which blacks and women should not be excluded. French and German theorists made me aware of assumptions which even the critics of North American sport have internalized. I am not maintaining that European theorists are superior to North American theorists, but I do insist that their perspectives are different from ours. They represent an otherness which can stimulate and enlarge our sociological imaginations. I do not think I could have written *From Ritual to Record* if I had not been excited, provoked, fascinated, and annoyed by European theorists.

Since I have saddled up one of my hobby-horses, I shall gallop a bit further. If cross-cultural analysis is truly to be fruitful, it must be what it was when Talcott Parsons actually went to Heidelberg to study German sociology *in situ*. It has to be an interaction that includes familiarity not only with major works but also with monographs, articles, reviews. Ideally, it should involve debates, conversations, and letters as well. I recognize that all this costs time and money, but the distributing of questionnaires, the conducting of interviews, the processing of computerized data are also expensive propositions. It is a question of marginal utility. The next step in factor analysis may bring one less than the intellectual gains of a semester devoted to contemporary German *Sportwissenschaft*. Or to sport history.

If my admittedly less than perfectly informed perceptions are correct, sport sociology shares with the larger discipline of sociology a regrettable tendency to ignore the possibilities of historical scholarship. To the degree that contemporary sociologists fail to work diachronically, they turn their backs on the founders of modern sociology. Tocqueville wrote on the *ancien regime* as well as on democracy in America. Marx studied Greek philosophy before he turned his attention to 19th-century Manchester's dark Satanic mills. Weber's detailed historical discussions of Confucianism, Taoism, Hinduism, Buddhism, Judaism, Christianity, and Islam testify to his readiness to devote not months but years, perhaps decades, to the study of history in order to formulate his famous theses about the gamut of possible relationships between the spiritual and the material, between religious tradition and capitalist development. It is not simply that such men knew what was once called "universal history"; it is also that they sought to locate the values and the institutions of the modern world within a historical process. They were historical sociologists; they were sociological historians. While C. Wright Mills and Alvin Gouldner may not belong in the exalted company of Marx and Weber, they have both called for a greater attention to historical studies and have both attempted in their praxis to account for historical developments.

I see very little concern for the otherness of the past in the published work of North American sport sociologists. And I have seen occasional remarks, which I will not cite, that indicate a sense of the past so enfeebled that Hammurabi, Hannibal, and Herbert Hoover appear almost as contemporaries.

I can most readily illustrate the uses of history by immodest comments on my own past and present research. About ten years ago, I decided that someone ought to investigate the differences between European and American sport. I was at that time struck by the fact that German spectators are very nearly insane about soccer while Americans prefer to become hysterical about football, baseball, basketball, or hockey. I began with the assumption that cross-cultural differences are the significant ones and I read sport psychology on the psychological correlates of sport preferences. Are soccer players psychologically different from football players? Are runners different from swimmers?

I discovered that the psychologists are in a state of near despair because their primary instruments—personality tests—have produced a chaos of contradictory results. It did, however, seem clear that a preference for individual sport implies a somewhat different personality structure than does a preference for team sport and that Americans are more likely than Europeans to prefer team sport. By the time I came to that conclusion, however, I had arrived at other conclusions which still strike me as considerably more important, namely, that chronological differences within Western ludic culture are far more significant than the differences between Europe and North America. Within western civilization, the historical factor outweighs the geographical one.

Coming to the conclusion that all modern sports are fundamentally similar in that they share what I have asserted are the universal characteristics of modern sport, I realized that some of these characteristics are uniquely modern. I was especially struck by the importance of quantification and the search for records, two characteristics which, if not uniquely modern, are at the very least emphasized in modern sport to a degree unknown even in Roman times. I doubt if I would have been so struck by this realization if I had not learned that the ancient Greeks were almost completely uninterested in quantification and lacked even the words to express what we mean by setting a record. For the Greeks who celebrated the sacred games at Olympia, Delphi, Corinth, and Nemea, victory was the goal. The dimensions of the victory were unimportant. Obsessed with the desire to be first, they never bothered with the numbers. They never compared the length of the leap at Olympia with that at Delphi, a task which would have been especially difficult since the Olympic foot differed from the Delphic foot. In fact, they never bothered to compare the victor's leap at one Olympiad with that of his predecessors or successors at prior or subsequent Olympiads. Although the failure to measure times may be attributed to the absence of accurate chronometers, the failure to measure distances cannot be explained by technological factors. The Greeks were perfectly well able to measure the distances if they had wanted to. But they didn't want to. For them, "man was the measure of all things," and not the object of endless measurements.

Given their lack of interest in quantified results, they were ill-equipped to invent the concept of the record. In *From Ritual to Record*, I attempted to describe the uniqueness of this concept: "What is a record in our modern sense? It is the marvelous abstraction that permits competition not only among those gathered together on the field of sport but also among them and others distant in time and space. Through the strange abstraction of the quantified record, the Australian can compete with the Finn who died a decade before the Australian was born. The record becomes a psychological presence in the mind of everyone involved with the event, as it was at Iffley Road Track in 1954 when

Roger Bannister ran the first four-minute mile. The record is a number in the 'record book' and in the upper-right-hand corner of the television screen; it is a stimulus to unimagined heights of achievement and a psychic barrier which thwarts our efforts; it is an occasion for frenzy, a form of rationalized madness, a symbol of our civilization. In a lyrical moment, a French athlete of the 1920s hoped that his daughter would 'one day recite the litany not of our battles but of our records, more beautiful than the labors of Hercules.' "

I do not assert that an awareness of the significance of records in modern sports occurs only when one contrasts modern sports with those of primitive peoples, with those of antiquity, the Middle Ages, the Renaissance, but I am convinced that the fullest awareness is the reward of those who have actually studied the sports of ages prior to our own. Although I have in a certain sense "known" baseball since childhood, it was only when I read about Greek and Roman sports that I realized that our national game is almost bizarrely quantified. What had seemed "natural" to me—doesn't everybody memorize batting averages?—now appeared in all its outlandish peculiarity. No, not everybody expresses hero-worship in three decimal places. Since European and Japanese sports are almost as number-obsessed as American sports, the historical dimension best enables us to perceive ourselves from a different angle of vision.

I have exemplified my argument about the uses of history with references to my book. Another project illustrates similar possibilities. In writing *From Ritual to Record* and discussing rationalization as one of the characteristics of modern sports, I asked, "How shall we transform hunting into a modern sport?" My answer was, I believe, correct but insufficient. I quote briefly: "The answer, of course, is to create an 'animal' which symbolizes the equality of all animals, i.e., a target. The target is of a standard size. It stands in one spot and it does not roar. With the target, we can rationalize hunting into archery or pistol-shooting. Rationalization is the key to the development of all sports which utilize a target. Shooting at a bull may be more satisfying than shooting at a bull's eye, but it is less modern."

This answer is correct because the modern sport of archery does indeed substitute a target for the animals shot at by Egyptian pharoahs whose prowess proved their fitness for rule. But the answer is insufficient because there are targets and targets. The sport of archery was a favorite of the medieval middle class and the rationalizing process was far enough along in the Middle Ages for living birds to be transformed into wooden ones which were often intricately and imaginatively carved, but the substitution of wood for flesh and blood was only a single step, one, incidentally, which was also made within the world of Islamic culture. Another step on the route to modernity was the association of different numerical values with the different parts of the wooden bird. Shooting off a wing earned more points than shooting off a single feather. Some targets were apparently constructed so that a well-placed arrow knocked the entire bird to pieces. Hence the German idiom, *"den Vogel abzuschiessen."* The next step seems to have been to replace the simulated animals with a purely geometrical shape. We move from wooden bird to a white disk with a black center. Since the center was originally a flat-headed nail, we have—in several languages—the idiom, "to hit the nail on the head." The final step, visually, is the addition of progressively larger superimposed fields, i.e., concentric circles. It may have been that such circles originally served merely to locate the arrow lodged closest to the center, but the ultimate stage may have been perceived immediately, that is, the association of different quantified values with each field. Once the point-system is imagined, quantified comparisons precisely determine the outcome of the contest. Archery has become a modern sport.

When was the modern target, with its set of concentric circles, invented? My best guess is that it was invented in Holland or northeastern France somewhere in the early 17th century, but I really won't know until I can visit some of the folklore museums of the area.

What have I gained if I do pinpoint the invention chronologically? In the first place, I have demonstrated that modernization in the sport of archery occurred in the same place and at the same time as the incipient modernization of other areas. Brabant, for instance, was one of the places where early forms of capitalism were most advanced. Holland was one of the places where the scientific spirit first appeared. In the second place, I have demonstrated that the most advanced class ludically considered was also the most advanced class in other ways; I mean, of course, the urban middle class. While the upper class was still worried about whether or not a tournament challenger had the requisite number of noble ancestors, the middle class had turned the sport of archery into a world of numbers.

None of this may strike you as particularly noteworthy, but

I am on the track of another possibility which intrigues me enormously. Although the modern archery target does not seem to have been invented independently by Islamic or Hindu or Confucian culture, the Japanese may have anticipated the Dutch and the French. Seventeenth-century illustrations of the Japanese classic, *The Tale of Genji*, show the courtiers of Kyoto shooting at what are unmistakably modern targets. In fact, documentary evidence suggests that the archery contests at Kyoto's Sanju-sangen-do Temple may have been—as early as the 17th century—attempts to set quantified records. In other words, while Persian and Turkish archers were still content to fire away at the *qabaq* or gourd mounted upon a mast, the Japanese seem to have invented the modern sport of archery. What this possibility suggests to me is that the stunningly rapid modernization of Japan in the late nineteenth century was the result of factors long present in Japanese culture. Even if it were shown that the modern target was introduced to Japan by the Dutch, who were allowed to carry on a minimal trade with Japan even after the islands had shut themselves off from the West, it is still important to recognize that the Japanese were receptive to this abstraction while Persians and Turks preferred less abstract and more representational gourds, melons, bags, and baskets.

All this may strike one as either too little, or too much, to be teased from the nature of the mark at which the archer shoots, but this bit of research is an example of historical sociology or sociological history. The research is obviously historical (and cross-cultural); it is just as obviously sociological in that the questions asked are not simply of antiquarian interest but are, on the contrary, similar to the questions asked by Max Weber in his momentous investigations of the origins and development of modern society. And I should probably add that the research of this sort is an immense frustration because one continually discovers one's inadequacies: I wish fervently that I knew enough Japanese to investigate the cultural significance of seventeenth-century Japanese archery, and I admit with shame that it's all I can do to say, "Dorisu-wa kokuho des." Japanese scholars have promised to help me; they are, I suppose, the historian's equivalent to the computer-intoxicated sociologist's collaborator from the math department.

Having contended that one can operationalize the sociological imagination by serious involvement with European sport sociology and by an equally serious commitment to the kinds of otherness investigated by the historian, I wish now to comment on the third of my three categories. Literature, by which I mean poems, plays, novels, short stories, and other works of the imagination, can almost be defined as the fictive exploration of otherness. (I say "almost" to take into account writers like Thomas Wolfe, whose seemingly endless novels are peopled by hundreds of different versions of Thomas Wolfe.) Literary evidence, if used properly, is a revelation of what Truman Capote called "other voices, other rooms." John Keats wrote of the mysterious, inexplicable "negative capability" which enabled the poet suddenly to see the world through another person's eyes. The twentieth-century American poet Wallace Stevens wrote of the imagination as "the necessary angel," which, if I may quote one of his titles, provided 13 ways of looking at a blackbird. I said a moment ago that literary evidence is a revelation of otherness, if used properly. The qualification is a troublesome one. C. Wright Mills wrote in *The Sociological Imagination* that sociologists ought to be able to write about developments in contemporary poetry as well as conditions in the oil industry, but North American sociologists—less adventuresome than the French—have spent considerably more time analyzing OPEC than T. S. Eliot. The reasons are obvious: few sociologists want to be fools rushing in where angels fear to tread. The reluctance of the empiricist to investigate the fictive is intensified by the tendency of Departments of English to ridicule what they ought to encourage. Too many professors of literature emulate the Confucian mandarins who, having passed a strenuous series of examinations, stand jealous guard over their hierophantic wisdom. I feel as strongly about this form of perversity as I do about the tendency of some sociologists to speak and write a special language unknown to ordinary mortals.

Of course my colleagues in English have a point. There are difficulties in the investigation of otherness as it is found in literary texts. One must be sensitive to tones of voice, ironies: "Brutus is an honorable man," says Mark Antony, and stirs the mob against the high-minded assassin. One must infer from Antony's tone that Brutus is *not* all that honorable. One must also distinguish authors from their characters: Shakespeare did not say "Neither a borrower nor a lender be"; Polonius says this, and Polonius is a tedious fool; Polonius isn't ironic in his advice; Shakespeare is ironic about Polonius. One must also accept the fact that the most profound insights of the literary imagination are likely to be expressed symbolically, metaphorically, ambiguously. Melville's great white whale is an almost Marxist symbol of the capitalist's conception of nature as a commodity, but the whale also symbolizes the hopelessness of Captain Ahab's attempts to wring from nature the answers to his epistemological questions; the whiteness of the whale, says Melville's Ishmael, is "the colorless all-color of atheism." One must also constantly be aware of the fact that no novel, no poem, not even the greatest, not even the most profound, can be taken as fully representative of the society within which its author lived and wrote. *The Adventures of Huckleberry Finn* is a great novel and a powerful representation of the theme of American innocence, but the book is, finally, one man's interpretation of his world. That millions of Americans have read the book and have made Mark Twain's hero a part of their consciousness suggests that the book is sociologically as well as aesthetically important, but the novel, like all works of the literary imagination, should be considered by the sociologist as a hypothesis or an interpretation to be tested against the empirical evidence in the context of other hypotheses and interpretations. One of the least avoidable of pitfalls is the tempting assumption that the great work—Emile Zola's *Rougon-Macquart* for instance—dramatizes reality rather than the author's interpretation of reality. After all, the author may, like the great German poet Hölderlin, have been insane; the author may, like the great French poet Mallarmé, have sought to portray a world as far removed as possible from the bourgeois institutions of nineteenth-century France. If one does rush in where angels fear to tread, one must rush cautiously, thoughtfully, armed with a certain amount of preparation. Clearly, the problems of poetry, where formal elements are extremely important, are usually greater than the problems of prose fiction. Clearly, the problems presented by earlier writers—Rabelais for instance—are greater than those presented by writers whose culture we more or less share. The problems are, however, not insurmountable, and the insights available in literary form are inestimable.

Having claimed that literary evidence is immensely important and having commented on some of the difficulties inherent in the exploitation of literary resources, I wish to turn to a single, widely known work which is importantly concerned with sports: Ernest Hemingway's *The Sun Also Rises*. The choice of an example incidentally, is difficult because—contrary to what one is liable to read—the number of sports-related literary works, from Homer and Pindar to Robert Coover and Uwe Johnson, is enormous. The number of *important* sports-related literary works is far larger than most people have supposed.

The novel has two epigraphs, one from Gertrude Stein, the other from the Book of Ecclesiastes. The title, in the American edition, is taken from the latter: "One generation passeth away, and another generation cometh; but the earth abideth forever. . . . The sun also riseth, and the sun goeth down, and hasteth to the place where he arose. . . . All the rivers run into the sea; yet the sea is not full; unto the place from whence the rivers come, thither they return again." Against the sonorities of the King James Bible, the first epigraph is flatly American: "You are all a lost generation." The two epigraphs form a contrast because Stein's remark asserts a singularity of history while the Book of Ecclesiastes proclaims the endless repetitions of nature. Within the novel, the narrator is a victim of history in search of nature. Jake Barnes, the American journalist who tells the story, is a veteran of World War I, living now in Paris, tormented by the fact that a war wound has left him sexually impotent. He is hopelessly, frustratingly in love with Lady Brett Ashley, a young, beautiful, wealthy, witty, unconventional, promiscuous English woman. Jake has two important rivals. One of them, an American named Robert Cohn, is the villain of the novel; the other, a Spaniard named Pedro Romero, is the hero. Robert Cohn is an amateur boxer and Pedro Romero is a professional bullfighter. Hemingway's choice of these sports, and of the other sports which occur throughout the novel, is immensely significant. Perhaps a better way to express the point is to say that Hemingway, using sports as means of characterization, makes something immensely significant of boxing, bullfighting, tennis, fishing, bicycle-racing, and swimming.

Before I attempt to indicate exactly how Hemingway uses sports as a means of characterization, I should say a word about the setting. When the novel begins, Jake Barnes, Robert Cohn, and Lady Brett are in Paris, busy with the strenuous business of amusing themselves. They move through dance halls and cafes, drinking champagne, listening to jazz, passing off prostitutes as someone's fiancee. The dialogue is witty and the soliloquies are tragic. As Jake Barnes demonstrates in his moments of solitary nocturnal despair, he and his friends are, despite the parties and the clever talk, a lost generation. His physical impotence is a metaphor for a spiritual affliction which has damned them all.

The war is a metaphor for the sickness of an entire civilization. Hemingway's Paris is another version of T. S. Eliot's mythic waste land, spiritually arid, sterile despite the orgiastic sensuality of its doomed inhabitants.

But Paris is not the only scene. Jake Barnes, Robert Cohn and Lady Brett go to Pamplona in Spain to see the yearly festival and the bullfights that are a part of the rituals. Pamplona is all that Paris is not. The peasants of Spain symbolize primitive virtues, like stoicism, and Pedro Romero, the bullfighter, appears as a figure of grace. Predictably, Lady Brett falls madly in love with him, which drives the jealous Robert Cohn into childish displays of infantile rage. Jake Barnes suffers as well but controls himself with Hemingwayesque fortitude. The novel comes to a climax when Lady Brett runs off with Pedro Romero and then realizes that she, dazzlingly sophisticated and deeply cynical, is not right for him. "You know," she says to Jake Barnes, "I'd have lived with him if I hadn't seen it was bad for him. We got along damned well." Rather than ruin *him*, she breaks off the affair and returns to Paris, where she tells Jake Barnes, in some of the most marvelous lines in American literature, "You know it makes one feel rather good deciding not to be a bitch. . . . It's sort of what we have instead of God."

The last scene demonstrates the need for stoical acceptance: Jake Barnes and Lady Brett are in a Parisian taxi when she blurts out: "Oh, Jake, we could have had such a damned good time together." Hemingway interrupts the dialogue with a symbol of authority: "Ahead was a mounted policeman in khaki directing traffic. He raised his baton. The car slowed suddenly pressing Brett against me." And Jake Barnes has the last word: "Yes, isn't it pretty to think so?" In other words, it's marvelous to imagine what might have been, but we must never forget what actually is and the need to accept it.

And now for sports. Robert Cohn is a boxer and Jake Barnes, who is surely Hemingway's spokesman in this, has only contempt for Robert Cohn's pugilistic achievements: "Robert Cohn was once middleweight boxing champion of Princeton. Do not think that I am very much impressed by that boxing title, but it meant a lot to Cohn. He cared nothing for boxing, in fact he disliked it, but he learned it painfully and thoroughly to counteract the feeling of inferiority and shyness he had felt on being treated as a Jew at Princeton." Hemingway, as everyone knows, was fascinated by boxing, by the matching of man against man in a metaphoric, premodern re-enactment of the struggle for survival. The trouble with Robert Cohn is that he doesn't like to box. For him the sport is not a Darwinian opportunity to test his fitness to survive but simply an instrument to be used against anti-Semitism. One might say that Robert Cohn took up what was, for Hemingway, an authentic sport but for inauthentic reasons.

And he is not the only one to dramatize the misuse of the sport. Another of Barnes' friends, Bill Gorton, arrives from Vienna with a marvelously comic account of a fixed fight that came unfixed. The luckless protagonist of the incident is a black boxer from the United States. Here's Bill Gorton's account: "Wonderful nigger. Looked like Tiger Flowers, only four times as big. All of a sudden everybody started to throw things. Not me. Nigger'd just knocked local boy down. Nigger put up his glove. Wanted to make a speech. Awful noble-looking nigger. Started to make a speech. Then local white boy hit him. Then he knocked white boy cold. Then everybody commenced to throw chairs. . . . Injustice everywhere. Promoter claimed nigger promised to let local boy stay. Claimed nigger violated contract. Can't knock out Vienna boy in Vienna. 'My God, Mister Gorton,' said nigger, 'I didn't do nothing in there for forty minutes but try and let him stay. That white boy musta ruptured himself swinging at me. I never did hit him." Although the black fighter is more attractive than Robert Cohn—in Hemingway's eyes—he too betrayed the savage values implicit in boxing.

When the characters leave the waste land of Paris and Vienna behind them and go to Spain, they find not one but two physical activities which form a contrast to boxing. But I should probably say something about another sport that appears in the first pages of *The Sun Also Rises*. Jake Barnes says that he and Robert Cohn are tennis players, but there is no effort whatsoever on Hemingway's part to describe them at play. The reason is that tennis is a game for sissies. Robert Cohn plays it because he's a sissy, and Jake Barnes plays because he's too nice a guy to say no to Robert Cohn. The reason that tennis is a game for sissies, of course, is that it's a mediated contest in which players hit balls with rackets instead of each other with their fists. And besides, there's a net between them. Hemingway leaves it to writers like Wright Morris to publish novels about tennis. Real men risk their lives against bulls. Off to the ritualized fiesta of Pamplona.

Before the characters witness Pedro Romero in action and respond to his dramatic enactment of the human condition, there is an important interlude, a pastoral moment of male bonding during which Jake Barnes and Bill Gorton go fishing. The scene in the Irati Valley near Burgete is idyllic; it is also something of a literary joke for insiders since the central figure in T. S. Eliot's *The Waste Land* is the sexually wounded fisher-king, but I will avoid further comments on Eliot except to say that his poem was also the inspiration for Bernard Malamud's mythic baseball novel, *The Natural*. Hemingway's pastoral interlude is an occasion for profound communion and absurd conversation. It is the intermezzo before the fiesta.

The fiesta begins with the running of the bulls through the streets of Pamplona. One of the men running before the bulls is caught and gored, and another Spaniard remarks bitterly, "All for sport. All for pleasure," which indicates that the modern world's inability to respond to ritual has begun to destroy Spain even as it destroyed France and the United States.

There are even inauthentic bull-fighters who pretend to take greater risks than they actually do, who deceive, distort, twist, pervert, and disgrace. When I say "disgrace," I mean that they destroy the grace of the sport in a religious sense. For them Hemingway has a contempt even greater than his contempt for boxers who enter the ring to prove a point or, worse yet, to throw a fight. Pedro Romero is the authentic bull-fighter, the almost god-like hero who embodies the virtues Hemingway most admired in primitive man and most missed in the modern waste land. The most passionate moments of the book are devoted to Pedro Romero's heroic encounter with his bull, and they are rendered especially heroic by the farcical demonstration of Robert Cohn's villainy which precedes them.

En route to Spain, Lady Brett had had a brief affair with Robert Cohn. She quickly tired of his hang-dog devotion and now, in Pamplona, he is in a frenzy of miserable jealousy which he expresses by beating up everyone who crosses his path. He knocks down Jake Barnes and Mike Campbell (Lady Brett's fiance). And he beats up Pedro Romero. The fight with Pedro Romero is an allegory of technique versus innate virtue. Bill Gorton, whose clipped and incomplete sentences told of the black boxer in Vienna, now tells of the fight between Pedro Romero and Robert Cohn: "The bull-fighter fellow was rather good. He didn't say much, but he kept getting up and getting knocked down again. Cohn couldn't knock him out. . . . He'd been knocked down about fifteen times and he wanted to fight some more. . . . Then Cohn said he wouldn't hit him again. Said he couldn't do it. Said it would be wicked. So the bull-fighter chap sort of rather staggered over to him. . . . So the bull-fighter chap sort of rather hit him just as hard as he could in the face, and then sat down on the floor. . . . Cohn wanted to pick him up and carry him to the bed. He said if Cohn helped him he'd kill him, and he'd kill him anyway this morning if Cohn wasn't out of town. Cohn was crying, and Brett had told him off, and he wanted to shake hands. . . . Then Cohn leaned down to shake hands with the bull-fighter fellow. No hard feelings, you know. All for forgiveness. And the bull-fighter hit him in the face again." In short, Pedro Romero beats Robert Cohn at his own game by transforming the contest from one of skill into one of courage.

The day after the fist-fight, Pedro Romero faces the bull in a symbolic encounter of man and nature. If the other characters represent the historically lost generation that Gertrude Stein spoke of, Pedro Romero symbolizes the eternal return of natural virtue. Hemingway, who devoted an entire book to the art and significance of bull-fighting, writes at length of Belmonte and then of Romero. I quote only a small part of the homage to Romero: "The fight with Cohn had not touched his spirit but his face had been smashed and his body hurt. He was wiping all that out now. Each thing that he did with this bull wiped that out a little cleaner. It was a good bull, a big bull, and with horns, and it turned and recharged easily and surely. He was what Romero wanted in bulls. When he had finished his work with the muleta and was ready to kill, the crowd made him go on. They did not want the bull killed yet, they did not want it to be over. Romero went on. It was like a course in bull-fighting. All the passes he linked up, all completed, all slow, tempered and smooth. There were no tricks and no mystifications. There was no brusqueness. And each pass as it reached the summit gave you a sudden ache inside. The crowd did not want it ever to be finished." One has the sense here that Hemingway really has imagined that mysterious otherness represented by the Spanish *corrida*. If this is not truly the fascination of bull-fighting, I cannot imagine what is. It is only Hemingway's interpretation, but it rings true when sounded in the context of other attempts— literary, historical, anthropological—to explain the attraction of this premodern ritual sport.

Between this climactic moment of grace and the stoical acceptance in the taxi which brings the story to an end, there are two
scenes especially significant for our special interest in sports. First,
there is a ritual swim in the sea, the function of which is to cleanse
and to calm, to immerse Jake Barnes in a kind of baptismal font
before he faces the modern waste land once again. Strictly speaking, there is no contest and hence the ritual swim is not a sports
event, but it is nonetheless close in spirit to Pedro Romero's encounter with the bull. And then there are the bicycle racers, whom
most critics of the novel have ignored. The movement of the novel
has taken us from the perversion of boxing in the modern world
to the survival of bull-fighting in the primitive context of the
Spanish fiesta. We return now to the world of inauthenticity, lack
of seriousness, fixing, deception and self-deception. Jake Barnes
meets a group of professional cyclists at San Sebastian. "The
bicycle-riders," he tells us, "drank much wine, and were burned
and browned by the sun. They did not take the race seriously
except among themselves. They had raced among themselves
so often that it did not make much difference who won. Especially
in a foreign country. The money could be arranged." There is
vulgarity as well as corruption. The leader in the race suffers
from boils and the others ridicule him because of his ignoble
affliction. "Listen," he replies, "to-morrow my nose is so tight
on the handle-bars that the only thing touches those boils is a
lovely breeze." The physical position suggested is about as far
removed as possible from Pedro Romero's graceful stance.

Hemingway goes on with his dissection of the cyclists. The
ritual in Pamplona was a part of the traditional Catholicism of
the Basque country, an expression of faith; the bicycle race is
sponsored by the bicycle manufacturers, an instance of commerce.
The manager of the team explains to Jake Barnes that the Tour
de France is the greatest sports event in the world. In fact, the
manager goes on, soccer and cycling have made France the most
sportif county in the world. Jake Barnes comments: "He knew
France. *La France sportive*. He knew road-racing. We had a cognac."
The manager invites Jake Barnes, once they are both back in Paris,
the most *sportif* city in the world, to have a drink at the Chope
de Negre, but we can be sure that Jake Barnes will never show
up at the Chope de Negre. It is one thing to accept one's fate;
it is quite another to welcome it.

The study of literature, the utilization of historical research, the *"Auseinandersetzung"* with European sport studies—these are three forms of the quest for otherness and, if I am correct about the importance of otherness for the sociological imagination, three ways to link biography with history, private troubles with public issues. Or, if C. Wright Mills' rhetoric seems too gloomy and problem-oriented, three ways better to understand the role of play in a world of work.

THE SOCIOLOGICAL IMAGINATION, THE NEW JOURNALISM, AND SPORT[1]

Alan Tomlinson, Brighton Polytechnic

THE SOCIOLOGICAL IMAGINATION

NO SERIOUS EXAMINATION of the sociological imagination is possible without recognition of C. Wright Mills' seminal statement. At the risk of repetition bordering on superfluity, then,[2] I will consider some of his main points. For Mills, (1970 :11), the sociological imagination comprises the capacity to make connections between the 'larger historical scene' and the individual's "inner life" and "external career." Precisely the same point is made in several different ways. Through the sociological imagination we can grasp the relations between history and biography and are able to see the relations between the remotely impersonal and the "most intimate features of the human self" (Mills, 1970 : 12,14). A primary distinction with which the sociological imagination works is that between "personal troubles" and "public issues." Sociological insight is particularly focused upon cases where personal troubles outgrow particular individual settings (or "milieux" as Mills calls them) and become public issues of social structure. For Mills, the main problem with which the sociological imagination should deal is that of reason and freedom in modern society. I want to argue in this paper that unorthodox sources can operate in a sociologically imaginative fashion which can help us explore some dimensions of this problem.

To broaden the base from which this argument will be expanded, it is necessary to illustrate the scope of the sociological imagination. It is, in Mills' view, "coming to be felt as a need" in the contemporary world, and it has also flowered in many areas beyond academic sociology, emerging as "the major common denominator of our cultural period" (Mills, 1970 : 29, 20).

Some of the most perceptive social commentators have exhibited what is undeniably their own particular version of the sociological imagination, sometimes in marked preference to early forms of scientific sociology. Randolph Bourne, for instance, moved from traditional English studies at Columbia, just prior to the First World War, into the area of sociology. In Max Lerner's view, Bourne saw the term "sociology" as a catalyst which "included loosely within itself all the groping toward collective living that (his) generation was making" (Schissel, 1965 : xx). But rather than slot into the scientific sociology of the time, Bourne's thinking operated on the level of the social commentator and social critic, producing innovative and penetrating writings on education, the pacifist question and the state. His central preoccupations became, in Max Lerner's words again, "the relation between political power and cultural creation, and the new world forms and modes of thinking that can be fashioned to replace nationalism" (Filler, 1943 : vii). Bourne epitomized the attempt of his own generation to give adequate consideration to the individual in the machine age and to recognize that "culture" was a necessity rather than a luxury of civilization (Filler, 1943 : 133). In his own way Bourne pointed to the paramount importance of an understanding of the creative dimensions of human action. In his concern with the agency of the intellect or the role of the intellectual and with the oppressive nature of the state, Bourne could be seen as a North American, albeit less theoretical or revolutionary, version of the Marxist critic Antonio Gramsci.

In this context Bourne also offered some thoughts on the social significance of collegiate sports. He was not the first to do this. Thorstein Veblen had already argued that athletic games combined futility with a "colorable make believe of purpose," whilst at the same time functioning in an economic sense as a significant form of training and organization (Veblen, 1953 : 172, 245). Bourne's comments of 1915 on college sports, though, highlighted still further the formative influence of "the good old Anglo-Saxon conviction that life is essentially a game where significance lies in terms of winning or losing" (Schissel, 1965: 69). He was more concerned than Veblen to get at the core values of sports (Veblen tended to see them all as predatory). These in Bourne's view were inextricably linked to the values of an essentially practical, winner-take-all society. Bourne argued that critical thinking was dismissed in undergraduate life in favor of a Peter Pan world of sporting techniques and races for different goals. He saw sports as the embodiment of American cultural values. The task, he then implied, was to contest the terrain that they occupied in college life and to foster instead the critical spirit of the intellect.

This was provocative stuff, critical in a classically sociological fashion and pointing to the central critical issues of the age. The social critic has been an important bearer of the sociological imagination and offers insights into our social experience which must be taken seriously and might have the status of the hypothesis. George Orwell, for instance, observed that international sport was simply a surrogate form of war (Orwell, 1968 : 40-44). It is thinkers like Bourne and Orwell who show us that imaginative sociological thinking about sport is not confined to the halls of academia and to the funded research project.

Other spheres in which the sociological imagination has operated include the writing of fiction and sports writing. C.L.R. James looked at Melville's *Moby Dick* and asked how a book from the world of 1850 could contain so much of the world of the 1950's. Melville's work, he suggested, was a journey towards the creation of Captain Ahab, a character who sums up "the whole epoch of human history." In creating types in the context of historical settings and social processes, fictional constructions can formulate problems in the classical sociological sense. Thus, in James' view, Melville is a key representative writer of industrial civilization in whose work "the divisions and antagonisms and madnesses of an outworn civilization are mercilessly dissected and cast aside" (James, 1977 : 159). This is why fictional forms can be of genuine interest to the practitioner of critical sociology. They highlight the values characteristic of particular social formations and are indicative of both the constraints and possibilities which are so often in tension within specific forms of cultural expression and practice. I have illustrated this elsewhere with reference to the representation of masculinity in selected sports novels (Tomlinson, 1983).

Our insight into social phenomena can also be enhanced by social actors who develop into social observers of their own spheres of activity or, frequently, former spheres. In this category we can place the previously unreflecting, or coercively constrained, social actor who breaks through and "tells it like it really is." The pro football establishment in America has been exposed as a big problem in itself by savage contributions to radical critique and the genre of the sports novel (Parrish, 1972; Gent, 1973).

More generally, Charles Page has observed that painters and sculptors have made "insightful imaginative reconstructions" of sport, and that it would be shortsighted to ignore these when we are considering the relationship between sport and society. He argued against a sociological provincialism which ignores the contributions of non-sociologists and suggested that sports writers have often contributed "meritoriously" to the sociology of sport. Page called George Plimpton a "participant observer" and noted that other writers work in distinctively sociological ways. Such writing might be of general interest, but it is also a literature "of sociological utility" (Page, 1973 : 14). But he said nothing about the sorts of uses to which such writing could be put. In the second section of this paper I explore the characteristics and the thrust of selected examples of "new journalistic" writing on sport in an attempt to illustrate more specifically the utility of one category among such sources.

SELECTED 'NEW JOURNALISTIC'
TREATMENTS OF SPORT

Big claims have been made for the new journalism, most of all by Tom Wolfe, the most successful new journalist of all. Wolfe actually saw this type of writing as a successor to the novel, a successor so effective that it "would wipe out the novel as literature's main event" within ten years (Wolfe, 1975 : 22). We need not take too seriously a contention so trenchantly put, but it is worth dwelling on the excitement that early writers in this genre felt over what was in many respects a revelatory innovation. Wolfe attributed the breakthrough to Jimmy Breslin, who discovered that "it was feasible for a columnist to actually leave the building, go outside and do reporting on his own, genuine legwork" (Wolfe, 1975 : 25). Breslin's background as a freelance writer for *Sports Illustrated* and other magazines and his columns from 1963 onwards for the *Herald Tribune* made him an influential as well as pioneering figure. Wolfe pointed out that Breslin made it his business to be at a scene before any main event, so that he could gather off-camera material, the novelistic detail that gave life to his writing. Wolfe himself started work on the *Herald Tribune* and experimented with the techniques of fiction for the documentation of real events. His particular interest was in point-of-view.

It is not appropriate to develop here a critique of Wolfe's account of the characteristics and significance of the writings of new journalism. I want simply to raise some points about why this writing has focused, among other things, upon sport, and how the writings are of use to the sociologist. In Wolfe's (1975 : 41) terms, the new breed of journalists "somehow had the moxie to talk their way inside of any milieu, even closed societies, and hang on for dear life." John Sack, for instance, joined an infantry company as a reporter and went to war. Hunter Thompson ran with Hell's Angels in California for eighteen months. This capacity for empathy was a central part of the new journalist's method. And, as I have already noted, Charles Page referred to George Plimpton as a participant-observer and in so doing gave sociological recognition to Plimpton's enterprise.

Wolfe (1975 : 67) referred to Plimpton's work as "extraordinary feats with the sports world" and to his strategy as one of "hanging back in the shadows with a diffidence and humility that provoked his 'subjects' into asking him to join in as one of them." I would not want to suggest that such adventures have always been greeted with rapturous praise. Morris Dickstein referred to "the harmless participatory manner of a George Plimpton" in his dismissal of Tom Wolfe's writing (Dickstein, 1977: 140). But if Plimpton's achievements are harmless in terms of the wider issues of the age, his technique did enable certain revelations to be made. In his inside story of the breaking of Babe Ruth's lifetime home run record he employed the novelistic technique of varied point-of-view in the context of a single event, managing to evoke some of the resonances in the life of a society which can be set off by a seemingly superfluous sports event (Plimpton, 1974). This is one of the kind of things Charles Page (1973 : 9) was suggesting could be done by the sociologist of sport when he wrote of the study of particularly dramatic, at times traumatic, events in the world of sport. Spending time with the Detroit Lions in 1963, Plimpton also opened the window upon some specific characteristics of group culture in professional football. Consider this passage following Plimpton's account of the rendition of an old college song at pre-season training:

> Nobody put down their forks to listen. It was apparent that the singing was secondary to the indignity to which the rookie was put; he was being embarrassed, so that he would keep the rigorous caste system firmly in mind (Plimpton, 1964 : 23).

This is an astute and first-hand interpretation of an initiation rite—hazing—in a particular occupational subculture. In making his own "rookie" mistakes, Plimpton (1964 : 41) revealed to us the unwritten rules of football life, its normative code, including the preferential treatment of the quarterback. Plimpton was a genuine participant, not just an observer. This gave him access to initiation ceremonies such as the rookie show on an unprecedentedly accessible scale. As one of the rookies, he actually "oversaw" it himself. Plimpton (1964 : 308, 322) evoked the paradoxes of the sporting life, the exhilaration of fitness and camaraderie along-side the constraints of control and discipline. He used contrasts in his observations—two girls playing purposeless, spontaneous tennis contrasted with the team, drilling with machine-like precision in its training routines. This implied, but neither stated nor developed, an interpretation of the significance of different types of sports. In the end the interpretation faded out on a note of ambiguity. In some ways, then, Plimpton is harmless, and his biography of the team is not placed in any hard context of history. But after reading Plimpton, we feel we know more about the experience of the professional football player and the sport's cultural patterns. Plimpton's work offers the sociologist an ethnographic source full of useable detail.

The other writers considered in this section are Norman Mailer, Gay Talese and Hunter Thompson. Wolfe himself has not really written a great deal on sport, and his writing is in many ways less penetrating anyway than the other writers considered. For Wolfe (1975 : 66), the demonstration of moral points is subservient to the attempt to prove "one's technical mastery as a writer." In other words, form dominates content in his work. Dickstein condemned him for failing to let himself go, and for abandoning any critical perspective. Wolfe's work has, in the end, no sense of context at all.[3] Wolfe (1975 : 66) himself claimed that the new journalists work with a "strange sort of objectivity, an egotistical objectivity. . . an objectivity of sorts." An English critic, Richard Hoggart, has suggested that Wolfe's work is actually a search for poise, style or form. Wolfe, as indicated above, is aware of this. Hoggart suggested, though, that this tendency prevents Wolfe's work from becoming representative of anything. It remains a mere symptom of the age of modern mass communication, an age in which the medium and the stylistic poise are more important than the message; in such circumstances manner triumphs over matter (Hoggart, 1970). Style and content combine most effectively in the sports writing of Norman Mailer, Gay Talese and Hunter Thompson.

In Norman Mailer's book on the George Foreman/Muhammed Ali fight, for instance, we see a writer, to use Dickstein's (1977 : 143) words again, reporting "most deeply on what was happening both inside and outside his own head." In this way Mailer managed to situate the actor—and himself—in wider social and historical contexts. And at certain points Mailer moved explicitly into the realms of the sociological imagination. He was trying to find an appropriate context in which to place the boxing match, and given that this fight was to take place in Zaire, he had been reading his way into African culture by consulting authorities on Bantu philosophy. His source excited him, pointing out that the Bantu philosophy "saw humans as forces, not beings." That is, men and women are more than just the parts of themselves, more than the result of heredity and experience. They have, Mailer's (1977) reading implies, a future, a projective, a creative potential which is framed in terms of past influences:

> A man was not only what he contained, not only his desires, his memory and his personality, but also the forces that came to inhabit him at any moment from all things living and dead. . . . So the meaning of one's life was never hard to find. One did one's best to live in the pull of these forces in such a way as to increase one's own force (p. 42).

This is the framework in which Mailer began to make sense of the Foreman-Ali fight. It is clear to any of us that boxing is more than a mere contest between two opponents. It is also more than just a form of entertainment available to the highest bidder. Mailer began to probe into the context of the contest, showing how the commercial dimensions of the sport and the undeniable personal rivalries have deeper resonances. The social meanings of sports are not simply there to read off from the activity. Mailer believed that Ali's mind had been built upon whims and contradictions. His response to Ali's incredible victory over Foreman changed this. Ali fought as a Black Muslim, as the representative of the black race in a sport whose champions are almost exclusively black. Mailer's great insight was this: that Ali gained his inner resources of strength from his sense of himself as a significant human agent, as a force for change.[4] Mailer (1977 : 42) concluded that Ali lived with a highly developed sense of anxiety, given "the size of his world role and his intimate knowledge of his own ignorance." In this book Mailer began to link a cultural event to vital social processes, and in doing so could offer an interpretation of the cultural event which is framed in terms of that event's external determinants. Without the participatory techniques of the new journalism and the use of fictional devices for documentary writing, these insights could not have been arrived at or presented in such an effective way. Mailer talked to and ran with an apparently unfit and lethargic Ali just a few days before the fight. Such intimacy with the subject matter enabled Mailer to move towards an interpretation of the fight in terms of supra-individual forces.

It was a piece written in 1962 which first alerted Tom Wolfe to the existence of a style of writing which was to influence him so dramatically. The piece was written by Gay Talese, on Joe Louis. Wolfe's recollections of the piece show his own specific concern with style rather than substance. To Wolfe, the qualities of the piece derive from its use of literary devices such as point of view, scene-switching and use of time sequences. Wolfe nowhere talked about what the piece actually said about a famous sports figure.

Talese, though, is not merely a technician. He does have something to say. As a middle-aged man, he was implying, Joe Louis was learning to live with a dignity appropriate to his former fame. In other pieces, too, Talese offered memorable interpretations as well as observations. Although Talese (1981 : 9) himself saw the new journalism as a "more imaginative approach to reporting," and then went on to discuss briefly a few ways in which this can be achieved, his real significance is bound up with the interpretative shape which he imposed on his material. This is worth looking at in more detail, with reference not just to the piece on Louis but to one on Floyd Patterson.

If ever we are tempted to understand sport on the basis of a kind of reductionism which sees only the commercial base to and economic dimensions of the sporting spectacle, we should turn to Talese's (1981) picture of the 29-year-old, financially secure and physically unmarked Floyd Patterson in his mountainside retreat after being knocked out for the second time by Sonny Liston:

> But Patterson. . . cannot believe that he is finished. He cannot help but think that it was something more than Liston that destroyed him—a strange, psychological force was also involved, and unless he can fully understand what it was, and learn to deal with it in the boxing ring, he may never be able to live peacefully anywhere but under this mountain. Nor will he ever be able to discard the false whiskers and moustache that, ever since Johansson beat him in 1959,

he has carried with him in a small attache case into each fight so he can slip out of the stadium unrecognized should he lose (p. 69).

Patterson conquered his fear of heights in order to learn how to fly. This was a way of ensuring that after a defeat he could get "out of town, fast." Talese showed us how a champion boxer can be a mass of contradictions, a cowardly winner. In defeat Patterson would never face people. Here we see the dilemma of the dramatically successful individual whose background leaves him few resources to draw upon when success in the sphere of his expertise is no longer guaranteed. Talese showed us the raw human emotions behind the surface layer of stardom. This same general point is true of Talese's portrayal of the legendary baseball player, Joe Di Maggio, who set a record of hitting safely in 56 consecutive games in 1941. Talese wrote his piece 25 years later and captured the meaning of Di Maggio to millions of fans. The scene was the stadium in New York one day in 1965, when a veteran player has been talked out of retirement. Di Maggio was present on the occasion:

> The banners had been held by hundreds of young boys whose dreams had been fulfilled so often by Mantle, but also seated in the grandstands were older men, paunchy and balding, in whose middle-aged minds Di Maggio was still vivid and invincible, and some of them remembered how one month before, during a pre-game exhibition at Old-timers' Day in Yankee Stadium, Di Maggio had hit a pitch into the left-field seats, and suddenly thousands of people had jumped wildly to their feet, joyously screaming—the great Di Maggio had returned, they were young again, it was yesterday (Talese, 1981 : 124).

Sport has the capacity to do this sort of thing to people, to offer them unforgettably intense and meaningful moments, and is all the more effective because it could be you or me out there performing. As Di Maggio remarked to a "man from New York" who called him a great man—"I'm not great. . . I'm not great. . . I'm just a man trying to get along" (Talese, 1981 : 117). Talese showed us how sport and sports celebrities can live on in the popular memory, even though the former sports star is an individual just like any other individual, "trying to get along."

But it is in some of the writing of Hunter Thompson that the sociological imagination meets the new journalism with most devastating effect. Thompson's writing is made up of what he calls *gonzo* journalism—a "style of 'reporting' based on William Faulkner's idea that the best fiction is far more *true* than any kind of journalism" (Thompson, 1980 : 114). To do this sort of reporting effectively, Thompson (1980 : 115) believes, requires the skills of the journalist, the photographer and the actor, "because the writer *must* be a participant in the scene, while he's writing it—or at least taping it, or even sketching it." In Thompson's view Tom Wolfe fails to break genuinely new ground mainly because of his reluctance to participate.

The participant observer of California's Hells Angels attributed this failure to Wolfe's crustiness: "Wolfe's problem is that he's too crusty to *participate* in his stories. The people he feels comfortable with are dull as stale dogshit, and the people who seem to fascinate him as a writer are so weird that they make him nervous" (Thompson, 1980 : 116).

Thompson has no problems in this department, bursting his way into any setting that the job demands—football teams (1980 : 51-84); Muhammed Ali's inner circle (1980 : 578-622); international deep-sea fishing contests (1980 : 445-477); Jean-Claude Killy's aeroplane (1980 : 84-103). Thompson's writing on sports is also bound up with writing about his own drug-crazed 1960's existence. Setting out as a sports reporter to watch both horse and motor racing (Thompson, 1980 : 29-43; Thompson, 1972), he produced a "vile epitaph for the drug culture of the Sixties" (Thompson, 1980 : 118). But this is part of his achievement. By entering sporting settings on his own *terms* he was able to emphasize the nature of sports values by looking at them through the eyes of the marginal individual.

John Leonard of the *New York Times* called him "our official crazy, patrolling the edge." Nelson Algren suggested that his hallucinated vision of the 60s "strikes one as having been the sanest" (Thompson, 1980 : dust-jacket). By pitching himself into particular milieu, Thompson was able to depict the main characteristics of those settings. He (Thompson, 1980 : 65) showed us the *owner* of the Oakland Raiders maniacally coaching three of his key players on a training field at twilight. The international deep-sea fishing champion in Cozumel is shown up for the charlatan—in sporting terms—that he really is, and we are given behind-the-scenes detail on the elitist sports culture (Thompson, 1980 : 445 ff.). In going behind the scenes here, Thompson produced material which undermined official versions of social reality (Peter Berger's first motif of debunking in his model of sociology as a form of consciousness), and in his investigative voyeurism he was able to show what can actually go on under the surface of social life (Berger's unrespectability motif applied to the respectable [Berger, 1966 : Chapter Two]).

Thompson (1980) showed us an aging Muhammed Ali still finding sources of motivation in his role as underdog after his defeat by Leon Spinks. Ali, for Thompson, was a perfect contemporary myth:

> Myths and legends die hard in America. We love them for the extra dimension they provide, the illusion of near-infinite possibility to erase the narrow confines of most men's reality. Weird heroes and mold-breaking champions exist as living proof to those who need it that the tyranny of the 'rat race' is not yet final. Look at Joe Namath, they say; he broke all the rules and still beat the system like a gong. Or Hugh Hefner, the Horatio Alger of our time. And Cassius Clay—Muhammed Ali—who flew so high, like the U2, that he couldn't quite believe it when the drone bees shot him down (pp. 429-430).

At his most effective Thompson pointed to connections between individual experience and social forces. One of his most perceptive pieces was written in 1970, on 26-year-old French ski-champion Jean-Claude Killy. Killy won three gold medals at the 1968 Winter Olympics and then put himself in the hands of an agent, Mark McCormack: ''The only sure thing in the deal was a hell of a lot of money, both sooner and later. Beyond that, Killy had no idea what he was getting into'' (Thompson, 1980 : 90). Thompson's piece covered Killy's appearances at the Chicago Auto Show and in Boston, where the skier was selling Chevrolets. Here is Thompson's (1980) description of Killy at work:

> There was a hint of decency—perhaps even humour—about him, but the high-powered realities of the world he lives in now make it hard to deal with him on any terms except those of pure commerce. His handlers rush him from one scheduled appearance to the next; his time and priorities are parcelled out according to their dollar/publicity value; everything he says is screened and programmed. He often

sounds like a prisoner of war, dutifully repeating his name, rank and serial number. . . and smiling, just as dutifully, fixing his interrogator with that wistful, distracted sort of half-grin that he 'knows' is deadly effective because his handlers have showed him the evidence in a hundred press-clippings. The smile has become a trademark. It combines James Dean, Porfiro Rubirosa and a teenage bank clerk with a foolproof embezzlement scheme.

Killy projects an innocence and a shy vulnerability that he is working very hard to overcome. He likes the carefree, hell-for-leather image that he earned as the world's best ski racer, but nostalgia is not his bag, and his real interest now is his new commercial scene, the high-rolling world of the money game, where nothing is free and amateurs are called losers. The wistful smile is there, and Killy is shrewd enough to value it, but it will be a hard thing to retain through three years of auto shows, even for $100,000 a year (p. 86).

The smile was not always retained. When Killy was asked to comment on Avery Brundage's request that he return his Olympic medals, the response was not the programmed one:

But when a Montreal *Star* reporter asked Jean-Claude how he felt about turning in his Olympic medals, he replied: "Let Brundage come over here himself and take them from me."

It was a rare public display of "the old Jean-Claude." His American personality has been carefully manicured to avoid such outbursts. Chevrolet doesn't want him to say what he thinks, but to sell Chevrolets—and you don't do that by telling self-righteous old men to fuck off. You don't even admit that the French Government paid you to be a skier because things are done that way in France and most other countries, and nobody born after 1900 calls it anything but natural. . . when you sell Chevrolets in America you honour the myths and mentality of the marketplace: You smile like Horatio Alger and give all the credit to Mom and Dad, who never lost faith in you and even mortgaged their ingots when things got tough (Thompson, 1980 : 92).

Thompson here demonstrated the way in which the sport performer was transformed into a commodity form, caught up in the inexorable economic forces of a particular mode of production. Killy's partner in promotion for Chevrolet was O. J. Simpson:

> O.J.'s mind is not complicated; he had had God on his side for so long that it never occurs to him that selling Chevrolets is any less holy than making touch-downs. Like Frank Gifford, whose shoes he finally filled in the USC backfield, he understands that football is only the beginning of his TV career (Thompson, 1980 : 94).

Simpson was presented as a black capitalist, using his blackness as a market force, rather like the Joe Louis of Gay Talese's pioneering piece of reporting (Talese, 1962). Killy understood his new life but did not warm to it:

> locked into a gilded life-style where winning means keeping his mouth shut and reciting, on cue, from other men's scripts. He is a handsome middle-class French boy who trained hard and learned to ski so well that now his name is immensely saleable on the marketplace of a crazily inflated culture-economy that eats its heroes like hot dogs and honors them on about the same level. . . .
> His TV-hero image probably surprises him more than it does the rest of us. We take whatever heroes come our way, and we're not inclined to haggle (Thompson, 1980 : 103).

Thompson did not simply dismiss Killy as a "witless greedhead." He saw him as a victim of social forces, but as a willing one too—a "good soldier" of capitalism (Thompson, 1980 : 104), who corrupted his "completed original act" by working as hard at selling Chevrolets as he did at his sport.[5] Thompson's interpretation of Killy as an instance of advanced commodity exchange was given further emphasis by his own romanticism. He saw Muhammed Ali as a black Gatsby (Thompson, 1980 : 622) and compared Killy's smile to Gatsby's (Thompson, 1980 : 88). They were both presented as doomed romantics, individuals who were almost wholly taken over by specific socio-economic forces. So Thompson offered us a sense of how social forces are lived, of the interrelationships between different elements of our social life. Sport cannot be seen as a merely non-productive phenomenon. It is play, but it is also a focus for consumption. Sports performers can never be detached, innocent actors in a cocooned world of sport and play. They might come into our consciousness as exciting performers. In order to stay there, other than in the popular memory, they must become subservient to the forces of their time and place.

Thompson's most recent piece, after a decade of retirement, was on the Honolulu marathon of 1980. He (Thompson, 1981 : 24) started his piece off in typical challenging fashion, asking why "8,000 supposedly smart people. . . get up at four in the morning and stagger at high speed through the streets of Waikiki for 26 ball-busting miles in a race that less than a dozen of them have the slightest chance of winning?" He believed that the marathon might represent the "last refuge of the liberal mind, . . . the last thing that works. Physical Fitness" (Thompson, 1981 : 26). Doctors, lawyers, relatively affluent professionals, and many others from "two generations of political activitists and social anarchists" are now, after "politics failed and personal relationships proved unmanageable," into running. In doing this, they have also created a major rapid-growth industry. But why running? "Nothing else has worked, and the ability to run 26 miles at top speed might be a very handy skill for the coming ordeal of the 80's" (Thompson, 1981 : 83). This reading of contemporary American culture places sports firmly within the context of general social and cultural life. We cannot always take for granted the reasons social actors might give us for their actions. To contextualize individuals, it is necessary to make connections between individuals and contexts. In locating marathon running within a context of failed dreams, unachieved interpersonal Utopias and frightening futures, Thompson addressed issues central to the sociological imagination.

THE SOCIOLOGICAL PERTINENCE OF THE NEW JOURNALISM

At its most effective, then, new journalistic writing can inform sociological work. When the writer balances content with form then it can be a rich source indeed. This balance, though, must be carefully maintained. Wolfe was so impressed with form that he recollected Gay Talese's piece on Joe Louis almost purely in terms of its literary techniques. It is a beautiful piece, playing with time and mood in extremely evocative ways and starting and ending with the same scene. But, as Hoggart pointed out, to concentrate on manner rather than matter is to run the risk of offering a partial and incomplete reading. Generally, though, when the balance is there, new journalistic writing can show what lived realities are really like and can situate these realities in the context of their external determinants.

It can do this by shifting from one perspective to another, as Mills recommended; by suddenly talking not just about sport but about economic and political processes with which sports are connected. It can also, at its best, illustrate contradictions and tensions. Joe Louis' work as a black salesman is hardly the best way of acting out his sense that blacks are unequal and exploited. When Killy's Gatsby-like smile slips, we see a human being and not a commodity. The new journalistic sources can help us formulate the biggest sociological problem of all: sports may be repositories of inner meanings, but they do not exist in autonomy. They represent the value systems of the time and in so doing can embody the tensions, contradictions and anatagonisms of the age. Hunter Thompson, in particular, recognized this. His strategy in seeing the mainstream as problematic, as a problem to be explored, was a genuine sociological premise.

The sociological imagination can work in many ways. Anthony Giddens (1982) suggested a threefold exercise of it, involving three types of sensitivity—the historical, the anthropological and the critical. This first form of sensitivity does not characterize new journalistic writing on sports. Such writings contribute, obviously, to the investigation of particular contemporary moments. But the anthropological and the critical dimensions combine in the most effective pieces. In entering scenes from the outside, the new journalist can undermine the ethnocentric basis of commonsense views of the world and in showing what things are *really* like can be critical, albeit in an iconoclastic rather than future-oriented or projective way.

New journalistic writing highlights sport as a problem in the classical sense. The sociological imagination is not the exclusive property of the trained, professional social scientist. Problems should not be reduced to "social problems" in the sense of the "liberal practicality" in which a middle-class public makes an issue out of the troubles of lower-class people (Mills, 1970 : 96). Sociological knowledge should not be ordered into organized facts for ready transmission as the settled view of things. And the exploration of values, value conflicts and the varied nature of cultural experience cannot be collapsed into tidy and quantifiable generalizations. New journalistic pieces on sport formulate sport as a problem of values, and when "the interplay of ideas and facts" (Mills, 1970 : 99) works, they are of genuine use to the sociological researcher into sport.

In this paper I have sought to show just how far-reaching the sociological imagination is and to demonstrate some of the qualities and defects of new journalistic sources. To conclude on a bold note I will suggest just what "sociological utility" these sources have. They can be critically framed presentations of lived sports experience, and they can also highlight how general social processes are lived and experienced in specific settings. They are, at their best, a form of mediated ethnography. All reported experience is, of course, to some degree mediated by the ethnographer. I simply mean to point out that the new journalistic writer is, primarily, a professional journalist rather than a social researcher. But in our formulation of the problem of the function of sport in society, mediated ethnographies may be better than no ethnography at all. Until genuinely ethnographic data produced by covert and/or overt professional observers become available, the penetrative push of the new journalist will remain one source, albeit an uneven and bizarre one, on which the sociologist should draw in the exercise of any genuinely sociological imagination.

NOTES

1.   An earlier draft of this paper was written during a spell at the Center for Sport and Leisure Studies, School of Physical and Health Education, Queen's University, Kingston, Ontario. Many thanks to Hart and Sandra Cantelon, Rick Gruneau, and Bob Hollands for reassuring me that the paper was worth doing. At the NASSS Conference Alan Klein put me on to the collection of Gay Talese's pieces. In my earlier draft I had only mentioned one of these pieces, and so I would like to acknowledge the usefulness of conference exchanges as factors in intellectual production.

2.   Mills' vision of how sociological work should be done is not news, of course, to sociologists of sport. His vision is at the heart of one of the most sophisticated early discussions of sociological perspectives on sport in Richard S. Gruneau's (1976) "Sport as an area of sociological study: *an introduction to major themes and perspectives:*"

3.   It is worth quoting Dickstein at length on this:

Wolfe has no notion of the kinds of social forces that impede both manners and morals *and* politics, no feel for what Trilling calls 'a culture's hum and buzz of implication', 'a dim mental region of intention' that underlies a culture and shapes its character at a given historical moment. This is the implicit unity of mood or moral temper that the cultural observer must seek out, by which, for instance, the style of confrontation in the politics of the sixties is closely related to the style of self-assertion in the poetry and sexuality of the period, which in turn is related to the unexpected impulse of the journalist, in covering these and other developments, to do *his* own thing in an authenticating subjective way. And to determine *why* the whole culture should be moving in this direction, and to make some distinctions and judgments about it, required someone with greater analytical acuity, with more political sensitivity and novelistic vision, than Tom Wolfe (Dickstein, 1977 : 143).

4. This insight is all the more revealing when looking at the predictably brain-damaged figure of the Ali of today. Whether he *in fact* changed things is not so much the issue as the fact that he himself, and many followers, believed that he had the capacity to change things. Revolutionaries do not always initiate revolutions but this does not mean that they are not dynamic human agents themselves. For a few years at least Muhammed Ali fought for his own beliefs, whilst also acting out the dreams of millions. If nothing has changed, and if Ali has now exchanged his dramatic role for the role of the pathetic clown, this in no way eradicates his former significance as a symbol of his time.

5. Thompson, in one of his bizarre references, also added a final note, quoting Karl Marx on "the eunuch of industry."

REFERENCES

Berger, Peter
1966 Invitation to Sociology—A Humanistic Perspective. Harmondsworth: Penguin.

Dickstein, Morris
1977 Gates of Eden—American Culture in the Sixties. New York: Basic Books.

Filler, Louis
1943 Randolph Bourne. Washington: American Council on Public Affairs.

Gent, Peter
1973 North Dallas Forty. New York: Signet.

Giddens, Anthony
1982   Sociology: A Brief But Critical Introduction. New York: Harcourt Brace Jovanovich.

Gruneau, Richard
1976   "Sport as an area of sociological study: an introduction to major themes and perspectives," Pp. 8-43 in R. Gruneau and J. G. Albinson (eds.), Canadian Sport: Sociological Perspectives. Don Mills, Ontario: Addison Wesley.

Hoggart, Richard
[1966]   " 'The dance of the long-legged fly': On Tom Wolfe's
1970   poise," Pp. 129-143 in R. Hoggart, Speaking to Each Other: Volume II About Literature. London: Chatto and Windus.

James, C.L.R.
[1953]   "Fiction and reality," Pp. 142-159 in C.L.R. James, The
1977   Future in the Present. London: Allison and Busby.

Mailer, Norman
1977   The Fight. London: Panther Books.

Mills, C. Wright
[1959]   The Sociological Imagination. Harmondsworth: Penguin.
1970
Orwell, George
[1945]   "The sporting spirit," Pp. 40-44 in The Collected Essays,
1968   Journalism and Letters of George Orwell Volume IV: In Front of Your Nose 1945-50. London: Secker and Warburg.

Page, Charles
1973   "The world of sport and its study," Pp. 3-39 in John T. Talamini and Charles Page (eds.), Sport and Society. Boston: Little, Brown and Company.

Parrish, Bernie
1972   They Call It a Game. New York: New American Library.

Plimpton, George
1964   Paper Lion. New York: New American Library.
1974   One for the Record—The Inside Story of Hank Aaron's Chase For The Home-Run Record. New York: Harper and Row.

Schissel, Lillian (ed.)
1965   The World of Randolph Bourne. New York: E.P. Dutton and Co. Ltd.

Talese, Gay
1962   "Joe Louis—the King as a Middle Aged Man." Esquire Volume. LVIII No. 6 (Whole No. 343), June: 92-98.
1981   Fame and Obscurity. New York: Dell.

Thompson, Hunter S.
1972   Fear and Loathing in Las Vegas—a Savage Journey to the Heart of the American Dream. London: Paladin.
1980   The Great Shark Hunt—Strange Tales From a Strange Time. London: Picador.
1981   "The charge of the weird brigade," Running, March/April 1981.

Tomlinson, Alan
1983   "Sports fiction as critique: the novelistic challenge to the ideology of masculinity," In Michael Green and Charles Jenkins (eds.), Sports Fiction. Birmingham: Centre for Contemporary Cultural Studies, University of Birmingham.

Veblen, Thorstein
[1899] The Theory of the Leisure Class—An Economic Study of In
1953   stitutions. New York: Viking Press.

Wolfe, Tom
1975   The New Journalism, edited by Tom Wolfe and E.W. Johnson. London: Picador.

IMAGES OF WOMEN IN CANADIAN SPORTS FICTION[1]

Robert G. Hollands, University of Birmingham

THE INTENTION OF THIS PAPER is to situate a concrete analysis of the portrayal of women characters in three recent Canadian sports novels in the broader context of feminist and Marxist literary criticism. Initially this task poses some definite problems. On the one hand, both feminism and Marxism encompass a broad range of topics and subject matters. Further, both of these traditions are made up of various sets of competing perspectives. For example one need look no further than the heated polemic between radical, socialist, and liberal feminist scholars or the plethora of debates between English Marxists.[2] On reading feminist research one soon realizes that the socialist faction is steeped more in the tradition of historical materialism than it is in liberal democratic philosophy.[3] While much of this general material and debate is beyond the scope of this paper, I do want to suggest that there are important areas of convergence between particular variants of Marxist and feminist forms of literary criticism. I also want to suggest that these areas of convergence can help us understand more fully the characterization of women in sports fiction.

The paper will proceed in two parts. The first section will briefly provide some necessary background and pursue the notion that there are some basic similarities between recent developments in feminist and Marxist literary analyses. The second part of the paper will focus on the characterization of women in three contemporary Canadian sports novels. The purpose of this latter section is twofold: (1) to demonstrate how a socialist feminist critique might work, and (2) to show that a cooperative alliance between these two perspectives provides a useful and viable alternative to traditional liberal-patriarchal types of literary analysis.

MARXISM, FEMINISM AND LITERATURE

It is only possible to provide a cursory overview of some of the recent developments within Marxist and feminist approaches to literature. I will preface this discussion with some general remarks about Marxism and its relationship to feminist research. In his recent introduction to sociology, Anthony Giddens (1982) argued cogently that a comprehensive understanding of modern society is impossible without at least a basic grasp of Marx's analysis of capitalism. Furthermore, Giddens correctly pointed out that Marxism is not simply limited to Marx's own work, but "represents an internally diverse body of thought" which has "undergone continual development since Marx's time" (Giddens, 1982 : 31). However, for the purpose of this paper, Giddens' (1982) conclusion in the final chapter of his book is of greatest interest. He writes:

> In addition to the basic issue of totalitarian political control, there seems to me to be four further sets of questions linked to human emancipation which are inadequately analyzed both in Marx's texts and in the writings of most subsequent Marxists. . . (p. 169).

One of these sets of questions concerns the problem of sexual oppression.

Giddens' remark is highly significant in a contradictory sort of way. In the first place, it is a careful reminder that there remain fundamental splits and disagreements between feminists and socialists on many issues, including cultural ones.[4] On the other hand, a flexible use of Giddens' terms such as "inadequately analyzed" and "most subsequent Marxists. . .," with the emphasis on "most," seems to hint at the possibility of a compromise between these two perspectives. I feel compelled at least to pose this dilemma as a frame of reference for my discussion and analysis. Marxist and feminist theories of culture have important consequences for the way that we study and conceptualize literature and popular forms of literary production such as the novel, magazines, pulp fiction and news reports.[5] They also provide converging critiques of traditional literary criticism and capitalist culture in general. In order to argue for a socialist feminist theory of culture and literature, it becomes necessary to pose the question: what is feminist literary criticism?

What is Feminist Literary Criticism?

Perhaps the best way to frame this question is to state what feminist literary criticism is not. Contrary to the prevailing popular opinion, it is not simply the exposure of sexist attitudes and biases, nor is it an empirically based theory concerned with comparing the number of female and male writers. Equality of opportunity and equal representation within capitalist society are demands which characterize only certain elements in the women's movement.[6] These last two statements should be qualified. I am not trying to imply that the exposure of stereotypes and the recovery of ignored works of fiction are not by-products of feminist literary criticism, but rather, that they are not the sole analytical basis for it. What informs this type of analysis, is an understanding of the social and material basis of culture and consciousness and the way in which relations of power and authority structure various cultural products such as literature (cf., Millett, 1970).

This point deserves further clarification. An understanding of the social character of literary production and the manner in which power is exercised and distributed in a given society provides a great deal of insight into how those power relations are inscribed in cultural formations. In the case of the novel, for instance, one might ask the question: what have been the major literary conventions adopted and how does their utilization by both men and women writers result in the portrayal of women characters as subordinate? An example of this style of work can be found in Kennard (1978). She argued that the convention of the two suitors in Victorian fiction worked to structure the female character's maturation process, while consolidating her eventual subordination. Kennard's (1978 : 160) assertion that a revised version of this convention has surfaced in some modern feminist fiction[7] has some relevance to the three sports novels analyzed in the next section of the paper.

Feminist literary critics also have been interested in how the relationships between power, culture and literary form have influenced the work of mainstream critics and reviewers. For example, numerous feminist scholars have begun the job of deconstructing and reinterpreting classical theatrical productions by demonstrating how past reviews have relied almost exclusively on the main male character for their analysis. They argue that new insight and interpretation can be gained by listening to the "woman's part" and her understanding of the situation, especially her relationship with the male characters (Swift, *et. al.*, 1980). Much of this work revolves around the two interrelated themes of the *idealization* and *degradation* of women characters, both forms of subordination. There have also been attempts to recover lost or ignored works of fiction dealing with themes dismissed as trivial by patriarchal institutions and literary traditions (cf., Kolodny, 1980). Research of this type has been supported and accompanied by theories of women's literature as a distinctive sub-culture and the search for feminine consciousness in the British novel (cf., Showalter, 1977; Kaplan, 1975).

In a very important way, feminist literary criticism provides both a critique of and alternative to traditional criticism and aesthetics. Feminist critics increasingly want to know just what constitutes classic literature and what aesthetic criteria have been used to formulate that judgment. These questions are reminiscent of Raymond Williams' (1965) notion of a "selective" culture, one in which the power relations of a particular society figure heavily in deciding what forms of culture are to be valued and revered and what forms are to be excluded or appropriated. These questions also have helped to break down the high/low culture distinction, the result being that feminists are becoming increasingly concerned with more popular forms of culture. Gender-related research in the sociology of sport is one indication of this transformation. Research into "isolation as oppression," the relationship of leisure to domestic labor, the study of the working class household and the "cult of femininity" in teen magazines are other examples of this growing body of work (Women's Study Group, 1978; Luxton, 1980). In fact, it is in the area of culture and popular culture that Marxism and feminism run somewhat parallel courses.

Uneasy Alliances: Socialist Feminism, Marxism and Literary Production
Despite their differences and disagreement, numerous individuals have put forth the argument that Marxism and certain variants of feminist literary theory occupy somewhat common ground. For example, Gayle Greene (1981) in her argument for alliances, has written:

The understanding of the social basis of consciousness and

ideology, shared by feminists and Marxists, informs their
approaches and concerns; and since ideology includes art
and the judgement of art, it is an assumption that has implications for the literary criticism practiced by both (p. 29).

This statement forms the foundation for understanding how both
feminism and Marxism attempt to undermine traditional literary
theory and criticism. Instead of conceptualizing literature as
something which is separate from society, both theoretical approaches prefer to ground the production of literary conventions
in the social structure and to the relations of power which cir-
cumscribe that society. Generally, feminist critics have come to
this understanding through examining the various literary forms
used to limit and subordinate women characters (cf., Kolodny,
1980). Similarly, Marxists have attempted to assess the complex
manner in which particular forms of literature are inscribed with
class-specific codes and are rooted in specific world views (cf.,
Lukacs, 1964; Goldmann, 1975). This is not to say that either
perspective can simply be appropriated by the other. Indeed,
there has been enough disagreement even within Marxist circles
to prevent the construction of a unified body of theory (cf.,
Williams, 1977; Eagleton, 1976a; Jameson, 1971). The point is that
both feminism and Marxism are cognizant of the social basis of
art and literature.

There are a number of other parallels between these two
perspectives. In a very important way both Marxism and
feminism provide a ready-made critique of traditional literary
criticism and aesthetics. Both forms of criticism ask us to:
(1) reinterpret and even resist traditional readings of the text (cf.,
Fetterley, 1978; Eagleton, 1976a) and (2) reconceptualize our whole
notion of what literary criticism should be. With regard to this
latter point, Annette Kolodny (1980 : 8) argued that traditional
criticism "invites students to offer only increasingly more in-
genious readings and interpretations, the purpose of which is
to invalidate the greatness already imputed by canonization."
In other words, traditional criticism already has decided what
literature is worthy of study. Terry Eagleton (1976b), a Marxist
literary critic, made a similar point about literary criticism working to "add on" or complete the text, rather than analyze its incomplete nature.

A final area of convergence concerns the purposes of literary
criticism and, ultimately, a theory of aesthetics. There is a strong

sense in which both Marxism and feminism make the study of literature of the past part of the present and future. That is, in reinterpreting the production of literary forms in past societies and tracing their development through history, researchers can: (1) understand more completely the relationships between culture and social and political organization, and (2) devise strategies for alternative forms of literature and culture. This is not to imply that Marxists and feminists will always agree on these relationships and strategies. Nevertheless, it is difficult to imagine the creation of a socialist culture without addressing some of the fundamental questions raised by the women's movement; nor is it likely that feminism can make any real change without a corresponding grasp of the specific nature of women's oppression under capitalism (cf., Edwards *et. al.*, 1978; Barrett, 1980). As Rowbotham (1972) notes:

> Their synthesis cannot be merely intellectual, but will come out of the ideals we make practical, dissolving, preserving and exploding our conceptions of both (pp. 245-246).

THE CHARACTERIZATION OF WOMEN IN THREE CANADIAN SPORTS NOVELS

Before the discussion of three sample novels, a few general points about characterization should be made. At the broadest level, characterization in the novel obliquely reflects the vast changes in society as a whole. For instance, Alan Swingewood (1975 : 4) suggested that the ideology of individualism is reflected in the novels' portrayal of the hero/heroine and his/her conflict with the social order. Numerous analysts have advanced earlier versions of Swingewood's dichotomy in addition to developing their own theories of the novel form (cf., Williams, 1965; Goldmann, 1975; Fox, 1945). It is interesting to note, however, that very few researchers have extended the significance of these structures for understanding the dominant/subordinate relationships between male and female characters.

Why is characterization and the relationships between characters and the social structure in the novel important for a socialist feminist analysis? In the first place, it is generally accepted that the development of characters is perhaps the most important achievement of the novel form. Next to plot structure, characters are undoubtedly what most readers will remember when asked to explain what a novel was about. In addition, I would argue that the manner in which women and men are revealed and typified in relation to their social surroundings is probably the most significant structure to be analyzed by socialist feminist critics.

A final but important point needs to be made about characterization. In order to deal with the secondary position of women characters in Canadian sports novels, one must recognize two essential factors. The first has to do with the commercial logic of sport literature and the creation of an appropriate market. As Terry Eagleton (1976b) clearly pointed out:

> Books are not just structures of meaning, they are also commodities produced by publishers and sold on the market for profit. . . (p. 59)

The market which has been carved out for sports literature has largely been oriented towards a young male clientele, in much the same way that teen magazines have been aimed at a young female audience. It is not surprising then to find that the main characters and heroes of almost all sports novels are male figures.[8]

The second factor is not quite as straightforward as the commodity argument. It has to do with the type of qualities that the male hero possesses and the way in which he is related to the fictional social world. I have dealt elsewhere, in more detail, with the question of how the main male figure, or "positive hero" has been developed in Canadian sports fiction (cf., Hollands, 1981; Sattel, 1977). However, the point is sufficiently important to provide at least a skeleton sketch of how the characterization of the positive hero influences secondary characters, some of whom are women.

In a sample of Canadian sports novels, characterization was achieved by assigning to the main male character a core group of homogeneous traits. These traits included an over-emphasis on physical stature and body type, an implied socio-biological theory of personality, and the capacity of the sports hero to control and define social situations and structures (dominance). This latter quality has perhaps the greatest impact on the role and development of secondary characters. First, the plot structures of the novels tend to revolve around and be controlled to a large extent, by the hero's physical and mental capabilities. Second, due to the process of hierarchization (the idea that one character's actions are more important than are other's), the reader tends to focus on the activities and interpretations of the hero in his relationship to social situations. Finally, in order to understand the limited characterization of women in sports fiction, one must be aware that the forerunner to the women antagonists was the sports bully. The central, but limited role given to this character was: (1) to provide a target for the hero's morally correct response to social situations, and (2) to use this adversary to legitimate and enhance the virtues and strengths of the positive hero (cf., Hollands, 1981; Hollands, 1982). The importance of these and other factors in limiting the characterization of women in sports fiction will become clearer in my analysis of three contemporary Canadian sports novels.

Women as Antagonists in the Canadian Sports Novel
   The three novels selected for analysis are Scott Young's *Face-Off* (1972), Clive Doucet's *Disneyland, Please* (1978) and John Gault's *Crossbar* (1979). Their selection is neither random nor scientific. All three novels, written in the 1970s, represent attempts to utilize sport as a cultural theme without lapsing totally into traditional plots and formulas.[9] Additionally, each novel centers around a different sport (hockey, football and athletics), and interestingly enough, each main character comes from a particular region of Canada (Ontario, Cape Breton, and Saskatchewan). Most important, however, is the fact that each story contains a central woman character who acts as an antagonist to the male hero. Herein lies the major reason for their selection in this analysis.
   Certain questions must be asked in the context of the theoretical basis of socialist feminist literary criticism. For example, what structural roles are women characters given (or left with) in the creation of a sports plot? How does their relationship to the hero lead to a subordinate form of characterization? In what ways do women characters either affirm or challenge the masculine ideology of the Canadian sports story? If they do challenge the male hero, how is their alternative ideology subverted? How is male sexuality used to consolidate an impression of the "correctness" of male domination in other areas of social and cultural life? These are just some of the questions a feminist critic might pose.
   Scott Young's novel *Face-Off* (1972) is about Billy Duke, "the hottest prospect to hit the National Hockey League (N.H.L.) since Bobby Orr." *Face-Off* is Billy's story, and he tells it through his perceptions and feelings. This is an important place to begin the analysis. From a feminist point of view, it is essential to under-

stand the story as structured through a masculine ideology and consciousness. We receive only limited exposure to the consciousness of the antagonist, Sherri Lee Nelson. In fact the very reading of the novel is biased in the sense that we only see the world through the haze of Billy's masculine logic.

Billy is not a typical sports hero, however. While he could be described as a "superjock," he is at the same time equally cynical about the structure of professional hockey. He berates sportswriters who "flick a glance at your prick before meeting your eyes" (Young, 1972 : 1), his teammates for all the meaningless "rah, rah" stuff, and the corporate owners for their condescending and contradictory moral attitudes. Yet he accepts all of this because he loves the game of hockey, its thrills, excitement and stardom. Despite his cynicism, Billy is also caught up in the masculine world of high-level professional sport which breeds inflated egos, violence, and dominant behavior patterns. These traits are shown to permeate Billy's relationship with the antagonist, Sherri Lee Nelson. His desire to consume and own her (in much the same way that he is owned) becomes apparent to him too late in their relationship. In a very straightforward manner, Billy can be seen as one of Sherri's suitors; he wants to bring her into his world (which itself is a world of consumption) to protect her from a music subculture which he sees as both subversive and dangerous.

Sherri is everything that Billy is not. She is a star in her own right, yet she never seems to take on the status or importance of Billy. He is the central character who makes things happen; Sherri merely reacts to those changes. While Sherri possesses admirable characteristics—gentleness, sensitivity, and genuine caring—they are undermined by her inability to cope with problems without retreating into the illusory world of drugs and music. If Sherri's world is supposed to provide a challenge to the masculine structure of professional sport, then it is subverted by her weakness and paranoia in certain social situations.

Ultimately, Sherri is cast into a position where she simply cannot win. If she chooses Billy's world, she subordinates herself to him and the forces that control him. If she returns to her own world she is regressing into a subculture of escapism. Sherri is defeated halfway through the novel when she realizes "that a telephone bell could destroy an act of love and snatch him from her" and that she could not "contend with the other forces that controlled him" (Young, 1972 : 125). Her subordination to Billy's dominance is depicted in this particular scene:

> She felt herself wince under the pressure of his grip. "You're no different from the rest of those apes," she whimpered, starting to squirm with pain. "Yes I am," he said pulling her close until her face was almost touching his. "Because I'm younger, and stronger, and tougher!" Sherri gave a little cry, more to fend off his words than to protest his roughness. "That's why you dig me!" he went on, and even as she mouthed a denial she knew he had found the truth (Young, 1972 : 129).

Billy consummates his dominance sexually, in a reenactment of the way in which his father finally stood up to his mother, "the way a man should," earlier in the novel. His father's words, "Don't ever let a woman own you, Billy," echo in the background. The contradiction is that Billy is already owned by the barons of professional hockey.

The story ends with an unnecessary confrontation between Billy's love for Sherri and the inflexible and authoritarian logic of professional sport. Sherri's death, more correctly understood as virtual suicide, is also unnecessary for she had long given up trying to construct a viable alternative to Billy's acceptance and incorporation into the patriarchal structure of sport and society.

Clive Doucet's *Disneyland, Please* (1978) is strikingly similar to *Face-Off* in some central respects. Doucet's novel is concerned with the rise of an Acadian superjock to the world of American college football. Guy Lablanc, the hero of the story, is not so much caught up in the authoritarian structure of pro sport as he is torn between his fantasies of California and Cape Breton. His fantasies are also extended to his relationships with women characters, giving the plot an extra dimension. Again, what is striking is that the entire novel is written in the first person, which means that the reader can only experience the story through the consciousness of the main character. We know the major antagonist, Josie Caulie (again a singer), only from the protagonist's perceptions and sensibilities. Guy acts and interprets his actions, Josie reacts, and again Guy interprets her reactions.

There are other women characters presented throughout the novel. For the most part they are given supporting, if not subordinate roles. Guy's interpretation throughout the story is that women are basically objects to be consumed. His first real exposure to members of the opposite sex occurs in high school in Ottawa and can be characterized as follows:

Mostly high school had to do with being horny. Very, very horny. Ripening thighs attracted on each side. Rich young chests bowed down over desks. Straining for a glimpse. Hours and hours spent wondering. "What would it be like? On top of her? Underneath her? Inside her?" (Doucet, 1978 : 58).

The promise of a macho existence (fast cars and fast women) with the entry into professional sport is echoed by Guy's hockey friend, Reilly:

". . . Man, if I make it, the first thing I'm going to do is buy me the biggest, bluest, Corvette you've ever seen and right beside me is going to be this babe that'll melt your balls" (Doucet, 1978 : 79).

Also there is Guy's French teacher, Jane Johnson, who seduces him when he is fifteen. The impression is that Jane is liberated— "Miss Johnson had been to Europe and in Europe women did not shave their legs. Nor did she" (Doucet, 1978 : 88)—but one wonders how she spends two years of her life with a fifteen year old whose only interests are sex and hockey? The story indicates that Jane hates hockey, so her interest is clear. She calls Guy "meat," and although it is she who leaves, ". . . to be Jane Johnson," her character is symbolic of the denigrated woman. The point is not that the circumstances do not reflect the position of some women living in a sexist society but rather that these novels tend to "naturalize" such sex roles (Berger, 1972).

Josie Caulie, the antagonist in Disneyland, Please, enters the plot when Guy begins to play football and moves to California. She, like Sherri Lee Nelson in Face-Off, is a rock singer and in a similar fashion is the antithesis of professional sport. In Guy's words: "For me Josephine Caulie was the quintessence of everything the football world was not. . . she didn't have the season planned down to the last play. Nor did she care to" (Doucet, 1978 : 153). Josie is also torn between two worlds, symbolized by her two suitors—Harry, a drummer in the band and Guy, football player and "bearer of an independent and ancient culture." Again, like Sherri, she is caught in a no-win situation. Josie comes from a rich Californian family and realizing the phoniness of her position and heritage, searches for an existence rooted in genuine caring and feelings. Guy's homeland in Cape Breton can provide that existence. What Josie fails to realize, is that Guy's idealistic construction of his village, Bel Etang, is but one aspect of his fantasy of making himself more than he really is. This realization occurs too late in their relationship, and Josie quickly fades into the background of the novel and becomes yet another of Guy's fantasies.

John Gault's *Crossbar* (1979), is the final sports novel that I wish to examine. *Crossbar* is a fictional account of an Olympic high-jumper, Aaron Kornylo, who loses his leg in a farming accident. Katie Barlow is a world-renowned pentathlete who helps Aaron to believe in himself once more as he attempts to make the Canadian Olympic team.

Of all the women characters analyzed, Katie is adequately developed through her relationship to Aaron's family and through her own athletic talents. She is strong, sure of herself and her opinions. In a central way, Katie is given her identity in much the same manner as male heroes of Canadian sports fiction. This is a significant point. Katie is not so much a fully developed woman character as she is a woman developed through male categories.

There is a deliberate attempt to portray Katie as a liberated woman. When her conservative aunt sends her a copy of *Fascinating Womanhood*, Katie responds by mailing her *The Female Eunuch*. Her relationship with Aaron's father, Myles, also contributes to this characterization. To Katie, Myles is old school—masculine, self-centered, hard-shelled—and Aaron's attempted suicide causes her to lash out at him; "You still see it as some kind of big macho adventure, don't you" (Gault, 1979 : 51). In a later episode, she checks Aaron's amorous advancement by boldly announcing "Well, if that's all it is, let's get it on. Up in the hayloft?" (Gault, 1979 : 87). Everything about her suggests that she is in control. She continues her confrontation with Aaron by explaining:

". . . but Greg doesn't run my life. Not Greg, not you, not anybody. I'm my own woman, Aaron, I do what I want to do. I'm grown up and I can make my own choices" (Gault, 1979 : 88).

Yet, in the final analysis, what is Katie's real status in the novel?

In her relationship with Aaron she is cast in a supportive role; "In her mind, she was—has been—just a good friend, helping out" (Gault, 1979 : 75). She nurses Aaron over his depression, she helps him to believe in himself, and she trains him to qualify for the Olympic team. Katie's own athletic talents fade into background and the spotlight remains on Aaron, as it did at the beginning of the novel. Katie's talent is that she is a helper, a kind of Florence Nightingale of the sports world. The fact that she chooses to go with Greg (her other suitor) at the end of the story is also inconsequential. Aaron has found another helper and, besides, he is a man (albeit with one leg) who can make it on his own now. If Katie was portrayed as Aaron's equal in the first part of the novel, it was because he was less than a man then (emasculated through the loss of a limb).[10] Through sheer determination, and Katie's help, Aaron is whole again. She, like the other characters, stands in awe of him and his achievement. In a very real sense, Katie has been released from her task and placed back into the natural order of things, which can be no better than second place.

I want to conclude this paper on a more positive note than my previous comments imply. I am not suggesting that women characters in sports fiction will always find themselves relegated to a subordinate or supportive role. Nor am I arguing that novelists should simply insert women characters into a sports role which is nothing more than a surrogate male hero. On a broader level, it is still debatable whether sports fiction can provide an adequate critique of the ideology of masculinity. Alan Tomlinson (1982) has argued that some sports novels can function as a potentially counter-ideological form and can work to challenge some of the dominant values epitomized by male sport forms. In this regard, sport has never been a highly regarded subject in feminist fiction. Yet, there are exceptions. Oliver Leaman (1982) has discussed how Marge Piercy's novel, *The High Cost of Living* (1978), is an attempt to struggle with the dilemma feminists face when they adopt and try to transform male sports forms. More effort on the part of feminists needs to be directed to the ways in which they can work to deconstruct and transform existing cultural practices and formations, in the context of the existing political, cultural and economic structures of our society. Only then can a truly humane and egalitarian culture flourish.

NOTES

1. I would like to thank the following people who aided in one way or another in the creation of this paper: Alan Tomlinson, Rick Gruneau, Hart Cantelon, Cathy Bray, Rob Beamish and Ann Hall. Special thanks goes to Mrs. E.L. Hollands for her typing skill and to Susan Harcourt for her patience and support in my long absences.

2. The terms of this debate can be found in Anderson (1980) and Thompson (1978).

3. For example, see Sarachild (1975), Hanish (1975) and Barrett (1980). Feminism, as such, is a somewhat schizophrenic category. However, because my sources for this paper range from radical to socialist to structuralist feminists, I have kept the problematic term. I will try whenever necessary to differentiate between these various schools of thought.

4. For a sensitive, historical discussion of the fractures and alliances between feminist and socialist movements and thinkers, see Rowbotham (1972).

5. Examples of a perspective which combines elements of Marxism and socialist feminism and applies this approach to cultural forms such as popular literature can be found in the Women's Study Group (1978).

6. The liberal ideology of the media often tends to characterize the women's movement as one in which women want equal status with men within the structure of capitalist society, rather than the more radical notion that women's liberation is impossible without completely restructuring the social order. Fundamentally, this is the difference between liberal and socialist feminists. For an interesting and somewhat surprising discussion of what women can achieve under capitalism, see Barrett (1980).

7. Kennard (1978 : 160-63) makes this point primarily about Lessing (1974) and Jong (1974).

8. With women's sports increasingly becoming a commodity, one could easily predict the advent of women sports heroes in various fictional forms (cf., Lear, 1978).

9. This is not to say that these novels do not use modified versions of traditional sports plots. For a discussion of early American sports fiction see Evan (1972).

10. This point comes from a conversation I had with Alan Tomlinson. I would like to thank him for his many insights.

REFERENCES

Anderson, Perry
1980   Arguments Within English Marxism. London: Vevso.

Barrett, Michele
1980   Women's Oppression Today. London: New Left Books.

Berger, John
1972   Ways of Seeing. London: The British Broadcasting Corporation and Penguin Books Ltd.

Doucet, Clive
1978   Disneyland, Please. Toronto: Fitzhenry and Whiteside.

Eagleton, Terry
1976a   Ideology and Criticism. London: New Left Books.
1976b   Marxism and Literary Criticism. Berkeley: University of California Press.

Edwards, Richard, Michael Reich and Thomas E. Weisskopf
1978   The Capitalist System. New Jersey: Prentice Hall Inc.

Evan, Walter
1972   "The all-American boys: a study of boys sports fiction." The Journal of Popular Culture 6:104-121.

Fetterley, Judith
1978   The Resisting Reader: A Feminist Approach to American Literature. Bloomington: Indiana University Press.

Fox, Ralph
1945   The Novel and the People. New York: International Publishers.

Gault, John
1979   Crossbar. Toronto: Seal Books.

Giddens, Anthony
1982   Sociology: A Brief But Critical Introduction. New York: Harcourt Brace Jovanovich.

Goldmann, Lucien
1975   Towards a Sociology of the Novel. London: Tavistock Publications Ltd.

Greene, Gayle
1981   "Feminist and Marxist criticism: an argument for alliances."
       Women's Studies 9:29-45.

Hanish, Carol
1975   "The liberal takeover of women's liberation." In Feminist Revolu-
       tion. New York: Random House.

Hollands, Robert G.
1981   "Canadian Sports Novels and Cultural Production." Unpublish-
       ed M.A. thesis, School of Physical and Health Education,
       Queen's University, Oct.
1982   "Canadian sports novels, Marxism and cultural production." In
       Sporting Fictions. Birmingham: Centre for Contemporary
       Cultural Studies.

Jameson, Frederic
1971   Marxism and Form. New Jersey: Princeton University Press.

Jong, Erica
1974   Fear of Flying. New York: Signet.

Kaplan, Sydney Janet
1975   Feminine Consciousness in the Modern British Novel. Chicago:
       University of Illinois Press.

Kennard, Jean
1978   Victims of Convention. Connecticut: Anchor Books.

Kolodny, Annette
1980   "Dancing through the minefield: some observations on the
       theory, practice and politics of a feminist literary criticism."
       Feminist Studies 6:1-25.

Leaman, Oliver
1982   "Sport and the feminist novel." In Sporting Fictions. Birming-
       ham: Centre for Contemporary Cultural Studies.

Lear, Peter
1978   Golden Girl. London: Mayflower Books.

Lessing, Doris
1974   The Summer Before the Dark. New York: Bantam.

Lukacs, Georg
1964   Realism in Our Times. New York: Harper Torchbooks.

Luxton, Meg
1980   More Than a Labour of Love. Toronto: The Women's Press.

Millett, Kate
1970   Sexual Politics. New York: Doubleday and Company Inc.

Piercy, Marge
1978   The High Cost of Living. New York: Harper and Row.

Rowbotham, Sheila
1972   Women, Resistance and Revolution. Middlesex: Penguin.

Sarachild, Katie
1975   "The power of history." In Feminist Revolution. New York: Ran-
       dom House.

Sattel, Jack
1977   "Heroes on the right." The Journal of Popular Culture 11:110-125.

Showalter, Elaine
1977   A Literature of Their Own. Princeton: Princeton University Press.

Swift, Carolyn Ruth, Gayle Greene and Carol Thomas Neely
1980   'The Woman's Part': Feminist Criticism of Shakespeare. Urbana:

Swingewood, Alan
1975   The Novel and Revolution. London: MacMillan.

Thompson, E.P.
1978   The Poverty of Theory and other essays. London: Merlin.

Tomlinson, Alan
1982   "Sports fiction as critique: the novelistic challenge to the ideology
       of masculinity." In Sporting Fictions. Birmingham: Centre for
       Contemporary Cultural Studies.

Williams, Raymond
1965   The Long Revolution. Middlesex: Pelican Books.
1977   Marxism and Literature. Oxford: Oxford University Press.

Women's Study Group, Centre for Contemporary Cultural Studies
1978   Women Take Issue: Aspects of Women's Subordination. Lon-
       don: Hutchinson.

Young, Scott
1972   Face-Off. Richmond Hill: Simon and Schuster of Canada Ltd.

SECTION II

Feminist Analysis
and the Study of Gender
in Sport

ONE OF THE DEVELOPMENTS within contemporary sociology that reflects the promise of the sociological imagination is the analysis of gender relations and gender inequality. Mills' concern for the unity of theory and practice and his conviction that sociologists should devote their efforts to the major issues of their time find ready application in current efforts to identify the sources of gender inequality and the strategies that may be employed to transform social relations between women and men. Indeed, many would hold that these issues present the fundamental challenge to contemporary sociology and as well, to modern societies.

One indication of the enormity of the challenge posed by these concerns is the intensity of theoretical discussion and debate about the sources of gender inequality. The first three articles in this section present analyses of the contributions of several approaches to understanding gender inequality in sport. The first of these articles is Rob Beamish's discussion of the capacity of a materialist perspective to account for the condition of women. Rooted in Marx's *oeuvre* and subsequently developed in the writings of others, the materialist position takes the labor process and class as its major concern. Beamish illustrates the use of the materialist position by examining the relationship between gender and opportunities for participation in sport. The conclusion he draws is that gender issues can adequately be treated in a materialist framework without any substantial revision of the principles of the framework.

Ann Hall's "Toward a Feminist Analysis of Gender Inequality in Sport" begins with an account of her own work in the sociology of sport and how it has been influenced by feminism and feminist scholarship. Feminism, she writes, is a theory of power, and the task of the feminist scholar is to explicate the nature of power relations between men and women and the sources of the subjection of women. Hall reviews the main strands of feminist social theory: a Marxist-feminist analysis, an analysis that focuses on sexuality as the main area of women's oppression, and an analysis that attempts to incorporate considerations of both class and sexuality to explain power relations between the sexes. She concludes with some observations about the relationship between feminism and positivism and suggests that feminist social theory is "critical, humanist and value-oriented. . . . It rejects positivism but supports an interpretive model of social science."

While the papers by Beamish and Hall have a number of differences, there is an important implicit agreement between them that can easily be overlooked. Although Beamish's materialism draws from Marx's work, he also points out that Marx's work is incomplete, Beamish looks to a developing materialist position which will incorporate the work of many authors to establish an analytic framework that would adequately explain gender inequality in sport. Hall makes a similar point but in another way. Her critique of the Marxist paradigm is essentially directed at those who think Marx's writings represent a wholly completed system that can already adequately explain gender oppression. Thus both authors agree that current radical sociological theory does not deal satisfactorily with gender issues, although Beamish sees a partial solution within a more sophisticated materialism and Hall suggests that feminist and class theories themselves can, with more work, be successfully brought together to serve as the needed problematic.

The third article in this section is Cathy Bray's "Gender and the Political Economy of Canadian Sport." Grounded in Marxist and neo-Marxist theory and primarily Canadian, the political economy of sport utilizes dependency theory, class analysis and elite studies to explore issues of power and dominance. While offering an important alternative to traditional interpretations grounded in liberal democratic theory, the new political economy of sport is deficient in its analysis of gender issues. In her critique of some of the work in this area, Bray identifies three issues that need to be incorporated into the political economy framework: sexuality, the family, and domestic labor.

She argues that a comprehensive analysis of social relations in Canadian sport must contain a synthesis of the political economy tradition and a feminist analysis of these issues.

The final selection in this section is Susan Birrell's "Studying Gender in Sport: A Feminist Perspective." Based upon a content analysis of literature in the field, Birrell offers a review and critique of the conceptualization of gender as a variable in the sociology of sport. She shows that most of the research either ignores considerations of gender or perpetuates a false model of gender arrangements as complementary. Birrell calls for a revised understanding of the meaning of gender that embodies a feminist perspective and attends to the particular experiences of women. Like Hall, Birrell argues that to attain such a perspective, social scientists must look beyond the confines of traditional research methodologies. Birrell specifically recommends adoption of research strategies that enable the development of grounded theory based on the experiences of women. In this way, she believes, we may better attain the promise of the sociological imagination in the study of women's sport experience.

MATERIALISM AND THE COMPREHENSION OF GENDER-RELATED ISSUES IN SPORT[1]

Rob Beamish, University of Toronto

THE TASK THAT I WILL ADDRESS IN THIS PAPER—the presentation of the materialist position concerning gender-related issues in sport study—is an impossible one. It is impossible in what I understand is the military's sense of the term: "The difficult we do immediately," their axiom exhorts, "the impossible takes a little longer." I am not even sure that a few substantial books or a two-term graduate seminar would be long enough to explore fully the debate surrounding materialism and feminism as frameworks for sport study but certainly an article is not. Nevertheless, despite the constraints of available time, some headway can be made in outlining a few key issues concerning the materialist position as it clarifies gender-related questions in sport.

To make this headway, however, the march cannot be resolutely straight forward. It is imperative to begin with a theoretical excursus that establishes the background and context for the ensuing analysis of some specific gender-related sport issues. Thus the paper is divided into two parts. Part one examines, in a rather cursory manner, three issues: (i) Marx's *oeuvre*, since my materialist position is rooted in his work, (ii) the notion of a theoretical *tableau* or problematic and finally (iii) the notion of dialetic. In part two, I use the materialist position to discuss elements central to gender and opportunities for participation in sport. In that section I discuss (i) sport opportunity and the value-form of production, (ii) the hidden injuries of class and their manifestation in sport participation and finally, (iii) the media image of sport.

THEORETICAL EXCURSUS

Marx's Oeuvre.

Stripped to the absolute core, the materialist position contends that "[t]he history we make is nothing other than the processes of the relation of labour with nature, the interaction within society, and the mental and spiritual representations which arise from these relations and interactions" (Krader, 1982: 200). While this apparently simple statement is deceptively laden with considerable information, its aphoristic nature still leaves much to be fleshed out and explained. Unfortunately, the available writings of Marx are themselves only partially helpful for exploring all aspects of this aphorism. The young Kautsky was as much as told so when he visited Marx in 1881 asking if the time had not come to edit and publish Marx's complete works. Marx replied that they would first have to be written (see Kautsky, 1935: 53).

Marx's reply was not motivated by any false modesty concerning what he had already published and drafted in various degrees of completion to that point in time. As a comprehensive whole Marx's writings were, and are, deficient; he was unable to address all of the intellectual agenda he had established for himself. But attempts by Kautsky and the German Social Democratic Party (with at least some tacit support from Engels) to present Marx's work—supplemented by some of Engels' later writings—as a fully completed systematic science of society lead many to forget the incomplete nature of Marx's *oeuvre.* The idea that Marx's work represents a completed whole is myth on the one hand and impossibility on the other.

The myth side of the question is relatively easy to dispense with. Even though *Capital* (Volume One) was the crowning achievement of decades of labor, it did not exhaust, or really even approach the full intellectual project Marx had worked on throughout his life and had in mind in his reply to Kautsky.

As early as 1844, Marx had written an extensive critique of Hegel's *Philosophy of Law* in draft form and published an introduction to his intended full-scale critique of jurisprudence. But these efforts only showed Marx that an embracing critique of civil society would require a far more lengthy and complex analysis. In the preface to his *Economic and Philosophic Manuscripts*, Marx (1964: 226) indicated that he would publish "various independent booklets *[Broschuren]*" on the critique of law, morality, politics, political economy, etc., followed by a single work that would present them as a whole and the connections between the various parts. On February 1st, 1845, Marx signed a contract to publish a two-volume study entitled *Critique of Politics and Political Economy* (Marx and Engels, 1964, Bd. 2: 692). The contract is significant to more than Marx trivia collectors because, as Rubel (1981a) argued, Marx's so-called *Economics* was always intended to be more than a discussion of economic matters; politics and the state were considered significant aspects of the project from the outset.

The unity of politics and political economy was maintained in the *German Ideology* (see Marx, 1964: 367-368) although between 1848 and the mid-1850's Marx did not work systematically on the unified project. This period was filled with intense political activity followed by attention to specific components of political or political economy questions. Nevertheless, by 1857, Marx again drafted a project encompassing political economy and politics. Of six proposed books, the first triad (capital, landed property and wage-labor) is concerned primarily with economically oriented matters while the second triad (the state, foreign trade and the world market) would presumably have examined the state and its legislative role in the flow, exchange and distribution of social resources.

Now whether one agrees with Rosdolsky (1977: 10-62) that Marx subsequently modified this plan and incorporated all or parts of books two and three into the first three volumes of *Capital* or with Rubel (1981a; 1981b) that Marx's aspirations for the full project were never really abandoned, it is evident that Volume One of *Capital*—the only volume completed by Marx—or even the four volumes of *Capital* are merely part of a much larger whole envisaged by Marx. This conclusion does not even take into account Marx's early plan for a collection of the best non-German socialist writers or a "mak[ing] accessible to ordinary human intelligence. . . what is rational in the method which Hegel discovered. . ." (Marx and Engels 1964, Bd. 37: 235) nor his studies in ethnology (Marx, 1974).

Whether Engels' later writings complete Marx's project is contentious at best. He edited Marx's notebooks for Volumes Two and Three of *Capital* but deliberately refrained as much as possible from inserting his own ideas into the unfinished material. *Anti-Duhring* is foremost a reluctantly written polemic against a localized position which was gaining strength in the German social democratic movement (see Jones, 1982: 293). It elaborated upon aspects of *Capital* but did not supersede the latter in any way. Finally, the philosophic position advanced in *Ludwig Feuerbach*, which actually began as a somewhat reluctantly written review of C.N. Storke's book on Feuerbach, cannot be considered a faultless systematization and popularization of Marx's position.

Consequently, it is correct to conclude that even though the available writings of Marx provide tremendous insight into his ideas about the problems he saw as central to social study and indeed provide some exhaustive and complete analyses on certain questions, Marx's *oeuvre* does not represent a finished system. In fact, from a somewhat different angle of interpretation it is apparent that it could not be one.

On the basis of its own ontological premises, Marx's work, even if he had written all he had intended, could not constitute a closed, completed system. Korsch (1975) made this point forcefully in 1950. "Today" he wrote, "all attempts to re-establish the Marxist doctrine as a whole in its original function as a theory of the working class's social revolution are reactionary utopias." (p. 40). Korsch did not make this statement to reject the materialist position but rather to affirm it. The materialist position emphasizes the relationships between material conditions of existence and consciousness of those conditions, between practice and theory.

Since 1883 much has changed both materially and ideationally. Previously unknown manuscripts have changed our conceptions of Marx. We know Marx made errors and was himself limited by the *Weltanschauung* of his own epoch (see Krader, 1982: 218, n.10, 203, 212). Debates concerning Marx's and later Marxists' conceptions of society and social history have sharpened and altered perceptions considerably. Finally, capitalism's objective aspect—the social relations themselves—have changed markedly (though not qualitatively).

All of these changes have constituted part of the continuing development of the materialism initiated by Marx and Engels, and it is this theory/practice dynamic that necessitates resistance to ossification and canonization. In view of its open nature and the emendations made to the framework, the materialism initiated by Marx represents a powerful conceptual apparatus for comprehending and acting within contemporary society. Furthermore, I contend, the framework, as it has been developed, may be used to examine issues and answer questions the classical Marxists (including Marx) did not consider, without having to recast its structure.

The notion of a theoretical tableau or problematic (complete)

Following the attack upon positivist empiricism, there is more awareness concerning how much theory selects and elevates some parts of empirical reality to the status of fact while unconsciously suppressing other aspects from observation. This sifting process is found at all levels of observation from the everyday to the scientific (see Foucault, 1966: 11-13). Foucault (1966) noted that "[t]he fundamental codes of a culture—those that govern its language, its perceptual schemas, its exchanges, its techniques, its values, the hierarchy of its practices—fix at the outset for every man the empirical orders which he will be dealing with and in which he will find himself" (p. 11).

To conceptualize this organizing (and excluding) process, Foucault (1966) referred to an analytic grid or employed the image of a tableau. "[The *tableau*] permits thought to operate on things [*les etres*] to bring order, to divide them into classes, to nominally group them designating their similarities and their differences—the tableau [is] where, since the beginning of time, language intersects with space" (p. 9). Foucault's notions of grid and tableau have not enjoyed wide-spread currency in the social sciences even though they conceptually portray the process they are describing very well. More popular is the notion of problematic. Johnson (1979) stated, "'Problematic' may be defined as a 'definite theoretical structure,' a field of concepts, which organizes a particular science or individual text by making it possible to ask some kinds of questions and by suppressing others" (p. 201).

The way a problematic operates may be understood with reference to the concept of class which is a major term in the materialist tableau or problematic. At the same time the concept shows that the location of concepts within problematics does not make analysis simplistic. Class, as part of the problematic, retains subtle objective/subjective and abstract/concrete dimensions that make it an analytical philosopher's nightmare (and dialecticians often fare little better).

For the materialists following Marx, the objective dimensions of class emerge in the breakup of communal societies and the formation of civil societies. Work which was formerly concrete and directed by the recognized and articulated wants and plan of the community becomes divided into concrete and abstract and progressively subordinated to imperatives and pressures external to the community's interests as a unity (Krader, 1976: 196-197). The communal interest also becomes divided into realms of public and private, providing the context for the abstract, juridical, individual and a state structure. Most significant, a class division of immediate workers and non-workers (who may ostensibly assume some planning or protecting capacity) emerges.

The materialist problematic puts labor and the objective dimensions of class at the center of its tableau for basically three reasons. First, the primary alienation of humankind from nature creates production (or labor) as the negative ontology of social history (see Krader, 1979: 47-101; Lukacs, 1980; Marx, 1964: 346-347; Schmidt, 1971: 19-50, 76-94).[2] Second, the separation of labor into private and social, abstract and concrete, is the substance of class-divided or civil society. Finally, the eventual practical objective of the materialist problematic is the transcendence of the unbalanced, exploitative distribution of productive responsibility and rewards (material and cultural) that are inherent to the social relations of civil society.

As a tableau (or problematic) the inequalities emanating from class-divided production are given center court but, it must be asked if the apparent silence on the question of gender is one of total and necessary omission? I think the answer is no. Marx, we know, spent negligible time on the question but, as I have argued above (and will add to in the next section), the incomplete nature of Marx's *oeuvre* and the imperatives of his materialist ontology do not rule out the use of his problematic to investigate gender issues. I would contend that the questions associated with gender are always potentially present and they become increasingly central within the tableau as they raise, first, issues of social freedom and equality *pro forma* and, then, substantial issues of freedom, equality and human emancipation. But to articulate these questions fully, one has carefully to employ the abstract tableau with concrete questions of social history. In a sense, gender questions are not much different in terms of treatment than questions of class (although a little more mileage can be extracted from abstract formalism in the case of the latter).

Thompson's (1961) work on class helps clarify this last paragraph. He notes that in the study of class, the tableau of abstract conceptualization tends to remove class from the flux of time, and since class is more than an objectively determined category—it is also behavior and consciousness within time and social context (see also Thompson, 1978: 106-108)—this creates problems with purely abstract, categorial analyses of class. Thompson's work, like Marx's own concrete historical analyses, exemplifies the elucidation of class through the interrogation of concrete events with the abstract problematic of class. I would argue that work investigating the relation of gender-focused issues to class would have to follow that type of analysis and elaboration of abstract theory and concrete events.

The pressing concern to many at this point would be the question of biological reproduction in human history. There has been a movement toward the inclusion of biological reproduction alongside material production as co-determinants of the so-called social infra-structure (see Harris, 1980: 51-76). I would argue that such an attempt is incorrect, confusing and detrimental to analysis. The error in its inclusion has already been pointed out above concerning labor and the negative ontology of Marx-inspired materialism (see especially note 2). But even more significant than plain error, if that is possible, is the confusion it introduces to gender-related issues which is, I would maintain, detrimental to their study rather than enhancing.

The principal reason for my claim stems from the relation of logic and history. A consciously developed problematic (or tableau) in the hands of a researcher is a synthetic logical construction which organizes knowledge to a limited extent and generalizes the concrete abstractly so that penetrating questions of other concrete events may be asked and answered. Marx (1953: 22-29) was keenly aware that history (the concrete) could not be subordinated to logic (the abstract) and it was the strong temptation to reduce his critique of political economy to a manipulation of logical categories that he consciously resisted (see Marx: 1953: 69). In addition, he was fully aware that only certain dimensions of the social whole were fruitfully amenable to logical abstraction (see Korsch, 1963: 183-188; Marx and Engels, 1964, Bd. 13: 8-9)[3].

At this point in time there has not been any evidence suggesting a logical link between particular forms of the social organization of reproduction and forms of labor, class structure, class inequality or class domination, nor to the various forms of gender inequality and domination. On the contrary, the evidence suggests that a wide variety of kinship structures, clan structures, families—in short, forms of socially organized reproduction—are associated with variable forms of class domination and gender inequality (see for example Mead, 1978). As a result, to comprehend the role of socially organized reproduction in issues of class consciousness and structure or gender consciousness, one must abandon the formal sphere of abstraction and construct linkages at the level of the concrete. Unlike the law of value, which is somewhat amenable to logical elaboration, socially organized reproduction demonstrates such variable association that our understanding of its impact is more profitably pursued at the level of the concrete and not the abstract.

The dialectic.

Because the flux of social reality is the result of its own internal dynamic tension and contradiction, the intellectual framework necessary to grasp its movement must have the structural capacity to reflect reality's complex nature. Prior to Marx, Hegel had worked to develop just such a framework and a key concept of his thought was the overworked but highly misunderstood term dialectic. The most common injustice with which speculative content is being inflicted [*angetan*], Hegel (1969: 94) argued "is to make it one-sided, that is, to stress only one of the propositions [*Sätze*] into which it can be resolved." To grasp the multi-sided nature of reality, Hegel proposed and developed the classical Greek conception of dialectic.[4]

Hegel (1959: 103) argued that "dialectic is the *immanent* outward movement [*Hinausgehen*] in which the one-sidedness and limitedness of the determinations of understanding [*Verstandesbestimmungen*] represents itself as that which it is, namely as its negation." A simplified example will help clarify Hegel's idea.

When an individual first observes a soccer player in action, the observer tends to separate the player from all the other players on the field and while this separation process provides some immediate knowledge about the player, that understanding is limited. The focus of observation must be expanded. What is his or her relation to other players on the field in the same uniform? What is their relation to others observing the game? What are the players' relations to others of different socio-economic status, class and/or conditions of athletic participation? To really know our individual player, he or she must be progressively located within the ambit of ever more complex relations.

Hegel pointed out more than this. He indicated that the movement away from immediate, analytic differentation meant the drawing together of logically contradictory pieces of information: our player is both an individual and a team member (the one and the many). Hegel (1969: 450-458) argued that the synthetic logic of dialectical analysis held together logical contradictions so that knowledge could fully grasp the complex totality of reality and thereby overcome the one-sidedness of analytic syllogisms (see Hegel, 1969: 442-450). Marx went still further.

Marx argued that the dialectic of reality was the dynamic unity of actual contradiction in the concrete world and it was the tension of the concrete that created change and had to be grasped intellectually to direct such change insofar as this was possible. In terms of comprehending reality, however, Marx's synthetic logic was not markedly different from Hegel's.

That is one issue, but another remains for the purpose of this particular discussion. Earlier, I noted that the materialist problematic places labor and class in the center of its tableau but I also maintained that gender was not an irrelevant issue (especially in contemporary society). The link between class and gender may now be seen from a different angle. In grasping the dialectic of reality concerning class, the materialist must explore social labor. This can be initiated exclusive of gender (see for example Braverman, 1974: 1-292). But once this line of analysis has been pursued at some length the dialectic of reality, if it is to be intellectually apprehended, compels the investigator to at least examine (i) the realms of private and domestic labor, (ii) gender segregation in the work place, (iii) legislative regulation of work and gender and (iv) consciousness formation concerning work, ideology, etc. (see Braverman, 1974: 293-358). Thus it is via the dialectic of reality and attempts to comprehend it that synthetic class analysis encompasses more (or less) directly issues related to gender.

In this part of the paper I have sketched out three aspects of the materialist position which show (i) that gender issues can be treated by the framework without any real revision of the problematic; and (ii) indicated approximately how gender is a component of the tableau. In part two I will look at some particular problems related to gender and sport opportunity using the materialist position.

THE MATERIALIST FRAMEWORK AND GENDER-RELATED ISSUES IN SPORT PARTICIPATION

In this section I will superficially explore certain issues related to opportunity in sport. My intention is not to be exhaustive in either depth of analysis or breadth of scope—space constraints and the paucity of sport study research in this area preclude such treatment anyway—but rather to indicate how the materialist tableau can be used to inform gender-related questions in sport study.

Sport and the value-form of production.

Without sketching out the argument, it may be said with confidence that modern sport is clearly marked by the context of its birth and development. Indeed, some features of the sport world are almost totally subsumed under and dominated by the essential logic of industrial capitalism while others are less so. For the materialist then, a central question is the extent to which sport is permeated by the dominant value-form of production characteristic of capitalist society and subsequently, how that permeation contours participation opportunities.[5]

To begin with, what does the value-form of production represent? Rubin (1973) has treated this question at length. He (1973: 13) noted that "[t]here is a close connection and correspondence between the process of *production of material goods and the social form* in which it is carried out." Within the commodity-based economy—or the value-form of production—individuals are not connected to one another by permanent connections determined in advance by tradition, mechanical solidarity or community unity. "In the commodity economy" Rubin (1973: 15) argued, "the commodity producer is connected only with the indetermined market, which he enters through a discrete sequence of individual transactions that temporarily link him with determined commodity producers." The implications of this arrangement are profound.

First, the arrangement means that all individuals have access to and a legal claim over the material and social resources of capitalist society exclusively through their location within the cash nexus of the market economy and the mediate social relations that result from it. It also means that the creation of social goods and services is mediated primarily through the market, and it is via this rather chaotic mechanism that social wants are met. At the same time, profit—the creation and extraction of surplus value—possesses an over-riding prominence vis-a-vis the actual wants of the society so that social production and the actual social wants may not fully coincide (see Sombart, 1937).[6]

Now most physical educators and growing numbers of other professional and social groups regard physical activity in general, and sport in particular, as a valuable pastime and resource. But relying upon the market as the means of distribution for the resources associated with physical activity has significant problems. Within the market economy, income represents a major barrier (or facilitator) to athletic participation and enjoyment. The National Council of Welfare's report *Poor Kids* indicated the general impact of this circumstance on numerous Canadian families. The report (1975) noted:

> The idealized North American family is one that participates together—family outings to the ball game, the museum and the movies, and picnics in the country. But ball games and museums and movies have admission charges, and there can't be picnics in the country without a car to get there in. Summer vacations—with the whole family living a common experience, rediscovering one another and restoring the fabric of relationships worn thin over the year—play an important part in modern family life; but like picnics and ball games, these too are denied the children of the poor (p. 25).

A 14-year-old boy's comments make the point even more forcefully. "I love sport" he wrote, "but I can't participate in anything because we have no money for equipment. We can never do anything because of lack of money. I feel as if it will always be this way" (*ibid:* 9). Income and a family's location within the cash-nexus of the market can be harsh deterrents to many Canadian children's desires to play sport.

The hidden injuries of class: Gender-based issues.

As starkly true as the above condition is for more children than many would like to know or admit, income and family location in the market's cash nexus have a more subtle influence that requires further gloss. Gruneau's (1976) Canada Games study suggested that for children who can afford to participate in sport, income level affects male and female participation differently. The female participants in the 1971 Canada Games tended to come from significantly more privileged families than the males. Low and even medium levels of socio-economic status, the study suggested, create a greater impediment to participation in elite sport for females than males. Why is this the case?

The answer to the question still requires considerable empirical research but some work in sport study, class analysis and feminist inquiry can indicate, in a preliminary way, parts of the answer. First, one must consider the family environment and its relation to the work world. For the most part, parents in working class (or low socio-economic status) families work in low esteem, de-skilled jobs that are monotonous, dull, and intellectually stagnating. Little or no initiative is expected or welcomed from workers so that almost a third of their lives is spent in dull, concrete toil. This constant mediation of subject (the worker) and object (the work environment) has predictable consequences.[7]

Sennett and Cobb's *The Hidden Injuries of Class* has done much to sensitize sociologists to the complex ways the work place and the class structure mediate with private and domestic life and labor. I will touch on only three themes drawn from their closely knit argument and indicate their applicability for the issues at hand.

The first theme concerns passivity. Lower income workers, Sennett and Cobb demonstrated, tend to see themselves as passive actors in their own individual fates. Unlike professionals who control their work environment, plan and execute long term programs, etc., and thus possess self-confidence and self-assurance in all realms of life, the lower SES worker is far less apt to assert himself or herself, to counter convention or to explore even tentatively significantly new avenues of conduct outside the work place. It does not require great powers of logic to infer what influence this will generally have upon family attitudes to female sport participation within contemporary society. This inertia opposing female participation in sport could be easily coupled with a second theme that Sennett and Cobb (1973: 131-150) treated under the sub-title "Sacrifices and Images of Betrayal." They basically argued that parents in working class families willingly and consciously make sacrifices so their children will escape to better lives. The unsuccessful nature of this strategy is insignificant here; the point is that sacrifice on the part of parents means sacrifice on the part of the family and by the children. A major, unconscious sacrifice is the maintenance of the status quo with respect to male/female work norms. Some have termed this "hard hat conservativism" but others like Sennett and Cobb see it as an existential realism. Males in contemporary capitalist society

have more numerous and remunerative employment opportunities than females (see Armstrong and Armstrong, 1978;
Kanter, 1977). If one wants to bet on an offspring leaving the working class ghetto, males currently and historically represent the
better odds. Thus females are quite directly discriminated against
in overt and subtle ways as they are channelled into a traditional
outlook and role. Furthermore, the sacrifices made by parents
often reinforce traditional occupational stereotypes. As a father
increases his overtime or moonlights, the burden of domestic
responsibility falls increasingly upon the mother. The longer
hours of work also reduce the father's direct contact with his
children; his role is increasingly defined as material provider,
and nurturing becomes a task in the division of labor he rarely
assumes.

How does this link to sport? I am not aware of any in-depth
qualitative studies that have been carried out in Canada or the
U.S. which would answer the question but I expect the following would be found. Given all the confusing myths surrounding sport as a natural male activity, building corporate character,
enhancing natural assertiveness, aggression and competitiveness
and preparing participants for their roles in the real world, as
well as the mythical female stereotype/athlete stereotype contradiction, it would not be surprising to see such beliefs operating
overtly and covertly to encourage working class male participation and discourage female participation. The interesting answers
that studying this relationship would reveal are exactly what overt
and covert mechanisms operate and where they find their
legitimacy and truth.

A third theme discussed by Sennett and Cobb (1973: 149-150)
concerns the question of individual blame and responsibility.
The dynamic is an intricate one so citing their statement at length
is helpful:

> For the betrayed, what is the alternative to individualism?
> You assert a common humanity, equality, you desire to get
> those who are in higher social positions to admit the wor-
> thiness you share with them, you want them to stop treating
> you as an object. But what if you believe your social burden
> is your own burden, a matter of your character? How can
> you legitimize such an assertion of equality?

A paragraph later they continued:

> Work and warfare move to the same end: the more they

make a man feel he has denied himself for the sake of others, the more right he feels he has not to submit to the moral domination of anyone else. The feeling of having acquired the right to equal dignity is, however, complex. Neither Bertin [an industrial equipment painter] Bowers [a war veteran] nor Myra [a mother and housewife] is thinking about doing away with the class structure. They, too, are individualists, concerned with their right to be exempted personally from shaming and indignity. In turning people against each other, the class system of authority and judgment-making goes itself into hiding; the system is left unchallenged as people enthralled by the enigmas of its power battle one another for respect.

I cannot possibly unpack all of this statement—Sennett and Cobb's volume-long argument would be necessary—but aspects of it may be drawn out. First, Sennett and Cobb pointed out the paradox of equality and hierarchy. It is tremendously difficult to believe in class, or racial, or gender equality when, as an individual in an ideologically individualist society, one is in a position of subordination. Either your subordination and exclusion seems to be based upon the natural inferiority of your class, and/or race and/or gender or, if that is not true, then your subordination appears to be your own personal fault. In either case, as one who is part of a naturally inferior group, or as an individual who is inferior, the person is subjectively (as well as objectively) in a disadvantaged position from which to advocate reform or entertain innovative activity on his or her own. Second, as a disadvantaged individual, respect can often only be apparently won through denial in work (social or private in form) but such denial is conservative in praxis—it does not act to change conditions. Finally, both of these points center upon individual strategies of existential freedom which place the individual within the confines of an ideological system that hides the frame of analysis necessary to at least comprehend his or her true situation; i.e., a class or holistic framework. I invite the reader to link the conservative inertia associated with all three of these points to develop a logical explanation of how these aspects of class position negatively influence female opportunity to participate in sport. Subsequent empirical research will be needed to substantiate and verify such a logical argument but the questions emanating from this logical elaboration will be a helpful precondition for such work.

Media images of sport: the political economy of power.

Throughout the discussion in this section, I have implied that the dominant image of women and sport is one of non-participation. Few would question the existence of this image but it is wrong to think of it as a monolithic one. Historically, there have been social groups and organizations, like the Workers' Sports Movement or Y.W.C.A., advancing progressive images of women in sport. Likewise, numerous Canadian women have participated in and continue to take part in a wide spectrum of sports, games and physical activities so that other women can identify with a long, illustrious athletic heritage (see Hall and Richardson, 1982). But the political economy is an economy of power and the central axis of power runs from production right through the market place. Furthermore, this axis of power insidiously operates to reinforce, mostly by way of default, the image of female non-participation and this tends to more than counteract the few weakly projected images of genuine athletic participation enjoyed by females.

Because the political economy of power is such a fundamental aspect of gender-related questions of sport opportunity, it merits some further consideration. Power is rooted in three sources; size, organization, and the control of both normative (or ideational) and material resources (money, equipment, etc.). Modern media in contemporary capitalist society possess all three bases of power in abundance, enough to make them the most powerful image creators in the history of the human species. And the media tend to fashion the image most people associate with gender 'appropriate' sport activity. Nevertheless, in spite of their power, the "gatekeepers of ideology" and the "captains of consciousness" do not act in a totally *sui generis* fashion imposing personally selected images of 'appropriate' conduct.[8] Owners and managers, it must be remembered, are tied to the fetishism of commodities as much as workers, and it is the objective imperatives of the market and the bottom line that significantly structure a limited set of image options.

Harold Innis once argued that in the modern newspaper the news only served to fill in spaces so that the ads would be held together. He should have gone further. As advertising has increased in price (it costs $7,933.33 per second to advertise on the Superbowl on an American network while advertising rates in the *Ottawa Citizen* jumped 25% and in the *Winnipeg Free Press* 37% shortly after Southam and Thomson established their monopolies), and as markets have become more fragmented and specialized, news material is structured to appeal to specific audiences in order to guarantee a particular type of customer to the advertiser. The media owners and the merchants both make more money that way. The conservative nature of this advertising strategy is unquestionable. The sports pages are used primarily to sell products to men; females are reached through the lifestyle section. Sports coverage becomes predictably biased.

When historians of the future use the records of today's media for sport study they will be apt to think that Canadians' participation in sport centered mostly on the majority enthusiastically following a tiny minority engaged in all-male professional hockey, all-male professional football (from two to three types—Canadian Football League, National Football League and depending upon the period, American Football League, World Football League, or United States Football League.), all-male professional baseball (National League and American League.), professional golf and tennis (which appeared to consist of a major all-male circuit and a minor—but growing—all-female circuit for each sport) and horse racing dominated by male jockeys. About every two years (with greatest emphasis on those divisible by four, except the summer of 1980) amateur sports, with more male than female participants, were followed for intense three to five week periods once in the summer and once in the winter.

To explain such a balance of coverage (which is a totally unbalanced representation of Canadian participation in sport) the historians will have to turn to the economics of professional sport monopolies and the symbiotic relationships between the media and the advertisers and the media and sport franchises (see Beamish, 1982).

Irrespective of their explanation, however, it is obvious at the everyday level of consciousness (and has been substantiated by limited research into the question) that the image of sport conveyed through the media is one of male domination. Since humankind employs its own socially created cultural images to inform its various teleological projects (see Beamish, 1981b; Krader, 1979: 59-65), it is little wonder that sport continues to perpetuate an image and reality of male domination. In addition, the logic and imperatives of the market place continually reinforce this imbalance by the magnitude of the resources deployed in projecting male sport images as well as the frequency of such projection. In short, a law of the market provides the legitimate rationality for employing vast resources insidiously to shape perceptions of gender-appropriate sport conduct and, as a result, those who wish to advance images of gender equality enter the equivalent of a 1500-meter race in which three minutes have already elapsed.

CONCLUSION

There is no doubt that the quality and quantity of athletic experience for both sexes differs significantly. In this paper I have concentrated upon the question of opportunity and narrowed that topic further by attending primarily to female exclusion from participation. I have not examined the problem of opportunity for males which, in male dominated sport creates a master/slave dialectic that has significant consequences which are too often ignored. The specific issue addressed in this paper and the companion piece by Hall (in this volume) surrounds the explanation of gender-related issues in sport; can an existing frame of analysis deal with gender-related questions or must a new one specifically focused on the gender variable be created and developed? On the basis of my argument here, I think a strong case can be made for the use of the materialist framework in the study of socially constructed gender-related issues. Not only is the materialist problematic comprehensive in terms of scope and depth concerning sociological questions outside the realm of gender, it can also be employed to study gender directly and incorporate findings into a holistic comprehension of society's dynamics. This is not to say that such work has been done in the past—clearly in sport study very little has—but the record by no means negates the possibility for such work.

Our objectives as scholars and scientists diverge in many ways but within that variety a common endeavor is the development of theoretical frameworks that are more inclusive than those used previously and more comprehensively insightful than others. The materialist problematic, I would argue, still provides this type of framework for social study as a whole and can be used to enhance our comprehension of gender-related issues in contemporary sport study in particular.

NOTES

1. This is a shortened version of the paper I prepared for the NASS conference. I have eliminated numerous references when they did not point to cited material and I have removed a section on women in positions of leadership. I would like to thank Nancy Theberge for asking me to take part in the session and for organizing the opportunity for this formal dialogue. In addition comments by Nada Beamish, Hart Cantelon, Marcia George, Richard Gruneau and Bruce Kidd have all been helpful in writing this paper.

2. Krader (1979: 300) makes the point very decisively. "That the social relations of labor are a part of the prime motor of history can be shown in the following way: Labor as the combination of past and present labor in the relations to nature and in society is a starting point in all discussion of human history. The relation of the human kind to nature is the relation of labor, and no other, whereby the materials of nature are brought into a material interchange with man. The immediate relation is at once a mediate one, whereby the products of past labor in crystallized form as the instruments of labor are applied in the present production. There being no other means of supplying human wants save by labor, the relation to nature by the combination of past and present labor in the material interchange with nature cannot be further reduced. It is the necessary condition of human life. Moreover, it is the *differentia specifica*, for the human kind alone of all like species applies the combination of labor living and dead in producing its livelihood. The labor is at the same time a relation in society, however simple in organization that society is."

3. For Marx's own critical treatment of thinkers who allowed logic to dominate both history and their analysis, see his discussion of Hegel's *Philosophy of Law* (esp. Marx, 1964: 30-4; 52-7) and his lash at Proudhon (esp. Marx, 1950: 29-34, 120-26). Thompson (1978: 117-122) examines the pitfalls of formal logic extensively in *The Poverty of Theory* although in the context of his zealous style a reader may construe it as a total denial of logical constructions. This conclusion, I think, would be more extreme than Thompson intended. His efforts were centered primarily upon asserting the central significance of the concrete for Marx and materialist sociology, an emphasis I support fully.

4. The dialogues where Plato presents the dialectic most explicitly are Parmenides, Theaetetus, and Sophist (see Plato, n.d., v. 4: 312-348). See Hegel's (1969: 491-494) brief overview of Plato's and Kant's contributions to the history of the dialectic.

5. Elsewhere I have tried to examine in some detail the interpenetration of the value-form of production into sport (see Beamish, 1982).

6. This is not to say that profit is the only consideration in production but the myth of the corporate-soul has been overblown to hide the underlying reality that tough economic times like the current reces-

sion bring the dominance of the bottom line to the surface very quickly. Even Adam Smith (1937, v. 2: 244-341), the so-called father of free enterprise and the laissez-faire economy, recognized that utilitarian philosophy and the pursuit of profit would not ensure that all social wants were met (see also Mill, 1893, bk. V; Wolff, 1968: 3-51).

7. To lay so much emphasis on the work place (production) and overlook non-work consumption is problematic but I can only cover so much in this sketch. I will touch on non-work consumption in terms of inter-personal relations below, but the question is far more complex.

8. I have discussed these mechanisms from a slightly different angle of inquiry elsewhere (see Beamish, 1981a). I will not repeat those arguments here.

REFERENCES

Armstrong, P. and H. Armstrong
1978   The Double Ghetto: Canadian Women and Their Segregated Work. Toronto: McClelland and Stewart.

Beamish, Rob.
1981a   "Sport and the fetishism of commodities: issues in alienated sport." Paper presented at the regional symposium of the International Committee for the Sociology of Sport, Vancouver, B.C.
1981b   "Central issues in the materialist study of sport as a cultural practice." In Susan Greendorfer (ed.), Sociology of Sport: Diverse Perspectives. West Point, New York: Leisure Press.
1982   "Sport and the logic of capitalism." In Hart Cantelon and Richard Gruneau (eds.), Sport, Culture and the Modern State. Toronto: University of Toronto Press.

Braverman, Harry
1974   Labour and Monopoly Capital. New York: Monthly Review Press.

Foucault, Michel
1966   Les Mots et les Choses. Paris: Editions Gallimard.

Gruneau, Richard
1976   "Class or mass: notes on the democratization of Canadian amateur sport." In Richard Gruneau and John Albinson (eds.), Canadian Sport: Sociological Perspectives. Don Mills: Addison Wesley.

Hall, Ann and Dorothy Richardson
1982   Fair Ball: Towards Sex Equality in Canadian Sport. Ottawa:
          The Canadian Advisory Council on the Status of Women.

Harris, Marvin
1980   Cultural Materialism. New York: Vintage Books.

Hegel, Georg
1959   Enzyklopädie der philosophischen Wissenschaften in Grun-
          drisse. F. Nicolin and O. Pöggeler (eds.), Hamburg: Felix
          Meiner Verlag.
1969   Wissenschaft der Logik (2 Bd.). Frankfurt am Main:
          Suhrkamp Verlag.

Johnson, Richard
1979   "Three problematics: elements of a theory of working class
          culture." In R. Johnson, J. Clarke and C. Chrichter (eds.),
          Working Class Culture: Studies in History and Theory. Lon-
          don: Hutchinson Press.

Jones, Gareth-Stedman
1982   "Engels and the history of Marxism." In E.J. Hobsbawm (ed.).
          The History of Marxism. Bloomington: Indiana University
          Press.

Kanter, R.
1977   Men and Women of the Corporation. New York: Basic Books.

Kautsky, Karl
1935   Aus der Frühzeit des Marxismus. Prague.

Korsch, Karl
1963   Karl Marx. London: Russell and Russell.
1975   "Ten Theses on Marxism (1950)." Telos 26:40-1.

Krader, Lawrence
1976   The Dialectic of Civil Society. Assen: Van Gorcum Press.
1979   A Treatise on Social Labour. Assen: Van Gorcum Press.
1982   "Theory of evolution, revolution and the state: the critical rela-
          tion of Marx to his contemporaries Darwin, Morgan, Maine
          and Kovalevsky." In E.J. Hobsbawm (ed.), The History of
          Marxism. Bloomington: University of Indiana Press.

Lukacs, Georg
1980   The Social Ontology of Being: Labour. Tr. by David Fernbach.
          London: Merlin Press.

Marx, Karl
1950   Misere de la Philosophie. Paris: Alfred Costes.
1953   Grundrisse der Kritik der politischen Oekonomie. Berlin:
        Dietz Verlag.
1964   Die Frühschriften. Stuttgart: Alfred Kroner Verlag.
1974   The Ethnological Notebooks of Karl Marx. L. Krader (ed.),
        Assen: Van Gorcum Press.

Marx, Karl and Frederic Engels
1964   Werke. Berlin: Dietz Verlag

Mead, Margaret
1978   Sex and Temperament in Three Primitive Societies. London:
        Routledge and Kegan Paul.

Mill, John Stuart
1893   Principles of Political Economy (2 Vols.). New York: Appleton
        and Co.

National Council on Welfare
1975   Poor Kids. Ottawa: Ministry of Supply and Services.

Plato
n.d.   The Works of Plato. Tr. and ed. by B. Jowett. New York: Tudor
        Publishing Co.

Rosdolsky, Roman
1977   The Making of Marx's Capital. Tr. by Pete Burgess. London:
        Pluto Press.

Rubel, M.
1981a   "A History of Marx's 'Economics.'" In J. O'Malley and K. Algzin
        (eds.), Rubel on Marx. Cambridge: Cambridge University
        Press.
1981b   "The Plan and Method of the 'Economics.'" In J. O'Malley and
        K. Algzin (eds.), Rubel on Marx. Cambridge: Cambridge
        University Press.

Rubin, Isaac
1973   Essays on Marx's Theory of Value. Tr. by Milos Samardzija
        and Fredy Perlman. Montreal: Black Rose Books.

Schmidt, Alfred
1971   The Concept of Nature in Marx. Tr. by Ben Fowkes. London:
        New Left Books.

Sennett, Jonathan and Richard Cobb
1973   The Hidden Injuries of Class. New York: Vintage Books.

Smith, Adam
1937   An Inquiry into the Nature and Causes of the Wealth of Na-
        tions. Chicago: University of Chicago Press.

Sombart, Werner
1937   "Capitalism." In The Encyclopedia of the Social Sciences (1st
        Ed.). New York: The Macmillan Co.

Thompson, E.P.
1961   The Making of the English Working Class. Harmondsworth:
        Pelican
1978   The Poverty of Theory and Other Essays. New York: Mon-
        thly Review Press.

Wolff, Robert
1968   The Poverty of Liberalism. Boston: Beacon Press.

TOWARDS A FEMINIST ANALYSIS OF GENDER INEQUALITY IN SPORT

M. Ann Hall
University of Alberta

IT IS TAKEN AS A GIVEN within the women's movement that in order to liberate ourselves, as women, from male supremacy we must develop a systematic theoretical analysis of gender inequality. Feminism, however, has been perceived as a "loose collection of factors, complaints, and issues, which, taken together, describe rather then explain the misfortunes of the female sex" and not as a systematic analysis (MacKinnon, 1982: 528).

I will argue in this paper that feminism *is* a social theory and that if we get it right, it has the power to transform certainly women's collective social experience and perhaps men's as well. The creation of an entirely new social theory is not an easy task. The work is proceeding slowly, but laborious as it is, there is an unprecedented and new dialogue amongst those who have chosen to take part in this marvellously exciting venture.

I wish to do several things in this paper. First, I will situate this particular essay in the context of the rest of my work. Quite simply, I wish to explain where I have been and where I believe I am going. I then take up my initial point that feminism is rarely perceived as a systematic theoretical analysis and explain first, what such an analysis must be and second, how as feminists our political practice must be informed by our theory. Next, I examine what I consider to be the current strands of feminist social theory, namely, a Marxist-feminist[1] analysis, an analysis whose central focus is sexuality, and thirdly some amalgam of the two. I examine these perspectives primarily for their usefulness in helping us to understand and explain gender inequality in sport.[2] Finally, I entertain the notion that feminism is not compatible with positivism and what that means for us either as social scientists who are feminists or feminists who happen to be social scientists.

Let me begin with a critical look at my own work. My purpose is to explain where I've been, where I am now, and where I intend to head. I do not offer this critique as an apology for my work but rather as an explanation for what probably seems on the surface a rather dramatic turnabout in perspective and orientation. It's important, I think, to understand how this came about.[3]

About twelve years ago, I was asking a relatively simple question: "Why do some women make sport and physical activity a significant part of their lifestyle and others do not?" My interest in women and sport stemmed less from my experience as an athlete than from a master's level study I completed concerning the historical growth of women's sport and physical activity patterns in Canada. This particular question was to preoccupy me for over three years because it was the basis of my doctoral dissertation. It was my baptism into sociological enterprise for I had no background in either sociology or the sociology of sport. At that time the sociological study of sport was barely emerging in North America as a distinct subfield. My training had been in mathematics and statistics along with physical education, consequently the natural science model seemed at the time most appropriate to answer my questions. I was interested in the whys of women's involvement in sport or the lack of it and building a causal mathematical model to explain it all seemed eminently worthwhile and challenging. Moreover our exemplars in the sociology of sport at that time were proponents of the quest for empirically verifiable, formal, propositional theory. In the end, I produced a substantial multivariate statistical analysis (see Hall, 1974, 1976) but my carefully constructed model was a dismal failure. It explained little, and my real findings could be expressed in one rather lengthy sentence. I felt at the time and still do that the technical aspects of my work were beyond reproach. I was proud of what Ingham (1979) calls technical pedantry but the problem was that the more caught up I became in technicism, the more elusive were the answers to my increasingly complex questions about female sport involvement in what my emerging feminist consciousness began to recognize as a male-dominated world.

I have been actively involved in the Canadian women's movement since the early '70s, and although I find it impossible to separate my roles as advocate and academic, what interests us here is the influence of feminism on my scholarship. I understand clearly the position of those who would accuse me of succumbing to ideologism (see Berger and Kellner, 1981 for example). Unfortunately I cannot take up the point here and provide an adequate defense. Suffice it to say that feminist scholarship does not necessarily reject objectivity, empirical verification, reproducibility, comprehensiveness, parsimony, and elegance. It does, however, challenge the very assumptions upon which modern science and social science have developed and the methods of creating scientific knowledge as well as the products of that knowledge. There is no question that feminist scholarship is a partisan enterprise. As one feminist colleague has put it so well: "Feminist theory has to be biased because it is anti-bias." (O'Brien, 1981: 12).

Recognizing the necessity of feminist scholarship was only the beginning for me in what has become an increasingly fascinating quest to understand the female experience in sport within an androcentric world. At first, my published work was a mere plea to both my professional and academic colleagues in physical education and the sociology of sport to recognize the relevance of feminism (see Hall, 1979a, 1979b, 1982b). At the same time, I tentatively began to apply a feminist critique to what I thought we knew, sociologically, about women in sport (Hall, 1978). My critique, I believe, has become increasingly more sophisticated mainly because the volume of solid theoretical and empirical feminist scholarship upon which I draw has increased dramatically. For instance, I have examined in some detail the supposed conflict between femininity and sport from a sex role and sex identity perspective in the early work of Eleanor Metheney through the more recent research on psychological androgyny (Hall, 1981). More recently, I have applied a feminist analysis to the role of play, games, and sport in sex/gender role socialization (Hall, 1982a). Presently, I am engaged in examining the social construction of femininity through girls' leisure activities. My purpose in all this is to point out the androcentric assumptions which have shaped our sociological knowledge about women in sport and to provide some guidelines for future non-sexist research.

At the same time and because of my self-imposed obligations within the women's movement, I have continued to document sex inequality within the sport and physical education worlds and to speak out against it. My suggestions for change have hardly been revolutionary since women in sport are only beginning to develop even a liberal feminist consciousness. Nonetheless, I have always argued that within the women's movement it is necessary at times to advocate reform and assimilation and at other times to press for radically alternative structures (Hall and Lawson, 1980; Hall, Cameron and Shogan, 1981; Hall and Richardson, 1982).

Feminism, as I will try to show presently, is a theory of power and its distribution. I see power in terms of relations of domination and subordination whereby one group of persons (women) is controlled by another (men). Power, then, is the basis of sexual relations just as it is the basis of class relations.[4] Power, however, is an abstraction which "can only be rendered analytically useful if it is given a material base and a historical content" (O'Brien, 1981: 81). In other words, structured relations of power, domination, and subordination are but relatively enduring and are susceptible to historical transformation (Isaac, 1982). Therefore what has been missing from my work is an analysis of the conceptualization of sexual relations in terms of power and exactly how these sexual relations of domination and subordination are reproduced in sport. It is something which I have taken more or less as an article of faith, as do most feminists. Just as Marxists see social class not only as a *distributive* question (examining factors such as income, property or family status which contribute to social ranking and inequality) but also as a *relational* one (the ways in which social groups, differentiated in a consistent way by these factors, are interrelated in a systemic matter), I too have come to realize that we must view the social relations between the sexes in precisely the same way. My task as a feminist scholar is to analyze systematically the ways in which the two sexes have been and are differentiated in a consistent way and to uncover the reasons male supremacy continues to persist. Coupled with this is the belief that unless we, as feminists, develop a sound theoretical component to our political practice, we will never liberate ourselves from male supremacy. My task, now and in the future, is that of creating an entirely different way of thinking about sport, indeed the whole of human experience (not just *male* experience), which transcends and corrects male-stream thought. In many ways this essay marks the beginning, for me at least, of my task.

FEMINISM AS ANALYSIS, THEORY, AND POLITICAL PRACTICE

I wish now to take up my first point: the view that feminism is considered at worst an ideology and at best a mere critique of both society and those disciplines whose focus it is to understand and explain the social world. Certainly feminism as it is lived by women who call themselves "feminists" is an ideology. Adrienne Rich (1977: xvii) expresses it well:

> Feminism begins but cannot end with the discovery by an individual of her self-consciousness as a woman. It is not, finally, even the recognition of her reasons for anger, or the decision to change her life, go back to school, leave a marriage (though in any individual life such decisions can be momentous and require great courage). Feminism means finally that we renounce our obedience to the fathers and recognize that the world they have described is not the whole world. Masculine ideologies are the creation of masculine subjectivity; they are neither objective, nor value-free, nor inclusively "human." Feminism implies that we recognize fully the inadequacy for us, the distortion, of male-created ideologies, and that we proceed to think, and act, out of that recognition.

As I have argued elsewhere (Hall, 1982b), there is no question that feminist scholarship is a very partisan enterprise. In the same way that Rich implores us to recognize the distortion of male-centered ideologies, feminist scholarship challenges the assumptions upon which modern science has developed; it further challenges the methods of creating scientific knowledge as well as the products of that knowledge. For instance, three themes seem to emerge at present from the feminist critique of sociology.[5] First, there is the growing recognition that a radical challenge to the sexist assumptions which pervade sociology itself is needed rather than a mere addendum to sociological content. A sociology for woman, not of women, is needed. Second, it is recognized that the critique of androcentrism in sociology is inseparable from that of its methodology. Not only are feminist sociologists being methodologically innovative, but there is a growing understanding of what it means theoretically, methodologically, and ethically to do feminist research. Finally there is a movement which goes beyond mere criticism and correction and seeks to transform social science to account meaningfully for all of human experience.

Central to this critique is the assumption that "distinguishing between two genders is the appropriate foundation from which to build research questions and theory" (Matthews, 1982: 30). Some (e.g., Matthews) suggest that feminist sociologists who perpetuate this process of gender reification are being ideological rather than sociological. In some ways I agree. However just as feminist scholarship is denounced by those who claim it is neither a science nor scientific, the unexamined assumption in Matthews' critique of critiques is that sociology is a science whereas feminism is but an ideology (Eisenstein, 1982). The dichotomization between science and ideology does not and cannot hold.[6] Insofar as sociology is rooted in a male world-view, it is as much an ideology as it is a science. Feminism is explicit about its bias. It is ideological but insofar as any social science reflects the systematic knowledge of the material world, feminism (and feminist analysis) is as much a science as it is an ideology (Eisenstein, 1982). Further, feminist scholarship, if it is to be good scholarship, must go beyond criticism and mere fault-finding. It must be transformative and to be so, it must develop a systematic theoretical analysis of "the roots and grounds and development of male history and male philosophy" (O'Brien, 1981: 3). It must, in other words, develop a theory. "Theory at its best is fundamentally a way of analyzing human experience which is at the same time a method of organizing that experience" (O'Brien, 1981: 3). Theory, in this sense, is a scheme of ideas which explains practice.

Where to begin in this mind-boggling task? The problem is that history, philosophy, sociology—indeed all of human intellectual history—are male thought, based on male experience. It is, in a sense, an "ideology of male supremacy" (O'Brien, 1981: 5). Therefore, it is no wonder that so much of feminist scholarship to date has been directed at demonstrating that main-stream thought is male-stream thought and prejudiced as a result.[7] Regardless, there can be no separation of feminism as analysis, feminism as theory, and feminism as political practice. Feminism is all three, and more importantly, analysis and theory are interconnected with practice.[8]

In the context of our discussions about gender inequality in sport, I have argued elsewhere (see specifically Hall, 1982b) that we could go on indefinitely showing that structural equality does not exist within the sports world, but we have failed to take account of the origins and causes of women's oppression (or male supremacy) which have produced the societal sex structure and inequality in the first place. To do so would mean we must recognize, use, and contribute to feminist social theory in one or more of its forms. It is to this current feminist social theory that I now wish to turn.

FEMINIST SOCIAL THEORY

What is it that is implicit in feminist theory? What is the fundamental social process under consideration? These are complicated questions because feminist theory is as divergent and sometimes as contradictory as is social theory in general. In this section I wish to deal with three notions essential to all feminist theory: patriarchy, reproduction, and sexuality. Next, I examine and discuss what I consider to be the three most recognized versions of feminist social theory: an analysis whose focus is class (essentially a Marxist-feminist analysis), an analysis whose focus is sexuality, and finally, theory which purports to reconcile class and sexuality.

Patriarchy, Reproduction, and Sexuality

The starting point for all feminist social theory is some notion of patriarchy.[9] According to Hartmann (1981), the crucial elements of patriarchy as we currently experience them are: (1) heterosexual marriage (and consequent homophobia); (2) female childrearing and housework; (3) women's economic dependence on men (enforced by arrangements in the labor market); and (4) the state and numerous institutions based on social relations among men—clubs, sports, unions, professions, universities, churches, corporations, and armies, to name but a few. Beyond this, however, patriarchy can be viewed as "a set of social relations which has a material base and in which there are hierarchical relations between men and solidarity among them which enable them in turn to dominate women" (Hartmann, 1981: 18).

What does it mean to say that a set of social relations (in this case patriarchy) has a material base? At the risk of grossly oversimplifying the concept materialism, I defer to Heilbroner's (1980: 21) definition here because I find it lucid and clear: "a perspective that highlights the central role played in history by the productive activities of humankind, and that therefore locates a principal motive for historical change in the struggle among social classes over their respective shares in the fruits of production." Therefore, inherent in this particular sense of patriarchy is the notion that men have control over women's labor power and that this control is maintained by excluding women from access to necessary economically productive sources and furthermore by restricting women's sexuality (Hartmann, 1981: 18). Some of the precise ways, it is suggested, in which men exercise their control are in receiving personal service work from women, in not having to do housework or rear children, in having access to women's bodies for sex, and in feeling powerful and being powerful.

Now, not all feminist theorists agree with this sense of patriarchy—specifically, that it has a material base, that it is analytically dependent on the capitalist or any other mode of production. Indeed this has been the theme of many radical feminist writers (such as Kate Millett and Shulamith Firestone) who posit patriarchy as a system of domination completely independent of the organization of capitalist relations. Hence, according to those who disagree (by and large Marxist-feminists), the ensuing analyses "fall into a universalistic, trans-historical mode which may shade into biologism" (Barrett, 1980: 15).[10]

In sum, and for the purpose of this essay, I suggest that patriarchy be viewed as a set of social relations between women and men which has a material base and through which men dominate women. Also for our purposes, and stemming from this perspective of patriarchy, sport is one of many social institutions based primarily among men only and through which men dominate women.[11]

The second theoretical concept inherent in any social theory which is purportedly feminist is that of reproduction. As with the concept of patriarchy, there is little consensus among feminist theorists as to its definition. Barrett (1980) argues that there are three analytically distinct referents of the concept reproduction—social reproduction (the need of any social formation to reproduce its own conditions of production), reproduction of the labor force, and human or biological reproduction. The problem for feminist theorists in general has been to reconcile these three separate analytical levels of the concept and, especially for Marxist-feminists, how to explore adequately the relationship between reproduction (in all three senses) and production.[12]

One way around both problems has been to see reproduction

as reproductive labor: "It begins with ovulation and ends when the 'product,' the child, is no longer dependent on others for the necessities of survival" (O'Brien, 1981: 16). In fact, for some theorists (e.g., O'Brien), feminist theory begins with the process of human reproduction. Central to O'Brien's analysis is that it is "within *the total process of human reproduction* that the ideology of male supremacy finds its roots and its rationales" (p. 8).

The final and third component implicit in any feminist social theory is that of sexuality. For some it has more analytical primacy than for others. From the "outside," it might also seem that the only issues of concern in the women's movement are those of sexuality—rape, domestic violence, birth control, abortion, pornography, prostitution, sexual freedom, sexual autonomy, lesbianism, incest, sexual harassment, and so forth. In fact, for some theorists, as we shall see shortly, sexuality is the center of all male power and male supremacy.

Sexuality, then, is a difficult and elusive concept insofar as feminist social theory is concerned, and I shall say much more about it as I examine what I consider to be the three most important strands of feminist social theory—a Marxist-feminist analysis, an analysis whose central focus is sexuality, and thirdly some amalgam of the two. At the same time, I wish to examine the usefulness of each perspective in helping us to understand and more importantly to explain gender inequality in sport.

A Marxist-Feminist Analysis[13]

Perhaps the most pervasive theme in all Marxist-feminist literature is that there is, at present, a very unhappy marriage between Marxism and feminism. Heidi Hartmann (1981: 2) sums it up best: "The 'marriage' of Marxism and feminism has been like the marriage of husband and wife depicted in English common law: Marxism and feminism are one, and that one is Marxism."

The issue here is a relatively straightforward one: from the viewpoint of those feminists who are not Marxists, and indeed among those who are, the categories of Marxism are sex-blind. No one disputes this, and frankly I doubt whether Marx would have either. However, from the standpoint of Marxist-feminists, "feminist analysis by itself is inadequate because it has been blind to history and insufficiently materialist." They argue that *both* Marxist analysis, particularly its historical and materialist method, and feminist analysis, especially the identification of patriarchy as a social and historical structure, must be drawn upon if we are to understand and explain women's oppression. What is not so straightforward, and certainly very complicated, is how and in what form the actual "marriage" is to take place.

What is meant by stating that the categories of Marxism are sex-blind? Marxism has certainly enabled us to understand many aspects of capitalist societies—the development of class society, the accumulation process in capitalist societies, the reproduction of class dominance, the development of contradictions and class struggle, the structure of production, the nature of the dominant ideology, and so forth. Marxist theory explains the generation of a particular occupational structure whereby capital creates occupational places for individuals to fill. However the categories of Marxist analysis (class, reserve army of labor, wage-laborer, etc.) do not explain why particular people fill particular places. "They give no clues about why *women* are subordinate to *men* inside and outside the family and why it is not the other way around" (Hartmann, 1981: 10). It is in this way that Marxist categories, like capital itself, are sex-blind.

Nonetheless and despite the problems a Marxist-feminist analysis presents, it would be enormously useful in helping us to comprehend gender inequality in sport. First, it would force us to go beyond the increasingly repetitive description and quantification we have at present. The problem with describing and quantifying is that it cannot change gender inequality and therefore, according to O'Brien (1981: 161), "shows the distinct tendency to collapse into utopianism, polemic or mere statistics, which tendency is a direct consequence of an inadequate theoretical ground." Second, the relatively new political economy tradition in sport sociology sees class not just as a distributive question but also as a relational one whereby sport as a cultural form is seen as tied to forms of domination. The central focus of this work has been to examine the extent to which play, games and sports are related to the broader problems of voluntarism and determinism, freedom and constraint, liberation and domination in human existence—more specifically the complex relationships that exist between play, games and sport and the various forms of domination and class inequality in the social development of Western, capitalist societies (see, for example, Gruneau, 1976, 1978, 1980a, 1980b, 1983; Helmes, 1978; Kidd, 1978, 1982). However, none of this work takes any serious account of gender because class is the central consideration and focus. Certainly another form of domination is race. Yet the domination of men over women is also another form, specifically through the institutions of marriage and family, both of which are buttressed by capitalism. As I have shown in a general sense, any Marxist analysis which does not integrate the complex relationships between class and patriarchy is woefully inadequate. The implications are obvious for the otherwise excellent work, primarily Canadian, progressing within the political economy tradition.[14]

Sexuality as the Focus of Feminist Analysis

Catharine MacKinnon (1982: 515), in her recent article, states: "Sexuality is to feminism what work is to Marxism: that which is most one's own, yet most taken away." She extends her analogy further and suggests that where the structure of Marxism is class, that of feminism is heterosexuality; the consequence of Marxism is production, but for feminism it is reproduction; the congealed form in Marxism is capital and in feminism, it is gender and family; but the issue of both is control. She suggests further that both work and sexuality are social processes: "work is the social process of shaping and transforming the material and social worlds, creating people as social beings as they create value" whereas "sexuality is that social process which creates, organizes, expresses and directs desire, creating the social beings we know as women and men, as their relations create society" (p. 515).

The questions MacKinnon asks are whether two social processes can be basic at once and whether two theories (Marxism and feminism) each of which purports to account for the same thing—power as such—can be reconciled? Although her answer to the first question is yes (both are the prime moments of politics), her reply to the second is definitely no. With regard to the question of reconciling Marxism and feminism, MacKinnon argues that "most attempts at synthesis attempt to integrate or explain the appeal of feminism by incorporating issues feminism identifies as central—the family, housework, sexuality, reproduction, socialization, personal life—within an essentially unchanged Marxian analysis" (p. 524).

MacKinnon is by no means the first feminist theorist to place sexuality at the center of feminist analysis and to see it as central to women's oppression. Early (i.e., early 1970s) radical feminism did just that. The titles of books from that period attest to this: *Sexual Politics, The Dialectics of Sex, The Female Eunuch, Vaginal Politics.* The general argument presented by the authors of these works was essentially the same: sexuality, with variations along a continuum of masculine aggression (from the celebration of penetration to the brutality of rape), is the site in which male power and male supremacy are expressed (Barrett, 1980: 44).[15]

In our concerns about gender inequality in sport we have skirted around the issue of sexuality. I think, in essence, we have been afraid to attack it head on. Perhaps the application of an analysis whose central focus is sexuality would change that substantially. Elsewhere (see Hall, 1981) I have argued that we have "psychologized" our work with an almost fanatical concern for preserving the femininity of women athletes. Our work here has never been situated within the possibility that sexuality *is* the center of male power and supremacy. I have often argued that the primary reason why it has been (and still is) so difficult to arouse even a liberal feminist consciousness in woman athletes and female physical educators is because to be athletic is to be considered not feminine which is in essence to be considered masculine which ultimately is to be suspected of being a lesbian. "Lesbians so violate the sexuality implicit in female gender stereotypes as not to be considered women at all" (MacKinnon, 1982: 530). Therefore, for female athletes and physical educators, being labelled both a lesbian and a feminist is simply too much to handle. We desperately need to change this: change would come through an analysis which pinpoints why, and under what historical and cultural circumstances, the "not feminine/masculine/lesbian" linkage came to be such a powerful deterrent and whose vested interests are being preserved through its continued domination. There are so many questions and areas to explore here—for instance, how do women "come to take themselves up as fragile," how are women trained in physical weakness, what is the relationship between female sexuality and physicality—one hardly knows where to begin.

Sexuality and Class—Can They Be Reconciled?

My immediate answer to this is that I don't know. Intuitively, I do not believe that a Marxist-feminist analysis will ever overcome the problem of Marxism first, feminism second, although admittedly at present I cannot adequately provide much of a rationale for this view. At best, it is speculation. However, as I have tried to make clear in this paper, I am convinced that an analysis which is both historical and material is essential. Much of feminist theory has been neither and therein lies its greatest weakness.

Patriarchy is not analytically independent of capitalism and to treat it as such often means we fall prey to explanations which are ahistorical and quite frequently biological.

On the other hand, to claim that "sexuality is the linchpin of gender inequality" because "a woman is a being who identifies and is identified as one whose sexuality exists for someone else, who is socially male" (MacKinnon, 1982: 533) does not make a great deal of sense to me either. Also, it restricts the definition of sexuality to a narrow meaning.

One attempt (and there are certainly others) to bring at least some sort of reconciliation between class and sexuality has been undertaken recently in Mary O'Brien's brilliant work entitled *The Politics of Reproduction*. What she argues is that "it is not within sexual relations but with *the total process of human reproduction* that the ideology of male supremacy finds its roots and its rationales" (O'Brien, 1981: 8). Sexuality, then, is but a part of the total process of reproduction, and it is through our understanding of this process that women will comprehend not only their oppression but also their freedom.

What O'Brien has done is to explore a dialectical analysis of the social relations of reproduction (in the same way that Marxism provides a dialectical analysis of the social relations of production). Marx's model is material, historical and dialectical, and so, too, is O'Brien's but the difference is that she has tried to transcend the limitations of the Marxist preoccupation with class struggle "as the only operative field of praxis" in order to provide at least a starting point for a genuinely feminist praxis. As Miles (1982: 64) commented in reviewing O'Brien's book: "Feminist theory here makes the qualitative and essential leap from being a marginal commentary of male-stream thought to appropriate centre stage, from making occasional interjections in male discourse to reshaping the discourse itself."

We learn from O'Brien's analysis of the social relations of reproduction that it is possible for there to be a uniquely defined body of feminist theory—a "metatheory from a feminist perspective." We learn also from her work and that of other feminist scholars (e.g., Dorothy Smith) that the exploration of women's reality must be done "from the standpoint of women." What this means for a feminist analysis of gender inequality in sport is that our analysis must be grounded *in the experience of women in sport* and not in some abstract notion of either gender or sport. I think that the Marxists have helped us to see that we risk betraying the very essence of the sociological imagination through our attempts to use the analytical tools of sociology in order to satisfy ends which we take for granted and do not define as problematic. Sport must be viewed culturally and historically as something which is socially constituted. Where they have not been at all helpful is with the notion of gender.

Why is gender, and more importantly, the dichotomization of gender into female and male so important? Why give it *a priori* significance? Why see the world in this way?[16] The answer, I think, lies in the fact that gender must also be viewed as a socially constructed phenomenon. Certainly the "confluence of capitalism and patriarchy arising in the practices of society's members constitutes gender as consequential" (Griffith, 1982: 36). It is important to discover what gender means for different people because men and women quite regularly respond to their social situations in different ways. Certainly some men and some women may respond to their situation in very similar ways (e.g., members of the same social class). But I do not think that this means we cannot assert, *a priori*, that gender is significant. What it is important to answer is "how" and "when." I do not think that we have even touched on these questions in our work on gender inequality in sport.

THE INCOMPATIBILITY OF FEMINISM AND POSITIVISM

I think it should be evident by now that I no longer believe feminism is compatible with positivism. By *positivism* I mean much more than the adoption of the natural science model of inquiry. To view it in this way is to posit a form of naive positivism. I am talking about something much more complicated.[17] It strikes at the very heart of the long-standing epistemological (relating to knowledge or knowing) and the ontological (relating to the nature of being or reality) debates within the philosophy of science.[18] It goes far beyond arguments over whether to quantify or not to quantify. It addresses fundamental issues which stem from differing views of knowledge and reality and how to access them. It is also impossible to disentangle popular notions of positivism from general arguments about empiricism and the scientific method (Williams, 1976: 200).

One thing certain, however, is that feminist scholars in the social sciences are increasingly rejecting the positivist or empiricist mode of social inquiry.[19] Feminist theory in social science is, more than ever before, critical, humanist, and value-oriented. It is increasingly taking on the characteristics of a critical social science—it rejects positivism but supports an interpretive model of social science; it seeks to uncover systems of social relationships; and it is interconnected with political practice (Fay, 1975).[20]

Feminist scholars cannot, as O'Brien (1981: 196) puts it so aptly, "afford the ahistorical indulgences of here-and-now empiricism." We must go beyond description and critique; we must engage in the process of analysis. Further, this analysis must be a feminist one rooted in feminist social theory which itself points to a genuinely feminist praxis. I wish that I could be surer than I am at this moment as to precisely what should constitute a feminist social theory, but I cannot because all the work we have at present is so new.

Finally, although I have concentrated here on the *sociological* analysis of gender inequality in sport, a necessity recognized by most feminist scholars is that we can no longer continue to divide up and fragment the social sciences. "A feminist social science, responding to the cultural pervasiveness of male supremacy, must be a unified social science" (O'Brien, 1981: 196).

NOTES

1.   This is a revised and expanded version of my presentation at the conference. It has benefitted enormously from my discussions and correspondence with Rob Beamish. His major criticism is that I must more fully work through the many questions and issues I raise. I could not agree more; hence the word "towards" in the title.

2.   I am using the term "gender" here rather than "sex" because I believe it more accurately describes the differentiation of male and female and the social relations between women and men which are areas I wish to address.

3.   Some of the material in the remainder of this section appears also in Hall (1983).

4.   Feminist theorists such as Shulamith Firestone in *The Dialectics of Sex* and Kate Millett in *Sexual Politics* were among the first to point this out. Such a conceptualization of power places my own analysis within a similar and so-called "radical" feminist theory. I am quite willing to accept the label but there is little agreement as to its meaning within feminist circles (see, for example, Jagger and Struhl, 1978 contrasted with Charvet, 1982).

5.   These are more fully addressed in Hall (1982b).

6.   I cannot do justice here to the intellectual argument this would entail because the defense is complex and intricate as are most themes in the philosophy of science and the sociology of knowledge. (See, for example, McCormack, 1981; Fee, 1981; Keller, 1978; Smith, 1979). I do, however, return to the point later in my brief discussion of feminism, positivism, and empiricism.

7.   Sometimes our scholarship has been "bad" (or gone wrong) because we have not been overly specific about exactly what it is about masculine experience that colors perceptions of reality. (O'Brien, 1981: 6).

8.   There is nothing particularly feminist about this notion either. Indeed, this is precisely the basis of a critical social science which, according to Fay (1975), has three main features: (1) it supports an interpretive model of social science and is at odds with the positivist model; (2) it seeks to uncover those systems of social relationships which determine the actions of individuals and the unanticipated, though not accidental, consequences of these actions; and most importantly (3) social theory is interconnected with political practice—thus it ties its knowledge claims to the satisfaction of human purposes and desires.

9.   It should be pointed out here that feminist theorists do not have an agreed upon understanding of patriarchy. See, for example, the commentaries following Heidi Hartmann's article in Sargent (1981). The basis of the debate centers first on the analytic independence and primacy of patriarchy as a fundamental system of domination vis-a-vis the capitalist or any other mode of production as a fundamental system

of domination. Second, there is a fundamental confusion among feminists between patriarchy as the rule of the father and patriarchy as the domination of women by men (see Barrett, 1980: 10-19).

10. Barrett is also quick to point out that where "attempts are made to constitute patriarchy as a system of domination in relation to the capitalist mode of production, these frequently flounder on the inflexibility and claims to autonomy to which the concept is prone" (p. 15).

11. Historically, this has never been shown. This observation merely points up the kind of theoretical work ahead of us. Certainly, feminist theorists have paid little attention to sport.

12. I look at this question in more detail in the section on Marxist-feminist social theory.

13. What I say in this section and the next two is very tentative as it is a not yet completely developed analysis of the many articles and texts which must be examined in order to understand fully the three positions. Moreover, no one who advocates one position over the other would claim that view as completely developed. I have also not discussed the attempts to reconcile feminism and psychoanalysis which some would see as a significant oversight.

Also, as is clear from Rob Beamish's contribution to this volume, he calls for a "materialist" rather than a "Marxist-feminist" analysis. He argues that feminists would be on firmer ground ontologically were they to begin with materialism. Kuhn and Wolpe (1978: 7) point out that as far as an analysis of the position of women is concerned, "materialism would locate that position in terms of the relations of production and reproduction at various moments in history." But, as they further point out, it is precisely this materialist analysis which is at the heart of Marxist-feminism. Therefore, a Marxist-feminist analysis begins with a materialist rather than a classic and traditional Marxist position insofar as the former constitutes an attempt to transform Marxism and move towards a construction of a Marxist-feminism. In sum, and in my opinion, Marxist-feminism is a much more accurate label for this developing feminist theory.

14. See Cathy Bray's contribution to this volume entitled "Gender and the Political Economy of Canadian Sport" for more detail on how class and gender could be integrated in that work.

15. MacKinnon develops her argument further in a subsequent article (MacKinnon, 1983) not published at the time of this writing.

16. I raise this issue here because it has recently been seen to be a point of contention among feminist sociologists (see Matthews, 1982 and the subsequent commentaries).

17. In what I mean by positivism, I am following Alexander (1982: 5-15) who outlines four essential postulates: (1) a radical break exists between empirical observations and nonempirical statements; (2) because of this break, more general intellectual issues (called philosophical or metaphysical) have no fundamental significance for the practice of an empirically oriented discipline; (3) since such an elimination of the nonempirical reference is taken to be the distinguishing feature of the natural sciences, any true sociology must assume a "scientific" self-consciousness; and (4) questions of a theoretical or general nature can correctly be dealt with only in relation to empirical observation.

18. For an excellent discussion of these debates as they relate to the sociology of sport, see Helmes (1981). For good general discussion see Keat and Urry (1975) and Alexander (1982). See footnote 6 for several references which discuss these issues in relation to feminist scholarship.

19. It is important to note that I distinguish between "empirical" and "empiricism." Empirical means reliance on observed experience, whereas empiricism, while obviously related, is always associated with a strict logical or inductive positivism. Feminist researchers do not necessarily reject empirical observation.

20. See footnote 8.

REFERENCES

Alexander, Jeffrey C.
1982   Positivism, Presuppositions, and Current Controversies. Berkeley: University of California Press.

Barrett, Michele
1980   Women's Oppression Today: Problems in Marxist Feminist Analysis. London: Verso Editions.

Berger, Peter L., and Hansfried Kellner
1981   Sociology Reinterpreted: An Essay on Method and Vocation. Garden City, NY: Anchor Books.

Charvet, John
1982   Feminism. London: J.M. Dent.

Eisenstein, Zillah
1982   "Comment to 'Rethinking sociology through a feminist perspective." The American Sociologist 17:36.

Fay, Brian
1975   Social Theory and Political Practice. London: George Allen & Unwin.

Fee, Elizabeth
1981   "Is feminism a threat to scientific objectivity?" International Journal of Women's Studies 4:393-413.

Griffith, Alison
1982   "Comment to 'Rethinking Sociology through a feminist
               perspective.'" The American Sociologist 17:336-37.

Gruneau, Richard S.
1976   "Class or mass? Notes on the democratization of Cana-
               dian amateur sport." Pp. 108-141 in Richard S. Gruneau
               and John G. Albinson (eds.), Canadian Sport:
               Sociological Perspectives. Toronto: Addison-Wesley.
1978   "Elites, class and corporate power in Canadian sport:
               Some preliminary findings." Pp. 201-242 in F. Landry
               and W.A.R. Orban (eds.), Sociology of Sport. Miami:
               Symposium Specialists.
1980a   "Freedom and constraint: the paradoxes of play, games
               and sports. Journal of Sport History 7:68-86.
1980b   "Power and play in Canadian society." Pp. 146-194 in
               Richard S. Ossenberg (ed.), Power and Change in
               Canada. Toronto: McClelland and Stewart.
1983   Class, Sports, and Social Development. Amherst: The
               University of Massachusetts Press.

Hall, M. Ann
1974   "Women and physical recreation: a causal analysis." Un-
               published Ph.D dissertation, The University of Bir-
               mingham (England).
1976   "Sport and physical activity in the lives of Canadian
               women." Pp. 179-199 in Richard S. Gruneau and John
               G. Albinson (eds.), Canadian Sport: Sociological
               Perspectives. Toronto: Addison-Wesley.
1978   Sport and Gender: A Feminist Perspective on the
               Sociology of Sport. CAHPER Sociology of Sport
               Monograph Series. Ottawa: Canadian Association for
               Health, Physical Education and Recreation.
1979a   "Sport and feminism: Imperative or irrelevant?" Pp.
               51-58 in John J. Jackson (ed.), Theory into Practice, Vic-
               toria: University of Victoria Press.
1979b   "Intellectual sexism in physical education." Quest 31:
               172-186.
1981   "Sport, sex roles and sex identity." The CRIAW
               Papers/Les Documents de l'ICRAF, No. 81-01. Ottawa:
               The Canadian Research Institute for the Advancement
               of Women.
1982a   "Sport and sex/gender role socialization." Presented at
               the Annual Meetings of the Canadian Sociology and
               Anthropology Association, Ottawa.

1982b   "The player, the woman, and the necessity of feminist
             scholarship." Pp. 48-55 in Proceedings of the National
             Association of Physical Education in Higher Education.
             Champaign, IL: Human Kinetics Publishers.
1983   "Advocates for radical change: two research odysseys."
             Journal of Health, Physical Education, Recreation and
             Dance 54: 24-26.

Hall, M. Ann, Jane Cameron and Debbie Shogan (eds.)
1981   Women in Athletic Administration in Canadian Univer-
             sities. Report of a National Conference, University of
             Alberta.

Hall, M. Ann and Patricia Lawson
1980   "Womansport: implications of the changing roles of
             women." Pp. 341-372 in Frank J. Hayden (ed.), Mind
             and Body in the 90s. McMaster University: The Cana-
             dian Council of University Physical Education Ad-
             ministrators.

Hall, M. Ann and Dorothy A. Richardson
1982   Fair Ball: Towards Sex Equality in Canadian Sport. Ot-
             tawa: The Canadian Advisory Council on the Status
             of Women.

Hartmann, Heidi
1981   "The unhappy marriage of Marxism and feminism: towards
             a more progressive union." Pp. 1-41 in Lydia Sargent (ed.),
             Women and Revolution. Boston, MA: South End Press.

Heilbroner, Robert L.
1980   Marxism: For and Against. New York: W.W. Norton.

Helmes, Richard C.
1978   "Ideology and social control in Canadian sport: a theoretical
             review." Working Papers in the Sociological Study of Sports
             and Leisure, Queen's University, Volume 4.
1981   "The philosophy of science and the problem of alienated
             sport labour." Presented at the 1st Regional Symposium of
             the International Committee for the Sociology of Sport, Van-
             couver.

Ingham, Alan G.
1979   "Methodology in the sociology of sport: from symptoms
             of malaise to Weber for a cure." Quest 31:187-215.

Issac, Jeffrey
1982   "On Benton's 'Objective interests and the sociology of power': a critique." Sociology 16:440-444.

Jagger, Alison M., and Paula Rothenberg Struhl
1978   Feminist Frameworks. New York: McGraw-Hill.

Keat, Russell and John Urry
1975   Social Theory as Science. London: Routledge and Kegan Paul.

Keller, Evelyn Fox
1978   "Gender and science." Psychoanalysis and Contemporary Thought 1:409-433.

Kidd, Bruce
1978   The Political Economy of Sport. CAHPER Sociology of Sport Monograph Series. Ottawa: Canadian Association of Health, Physical Education and Recreation.
1982   "Sport, dependency and the Canadian state." Pp. 281-303 in Hart Cantelon and Richard S. Gruneau (eds.), Sport, Culture and the Modern State. Toronto: University of Toronto Press.

Kuhn, Annette and AnnMarie Wolpe (eds.)
1978   Feminism and Materialism. London: Routledge and Kegan Paul.

MacKinnon, Catharine A.
1982   "Feminism, marxism, method, and the state: an agenda for theory." Signs: Journal of Women in Culture and Society 7:515-544.
1983   "Feminism, marxism, method, and the state: Toward Feminist Jurisprudence," Signs: Journal of Women in Culture and Society, 8:635-658.

Matthews, Sarah H.
1982   "Rethinking sociology through a feminist perspective." The American Sociologist 17:29-35.

McCormack, Thelma
1981   "Good theory or just theory? Towards a feminist philosophy of social science." Women's Studies International Quarterly 4:1-12.

Miles, Angela R.
1982   "Review of 'The Politics of Reproduction.'" Canadian Woman
             Studies 3: 63-64.

O'Brien, Mary
1981   The Politics of Reproduction. London: Routledge & Kegan
             Paul.

Rich, Adrienne
1977   "Conditions for work: the common world of women."
             Pp.xiv-xxiv in Sara Ruddick and Pamela Davis (eds.), Work-
             ing it Out. New York: Pantheon Books.

Sargent, Lydia (ed.)
1981   Women and Revolution. Boston, MA: South End Press.

Smith, Dorothy E.
1979   "A sociology for women." Pp. 135-187 in Julia A. Sherman
             and Evelyn Torbin Beck (eds.), The Prism of Sex: Essays
             in the Sociology of Knowledge. Madison: The University
             of Wisconsin Press.

Williams, Raymond
1976   Keywords: A Vocabulary of Culture and Society. Fon-
             tana/Croom Helm.

GENDER AND THE POLITICAL ECONOMY OF CANADIAN SPORT

Cathy Bray
University of Alberta

THE PRIMARY DETERRENT to formulating an analysis of women's sport in Canada within the new political economy tradition is the difficulty that this tradition has in coming to terms with gender. Before one can "fit" women's sport or any form of cultural production by women into the political economic whole, one must first place women themselves and their productive and reproductive labor into the parent body of theory.

This essay therefore begins with a challenge to the new political economy in Canada. In defining the adversary, I rely on Daniel Drache's (1978) summary characterization. For Drache the new political economy includes:

> the writings of Ryerson, Nelles, Watkins, Naylor and Clement, among others who, from a Marxist or neo-Marxist perspective, have revived the political economy tradition (p.3).

Drache (1978: 32) elaborates by suggesting that this school of thinkers has "cut through much of the obfuscation and mythologizing of the basic issues by effectively applying dependency theory, class analysis, elite studies, and contemporary models of capitalist development." This paper will suggest that much is still obscure about the "basic issues" of Canadian society, and the tendencies of the new Canadian political economy, admirable though they may be for rejuvenating our strong Canadian social science heritage and its classic traditions, perpetuates myths and obscurities. What is obscure in the new political economy is the rudimentary importance of gender to our social relations.[1]

In substantiating this critique I will dwell specifically on two prominent themes within Canadian political economy: dependency theory and elite studies. I will suggest that our concentration on Canada as a dependent nation, and on the elites who control our dependent economy has mitigated against an analysis of gender relations in Canadian society and has therefore precluded a complete understanding of our political economy. I will illustrate the lack of explanation of gender relations with prominent work in mainstream political economy and with work that analyzes sport within this tradition.

I will then outline the issues that have not been raised or raised only peripherally by feminist scholars, and therefore have not been absorbed into pivotal thought. The issues from which the veil of obscurity must be raised are threefold: sexuality, the family, and domestic labor. Prominent Canadian feminist writers such as Margaret Benston have laid a foundation for such an outline. I will couple their work with feminist and nonfeminist work in the sociology of sport. This latter coupling will be suggestive, but incomplete, as the territory in which the juncture lies is unexplored.

Finally, I intend to outline what a synthesis of the political economic tradition, and feminist analysis of sexuality, the family, and domestic labor will look like, if applied to sport. This will be done through positing questions which might be asked by the social scientist informed by both the tradition of Canadian political economy and feminist theory.

MYTHOLOGIZING TENDENCIES

Dependency Theory

We are confronted by Canada's dependency each day as we visit a newsstand, turn on the T.V. or watch a "Canadian" Football League game wherein the "imports" almost outnumber the Canadians and dominate the play. It is certainly not surprising that dependency is a key theme in the new Canadian political economy. First popularized by Kari Levitt (1970), this explanation of Canada's position as a nation which survives economically and politically at the behest of foreign, primarily American, capital has much salience for the student of Canadian society. Its proponents such as Naylor (1975) and Clement (1977) make a strong case for the usefulness of this perspective, originally imported from Latin America and the Caribbean. As Drache indicates (1978: 40), Clement's thesis that Canada's industrial revolution was necessarily incomplete because of the superdominant commercial sector and imperialism "takes him a considerable distance in uncovering the historic origins of Canadian dependency." However, Clement and others are open to criticism. A recent manifestation of this criticism is authored by Leo Panitch (1981) who suggests that the concentration on the industrial entrepreneur versus the financial capitalist as fractions of the capitalist class has caused the contradictory relationship between workers and capitalists to be overlooked. He says that: "an appreciation of class relations, of exploitation and struggle is essential to make sense of what is going on in society." (p. 9). Panitch is correct—understanding of class is essential. Without the explicit demonstration of class conflict in dependency theory based political economy, we can see Canada only as a creation of capitalists on Wall Street or of their compradors on Bay Street or worse, as the result of a massive, inhuman and impenetrable corporation." Without class conflict the reader is left to query, paraphrasing the student of constitutional history: "Is everybody in Canada a capitalist?"

Knowledge of class is essential, but insufficient. Demystifying class relations is merely a step toward a fuller understanding of society, including that aspect of society which is the theme of this paper—gender relations. The political economist must understand class relations before he or she can fully comprehend gender relations. This is not to say that a class analysis can subsume an analysis of gender. Seeing class structure is only partial preparation for seeing sex structure. Seeing both doubles one's vision (Kelly, 1979), initially causing a figurative headache, eventually allowing deeper perception.

Margaret Benston (1969) shows us why we must understand class together with sex oppression. A Marxian understanding of class introduces us to use-value and exchange-value and therefore allows us to see that women, because they produce use-value in the home, are unable to exchange their labor on the commodity market, i.e. they cannot be paid for their domestic labor. Thus, in a capitalist society where commodities must be purchased for survival, the unpaid woman working in the home depends on someone else to provide the money. This gives rise to the family—an important concept to be discussed later in the paper.

The class perspective designates a second point of departure in understanding gender relations. When women do sell their labor in the labor market, as more women are now doing, they sell it under competitive conditions. In the segmented labor market (Edwards and Gordon, 1975) where secretaries are women and truck drivers are men and the blue collar woman and male nurses are anomalous, women compete for each other's jobs. This has produced a female job ghetto, characterized by low pay, poor working conditions, and resulting high turnover. This ghetto can be tapped by the capitalist to secure cheap labor in order to increase profits.

Thus, in depriving us of class analysis, dependency theory, as taken up by many of the Canadian political economists, has deprived us of a necessary component in our search for the meaning of gender. It must be remembered, though, that in cleaning up the "intellectual messiness of the new Canadian political economy" (Panitch, 1981: 12) by bringing the concepts of class and dependency together, we are not automatically creating room wherein gender analysis will fit. Bringing class back in is only the beginning.

How have Canadian sport sociologists taken up the dependency argument? One good example is Bruce Kidd's "Sport, Dependency and the Canadian State" (1982).[2] Kidd has written a thorough, and happily readable, account of the centralization of popular culture (i.e. the National Hockey League and Canadian Football League) in the hands of rich and powerful American capitalists and the associated loss of community and nationalism in Canada. Kidd sees state support of Olympic and national teams as "the Liberal (government's) attempt to solve national, economic, political, and cultural discontents by accentuating the role of sport as a symbol of one 'Canada'" (1982: 298). These discontents, according to Kidd, arise largely because of a dependent national economy.

Colin Leys (1982), in a commentary on Kidd (1982), replicates the Panitch critique of the classlessness of dependency theory. He refers to: "the distinctly 'residual' role played in the analysis by social classes. . . Classes appear only as the source of particular forms of cultural hegemony in sport—the amateur code and so on. The struggles of the working class, in particular, don't figure in the account" (p. 307). Though the Leys critique perhaps overlooks the statement (Kidd, 1982: 300): "the democratic control of Canadian sport cannot be posed solely in terms of nationalism for classes as well as people are oppressed, and increasingly the state plays an active role in the process," the primary importance of class exploitation is not clearly demonstrated in Kidd's paper. As has been said above, it is therefore rather difficult to make the economic exploitation of women explicit.

But, the dimunition of class aside, Kidd (1982) can be criticized simply for his choice of illustrative material and the evaluations he makes of his material. For example, he refers nostalgically to the hockey leagues of old, and "the styles of play, norms of behavior, and team loyalties which once combined to enunciate a national sense of identity" (p. 289) and invokes Al Purdy's poetic label for hockey—"the national specific," and Ralph Allen's similar "national religion." If hockey, a sport played, coached, administrated and watched largely by males and at the professional level played exclusively by males, is a national specific or religion, then to be a Canadian one must first be male. The feminist, reading such statments in silent pain, admonishes such authors for believing that a national community has been formed without significant representation by women.

To be sure, recognition of the primacy of class won't rectify the problem of seeing the male nation as *the* nation. Leys (1982) says: "What (is it) about sport that makes it so important to the workers: why do they read the sports page first, why are team loyalties so central in people's consciousness, why should sports be an important arena or focus for the violence through which the frustrations of working class life are partly expressed, etc.?" (p. 311). However, sport is not important to most women. Women, if they read the sports pages at all, do not read them first. Team loyalties are not central to most women. Most importantly, sports are not an arena of violence for women. If sport sociologists ever begin to analyze sport as an expression of *male* violence carefully, seriously and in social context, we will have come a long way toward making sense of what is going on in our society.

But the concluding remarks of Leys' (1982) commentary are imaginative and synthetic. In calling for links between working class struggles for socialism and other non-class struggles. Leys suggests that an example might be: "the linking of the women's struggle with the workers' struggle by taking up the progressive implications of both for the question of women's participation in sport" (p. 314).

Elite Studies

From the critique of dependency theory and its implications for gender analysis, I will move on to a similar examination of elite studies. Clement, following Porter (1966), provides the new political economy with the benchmark definition of an elite as "a set of uppermost positions within any given institutional sphere that is arranged in a definite hierarchy. . . . The corporate elite is, according to this minimal definition, that set of positions known as senior management and directors within dominant corporations." (1975: 5). Women have been collectively defined out of the analysis. In Porter's economic elite "there are no women" (1966: 264). Clement's (1975) later study, which makes reference to women often enough to warrant inclusion of them in the index (an improvement over Porter's *The Vertical Mosaic*), notes that "women are probably the most underrepresented type in the economic elite." Their representation at various levels of the corporate higher echelons is on the order of .6 percent." (p. 266).

The reason women are defined out of the elite is because the determining factor of elite membership is one's relationship to the means of production. If one owns and/or exercises control over the means of production, one might be considered part of the elite, depending on the breadth of categorical restrictions. However, if one has an indirect relationship to the means of production or a direct relationship which is secondary to one's indirect relationship, one cannot be classified as a member of the elite.

Elite studies, handled properly, must be imbedded in class theory. Women cannot be stratified under the traditional class structure. Saying that women belong to the class of their husbands and that therefore husbands and wives are social equals raises a number of problems: 1) because the unpaid housewife has access to money only with the consent of her husband, she is not financially independent, and therefore, for this reason among others, cannot be considered her husband's equal; 2) the paid wife is usually occupied at a job in a lower class than her husband's job; and 3) in the rare cases that a husband and wife have equivalent occupations and receive equal pay, the wife usually performs most of the domestic labor and therefore receives less pay for each hour of her labor, making her "less equal." As Margrit Eichler (1980) indicates in an important critique of social science: "In its internal logic, class analysis is incapable of incorporating an analysis of the position of women in the family, since the central concepts developed and used for analysis—exchange-value and use-value, production and consumption, the relationship to the means of production, occupation and wages—are premised on a capitalist rather than a quasi-feudal type of relationship" (p. 115). This quasi-feudal relationship is found in the family, and it is family status that usually fully determines a woman's status.

Specifying the relationship between economic class and gender class is difficult, yet this specification is, I would suggest, the key problem in sociology presently. More importantly, the struggles against exploitation and oppression and for equal rights for workers and women are central practical activities which will change the future lives of human beings. It is not within the realm of this paper to prescribe a solution or outline a theory which conjoins the problems or directs the struggle. I can merely indicate an awareness of the problem, and carefully draw out ideas which may be tentatively attached to the new Canadian political economy tradition and to recent efforts in the sociology of Canadian sport. As Ann Oakley (1981) warns, our attempt to conceptualize stratification "must begin, not merely end, with the subtleties of women's situation. It must be prepared to acknowledge the dispensability of the notion of class—or at least the importance of a revised notion, of 'gender class'—in making sense of women's labour and relationships" (p. 292).[3]

To return to the narrow confines of this paper, however, a primary example of an elite study and the corresponding class analysis which should accompany a study of elites is Richard Gruneau's "Power and Play in Canadian Society." One of Gruneau's contributions to the sociology of Canadian sport in this paper is the demystification of colonial games as democratic (C.F. Howell and Howell, 1969: 54-6; Roxborough, 1966). Gruneau (1980) contends that "when organized games or sports did occur. . . they tended to affirm the logic of a pattern of domination that, if not really feudal, was nonetheless highly traditional and paternalistic in nature" (p. 161). However, Gruneau specifically addresses only one mode of domination, that of the aristocrat over small farmers and artisans and later *petit bourgeois* and a growing middle class. He fails to elucidate another clearly obvious power relation in nineteenth-century Canadian society, that of men over women. Women do not appear in "Power and Play," and more important, the sex homogeneity of Canadian players during this period is not seen as remarkable.

Yet Gruneau juxtaposes patriarchal and capitalist relations of power so closely that, through the filter of feminist awareness, we can see linkages. He says:

> In particular, the values of *manly* character and con-
> spicuous leisure that had characterized the ritual games
> and field sports of European life. . . served as a means
> of self-assertion and as weapons in the endorsement
> of a cultural legacy which stressed hierarchy, deference
> and class distance (emphasis added). (Gruneau, 1980:
> 163).

Surely it is but a small leap to suggest that *manly* characteristics endorsed a cultural legacy of a *gender* hierarchy, deference to *men*, and *gender-class* distance.

This small but important step can be taken with respect to the English public (i.e., males only) schools. "By indoctrinating the sons of the bourgeoisie as gentlemen," these schools not only served to thwart class conflict, but maintained the sex hierarchy by perpetuating male dominance. The collectivity to which the young bourgeoisie became committed was not only bonded by class but by sex. That this collectivity was also race homogeneous is equally important but cannot be adequately discussed in this paper.

The gender-specific terminology of Gruneau's piece is the thread which one must take hold of in order to unravel the webs of meaning and mystification in regard to gender. Upper Canada College was to discipline the *boys*, through *manly* British field sports. If we ask why it is impossible to replace these words with *girls* or *womanly* and answer ourselves in more than a flippant, superficial fashion, we will continue to demythologize power and play in Canadian social development. A footnote, a paragraph, or even a chapter devoted to "the women" is flip-pant when the rest of the article or book is characterized by a unidimensional vision which sees only economic class as a strati-fying variable and therefore sees only men as social actors.

ISSUES TO INCORPORATE

As promised in the introduction, I now wish to outline some issues that have not been raised by sport sociologists within the new Canadian political economy tradition. These issues have only recently been discussed by Canadian political economists. I would like to consider sexuality, the family, and domestic labor, their relationship to political economy, and how these concepts can be incorporated into an analysis of sport.

Sexuality

In a ground-breaking paper, Catherine MacKinnon (1982) links sexuality to the family and domestic labor in a challenging "Agenda for Theory" which frequently shakes both Marxism and feminism at their foundations. Her fundamental principle, that sexuality is to feminism as work is to Marxism, illuminates the relationship between women's labor, family and sexuality. Where the structure of work is class, the structure of sexuality is heterosexuality. The consequence of work is production; the consequence of sexuality is reproduction, or alternatively, domestic labor. The congealed form of work is capital; the congealed form of sexuality is gender and family. MacKinnon (1982) reminds us that both work and sexuality are "constructed yet constructing, universal as activity yet historically specific, jointly comprised of matter and mind" (pp. 15-16).

By defining sexuality as the primary determiner of male power and the constructor of family and the sexual division of labor, MacKinnon exposes the sexual basis of the social construction of women. She (MacKinnon, 1982: 531) says simply "What defines women is what turns men on." MacKinnon thereby clarifies the fact that the issues of the women's movement are sexual; they form a unity, and define a politics. Sexual harassment, for example, first seen as a nonissue, is now commonly viewed as a problem of personal relations, not as an issue where sexuality, i.e. male power, is the base cause. The discussion of rape, not seen as an issue of male sexual power, has revolved around questions of consent and violence. But issues such as sexual harassment, rape, incest, contraception, abortion, lesbianism, pornography and prostitution can, and must, according to MacKinnon (1982) be seen: ". . . as a cohesive whole. . . . The defining theme of that whole is the male pursuit of control over women's sexuality." (p. 532).

Sport sociologists interested in women and sport have realized that sexuality is an important concept. Unfortunately, however, most work concerning sexuality and sport has centered on narrowly defined psychological studies of sex roles. Masculine and feminine behavior expectations have been reified as sex roles, and the predominant issue in this sort of research has been whether there is a conflict between the role of athlete and the role of woman. Using such questionable instruments as the Bem Sex Role Inventory (Bem, 1974; Elazar *et al.*, 1979), sport sociologists have advocated the androgynous advantage, wherein individuals who combine both "masculine" and "feminine" behavioral traits are seen to be psychologically healthier. Hall (1981) critiques such work within the sociology of sport, indicating that the research tends to perpetuate the idea that there are two separate sex roles. Such research, Hall suggests, directs attention away from the historical, political and economic power differential in men and women. In other words, sex-role research in sport looks at the "sport-feminity conflict" as an issue in isolation from other issues of sexuality such as pornography and prostitution. If this analysis is inserted into the politics of male power that MacKinnon has identified, the "conflict" will be exposed as vacuous, and the reification of this conflict will be seen as a result of androcentrism.

This avoidance of the politics of sexual power is obvious in an article by Carole Oglesby. Oglesby (1978), after defining sexuality in a limited unisexual (heterosexual) manner which excludes the many variants of physical and nonphysical sexual expressions known to exist, makes the following statement about the construction of sexuality: "If we can make permeable the construct of sexuality, rid it of the false cloak of supernatural origin, we can create and live new definitions. We are in need of a construct which, in its brilliance and order, would expose and shatter the androcentric prison which destroys women. But as scientists we have read too much to honestly propose that women suffer more from this aberration of our society" (p. 85). While it may be granted that suffering should not be measured out like so many teaspoons of sugar, Oglesby's statement suggests a lack of awareness of the fundamental difference in power between males and females as a result of the androcentric construction of sexuality. Her statement that "there is no notion of femininity except as a female relates to males" (Oglesby 1978: 85) does not shatter any prison walls, but in fact buttresses them more firmly.

Family

Turning to the second new concept which, as I have suggested above should be integrated into a feminist political economy of Canadian sport, I will now discuss the family. Reiterating MacKinnon, the congealed form of sexuality is the family. In other words, because men are more powerful than women, due to the male centered definition of sexuality, the family has arisen in its present form. Ann Oakley shows how women's sexuality is "congealed" in the institutions of marriage and the family. She (Oakley, 1981: 236) suggests that the nature of women, as attributed by present modern industrial society, is to be contentedly "heterosexual, monogomous, and 'complementary' to the role and character of men." One reason for restricting female expression of sexuality to the nuclear family is that the family, as presently constituted, protects capital. "In a society based on private property, marriage ensures that fathers will know their children, and thereby upholds the patriarchal system of inheritance" (The Staff of Women, 1978: 311). Simplistically, fathers pass their capital on to their sons, maintaining the class structure through the institution of the family.

Evidence of awareness of the impact of the family on political economy in studies of Canadian sport vary from negligible (Helmes, 1981) to strong (Gruneau, 1976). Helmes (1981) discussing ideology and social control should perhaps have mentioned the family when he suggested that liberal ideology is disseminated through the "institutional structure" and that "political socialization experiences" produce an institutional elite hostile to socialist thinking. He also avoids mention of the family when discussing elite groups' collegiality, by concluding a list of the background characteristics "social class, educational, occupational" with the innocuous "etc." It would have been helpful to the Helmes paper if some discussion of the family had taken place in the context of social control.

Gruneau's (1976) paper refers to family members, usually to fathers, often mothers, sometimes parents, and sometimes families. His (Gruneau, 1976) summarizing statement is: "The data on Canada Games athletes indicates noticeable differences between athletes' families and those of Canadian families generally" (p. 127). He concludes that well-placed families are in a position to confer differential advantage on their children, enabling them to be overrepresented in Canadian sport. In other words, Gruneau does see the family as the carrier of class.

However, Gruneau and others within the new Canadian political economy tradition might do well to heed the advice of Margrit Eichler, warning against "The Monolithic Model of the Family." Eichler (1981: 368) suggests that "the family" as studied by sociologists is defined as an institution which serves a variety of functions "concomitantly and in a congruent manner." That is, if a family can solve, for example, economic problems, it can also solve legal problems. What Eichler (1981: 371) calls "high interaction" in one dimension of family life "is assumed to coincide with or result in high interaction in all other dimensions." Eichler defines seven "dimensions" of family interaction and schematizes them in an article which deserves a careful reading. Briefly, these dimensions are legal, procreative, socialization, sexual, residential, economic, and emotional.

Eichler (1981) points out the consequences of assuming congruency: "1) the assumption of congruence leads to 2) a bias in the data collection process, which leads to 3) an underestimation of the incidence of noncongruence and 4) inappropriate categorizations which in turn 5) lead to misdefinitions as to what constitutes 'problem' families and 6) neglect of vitally important questions." (p. 369). The implications of these consequences are many and varied. In relationship to the political economy of Canadian sport, I will discuss problems in data collection regarding the economic, residential, and socialization dimension.

A key problem for the political economist interested in sport in Canada is the use of sport in maintaining the class structure. As Gruneau (1976) has indicated, it is necessary to determine the social class of sport participants, administrators, etc. if we are to understand constraints placed on sport participation. Gruneau's (1976) work and a study of the social class of Canadian sport administrators by Hollands and Gruneau (1979) attempt to assess class. Their assumption in both cases is that parents pass capital, both economic and social, onto children. Paraphrasing Parkin (1972: 57), they suggest that class structure is partially generated by parents providing their children with an education and home environment conducive to achievement.

They (Hollands and Gruneau, 1979: 36) assert with Forcese (1975: 58-81) that "Canadian children tend to inherit the social class status of their parents."

Without belaboring the point made above, that fallacious assumptions of equality between women and men have been made if married couples are assigned to the same class, it must be reiterated that collecting data on solely father's occupation gives, at best, an incomplete picture of the social class of a family. Secondly, the assumption has been made that the Canada Games athletes and the sports administrators actually lived with their parents or in Margrit Eichler's terminology, that the economic dimension and the residential dimension were congruent. Thirdly, allowing the assumption that sports participants lived with their parents, it is further assumed in the Canada Games study that both spouses were involved in parenting and in conveying attitudes such as achievement motivation. Perhaps only one parent, or neither parent, had such a socialization effect.

What does all of this have to do with understanding gender relations? How will using a more adequate construction of the family, which allows for incongruencies, help to penetrate the myths about gender inherent in political economy? What this correction will do is take the family out of the private sphere, and therefore properly place women, who are so closely identified with the family, under the scrutiny of social scientists. What has heretofore been seen as private and personal—domestic and emotional life within the family—will be recognized as what it really is: an institution which constructs and is constructed by capitalism through the performance of socially necessary labor. Eli Zaretsky (1976) puts the case for bringing the study of the family into political economy strongly: "Childrearing, cleaning, laundry, the maintenance of property, the preparation of food, daily health care, reproduction, etc. constitute a perpetual cycle of labour necessary to maintain life in this society" (p. 11).

Domestic Labor

Zaretsky's statement leads directly to a consideration of what I have identified as the third component to be introduced into the political economic analysis of Canadian sport—domestic labor. Discussion of domestic labor was opened by Margaret Benston (1969) and important questions are now being addressed in a highly scholarly manner, yet with pertinence to the women's movement and to women's lives. *Hidden in the Household*, edited by Bonnie Fox, and *More than a Labour of Love*, by Meg Luxton, are two recent books which formulate and answer significant questions regarding women's household labor. Here I will attempt only to introduce some of these questions. The area of thought is emergent and burgeoning and requires a careful, knowledgeable perusal before incorporation into sport sociology or any other body of thought.

Before directing attention at these important questions revolving around women's domestic labor, the connection between women's sexuality and such labor must be restated. MacKinnon (1982) as quoted above, suggests that the product of sexuality is reproduction. "Reproduction" includes not only biological replication of the species but the care and maintenance of people in their homes for the labor market. Bonnie Fox (1980) expresses the connection between sexuality and reproductive or domestic labor thus: "In stark contrast with capitalist production in which the direct producer is clearly compelled by necessity to sell his or her capacity for work, domestic labour presents itself as a labour of love. . . . Domestic labour accompanies a personal commitment to family members. . . . Household labour is interwoven with 'personal life' and totally enmeshed in the worker's most intimate personal relationship. . . . The household worker is perpetually striving to meet personal needs." (p. 12). While this passage makes obvious the connection between sexuality and domestic labor, the cautions of Zaretsky and others that domestic labor is part of the socially necessary labor of capitalism must not be forgotten. That this labor is a result of both patriarchal and capitalistic constraints—constructed by both sexuality and work—is neatly manifest in the title of the Luxton book. Housework is indeed *More than a Labour of Love*.

Fox (1980) formulates many of the questions that will, I hope, be incorporated into coming discussions of Canadian political economy. She asks, for instance, about the consequences of the privatization of housework under capitalism, and whether or not the privately productive household is a structural necessity under capitalism; about the relationship between domestic labor and wage labor; about increasing numbers of married women in the labor market; about the trend toward industrialization of housework; about the possibility of complete socialization of domestic labor under capitalism; about the relationship between patriarchy and capitalism.

It would be foolhardy to attempt to deal with the answers to these questions here. What will be done is to indicate some information which has arisen from such discussion of domestic labor which might be immediately applied to an understanding of sport, particularly women's sport.

One salient feature of housework in relationship to sport is that it is "a twenty-four hour proposition." This has implications for the time which women might spend in leisure activities such as sport. Women's leisure does not fall into the usual categories identified by people studying men's leisure; it does not usually take place at a time and place separate from work. For example, the housewife might watch a soap opera while ironing a shirt or compose poetry while minding the baby. The sport sociologist, aware that sport has been rationalized in regard to time and place, must take this difference in women's leisure, as a result of her domestic duties, into account.

Another cogent aspect of domestic labor is that this labor includes meeting the emotional and socialization needs of children. Labor in this regard, it is beginning to be understood, is performed differently in different households, depending on the social class of the family. Dorothy Smith elaborates on this distinction. According to Smith (1977: 45), middle class women are "oriented to the values and standards of the externalized order." The corporate structure requires that the male manager be a "company man" subordinating himself to the ethics of his employer—the ethics of free enterprise such as liberalism, achievement motivation and privatization. The middle class wife, then, reproduces her husband and family in the corporate image and strives toward the externalized goal of consumption in order to do so. Reproduction or nonreproduction of such values in potential sport participants has been of interest to sport sociologists. Contextualizing such interests within an understanding of class structure will help sociologists to explicate social relations more fully by situating the athlete and the family within the economy and the polity.

I am aware of no significant reference to domestic labor within the study of Canadian sport which has been informed by the new political economy. Bruce Kidd (1978: 64), in a peripheral remark, notes that "it is not surprising (that women between the ages of twenty and twenty-nine are unfit) when we consider that during these ages the burdens of childrearing tend to be the most onerous." Perhaps such "unsurprising" details have not stimulated the need in Canadian political economists who study sport to ask "Why?"

We must turn to feminist sociology of sport to find reference to domestic labor. Ann Hall in an early article, makes the relationship between domestic labor and women's sport clear. Her (Hall, 1976) sophisticated mathematical analysis of a great deal of data notwithstanding, the conclusion is simple: "One of the real barriers to (sport) participation specifically for women is the fact that they, and not their husbands, are entrusted with the responsibility of childcare and housekeeping. . . . Their lack of participation is a result of an injustice in the realm of marriage and the family."(p. 194). It will be interesting and exciting to extend such empirical findings and associated judgments about "injustice" into the realm of Canada's political economy. Both the data and the theory are there; links must now be made.

Questions for the Future

In conclusion, I would like to pose a few questions which might arise at the juncture of Canadian political economy, feminist theory, and the sport experience. The questions are preliminary and will need readjustments, answers, and further revisions. In asking these questions, I believe Gruneau's (1980) postulate that sport is both reproductive and transformative should be kept in mind. Sport not only reflects society but in many ways can change social actors, who make their own society.

In relationship to sexuality, students of sport should ask the question: how does sport reproduce female sexuality? What qualities of "maleness" are demonstrated in our play? What "feminine" qualities? Women's sport could be assessed to see if it reproduces the qualities which MacKinnon (1982: 530) isolates as part of the female gender stereotype: vulnerability, passivity, softness, incompetence, domesticity, infantilization. Such questions are not, in fact, new. Metheney considered the relationship between sport and the feminine image as early as 1964. What would be new would be to situate the answers in the context of power relations between males and females, or as Gruneau (1975: 146) advocates, to concentrate on the relational aspects of sport as played by men and women rather than merely the distributive aspects. We should be asking not only what makes women's sport different but how these differences explain the association between women's sport and men's sport. In answering these questions one must remember the political and economic context of all social relations and ask follow-up questions: does sexuality as reproduced in sport express and maintain male/female power differentials? If so, in what ways does patriarchal power, as mediated through our sport activities, sustain capitalist relations?

Cognizance of the family and its relationship to the political economy of Canadian sport suggests questions of a more concrete nature than those discussed above in regard to sexuality. Of immediate importance is the determination of how the non-congruent familiy—the family that does not fit Eichler's "monolithic model"—is served by sport delivery systems such as governments, voluntary institutions, and schools. Can one-parent families donate the time and money required by the minor hockey league? How does the increasing adolescent contribution to family income and the concurrent decrease in adolescent free time in middle-class households affect the athletic population? Does the child of a family which is not legally defined have the same rights to engage in sport as a child from a legally defined family? How does sport affect marital breakdown?

Again, in asking such questions, it is important not to stay behind the door to the private sphere of the family. Going inside this sphere to ask questions is not enough; sociologists must re-enter the public world before they can complete their analysis. Thus, the supposed inability of the single mother, for instance, to permit her daughter to play hockey might be taken as an indication of other restrictions imposed upon the single-parent family. The next question becomes why is it easier for the nuclear family to support itself in a capitalist society? What conditions are more conducive to the two-parent family than to the one-parent family? Who benefits from these conditions? Who pays?

Finally, the relationship of domestic labor to sport is an area requiring consideration. In what ways could sport agencies provide services which would take advantage of women's time where work and leisure are intermingled? Do domestic workers need exercise? What physical activities can be enjoyed by mothers and their children together? Will collective organization of domestic labor affect sport provision? How does engaging in sports change a housekeeper's work habits? Some of these questions have indeed been asked, but again I am advocating putting answers in context. Suggesting merely that women have no time to play sport because of their domestic labor is not illuminating. We must ask further why women perform domestic labor in the manner they do and how this performance is related to the larger political economy. Only by making these connections can we trace the full meaning of sport and meanings behind the social practice of sport. We will then perhaps be able to identify a means of changing and improving this cultural practice.

NOTES

1. Though this topic has been delimited such that it concentrates on Canadian political economy, the class and gender struggles about which it speaks are similar in many other parts of the world.
2. See , Hart Cantelon and Richard Gruneau (eds.) *Sport, Culture and the Modern State* (Toronto: University of Toronto Press, 1982) for this and other papers first published as conference proceedings.
3. The third and equally difficult notion that must be incorporated in our new reconceptualization is that of class based on race.

REFERENCES

Bentson, Margaret
1969   "The political economy of women's liberation." Monthly Review 21:13-25.

Bem, Sandra L.
1974   "The measurement of psychological androgyny." Journal of Personality and Social Psychology 42:155-162.

Clement, Wallace
1975   The Canadian Corporate Elite: An Analysis of Economic Power. Toronto: McLelland and Stewart.
1977   Continental Corporate Power: Economic Linkages Between Canada and the United States. Toronto: McLelland and Stewart.

Drache, Daniel
1978   A Practical Guide to Canadian Political Economy. Toronto: James Lorimer.

Edwards, Michael R. and David M. Gordon (eds.)
1975   Labour Market Segmentation. Lexington, Mass.: D.C. Heath.

Eichler, Margrit
1980   The Double Standard: A Feminist Critique of Feminist Social Science. New York: St. Martin's Press.
1981   "The inadequacy of the monolithic model of the family." Canadian Journal of Sociology 6:367-388.

Elazar, J., J. Pedhazur and T. Tetenbaum
1979   "Bem sex role inventory: a theoretical and methodological critique." Journal of Personality and Social Psychology 37:996-1016.

Forcese, Dennis
1975   The Canadian Class Structure. Toronto: McGraw-Hill Ryerson.

Fox, Bonnie
1980   Hidden in the Household: Women's Domestic Labour Under Capitalism. Toronto: The Women's Press.

Gruneau, Richard
1975   "Sport, social differentiation and social inequality," in D. Ball and John Loy (eds.) Sport and Social Order Reading: Addison-Wesley.
1976   "Class or mass: notes on the democratization of Canadian amateur sport," in R.S. Gruneau and J. Albinson (eds.) Canadian Sport Sociological Perspectives. Don Mills: Addison-Wesley.
1980   "Power and play in Canadian society," in Richard Ossenberg (ed.) Power and Change in Canada. Toronto: McLelland and Stewart.

Hall, M.A.
1976   "Sport and physical activity in the lives of Canadian women," Pp. 170-199 in R.S. Gruneau and J. Albinson (eds.) Canadian Sport Sociological Perspectives. Don Mills: Addison-Wesley.
1981   Sport, Sex Roles and Sex Identity. Ottawa: The CRIAW Papers/Les Documents del 'ICRAF, No. 81-01 Canadian Research Institute for the Advancement of Women.

Helmes, Richard
1981   "Ideology and social control in Canadian sport: a theoretical review," Pp. 207-232 in Marie Hart and Susan Birrell (eds.) Sport in the Sociocultural Process. Third edition. Dubuque, Iowa: William Brown.

Hollands, Robert G. and Richard S. Gruneau
1979   "Social class and voluntary action in the administration of Canadian amateur sport." In Working Papers in the Sociological Study of Sports and Leisure, 2(3). Kingston: Sport Studies Research Group.

Howell, Nancy and Maxwell Howell
1969   Sports and Games in Canadian Life: 1700 to the Present. Toronto: MacMillan of Canada.

Kelly, Joan
1979   "The doubled vision of feminist theory: a postscript to the women and power conference." Feminist Studies 5:216-227.

Kidd, Bruce
1978   The Political Economy of Sport. Ottawa: CAHPER Sociology of Sport Monograph Series.

1982   "Sport, dependancy and the Canadian state." In Hart Cantelon and Richard Gruneau, eds. Sport, Culture, and the Modern State. Toronto: University of Toronto Press.

Levitt, Kari
1970   Silent Surrender: The Multinational Corporation in Canada. Toronto: Macmillan.

Leys, Colin
1982   "Comment on Kidd." In Hart Cantelon and Richard Gruneau, eds. Sport, Culture, and the Modern State. Toronto: University of Toronto Press.

Luxton, Meg
1980   More than a Labour of Love: Three Generations of Women's Work in the Home. Toronto: The Women's Press.

MacKinnon, Catherine
1982   "Feminism, Marxism, method and the state: an agenda for theory." Signs: Journal of Women in Culture and Society 7:515-544.

Metheny, Eleanor
1964   "Sports and the Feminine Image." Gymnasion 1(4): 17-22.

Naylor, R.T.
1975   The History of Canadian Business 1867-1914, 2 vols. Toronto: James Lorimer.

Nelles, H.V.
1974   The Politics of Development Forests, Mines and Hydro-Electric Power in Ontario, 1849-1941. Toronto: Macmillan.

Oakley, Ann
1981   Subject Woman. Oxford: Martin Robertson Press.

Oglesby, Carole A.
1978   "The masculinity/femininity game: called on account of. . .," in
       Carole A. Oglesby (ed.) Women and Sport: From Myth to Reality.
       Philadelphia: Lea and Febiger.

Panitch, Leo
1981   "Dependency and class in Canadian political economy." Studies
       in Political Economy: A Socialist Review 6:7-34.

Parkin, Frank
1972   Class Inequality and Political Order. London: Paladin.

Porter, John
1966   The Vertical Mosaic: An Analysis of Social Class and Power in
       Canada. Toronto: University of Toronto Press.

Roxborough, H.
1966   One Hundred—Not Out: The Story of Nineteenth Century
       Canadian Sport. Toronto: Ryerson.

Ryerson, Stanley
1968   Unequal Union: Confederation and the Roots of Conflict in the
       Canadas, 1815-1873. Toronto: Progress Books.

Smith, Dorothy E.
1977   "Women, the family and corporate capitalism," in Marylee
       Stephenson (ed.) Women in Canada, second edition. Don Mills:
       General Publishing.

The Staff of Women
1978   "Sex in a Capitalist Society." In Alison Jagger and Paula Struhl
       (eds.) Feminist Frameworks: Alternative Theoretical Accounts
       of the Relations Between Women and Men. New York:
       McGraw-Hill.

Watkins, Mel
1963   "A Staple Theory of Economic Growth." Canadian Journal of
       Economics and Political Science 29:141-158.

Wise, S.F. and D. Fischer
1974   Canada's Sporting Heroes. Toronto: General Publishing.

Zaretsky, Eli
1976   Capitalism The Family and Personal Life. New York:
       Harper-Row.

STUDYING GENDER IN SPORT: A FEMINIST PERSPECTIVE[1]

Susan Birrell
University of Iowa

WHILE THE TOPIC OF GENDER IN SPORT is of great significance within the area of sociology of sport, it has been treated with a marked lack of imagination, when it has not been overlooked completely. Thus it is entirely appropriate that this year, when the NASSS conference theme calls on us to engage our sociological imaginations in new and exciting ways, we should direct some of our attention to the use of gender as a variable in research in sociology of sport. The stance that will be taken in this paper is based on the assumption that to ask how gender is used as a variable in research in sociology of sport is to ask more than how understanding gender differences can add to our sociological understanding of sport; it is to ask how research designed to investigate the sport experiences of women should be conducted. My major thesis is that the way we as sociologists use gender as a variable is a reflection of our approach to women as social beings; until we recognize and seek to overcome the significant limitations that our biases place on our research, major barriers will continue to obscure our understanding of sport as a social phenomenon, and we will continue to see only half the world of sport.

The central issue revolves around the notion of the "proper use" of gender in sport research. Yet before one can make sound recommendations concerning how research on gender *should* be conducted it seems logical to ascertain how research on gender *has been* conducted in the past, for past patterns surely inform the research of the present. Thus the discussion turns first to the past.

A RETROSPECTIVE VIEW OF GENDER AS A VARIABLE

A content analysis of some of the major journals and proceedings in sociology of sport can furnish a starting point for an investigation of the uses of gender as a variable in past research. The purpose here is not only to give an account of the contents of those journals but also to generate categories that distinguish different treatment strategies for analysis. Once a catalogue of uses of gender has been established, the assumptions of each use need to be explicated. What does the treatment of men and women as research subjects in sociology of sport reveal about the way men and women are viewed in relation to one another in the social world?

Procedures

The sample consisted of all available issues of six journals (Arena, Canadian Journal of Applied Sport Sciences, International Review of Sport Sociology, Journal of Sport Behavior, Journal of Sport and Social Issues, and Review of Sport and Leisure) and the published proceedings of two sets of meetings (the 1968 and 1978 CIC Big Ten Symposia on Sociology of Sport and the 1980 NASSS conference).

The analysis proceeded in two stages: the generation of meaningful categories and the classification of articles according to that categorical system. The generation of meaningful categories was considered a purpose of the study rather than merely a starting point for the analysis. Thus the analysis began with arbitrary categories but proceeded in a manner that allowed the data to dictate readjustments to the categorical scheme. Finally, six logical categories emerged: (1) studies in which no gender was specified; (2) studies on males only; (3) studies including incidental analyses of gender differences; (4) purposive comparative studies of both sexes; (5) studies on females only; and (6) feminist analyses or commentaries on sport involvement.

In the second stage of analysis, each article was classified according to the categorical scheme. Only those articles concerned with sociological analyses of sport were included. Two readers independently classified the articles, and inter-coder agreement was over 90 percent. The frequency of occurrence of each category of gender use was recorded by journal issue.

Categorical Assumptions

A closer inspection of the categories generated for this study reveal some significant assumptions underlying the use of gender in research. These assumptions are most informative if the categories are discussed in pairs.

Categories 1 and 2
Category 1: those articles which specify neither gender. This category includes commentaries that assume that the sport world embraces both sexes, empirical studies which neglect to report the sex of the subjects, or empirical studies which assume that women and men are not distinctive sub-populations.
Category 2: those articles clearly focusing exclusively on male subjects.

Both categories 1 and 2 assume sport is a male domain. Category 2 is more honest in that assumption, clearly focusing on the male experience of sport. Category 1 more subtly implies a unisex model of the world by equating the human interpretation and experience of the world of sport, totally obscuring the female experience in the process. No doubt in some people's view of the best of all possible worlds, differences between the sexes will someday not exist and it will not be necessary to distinguish between the two, but we can hardly claim to have reached that point yet. In fact, there are some who do not believe gender differences will ever disappear, and some who hope that particular form of gender equality is never achieved.

Lest it be thought that these comments stray from the assigned topic, I assert that both these categories use gender as a variable but have provided only half the data and/or analysis by assuming that human norms and behavior patterns can be generalized from male norms and male behavior patterns.

Categories 3 and 4
Category 3: those articles which feature an incidental analysis of gender differences in sport.
Category 4: those articles focused on gender differences in sport.

Both these categories include some sort of gender comparison. They reflect the most direct and obvious use of gender as a variable. When the analysis began, these categories were considered one. However, close inspection of the studies including gender comparisons indicated that at least two different levels were presented, distinguished by important analytical strategies on the part of their authors.

At the first level (Category 3), gender is used as one of several social category variables, i.e., some of the data and relationships are reported by sex. Use of gender appears clearly superficial because nothing is ever elaborated about the differences in theoretical terms.

At the other level of analysis (Category 4), the gender comparison is more purposive. The study focuses on comparing the responses or behaviors of the sexes on some aspect of sport. In a few of these, gender is used not merely as a descriptive variable but as a category of analysis, and the analysis moves toward an attempt to explain the patterns with reference to some theoretical scheme.

Both the third and fourth categories assume that the existence of gender differences is an issue worth exploring. Some studies clearly were inspired by the question of whether gender differences do exist. However, most assumed a difference, in some cases, one suspects, throwing gender in as a variable in order to ensure that at least one significant pattern can be reported. Moreover, and more importantly, it appears that some sort of relationship is expected between male and female data. Research has progressed in some measure from the days when male and female traits and behaviors were conceptualized as polar opposites, and most researchers would be ashamed to be caught employing the ill-conceived reifications "masculine" and "feminine" as descriptors of any meaning, yet it has apparently been harder to rid our research of the perspective that women's experiences are variations on men's experiences. In its most extreme form, this is the Paul Weiss (1969) assumption of females as truncated males. Yet this is the conclusion that suggests itself when we refer to gender as a variable.

These research strategies imply that women are different from men, but are men different from women? Lamentably, we cannot answer because we use male experiences as our reference points and male behaviors as our standards: we know women only in relation to men.

Categories 5 and 6
Category 5: those articles clearly focusing on female samples, sometimes introducing a female sample into a topic previously explored only for males
Category 6: those articles that emanate from an attempt to redirect our way of conceptualizing and studying women in sport. These articles are both empirical studies and comprehensive analyses of women's status in sport.

Both Categories 5 and 6 assume the need to apply a corrective to the male domination of research by attempting to "bring women back in." The final category goes further in this attempt by incorporating certain feminist assumptions that will be spelled out in more detail below.

Categorical Frequencies
When the frequency of each category is recorded, some revealing patterns emerge. As Table 1 shows, 50 percent of the studies in these journals and proceedings make no mention of gender. 22 percent focus only on males, while 6 percent focus only on females. These figures suggest the strong possibility that 72 percent of the articles in sociology of sport journals and proceedings do not speak at all to the female experience of sport and thus do not take gender into account in any meaningful way.

Concerning the 22 percent of the articles which feature gender comparisons, we must ask whether such comparisons are enlightening to any significant extent. I suggest that they are not; indeed, they have disappointed curiosity and misled energies. But what could such studies hope to tell us? Gender comparisons of the sort already undertaken attempt to document in what areas and to what extent girls' and women's involvement in sport differs from boys' and men's. Thus they document structural inequality and differential socialization experiences. However, such strategies can provide only partial understandings. A more profound analysis is called for if we are to understand sport as it has meaning for both women and men. Current strategies obscure more than they clarify. They perpetuate a false model of gender arrangements as complementary. In some cases they serve a sort of *noblesse oblige* function and thus serve as a smoke screen for unconsciously sexist biases in research.

GENDER AS A VARIABLE:
A FEMINIST PROSPECTUS

Such a dismal conclusion obliges one to offer a remedy. If past research has made incomplete, perhaps "improper," use of gender as a variable, what might the future hold?

Clearly, the notion of "proper use" and its complement "improper use" depends upon what is envisioned as the goal of research. In my view, research that uses gender as a variable has a responsibility to do more than merely control for gender; it must provide more than a few superficial or gratuitous comments about sex differences in sport involvement. Such research should do more than describe the differential effects of social category membership on sport involvement and should provide more than a documentation of the underclass status of women. Research which uses gender as a variable should seek to inform us to some degree about the sport experience of women *per se*, and not only in relation to men. Finally, such research should provide some explanatory framework for understanding women's experience in sport.

My concern is clearly that we focus more attention on women but not merely by including women in our samples. Rather we must begin to locate our research within the rich theoretical framework that holds out the most promise for enlightening our analyses: we must incorporate a feminist perspective into our research.

This is an essential step if we are ever to understand the profundity of gender differences in sport, for the fact is that gender differences are far more profound than research strategies have yet acknowledged. The most enlightening research will follow from the assumption that women are different from men and that the significant differences do not lie in biological or physiological differences nor in any inherent psychological differences but in a profound way that emanates from women's very different social situation. I refer not merely to structural inequality or differential socialization experiences but to the fundamental difference in the way women experience the world by virtue of their being women.

Thus, I am calling for a feminist analysis of sport, because feminism holds out the greatest promise for providing an integrated theoretical understanding of women's involvement in sport. Feminism is to the study of gender what Marxism is to the study of social class: a theoretical framework that enables

TABLE 1. Treatment of Males and Females in Sociology of Sport Journals and Proceedings

Journal or Proceedings	No Gender	Males Only	Incidental Mention of Gender Differences	Purposive Comparisons	Females Only	Feminist Analyses/ Commentaries	Total
ARENA	48	14	6	3	6	1	78
CJASS	11	10	8	0	0	0	29
IRSS	128	61	41	11	9	2	252
JSB	27	5	7	7	1	1	48
JSSI	29	7	6	3	1	0	46
RSL	24	20	23	1	6	1	75
CIC 68	3	2	2	0	0	0	7
78	8	5	3	1	3	1	21
NASSS	10	4	0	2	1	2	19
TOTALS	288	128	96	28	27	8	575
%	50	22	17	5	5	1	

Volumes included: *Arena* 1-6; *CJASS* 2:7-3; *IRSS* 1-15; *JSB* 1-3; *JSSI* 1-6; *RSL* 1-6; CIC 1968, 1978; NASSS 1980.

scholars to move beyond considerations of gender and class as descriptive variables. But the task is not an easy one.

What is a feminist analysis of sport, i.e., on what basis were articles classified into the final category in the content analysis? Feminist analyses proceed from the assumptions of feminism,[2] the recognition of the fundamental oppression of women at the hands of patriarchal value systems and structures. Feminism is a strategy for understanding the way women organize their understanding of the world. A feminist analysis is one that begins with an appreciation of the neglect of women's concerns by scholars, that seeks to remedy that ignorance in some way, that continually reminds us of those oversights, that rails against methodological narrowness and problems of biased design, but mostly a feminist analysis is one that entertains interpretations of findings that are informed by and consistent with women's experience in the world. In these ways, feminist analysis furnishes a corrective to the limitations of past research on the female experience.

But there is a fundamental feminist dilemma: women's ideological imprisonment has been so complete, our social world so totally defined by male prerogatives that we have lost our sense of being women in the world. We can hardly envision what a world defined in answer to female needs and experiences would be. We can hardly comprehend what it would be like to define sport in terms that reflect our own experiences. Left to our own devices, for example, would women invent a model of sport that includes physical aggression, exclusive rewards, scholarships, sophisticated recruitment systems, free cars and carpeted offices for coaches, and powerful economic cartels? It may be tempting to think not, but we simply do not know. Given one dominant model of sport, today's women seem more than willing to accept their share, ignoring the fact, as we who do research often do, that alternative models could be employed.

Moreover, it is important to make explicit in this discussion on the proper analysis of gender the interrelationship of substantive, methodological and theoretical concerns. Biases in research extend beyond the choice of subject matter to beliefs about how it is possible to know the social world, the strategies for research, and the explanations for social phenomena that one is willing to entertain. As Roberts (1981:4) reminds us, "How far. . . the dominant rationality in social science is a male rationality is a complex question in the sociology of science and the philosophy of science." It is entirely possible that when research techniques and strategies developed primarily by men are used, the knowledge or understandings that are produced reflect male interpretations of the social world. Hall and Beamish[3] speak quite convincingly to this point.

This is the fundamental dilemma then: feminists call for an analysis of sport that proceeds from women's unique understanding of the world while not being able to agree upon the sources of that novel understanding, i.e., that oppression, be it sexuality, reproduction, rapability, physical stature, connection to principles of nature, or the like. Given this dilemma, what helpful strategies exist to keep us from abandoning in despair this challenging task?

Gender relevant research must attend to the hegemony of male developed methodology and theory while tapping into women's unique life experiences. An appropriate starting point would be to conduct research studies designed to build grounded theory from human experience. Such an approach takes various labels: definitionism, symbolic interactionism, phenomenology, ethnomethodology (cf., Ritzer, 1975). This strategy holds out the most promise for removing sex biases in research because it seeks to derive understandings of the social world from empirical information rather than by testing postulates or hypotheses derived or deduced from set-of-laws type theories. Since such hypotheses and theories contain a history of male-biased findings and explanations, by employing that traditional strategy in research, we run the risk of seeing comparative data on men and women interpreted and explained in male terms. Thus I suggest that those committed to exploring gender differences by attempting to understand the female experience of sport should examine the possibility that less traditional methodologies, specifically interactionist studies, and more imaginative theoretical conceptualizations, specifically feminist analyses, may provide new insight into this significant topic.

CONCLUSION

The intent of this exposition was to challenge the bases of research on women in sport and on gender differences in sport. An examination of research strategies of the past suggests to me that not only have we invested little effort in exploring either gender differences in sport or women in sport but that the strategies of the past may have obscured the very phenomena they sought to reveal. New methods may be called for, but certainly the theoretical assumptions underlying the use of gender as a variable in research in sociology of sport must undergo thorough and constant critical appraisal.

NOTES

1. The content analysis reported in this paper was accomplished with much assistance from Jan Rintala, University of Iowa.
2. The growing literature on feminism and feminist analyses of the social world is truly impressive. Some sources of interest include Jagger and Struhl (1978), Daly (1973), Carroll (1976), Degler (1982), Eichler (1980), Hall (1978), Millman and Kanter (1975), and Roberts (1981).
3. See Ann Hall "Towards A Feminist Analysis of Gender Inequality in Sport" and Rob Beamish "Materialism and the Comprehension of Gender-Related Issues in Sport," in this volume.

REFERENCES

Carroll, Bernice A. (ed.)
1976   Liberating Women's History: Theoretical and Critical Essays. Urbana: University of Illinois Press.

Daly, Mary
1973   Beyond God the Father. Boston: Beacon Press.

Degler, Carl
1982   "The legitimacy of scholarship by and about women." Chronicle of Higher Education, September 15, p. 56.

Eichler, Margrit
1980   The Double Standard: A Feminist Critique of Feminist Social Science. London: Croom Helm.

Hall, Ann
1978   Sport and Gender: A Feminist Perspective on the Sociology of Sport. Ottawa: CAHPER monographs.

Jagger, Alison M. and Paula Rothenberg Struhl
1978   Feminist Frameworks. New York: McGraw-Hill

Millman, Marcia and Rosabeth Kanter
1975   Another Voice: Feminist Perspectives on Social Life and Social
        Science. Garden City: Anchor.

Ritzer, George
1975   Sociology: A Multiple Paradigm Science. Boston: Allyn and
        Bacon.

Roberts, Helen (ed.)
1981   "Introduction." Pp. 1-6 in Helen Roberts (ed.) , Doing Feminist
        Research. London: Routledge & Kegan Paul.

Weiss, Paul
1969   Sport—A Philosophic Inquiry. Carbondale: University of
        Southern Illinois Press.

SECTION III
SPORT AND SOCIAL PROBLEMS

SINCE THE LATE 1960s much research has been conducted on the ills of sport. Violence, the negative effects of competition on children, the exploitation of scholarship athletes, and the various forms of discrimination evident in sport have all been the subject of sociological analysis and critique. To some extent there has been a "Millsian" recognition that these are social problems: "public issues" rather than "private troubles." There has, however, also been a tendency for the research to be descriptive and atheoretical or to employ theories of the middle range in an attempt to explain such problems as discrimination in sport. Only recently have there been attempts (e.g., research on gender discrimination) to study the specifics of discrimination in sport in the context of broader questions of structural inequality.

The four papers in this section deal with racism, sexism, handicapism, and a general lack of justice in the treatment of athletes. In the first paper, Roger Rees and Andrew Miracle address the frequently heard contention that sport is different and somehow "better" than everyday life. Proponents of this view often presume sport to be an arena in which all forms of social differentiation cease to exist. This presumption, however, is based more on faith than established fact. In an effort to assess the evidence, Rees and Miracle provide a review of related research. They note that two theories in social psychology, contact theory and superordinate goals theory, present rationales for the reduction of racial prejudice in sport. The results of research to date, however, do not provide convincing evidence for either theory. Rees and Miracle show that the research is both equivocal and methodologically flawed. The authors suggest that those who propagate the belief that sport is free from prejudice and discrimination may be guilty of wishful thinking. Even where interracial cooperation and support is evident in a sport setting, there is no evidence that such behavior will transfer to other settings or persist beyond the players' careers.

In "A Kind of Precipitate Waddle: Early Opposition to Women Running," Helen Lenskyj examines a specific incidence of sexism. Her article provides detailed documentation of the views of male "authorities" in the period from 1890 to the 1920's on the issue of women running. Some researchers have attempted to draw a direct path between women's initial involvement in cycling during the 1880's and the social and political progress they experienced in the 1920's. Others have suggested a conspiracy theory which indicates that women were "permitted" to participate in sports at this time in order to deflect their interest and energies from social and political matters, and that sport involvement actually delayed emancipation. Lenskyj's study indicates that the latter view should finally be put to rest. It is apparent that, far from being permitted to become involved in sports, substantial barriers were placed in the way of women who wished to become involved. What is evident is that in the struggle between hegemonic and counter-hegemonic forces the male power bloc was less committed to taking a stand over the issue of sport than over political matters, and that it was somewhat easier for women to "win space" in sport than in politics. The ingenuity and selectivity employed by males in their attempt to proscribe running for women is truly amazing. As Lenskyj notes, while it was quite acceptable for working class women to engage in heavy domestic or sweat shop labor, dire consequences were predicted for middle-class women who engaged in any form of vigorous exercise.

In the third paper, Nixon draws attention to an aspect of discrimination in sport that has previously received very little attention, namely, discrimination against disabled persons which is based on a prejudice he calls "handicapism." (As Nixon notes, persons have a disability, but we handicap them.) The author reviews the scope of the problem, the manner in which handicapism occurs, and legal and other measures that are being taken in order to overcome it. He concludes by posing a number of questions for future research by sport sociologists. Of particular interest are issues concerning the development of various competitions and games by and for disabled athletes and the attitudes and responses of non-disabled persons.

In the final article in this section, Mary Duquin reintroduces the idea of the separateness of the world of sport that was considered in the Rees and Miracle paper. The questions asked in the two papers are similar. Rees and Miracle are concerned with whether sport is free of the racial prejudice of the broader society, while Duquin asks whether the meaning of social justice in sport is different from its meaning in the broader social context. Duquin's analysis indicates that interpretations of what is "just" are situationally specific, and she suggests that the difference lies in the relative freedom of the athletic establishment to treat athletes in an inequitable manner, having desensitized the public to the fact that such treatment is unjust. The concept of blaming the victim is introduced here for the first time with respect to discrimination in sport. It is a concept that deserves more widespread attention from sport sociologists.

PARTICIPATION IN SPORT AND THE REDUCTION OF RACIAL PREJUDICES: CONTACT THEORY, SUPERORDINATE GOALS HYPOTHESIS OR WISHFUL THINKING?

C. Roger Rees, Adelphi University
Andrew W. Miracle, Texas Christian University

ON THE FIRST SATURDAY IN DECEMBER, 1981, the members of the Eastern Hills Highlanders, a powerhouse high school football team in the Dallas/Fort Worth metroplex, were interviewed by a reporter from a local paper after they had suffered a heartbreaking loss in the quarterfinals of the class 5A Texas State Championship. What they said they would remember most about the season was not the defeat but

> . . . how close they felt to the other team members, making no distinction between black and white players. "What makes me cry," said the captain Elisha Dickerson, choking as he spoke, "is I loved the white boys on our team. I was telling them last night, 'I just love you. I don't want to leave you.' I mean this is close, really close."

> The quarterback Vincent Spruell agreed. "We'll look back on this the most. The togetherness. We call ourselves the sock brothers—made up of soul and rock." (*Fort Worth Star Telegram*, December 7, 1981)

Such affirmations of the value of athletics are common from the mouths of athletic directors, coaches and athletes. Indeed racial togetherness is often acclaimed as one of the values of athletics at the high school if not the college level. However, sociologists who study the relationship between sports participation and racial integration have not been able to demonstrate the generalizability of the anecdote described above. This paper discusses some theoretical and methodological issues which confront them in their attempts to investigate the relationship between participation in sport and the reduction of racial prejudice.

Theoretical Perspectives

Two theories in social psychology present rationales for the reduction of prejudice in groups. The first is known as the "contact" theory discussed by Allport (1954) and extended by Pettigrew (1971); the second is the theory of superordinate goals developed by Sherif (1958).

While there is some evidence to suggest that interracial contact improves the racial attitudes of whites towards blacks (Deutsch and Collins, 1951), other studies have indicated that such contact either has no effect upon prejudice (Katz and Benjamin, 1960) or leads to an increase in prejudice (Katz and Cohen, 1962). These findings imply that it is not interracial interaction *per se* which reduces prejudice, rather interaction under certain conditions. Allport's "contact hypothesis" as summarized by Pettigrew (1971) specifies four such conditions. Prejudice is lessened through the interaction of two groups which, 1) possess equal status, 2) seek common goals, 3) are cooperatively dependent upon each other, and 4) interact with the positive support of authorities, laws, and customs.

According to Pettigrew, these characteristics are effective because they maximize the probability that interacting individuals will perceive themselves to have similar attitudes and beliefs. The characteristics of shared attitudes and beliefs have formed the basis of Newcomb's theory of attraction development (Newcomb, 1961). Furthermore, experimental studies (Byrne, 1971; Byrne and Nelson, 1965; Griffitt and Veitch, 1974) have shown attitude similarity to be an important source of positive attraction on the part of respondents for hypothetical others presented by the experimenter. Results from experimental studies also tend to confirm the importance of attitude similarity in the development of positive interracial attraction. A study by Rokeach, Smith and Evans (1960) indicated that belief was more important than ethnic or racial membership in the development of attraction among university undergraduates. For instance, a white Christian would accept a black Christian before he would accept a white atheist, all other things being equal. Further support for the importance of attitudes in interracial attraction is presented by Byrne and Wong (1962). Their study of interracial attraction among 120 introductory psychology students indicated that regardless of the prejudice of the subject and the race of the stimulus stranger, similarity of attitudes resulted in positive ratings while dissimilarity of attitudes resulted in negative ratings. A related study by the same authors indicated that highly prejudiced whites assumed a greater degree of dissimilarity between themselves and an unknown Negro than between themselves and an unknown white. Similar results were not found among low prejudiced whites.

In summary, therefore, Pettigrew's explanation of why contact functions to reduce prejudice is based upon the belief that the necessary characteristics governing interaction function to induce the perception of similar attitudes and values among interacting individuals. This perception leads to the development of positive attraction. Support for this rationale rests chiefly upon results from experimental research.

Sociologists examining the effect of contact or racial attitudes outside the laboratory have also encountered negative, positive and neutral results (St. John, 1975). For example, McIntyre (1970), in a study on racial integration on youth football teams, found support for the contact hypothesis. Slavin and Madden (1979), in a study of fifth through 10th graders in 40 high schools in 10 southern states, also found that playing with a student of another race on an athletic team was perceived by respondents to have a strong, positive effect upon racial attitudes and behavior, at least for white students. On the other hand, Chu and Griffey (1982), using the same questions as Slavin and Madden, found little support for the contact hypothesis. Such conflicting results suggest the need to examine the utility of the contact theory in the reduction of racial prejudice or at least the degree to which the context of sport and athletics satisfy the conditions necessary for the testing of the contact theory.

The Equal Status Condition

The assumption that blacks and whites interact in sport under conditions of equal status has been questioned by McClendon (1974). He distinguished between "extra-contact" equal status, contact between blacks and whites who share a similar socioeconomic background, and "intra-contact" equal status, contact between blacks and whites who are functional equals in the common task (McClendon, 1974: 49-50). McClendon argues that "extra-contact" equal status is primary in the Allport-Pettigrew theory because persons of equal status are likely to hold similar attitudes and values. Both status conditions do not necessarily characterize the interaction between whites and blacks in organized sport. While there is little empirical data comparing the socioeconomic status of white and black athletes, most researchers contend that blacks and whites grow up in different social environments, and learn sports skills under different conditions (Castine and Roberts, 1974; Jones and Hochner, 1973; McPherson, 1975). These differences are maintained in college (Castine and Roberts, 1974; Olsen, 1968) and also in professional sports, where blacks are said to see themselves as playing in a different style than whites (Jones and Hochner, 1973; Olsen, 1968). While these speculations have not been empirically investigated, they do imply that "extra-contact" equal status between blacks and whites does not occur in organized sport and this important condition for prejudice reduction, at least according to Allport and Pettigrew, has not been met.

"Intra-contact" equal status between racially dissimilar athletes may depend upon the level of participation. Studies have shown that blacks are underrepresented in central positions in professional sport (Curtis and Loy, 1979; Eitzen and Sanford, 1975; Loy, Curtis and Sage, 1979). The extent to which this state of affairs has changed in the last five years or is not replicated in colleges and/or high schools is not presently known. At any rate "extra-contact" equal status among blacks and whites must not be assumed and ought to be measured.

The Co-operative Dependent Position

The above discussion has implications for cooperative dependency. If black or white players play central or decision-making positions which are perceived as differentially important to the participants, this condition cannot be assumed in sport. The problem is evident in sports such as baseball and football where certain positions, e.g., pitcher and quarterback, are less dependent upon players in other positions than are those players on them.

The Positive Support Condition

While authorities and laws tend to support the idea of interaction between races in sport during the game, one cannot assume that the same motivation for interaction exists outside the game situation. It may be that "customs" or local community pressure exist to discourage that interaction. The implications of this point for the measurement of racial integration will be discussed later.

The Common Goals Condition

The most important Allport-Pettigrew condition for the application of the contact theory to sport is the assumption of common goals. According to Pettigrew the contact theory reduces racial prejudice through allowing the interacting individuals to perceive similarity between themselves and racially different others in the interacting situation. The perceived similarity leads to positive attraction.

However, McClendon (1974) contends that the interpersonal attraction rationale is not the only explanation of why interaction under the conditions specified by Allport can lead to prejudice reduction. Interaction by individuals pursuing common goals implies that the interaction is for some external reason other than for specific development of attraction; although positive attraction may be a by-product of this interaction. This argument leads to the second theory of prejudice reduction in groups, Sherif's theory of superordinate goals.

Sherif (1958: 349) has defined superordinate goals as "goals which are compelling and highly appealing to members of two or more groups in conflict but which cannot be attained by the resources and energies of the groups separately." Sherif tested his theory in a field experiment involving two groups of boys in a summer camp. Hostility between the groups was first encouraged by the experimenter, who then introduced a series of superordinate goals in order to restore harmony. Examples include the pooling of money from both groups in order to procure a popular movie to be viewed by everyone and the combined efforts of both sub-groups to push out of the mud the truck containing food for the whole group.

The only study designed to test Sherif's theory in a sport context was carried out by McClendon and Eitzen (1975) with a sample of biracial college basketball teams. Support was found for the theory among the white players, but not among the black players. The key point, however, for the contact theory, is McClendon's (1974) argument that the achievement of the superordinate goal is instrumental in reducing the potential conflict between races. This indicates a basic difference between the Allport and the Sherif theories since the former theory implies that the mere pursuit of common goals was enough to induce positive attraction among group members.

Based upon this argument we contend that in sport the common goal is generally a superordinate goal, that is, victory, and it is usually highly valued. The main function of athletic contests is not to provide situations in which blacks and whites can interact equally. Thus the context of athletics is not the ideal situation in which to test the contact theory, especially if goal achievement rather than the mere presence of common goals is the key factor in reducing prejudice. If the achievement of common superordinate goals is so important for the improvement of racial harmony in sports teams one is tempted to ask what happens to harmony when the goal is not reached.

McClendon argues that goal failure might be highly frustrating and consequently lead to one race using the other as a scapegoat, thus increasing rather than diminishing hostility. The scapegoat theory has been developed as a general theory of prejudice by Berkowitz and his associates (Berkowitz, 1959; Berkowitz and Green, 1962). Scapegoating is seen to apply in situations where aggressive tendencies generated by frustration cannot be directed against the actual thwarting agent, either because it is not visible, or because it is too powerful. The needed outlet for aggression is found through an attack upon an innocent minority group which is blamed for the frustration.

Support for the contention that scapegoating can function in interracial contact situations involving group failure is supplied by an experimental study by Blanchard, Weigel and Cook (1975). They examined the effects of competence of group members, and the extent of group success or failure, upon the interpersonal attraction of white subjects for both white and black workmates in cooperating interracial groups. The experimenters utilized a research design in which subjects, three per group, cooperated in a management-training activity requiring them to coordinate the operation of an imaginary railroad business. The race and performance of one subject in each of the 30 groups was controlled by the experimenters so that each group had either a black or white confederate who exhibited a greater, equal, or lesser degree of competence than the other group members. The main finding of the study was that white subjects exhibited less attraction for a black group mate when he performed less competently than when he performed competently but no parallel effect was found on attraction to white group mates. These findings were strongest for the conditions in which the group failed. The authors concluded that "group failure will lead to scapegoating in that combination of circumstances where a group member not only performs incompetently but comes from an ethnic group about which the research subjects hold stereotyped expectations of incompetence" (Blanchard, Weigel and Cook, 1975: 528).

To summarize the above discussion we have suggested that:

1. the requirements for the testing of the contact theory are not readily applicable to sport;
2. sport contexts may not be ideal situations in which to test the contact theory;
3. if the superordinate goals theory is applicable to sport situations there is a potential for these situations to increase racial tension via scapegoating as well as reduce it through the satisfaction of seeing the goal achieved.

We now examine the methodological implications of the two theories for the measurement of racial tolerance in sport.

METHODOLOGICAL CONSIDERATIONS

One methodological implication of the contact theory is that racial integration be measured as a form of interpersonal attraction, that is, feelings of affect that people have for others. These feelings have been defined as attitudes and consequently these attitudes have cognitive, affective and behavioral components (Segal, 1979).

While research in sport has tended to measure racial tolerance cognitively and affectively, few behavioral measures have been attempted. Athletes on biracial teams have typically been asked the degree to which they felt that integrated athletics promotes racial harmony (McClendon and Eitzen, 1975) or whether they would like to have more friends who are of a different race (Chu and Griffey, 1982; Slavin and Madden, 1979). Clearly such attitudinal questions are open to response bias.

While some behavioral measures were used by Slavin and Madden (1979) and Chu and Griffey (1982)—e.g., "Have you ever called a student of a different race on the phone?"—these have been questions directed to the athlete and have not been verified by an outside source.

The relationship between participation in sport and the interpersonal attraction of participants has not received much study by sociologists. However, there is no reason why those interested in racial tolerance within sports could not make use of the concept of interpersonal attraction. This could be operationalized by rating scales (attitudinal measures) and interpersonal choices (behavioral measures). This approach has been developed by Rees as part of a larger study on interpersonal attraction in sports teams (Rees, 1977). Of particular interest is the data on cross-racial friendship. Friendship implies a structural relationship, that is, friends spend time together and engage in mutually rewarding activities (Segal, 1979). Thus friends tend to choose each other for different activities.

Rees (1977) measured the degree of cross-racial friendship on an intercollegiate football team from Division 1 of the NCAA. Respondents chose the names of up to five teammates "you hang around with most," and were then asked for up to three choices for team members with whom "you most often play basketball, golf, etc.," "watch TV," and "sit with at training table."

Of the 59 players, seven, five whites and two blacks, made at least one cross-racial choice on one or more of the interacting situations. Of the five white players, three chose a black player in their five choices for general association or one in their choices for "playing sports with." None of these choices were extended to watching TV or eating at training table. The other two whites made their choices for black teammates across all interacting situations. Of the two black players, one chose two white players on association. One of these players was also named on all categories. The other black player chose a white teammate on association only.

While the tendency to choose teammates in different interacting situations may be a result of friendship, a more acceptable characterization of friendship is mutuality of choice. The white who chose the black across all situations was only reciprocated by that black on general association, although this was a first choice. However, the black who chose white teammates across all categories did not receive reciprocal choices from any of these players in any situation. Overall, the incidence of cross-racial choice among participants in the football team polled here is low. There is less evidence of choices generalizing across situations and/or being reciprocated, both characteristics which could be measures of friendship.

While this study asked players for their choices, it did not assess the amount of cross-racial interaction directly. Few studies in sport have employed a participant observation approach necessary to examine this. One which did utilize this approach was Miracle (1981). This study was an attempt to assess both the contact hypothesis and the superordinate goal hypothesis through an ethnographic analysis of interracial interaction on a desegregated high school football team. The study was conducted in two phases. The team, from a southern city in the United States, was studied during the 1972 and 1973 seasons by means of participant observation. The researcher observed practices, games and other events, conducted interviews, and became an active member of the parents' booster club. Follow-up interviews during 1975-76 comprised phase two of the project.

During the observational phase of the study, several behavioral measures were obtained. For example, careful records were kept of seat selection on the bus to games away from home, choice of "buddies" during pre-practice warm-ups as well as for drills, and general interaction during the football game and related activities. Team members also were observed in non-football-related activities during the season and off-season. Football players were compared to the general student population on several behavioral parameters.

Analysis of these data provided no support for the contact hypothesis, since there was no observable difference in the interracial behaviors of team members and other students in the school in spite of the increased interracial contact on the part of football players. However, it was concluded that commitment by the team members to superordinate goals was sufficient to effect cooperation and reduce conflict. Since the team did not have a winning season, it was concluded that goal achievement, as assumed by McClendon and Eitzen (1975), was necessary to reduce conflict. "As long as individuals maintain sufficient goal commitment to continue the task activities, cooperation will be evident" (Miracle, 1981:153). Furthermore, since voluntary interracial interaction by football players seldom occurred outside football-related events, it was concluded that inter-group cooperation may be limited to a specific sphere and may not be transferable or generalizable.

CONCLUSIONS

This discussion has examined sport as a possible medium for reducing racial prejudice. Two theories have been offered which suggest that participation on a biracial team should lead to a reduction in racial prejudice. Empirical testing of the contact hypothesis as posited by Allport and modified by Pettigrew has produced mixed results in non-sport settings. We question the applicability of the theory to sports, since it is unlikely that players on a team could meet the equal status condition—either intracontact or extra contact equal status—specified by Pettigrew. It also has been suggested that the other conditions Pettigrew assigns to the contact hypothesis cannot be assumed to be met by sports teams. For example, sports teams are not formed for the specific purpose of providing equal status situations in which black and white players can interact to reduce prejudice. Such interaction is a by-product of the main goal which is team victory.

Moreover, if the achievement of the superordinate goal is the key to the reduction of racial prejudice, sociologists also need to examine the effect of failure to achieve the goal upon racial integration. We suggest that stereotyping is the logical outcome in this situation.

It is suggested that future research consider these theoretical issues. In addition, we would urge researchers to employ behavioral measures to evaluate the theories. Most important, however, is the need to determine if there is any transferability or generalizability of behavioral or attitudinal changes from the sport setting to non-sport settings. In other words, it is essential that we determine whether at Eastern Hills the sock brothers' love for one another extended to non-football-related spheres and whether the sock brothers generalized from their favorable cross-racial attitudes towards one another to different cross-race individuals in other settings.

REFERENCES

Allport, G.
1954   The Nature of Prejudice. Cambridge: Addison-Wesley.

Berkowitz, L.
1959   "Anti-semitism and the displacement of aggression." Journal of Abnormal and Social Psychology 59:182-187

Berkowitz, L. and J. A. Green
1962   "The stimulus qualities of the scapegoat." Journal of Abnormal and Social Psychology 64:393-401.

Blanchard, F. A., R. H. Weigel and S. W. Cook
1975   "The effect of relative competence of group members upon interpersonal attraction in cooperating interracial groups." Journal of Personality and Social Psychology 32:519-530.

Byrne, D.
1971   The Attraction Paradigm. New York: Academic Press.

Byrne, D. and D. A. Nelson
1965   "Attraction as a linear function of proportion of positive reinforcements." Journal of Personality and Social Psychology 1:659-663.

Byrne, D. and T. J. Wong
1962   "Racial prejudice, interpersonal attraction, and assumed dissimilarity of attitudes." Journal of Abnormal and Social Psychology 65:246-253.

Castine, S. C. and G. C. Roberts
1974   "Modeling in the socialization process of the black athlete." International Review of Sport Sociology 3-4 (9):59-73.

Chu, D. and D. C. Griffey
1982   "Sport and racial integration: the relationship of personal contact, attitudes and behavior." Pp. 271-282 in A. O. Dunleavy, A. Miracle and C. R. Rees (eds.), Studies in the Sociology of Sport. Fort Worth, Texas: TCU Press.

Curtis, J. E. and J. W. Loy
1979   "Race/ethnicity and relative centrality of playing position in team sports." Pp. 285-313 in R. S. Hutton (ed.), Exercise and Sport Sciences Reviews: Volume 6. Philadelphia, PA: The Franklin Institute Press.

Deutsch, M. and M. Collins

1951   Interracial Housing: A Psychological Evaluation of a Social Experiment. Minneapolis: University of Minnesota Press.

Eitzen, D. S. and D. C. Sanford
1975   "The segregation of blacks by playing position in football: accident or design?" Social Science Quarterly 55:948-959.

Fort Worth Star Telegram
1981   "Highlanders remember team closeness as well as victories." Sports Section, December 7.

Griffitt, W. and R. Veitch
1974   "Preacquaintance, attitude similarity and attraction revisited: ten days in a fall-out shelter." Sociometry 37:163-173.

Jones, J. M. and A. R. Hochner
1973   "Racial differences in sports activities: a look at the self-paced versus reactive hypotheses." Journal of Personality and Social Psychology 27:86-95.

Katz, I. and L. Benjamin
1960   "Effects of white authoritarianism on biracial work groups." Journal of Abnormal and Social Psychology 61:448-456.

Katz, I. and M. Cohen
1962   "The effects of training Negroes upon operative problem solving in biracial teams." Journal of Abnormal and Social Psychology 64:319-325.

Loy, J. W., J. E. Curtis and J. N. Sage
1979   "Relative centrality of playing position and leadership recruitment in team sports." Pp. 251-284 in R. S. Hutton (ed.), Exercise and Sport Sciences Reviews: Volume 6. Philadelphia, PA: The Franklin Institute Press.

McClendon, M. J.
1974   "Interracial contact and the reduction of prejudice." Sociological Focus 7:47-65.

McClendon, M. J. and D. S. Eitzen
1975   "Interracial contact on collegiate basketball teams: a test of Sherif's theory of superordinate goals." Social Science Quarterly 55:926-938.

McIntyre, T. D.
1970   "A Field Experimental Study of Cohesiveness, Status, and Attitude Change in Four Biracial Small Sports Groups." Unpublished Ph.D. Dissertation, Pennsylvania State University.

McPherson, B. D.
1975 "The segregation by playing position hypothesis in sport: an alternative explanation." Social Science Quarterly 55:960-966.

Miracle, A.
1981 "Factors affecting interracial cooperation: a case study of a high school football team." Human Organization 40(2):150-154.

Newcomb, T.
1961 The Acquaintance Process. New York: Holt, Rinehart and Winston.

Olsen, J.
1968 "The black athlete—a shameful story." Sports Illustrated: July 1, 8, 15, 22 and 29.

Pettigrew, T. F.
1971 Racially Separate or Together? New York: McGraw-Hill.

Rees, C. R.
1977 "Interpersonal Attraction in Two Collegiate Football Teams." Unpublished Doctoral Dissertation, University of Maryland.

Rokeach, M., P. W. Smith and R. I. Evans
1960 "Two kinds of prejudice or one?" Pp. 132-168 in M. Rokeach (ed.), The Open and Closed Mind. New York: Basic Books.

Segal, M. W.
1979 "Varieties of interpersonal attraction and their interrelationship in natural groups." Social Psychology Quarterly 42:253-61.

Sherif, M.
1958 "Superordinate goals in the reduction of intergroup conflict." American Journal of Sociology 63:349-56.

Slavin, R. E. and N. A Madden
1979 "School practices that improve race relations." American Educational Research Journal 16 (2):169-80.

St. John, N. H.
1975 School Desegregation: Outcomes for Children. New York: John Wiley and Sons.

"A KIND OF PRECIPITATE WADDLE": EARLY OPPOSITION TO WOMEN RUNNING

Helen Lenskyj
Ontario Institute for Studies in Education

THE PATRIARCHAL IDEOLOGY which pervaded North American society in the late 19th and early 20th centuries provided a fertile context for the growth of the female frailty myth. Legitimated by medical and pseudo-medical opinion, the view of women as victims of their "peculiar" physiology had important implications for their participation in a physical activity like running. When women's performance was evaluated in terms of male-defined criteria—strength, speed and endurance—it was, in most cases, inferior to men's, a finding which lent support to the notion of female frailty, and to its corollary, women's susceptibility to injury. Especially vulnerable, according to this line of reasoning, were the female reproductive organs; variations in their "normal" functioning, which vigorous physical activity allegedly produced, were invariably treated as symptoms of disease. At a time when medical texts listed childbirth and menstruation, together with dysmenorrhea and cancer, under the general heading "diseases of women," this tendency was hardly surprising (Kelly, 1913, Huhner, 1923). By the late 19th century, the medical profession was well established as a cornerstone of patriarchal hegemony, a tradition which North American gynecologists upheld when women began to participate, in increasing numbers, in sporting activities.

In addition to the physical consequences of femaleness, women's child-bearing capacity was believed to make them, by nature, passive, nurturant, non-competitive and non-aggressive; "true womanhood" was defined in these terms. Therefore, it was argued, women lacked the prerequisite drive to succeed in athletic (or any other) competition, and those who engaged in such activities were not true women. The emphasis on sex differences was, of course, an effective means of perpetuating the patriarchal order. To explain women's sporting participation in terms of malformed gender identity was to reduce its political ramifications to the level of a personal abnormality. This tendency, moreover, was responsible for the inordinate amount of attention given to the alleged masculinizing effects of sport on women, an issue which continues to preoccupy contemporary critics.

In the late 1800's, many university departments of physical education in Ontario, Quebec and the Eastern part of the United States were administered by former doctors. These men were in a powerful position to influence both programs and opinion, and the texts which they produced were uniformly conservative on the question of women's sport, as were the articles they wrote for publications as diverse as the *Ladies' Home Journal* and the *Canadian Journal of Public Health* (Anderson, n.d.; Sargent, 1912; McKenzie, 1909; Lamb, 1927). Since it was not in their interests to issue a blanket condemnation of women's sports, physical educators assumed the responsibility for classifying activities as safe or unsafe. Their judgment in most cases rested on a strong reliance on social convention. Girls, according to one of these early leaders, Tait McKenzie, would not run a hundred yards of their own volition; if they did, it was simply "in imitation of their brothers," a statement which amply illustrated the no-win situation confronting the female athlete. Blaming their restrictive dress and upbringing for this incapacity, McKenzie, nevertheless, asserted that running and other track and field events were not suitable for girls and women: "They cannot possibly hope to do more than give a feeble imitation of what men will always do infinitely better" (McKenzie, 1909:286-287).

As well as the call to "nature" to legitimate the limitations which doctors and physical educators placed on women's sport, there were frequent allusions to religion. Motherhood, in the words of a Toronto doctor, was "the most sacred trust the almighty can bestow upon any woman" (Hastings, 1917). It was a patriotic duty to bear healthy children too, at a time when high immigration and alarming infant mortality rates fuelled fears of race suicide among the Anglo-Saxon middle class. With motherhood thus defined as a religious and patriotic duty, as well as a woman's *raison d'etre*, it was not only immoral and unpatriotic, but also foolish, for a woman to engage in any activity which might jeopardize her one avenue for social recognition and personal fulfilment. This was the message which the "experts"—the agents of hegemony—delivered. This was also the view of maternal feminists, whose conservatism on some issues can be explained in terms of their view of women's sphere. Having applied the notion of women's special nurturing talents to justify their earlier suffrage and reform efforts, they continued, in the post-war period, to stress the special function of women as moral guardians of society. If participation in sporting activities promoted, as they suspected, mental as well as physical toughness and independence, girls would not develop into the type of women for whom they had prepared a special place in society—women who understood, above all, the importance of the service ethos. For all women, this encompassed service to one's family; for the more privileged, there was the additional responsibility to serve the community (Knox, 1919; MacMurchy, 1930).

In this context, girls' and women's participation in all but the most slow-moving of physical activities was unlikely to receive medical or popular sanction. Up to the 1920's, the pervasiveness of vitalist explanations of human physiology was, to a large extent, responsible for the restrictive attitudes. The body was believed to possess only a limited supply of "vital force" or "nerve energy," which was in danger of becoming depleted by excessive exercise, brain work or sexual activity. For women, also referred to as "the sex," the situation was complicated by the menstrual cycle, which, it was claimed, demanded the lion's share of the vital force in order to function properly. This reasoning, which had formed the basis for earlier arguments against higher education for women, was easily adapted to meet other diverse contingencies, like their participation in the labor force, their political activities and their growing interest in sporting and leisure pursuits—in short, any activity which might bring about a change in women's traditional, dependent, domestic role as wife and mother. Even the telephone and the automobile were blamed by gynecologists for the problems of pregnancy and parturition: the excitement and strain of "social duties" left little vital force for the demands of childbearing, with the result that these women experienced difficult deliveries and produced inferior offspring. The specific problems predicted for athletic women were said to be related to their well-developed arm, leg and abdominal muscles: "the reproductive system is often dwarfed by the force going to overdeveloped arms and legs," according to a 1912 medical journal (Parry, 1912:347).

Another consequence of women's athletic activity which concerned doctors was the loss of body fat. For women, "a healthy, well-developed body is characterised by plumpness," according to William Anderson, a doctor and physical director at the Chautauqua School (Anderson, n.d.:27). The ideal depicted in health and beauty books was "plump" by contemporary standards, whereas athletic women (with the possible exception of long distance swimmers) were relatively thin. Breasts were a particular focus of attention, as a manifestation of "normal" sexual development and as an indication that lactation could be successfully established. Chest development was the goal of many physical culture exercises for girls and women, according to sources as diverse as Department of Education textbooks and women's magazines.

In addition to the medical rationales, the preoccupation with chest development can be explained in terms of the importance attached to sex differentiation in a patriarchal society: secondary sex characteristics, accentuated by the appropriate clothing and manner of moving, served to reinforce the relative status of men and women. The blurring of these differences brought about by any changes in women's lifestyles and dress was correctly perceived as a threat to the old order, where the image of the woman as frail and decorative legitimated her subordinate, protected status. One of the pioneers of gynecology in North America, John Todd (cited in Barker-Benfield, 1976), reflected this kind of thinking in his attack on women who tried to become "semi-men" by wearing the bloomer dress.

> Woman, robed and folded in her long dress, is beautiful. She walks gracefully. . . . If she attempts to run, the charm is gone. . . . So long as she is thus clothed, there is just enough mystery about woman to challenge admiration, almost reverence (p. 209).

Although Todd expressed these views in 1867, similar sentiments continued to appear for the next half-century. Clearly, a woman who wore bloomers or any functional clothing which revealed that she shared with men a common means of locomotion, could not hope to remain on the pedestal Todd had prepared for her. To defy these male-defined standards of female beauty was, in a sense, to reject the protected status which the pedestal offered. Arabella Kenealy, a doctor whose attacks on female athletes appeared in 1899, was clearly not prepared to forfeit this status. Among the attributes of the woman athlete which she con-

demned were assertiveness, strength, and masculinity of movement instead of "certain mystery of motion. . . an air of gliding
rather than striding." This level of confidence in one's physical
capacities was, it seems, a male prerogative. Like many of her
contemporaries, Kenealy recognized that a new body image
had ramifications beyond the playing field or the gymnasium
(Kenealy, 1899).

It is clear that doctors' interests were served by women's alienation from their bodies, which were depicted in medical and
pseudo-medical literature as a liability—a source of mysterious
diseases which only the health professionals were qualified to
treat. At the same time, the medical view of female health and
beauty was culturally embedded. The female body was a sexual
asset, even though it was a physical liability. This is not to suggest that doctors encouraged women to understand their sexual
nature. As long as they were ignorant in these matters, they
formed a receptive audience for the advice literature which served
to reinforce their subordinate status. A Baltimore gynecologist
noted with some satisfaction that, on questions of sex, "good
women, particularly, possess no language and no terminology,
either for their feelings or their anatomy" (Kelly, 1913:314). Such
women were ill-equipped to challenge the advice of the experts
on matters of female physiology; they were unlikely, too, to question conventional wisdom regarding the physical activities best
suited to their sex.

Observations of women's style of running provided some doctors with additional grounds for opposing this activity. Because
some women did not run like some men, it was claimed that
women, as a group, were not constructed for running. The explanation offered by Dr. Jesse Wiliams (1940), Physical Director
at Columbia University, deserves to be cited in full:

> The width of the pelvis interferes with the running ability
> of the girl, in all movements of the lower extremities, either
> in walking or running. There is a lateral sway of the pelvis,
> and the extent of this oscillation determines the speed of
> the individual. . . . It is this sort of biological evidence that
> one must understand and respect. . . .(p. 181).

Other critics depended less on science than on the power of the
pen. Women's running, according to one journalist, was "constrained and awkward. . . a kind of precipitate waddle with
neither grace, fitness or dignity" ("Modern mannish maidens,"

1890:260). Like Williams, this journalist led his readers to believe that *learned behavior*, "constrained" as it was by the clothing and conventions of the day, was *innate* behavior, a false assumption which has continued to plague women's sporting activities today.

The question of body type was, for the most part, ignored by doctors and physical educators at the turn of the century. An early exception was Dudley Sargent, Physical Director at Yale, who referred to the "conventional" and the "athletic" types of women. The former, also called "feminine," was characterized by "a narrow waist, broad and massive hips and large thighs," while the athletic or "masculine" type had less accentuated sex characteristics, with narrow hips, broad shoulders and muscular chests (Sargent, 1912). While Sargent's attempt at classification was a progressive step, his equating of "conventional" with "feminine" and "athletic" with "masculine" simply reinforced the popular suspicion that, if sports did not masculinize girls, then it was because sportswomen were masculine at the outset. A Wisconsin physiologist, commenting on the tendency for female gymnasts to be of the "athletic" type, suggested that "the glandular condition which leads to. . . large pelves" might also have been responsible for these women's greater interest in men's company than in competitive gymnastics (Dawson, 1934:904).

With so-called medical rationales colored by this preoccupation with the "femininity" question, it is not surprising that aesthetic considerations were a primary concern among the critics of women's running. Consistent with the view of women, in a patriarchal society, as possessing qualities like modesty, charm and passivity was the expectation that their clothing and general demeanor should reinforce this image. The air of mystery so revered by men like Todd served an important function in the maintenance of power relations between the sexes. The woman whose body was delicately decorative, whose face was appealingly empty, need not be taken seriously. Conformity to these standards of female beauty signalled adherence to the rules. The same criteria were used to evaluate women's sports: "Girls, stick to the things you do gracefully, beautifully, with rhythm, without strain. . . leave the rough, tough athletics to the men." The Canadian journalist who issued this warning in 1938 was more explicit than his earlier counterparts: "The men want the girls to stay beautiful, graceful and sightly." Runners, he claimed were usually "flat-chested, leather-limbed, horselike." One champion whom he labelled "Galloping Ace" had "as much sex appeal as grandmother's old sewing machine" (Ferguson, 1938:9, 32).

As well as the pressure to conform to certain beauty standards, women were warned of the dangers inherent in physical activities which produced strain or sweat. Here, too, medical and aesthetic rationales were indistinguishable. On one hand, it was claimed that women were emotionally unsuited for competitive sports like running: "the peculiar constitution of [a woman's] nervous system and the great emotional disturbances to which she is subjected" increased the likelihood of "nervous collapse" and hysteria (Sargent, 1912:72). On the other hand, sweat and strain were labelled "unfeminine." Kenealy, (1899:367) for example, lamented the passing of "a dainty, elusive quality" in the face of the athletic woman, whose "bicycle face" was characterized by "muscular tension" where formerly there had been sympathy and tenderness. Such concerns were, of course, class-bound. The critics who found strain so unappealing on the faces of young middle class women rarely agonized over its appearance on the faces of women who scrubbed floors or worked in factories. In the words of a Canadian journalist, "no one talks about a charwoman losing her bloom or her womanliness" (Luke, 1935:35). Clearly, the womanliness of her privileged sister was more highly valued and more easily damaged; her reproductive organs, too, were apparently more injury-prone. Doctors had been predicting for decades that the recreational activities of middle class girls and women were certain to produce conditions like uterine displacement and sterility, particularly if carried on during menstruation. In the 1920's, however, with the emergence of industrial medicine as a field of specialization, doctors testifying in compensation cases were remarkably reluctant to produce a causal relationship between workplace accidents and uterine displacements suffered by working class women (Mock, 1922).

Although there was a clear double standard in this area, one rule applied to women of all classes. Domestic work, however strenuous, carried none of the risks to health or femininity present in other forms of physical activity. The work ethic was, of course, operating here. Hard work, unlike hard play, needed little justification as long as it was "women's work." The "housework as therapy" idea was a popular one at the turn of the century, when young women were allegedly neglecting domestic chores for the pleasures of cycling or playing games. By the 1920's, the health benefits, as well as the character development which resulted from moderate, controlled participation in sport were recognized by many doctors and educators, but "enhancement of womanhood" remained a criterion which running failed to satisfy. It did not promote qualities like loyalty and obedience to the leader, as team sports did; it lacked the grace of swimming or skating and the charm of dance or gymnastics. Qualities like self-discipline, daring and independence, the by-products of a solitary sport like running, had limited application to the domestic destiny envisioned for every girl.

It can be seen, then, that running as an activity for women was subject to many of the same criticisms levelled at other so-called vigorous sports. There were three mutually reinforcing dimensions to the argument against running: the medical rationales, the aesthetic and the social considerations. Although some doctors and physical educators agreed that running developed body and mind, the specific nature of this physical and mental development conflicted with the popular image of "femininity" in a patriarchal society. There were, of course, women who did not accept the conventional view that strength, endurance and self-knowledge—physical as well as mental—were "unfeminine." For many women, however, the pattern of conformity was the only option. The economic security offered by marriage was conditional upon their "femininity" being beyond reproach. With "femininity" defined by the agents of patriarchal hegemony as the capacity to bear children and to please men, running, clearly, was not a "feminine" pursuit.

REFERENCES

Anderson, William
n.d.   Anderson's Physical Education. Toronto. Harold Wilson, Co.

Barker-Benfield, G.
1976   The Horrors Of The Half-Known Life. New York: Harper and Row.

Dawson, Percy
1934   The Physiology of Physical Education. Baltimore. Wilkins and Wilkins.

Ferguson, Elmer
1938   "I don't like Amazon athletes." Maclean's Magazine 51 (August), 9, 32.

Hastings, John
1917   "Are we giving the child a square deal?" Woman's Century,

Special Number, 152.

Huhner, Max
1923   A Practical Treatise On The Diseases Of The Sexual Function. Philadelphia. F. A. Davis and Co. 3rd Ed.

Kelly, Howard
1913   Medical Gynecology. New York. D. Appleton and Co., 2nd Ed.

Kenealy, Arabella
1899   "Woman as an athlete." Living Age 3:363-70.

Knox, Allen
1919   The Girl Of The New Day. Toronto. McClelland and Stewart.

Lamb, Arthur
1927   "Health education." Canadian Journal of Public Health 18:509-19.

Luke, Edith
1935   "No sex bar." Canadian Magazine 84:2, 32, 35.

MacMurchy, Helen
1930   How To Manage Housework In Canada. Ottawa. Department of National Health and Pensions.

McKenzie, R. Tait
1909   Exercise In Education and Medicine. Philadelphia. W. B. Saunders, 3rd Ed.

Mock, Harry
1922   "So-called traumatic displacements of the uterus." Journal of the American Medical Association 79:797-804.

"Modern mannish maidens"
1890   Blackwoods' Magazine 147:252-64.

Parry, Angenette
1912   "The relation of athletics to the reproductive life of woman." American Journal of Obstetrics 66:341-57.

Sargent, Dudley
1912   "Are athletics making girls masculine?" Ladies' Home Journal 29:11, 71-3.

Williams, Jesse
1940   Personal Hygiene Applied. Philadelphia. W. B. Saunders, 6th Ed.

HANDICAPISM AND SPORT: NEW DIRECTIONS FOR SPORT SOCIOLOGY RESEARCH[1]

Howard L. Nixon II
University of Vermont

IN HIS BOOK *Handicapping America* (1978), Frank Bowe argued that, "America handicaps disabled people. And because that is true, we are handicapping America itself" (p. vii). By this he meant that American society creates obstacles or barriers for disabled people that handicap them by interfering with the development or use of their abilities and in doing so, it deprives society of the contributions that could come from the fuller use of the abilities of disabled people. The institution of sport has contributed to this handicapping process in American society—and other societies—by denying disabled people opportunities to develop their physical and athletic potential and interests in the kinds of sports activities and roles routinely available to able-bodied or "normal" people and by denying disabled people chances to compete with, alongside, or against their nondisabled peers.

Sport sociologists have not paid much attention to the handicapping of disabled people in or through sport. What has been said about disabled people in sport sociology literature has tended to extol the virtues of events such as the Special Olympics without addressing the problems of disabled people in sport or the larger society. The general aim of this paper is to stimulate more interest among sport sociologists in studying disabled people and the social problem that has been created by handicapping processes in society. This paper will introduce sport sociologists to handicapism and its relevance to sport by examining its nature, the minority status of handicapped people, labeling and stigmatization of handicapped people, and the role of sport in creating and overcoming handicapism. The paper will conclude with a list of issues and questions about disabled people, handicapism, and sport that could become the focus of future research in sport sociology.

DISABILITIES, HANDICAPS, AND HANDICAPISM

Although it is common to refer to disabled people as "handicapped," it is important for the purposes of this analysis to distinguish between "disabled" and "handicapped" people. The basis for both disabilities and handicaps is impairments which are organic or functional disorders resulting from disease, accident, or a defective gene. When an impairment persists for several months and interferes with a person's ability to use certain skills, perform certain tasks, or participate in certain activities, that person can be called "disabled." A disabled person becomes "handicapped" when his or her disability interacts with a specific set of conditions in society or the environment constructed by members of society to make that person socially disadvantaged (Bowe, 1978:16). Some also have suggested that to be handicapped is to be adversely affected psychologically and emotionally as well as socially by societal reactions to one's disability (see, e.g., Fait, 1978:3).

When people consciously or unconsciously conspire to create physical and social environments with barriers to disabled people, they ultimately are responsible for making disabled people handicapped. For example, a deaf wrestler becomes handicapped—and disadvantaged—when his school prohibits him, as a disabled person, from trying out for the school wrestling team even though he has had several years of experience in wrestling outside the school. When people hold assumptions and engage in practices that contribute to the differential and inferior treatment of others because of apparent or presumed physical, mental, emotional, or behavioral deficiences, they are being handicapist and the result of their beliefs and actions is handicapism (Bogdan and Biklen, 1981:16).

THE MINORITY STATUS OF HANDICAPPED PEOPLE

It has been estimated that one out of six Americans—or nearly 38 million people in 1982—have physical, mental, or emotional disabilities (Bowe, 1978:vii). Disabilities are disproportionately found among older, male, nonwhite, lower- and working-class people (Nagi, 1969), and they tend to be more restrictive and last longer as people grow older (DHEW, 1973). While disabilities frequently are associated with the aging process, it is important to note that at the end of the 1970s, an estimated eight million American children and youths aged 3 to 21 were sufficiently disabled to require special educational services (Bowe, 1978:135).

When disabled people, of all ages, are made victims of handicapism, it is possible to conceptualize these people as a sociological, as well as statistical, minority. Safilios-Rothschild (1970:109-115) has argued that despite some minor differences between people whom we have called "handicapped" and other types of minority groups such as elderly, black, and poor people, handicapped people can be seen as having much in common with other minorities.

Like a number of other minority groups, handicapped people tend to be segregated in schools, housing, care facilities, and a variety of other institutional and interpersonal settings. In addition, like other minorities, handicapped people are treated by the nondisabled majority as inferior, and segregation is used to keep them at considerable social (and territorial) distance from majority group members. The segregation imposed by the majority is rationalized as "beneficial" for handicapped people because handicapped people are supposed to be more likely to find happiness and acceptance among their "own kind."

Probably the most fundamental way in which handicapped people are like other minority groups is that they are differentiated from other people and treated as inferior by the nondisabled majority solely or largely on the basis of their disability, which overshadows and qualifies all other qualities or abilities. That is, like other minorities, handicapped people are stereotyped, usually in negative terms, on the basis of their disability; as a result, the significance and visibility of other, potentially more positivly evaluated qualities and abilities, tend to be obscured or denied. Thus, the categorical or stereotypical treatment of people with particular disabilities and disabled people in general not only sets them apart from the nondisabled majority, it also often leads to handicapism. The minority handicapped status that is created for disabled people implies that by virtue of being disabled, they will have limited power, privilege, and prestige in society.

Handicapist beliefs and actions in both formal institutional and informal interpersonal settings can produce barriers that substantially disadvantage disabled people. However, disabled people with congenital and noncongenital disabilities and with disabilities of varying severity may be most handicapped when they accept the minority status imposed on them by the non-disabled majority and internalize stereotypical conceptions of their own incompetence and inferiority. This "personal" barrier (Bowe, 1978) by which disabled people contribute to their own handicapping is self-demeaning and self-inhibiting and reinforces both the occurrence and outcome of societal handicapping processes.

LABELING AND STIGMATIZATION
OF HANDICAPPED PEOPLE

It is possible to understand why society handicaps disabled people and relegates them to a minority status by focusing on labeling and stigmatization processes in societal and interpersonal reactions to disabled people. There is evidence from studies of blind people by Josephson (1968) and Scott (1969) that people with the same degree of visual impairment may be labeled blind or not-blind depending on whether or not they have come to the attention of an agency for the blind. Thus, it can be inferred from this evidence not only that disabled people are not necessarily perceived as disabled, but also that disabled people may escape minority status and many forms of handicapism if their disability is not recognized and labeled as a handicap. Of course, except in cases where disabilities are minor or difficult to detect, disabled people tend to be labeled and the labels tend to reflect negative or condescending stereotypes and feelings.

One reason perceptions of disabled people tend to be negative or condescending may be the historical pattern of treating perceived disabilities as a diffuse and undesirable status characteristic that fundamentally distinguishes disabled from nondisabled people. Though disabled people may be limited in function or activities by their condition itself, it can be argued that the perception and labeling of disabilities as forms of sickness (Gliedman and Roth, 1980) or deviance (Freidson, 1965) by others in formal institutional and informal settings constitute the major basis for the relegation of disabled people to a socially disadvantaged status as "handicapped." Thus, while impairments make people disabled, societal and interpersonal reactions through a labeling process may be substantially responsible for making disabled people a handicapped minority.

A key component in the societal labeling process that defines disabled people as handicapped may be stigmatization (Goffman, 1963; Katz, 1981). When the attribute of a disability is recognized and interpreted as a form of sickness or deviance, it may become a stigma and thereby cause a general discrediting of the disabled person's identity and a devaluation of his or her status in the eyes of others. The stigma of disability sets disabled people apart from the nondisabled majority, and as a result, stigmatized disabled people often feel shame and confusion in their efforts to manage their "spoiled identity" and adjust to their devalued status (Albrecht, 1976). Thus, as a stigma, disability is a diffuse status characteristic that is the basis for the negative stereotyping of disabled people. Once disabled people are stigmatized by being labeled sick, deviant, or handicapped, a self-fulfilling prophecy may emerge by which the handicapped minority status and spoiled identities of disabled people are reinforced (Becker, 1963; Erikson, 1964).

Although the outcomes of labeling and stigmatizing processes for disabled people are a socially disadvantaged minority status and a spoiled identity, these processes do not necessarily reflect uniformly negative—or intentionally negative—attitudes toward disabled people. On the other hand, the disability stigma may be tied to perceptions of deviance that arouse feelings of antipathy, disgust, or contempt because disabled people seem unable to meet valued cultural standards of health, self-reliance, independence, vitality, achievement, physical integrity, beauty, and/or success (Safilios-Rothschild, 1970). In addition, nondisabled people might feel threatened by people with disabilities because they are reminded of their own vulnerability to disability and its presumed negative consequences (Katz, 1981). On the other hand, the stigma of disability could be associated with perceptions of deprivation or disadvantage that arouse feelings of compassion, sympathy, or pity because embedded in Judeo-Christian culture is a norm of charity toward the less fortunate. Thus, as *deviant*, disabled people may be seen as inadequate, incompetent, or morally inferior or reprehensible, but as *disadvantaged*, disabled people may be seen as victims worthy of our compassion and charity.

Katz (1981:5) has proposed that this dual perspective creates ambivalent feelings that are a fundamental feature of attitudes toward stigmatized people such as those who are disabled. Ambivalence toward disabled people may suppress overt or intentional forms of handicapism. Nevertheless, conflicted feelings toward disabled people make interaction between disabled and nondisabled people uncomfortable and create a desire among nondisabled people to avoid others with disabilities. Furthermore, overt expressions of sympathy and charity toward disabled people, which may be well-intended but could be expressed in condescending or demeaning ways, may merely disguise a more deeply rooted and deeply felt aversion or antipathy toward these people.

In general, existing evidence (cited by Katz, 1981: 17) suggests that the common public expression of favorable or charitable attitudes toward disabled people tends to mask deeper, largely unconscious feelings that tend to be rejecting. Those underlying feelings of rejection are manifested in the superficial, anxious, or uneasy interaction of nondisabled with disabled people. The masking of underlying negative feelings toward disabled people contributes to handicapism by misleading disabled people about how they are perceived by others in interpersonal relations and by undermining chances for genuine intimacy between disabled and nondisabled people.

Labeling or societal reaction perspectives have had a major influence on a number of the most prominent sociological analyses of disability and rehabilitation over the past two decades (e.g., Freidson, 1965; Scott, 1969; Safilios-Rothschild, 1970, 1976). Even critics (e.g., Gove, 1976) who have pointed out the limitations of these perspectives in the analysis of disability and rehabilitation have acknowledged that labeling and stigmatization processes tend to be important elements in the handicapping of disabled people. From a labeling approach, a key to understanding how disabled people are handicapped as a minority is the identification of contextual variables that activate a deviant labeling of the disability attribute *and* transform the perception of that differentness into stigma. Among the kinds of contextual variables that may activate the labeling and stigmatization processes are the power and resources of disabled people, the social distance between disabled people and others who might label and stigmatize them, community tolerance for deviance, differentness, or disability, and stimulus properties of the disability, such as its severity, visibility, and type that could turn it into a stigma (Gove, 1975; Katz, 1981:121).

The capacity of disabled people to escape handicapism and become genuinely rehabilitated would seem to depend on a combination of personal and sociological factors. On a personal level, adjustment to the disability condition and rejection of handicapist attitudes and a minority status may be assumed to have a significant influence on the extent to which disabled people can escape or minimize being handicapped. To overcome their handicapped minority status, disabled people also need opportunities to interact directly, spontaneously, and/or freely with nondisabled peers. Such opportunities for interaction on informal interpersonal and formal institutional and societal levels could be especially important in overcoming handicapist attitudes and practices if they allow disabled people to demonstrate their abilities and similarities to nondisabled others and to defy or minimize handicapist stereotypes of them as sick or unable.

SPORT, PHYSICAL ACTIVITIES, AND HANDICAPISM

Since physical vitality, ability and achievement typically are strongly emphasized in sport, sports involvement and the sick status often accorded disabled people appear clearly contradictory. To the extent that handicapist beliefs and actions rather than disabilities per se prevent disabled people from participating in sport and less structured or less competitive physical activities, sport and these other activities help reinforce the minority deviant or sick status and stigmatization associated with disabilities. On the other hand, the successful disabled athlete is a contradiction of the popular handicapist stereotype of the disabled population as physically inept or sick and, hence, could help limit or undermine stereotyping of this sort.

The special significance of the handicapist exclusion of disabled children from vigorous physical activity and sport becomes readily apparent when we recognize how much childhood socialization and social acceptance are affected by participation in group play, games, and sports (Groves, 1979). Children who are deprived of group play or games lose potentially valuable opportunities to develop physical and social skills that would enable them to become integrated into group activities later in life. They also lose opportunities to develop a sense of physical fitness and competence that could become the basis for a positive self-image and confidence in interpersonal skills.

Until recently, disabled children and adults in the United States, and in many other countries, rarely have had opportunities to participate and compete in physical activities and sports with their nondisabled peers, and they have not had the same number, range and quality of chances for vigorous physical activity enjoyed by nondisabled people, even in segregated settings in the school or in the community (see, e.g., Sherrill, 1976; Weisman and Godfrey, 1976; Vannier, 1977; Fait, 1978; Orr, 1979; Aufsesser, 1981; Jackson and Fredrickson, 1981; Orr, 1981). One cannot discount the importance of disabilities per se in restricting opportunities for disabled people. However, over the past few decades the Special Olympics and other sports events for disabled people have demonstrated that people with a variety of disabilities can perform at levels equivalent to or even exceeding the best accomplishments of nondisabled people in certain sports (e.g., see Weisman and Godfrey, 1976; Nixon, 1982). Nevertheless, the myth that disabled people are generally or universally different *and inferior* as athletes continues to handicap them (Orr, 1979). Despite the widespread visibility of the accomplishments of mentally retarded people in the Special Olympics, the outstanding accomplishments of the vast majority of top disabled athletes are largely ignored by the popular press and unnoticed by the public, including disabled people themselves in many cases.

Victims of stigma, ambivalence, and misplaced sympathy, disabled people often are overprotected by the nondisabled who worry for them about excessive risks, the danger of accidents and injuries, inadequate supervision, and the possibilities of social rejection and failure. As a result, disabled people often are excluded from sports opportunities that provide their nondisabled peers with fun, excitement, and lessons about competition, achievement, success, and failure that could have value as part of their socialization for participation in the larger society. This exclusion is unnecessarily restrictive—and handicapping—when it is based more on popular handicapist stereotypes and misplaced sympathy than on actual limitations of disabled people. The impact of this exclusion may be doubly handicapping because it could discourage or prevent disabled people from pursuing activities that could enable them to prove to themselves as well as others that they are more able and more similar to their nondisabled peers than popular stereotypes would lead us to believe.

Two major legal developments in the United States in the past decade have been significant levers for changing these conditions of handicapism in school physical education and athletic programs: P.L. 94-142, the Education for All Handicapped Children Act of 1975, and Section 504 of the Rehabilitation Act (P.L. 93-112), which was passed in 1973 but was not implemented until 1977 (DHEW, 1977a, 1977b; Aufsesser, 1981; Auxter, 1981;

Nixon, 1982). These new legal developments and the educational, social, and political movements related to these legal changes have introduced into American society concepts such as least restrictive environment, right to treatment, delabeling, mainstreaming, and normalization which challenge handicapism and the barriers causing or embodied in it (Bogdan and Biklen, 1981). In addition, the new laws have given physical education and athletics in the schools a legally defined role in overcoming handicapism.

The combination of Section 504 with P.L. 94-142 and its mainstreaming or integration provision and its mandate of physical education for all disabled children has had an especially powerful impact on adapted physical education, which offers modified physical activities for students with physical disabilities (Aufsesser, 1981). However, it should be evident that even the provisions of these laws concentrating on physical education have potential ramifications going well beyond adapted physical education.

The demonstration effect of increasing numbers of disabled children and youths participating in an expanding range of physical activities in increasingly "normalized" (McClenaghan, 1981) settings could open many new opportunities for disabled people in sports both within the schools and outside. In addition, as children and youths with disabilities become increasingly involved in various types and at higher levels of sport, they may succeed in undercutting some of the basic myths and misconceptions about the physical capabilities and performance of disabled people that have been part of the stigma and have perpetuated the handicapping of disabled people in sport and the larger society.

SPORT AND HANDICAPISM:
ISSUES AND QUESTIONS FOR RESEARCH

The recent experience of women in American society has shown that a legally mandated and real expansion of opportunities for a minority group is not without problems, unfulfilled promises, and unanticipated and unwanted consequences. Historically well-entrenched deviant labels, stigmas, and structural barriers are likely to make escape from handicapism difficult, uncertain, and frustrating for most handicapped people. However, for sport sociologists, the possibility of changes in traditional patterns of handicapism in and through sport in America raises a number of interesting issues that could become the basis for important and socially relevant new research. Three major issues are of concern: (a) how to proceed with integration through sport of disabled people into the mainstream of society; (b) what types of sports and sports programs to develop for the appropriate integration of disabled people into sport and society; and (c) how to incorporate competition and opportunities for success and failure into sports programs involving disabled people. Each of these issues suggests a number of general sociological questions that could be reformulated as hypotheses for research concerning handicapism and sport. The paper will conclude with examples of the kinds of questions that could be generated by these issues.

1. *Integration.* What strategies of integration or mainstreaming in sports activities will be most conducive to the establishment of normalized relationships between people with disabilities and nondisabled people in sport and the wider society? How will different strategies and degrees of integration in school and community sports programs affect handicapist prejudices, stereotypes, and discrimination, and the self-image and aspirations of disabled people? To what extent must integration strategies be modified according to the type and degree of disability in order to be beneficial both for disabled and nondisabled competitors? To what extent do achievements by disabled athletes in segregated sports settings such as the Special Olympics facilitate subsequent mainstreaming efforts in sport and elsewhere in society? To what extent do achievements by disabled athletes in segregated settings reverse negative stereotypes and discrimination and remove prejudices and stigmatization toward disabled people in sport and elsewhere in society? Relevant references for expanding or refining these integration questions include AAHPER (1975), Winnick (1978), Williamson (1979), Auxter (1981), McClenaghan (1981), and Jansma and Krasnavage (1982).

2. *Types of Sports and Sports Programs.* What types and levels of sports participation allow people with different types and degrees of disability to develop and demonstrate their athletic and social skills most fully? In what types of sports participation are people with different types and degrees of disability likely to derive the most self-respect and respect from others? How does participation by disabled people

in risky or dangerous sports affect handicapist beliefs and actions? What types and degrees of supervision tend to be most appropriate for sports programs involving people with different types and degrees of disability? Among the many relevant recent references concerning this issue are Adams, Daniel, and Rullman (1972), Buell (1973), AAHPER (1975), Sherrill (1976), Weisman and Godfrey (1976), Vannier (1977), Peterson (1978), Sonka and Bina (1978), Barclay (1979), Jackson and Fredrickson (1981), and Orr (1981).

3. *Competition, Success, and Failure.* In what ways can competition be structured, modified, or controlled to maximize the opportunities for success and minimize perceptions of failure among disabled *and nondisabled* competitors? Under what conditions are officials and nondisabled competitors most likely to accept the Special Olympics model of competition for integrated sports? Under what conditions are the mass media most likely to publicize the abilities and successes vs. disabilities and failures of athletes with disabilities? To what extent does participation in integrated sports provide disabled people with skills that will help them participate more effectively in the competitive realms of the mainstream of society outside sport? How does competition among and between disabled and nondisabled athletes influence handicapist attitudes and behavior in sport and elsewhere in society? In addition to many of the references already cited, Owens' (1981) discussion of "maintreaming in the Every Child a Winner Program" and Coakley's (1982) discussion of the Special Olympics as "controlled competition" also are especially relevant to this issue.

NOTES

1.   I would like to thank Nancy Theberge and Peter Donnelly for their suggested revisions of my paper presented at the Third Annual NASSS meetings in Toronto. I found their comments helpful, and I substantially revised my original paper as a result of them.

REFERENCES

AAHPER
1975   Physical Education and Recreation for Impaired, Disabled, and

Handicapped Individuals. . . Past, Present, and Future.
Washington, D.C.: American Alliance for Health, Physical Education and Recreation. Date inferred.

Adams, R.C., Daniel, A., and Rullman, L.
1972   Games, Sports and Exercises for the Physically Handicapped.
Philadelphia: Lea and Febiger.

Albrecht, G.L.
1976   "Socialization and the disability process." Pp. 3-38 in G.L.
Albrecht (ed.) The Sociology of Physical Disability and Rehabilitation. Pittsburgh: University of Pittsburgh Press.

Aufsesser, P.M.
1981   "Adapted physical education: a look back, a look ahead." Journal of Health, Physical Education, Recreation, and Dance 52:
28-31.

Auxter, D.
1981   "Equal educational opportunity for the handicapped through
physical education." The Physical Educator 38: 8-14.

Barclay, V.
1979   "Competition for physically handicapped children." Pp. 49-80
in L. Groves (ed.) Physical Education for Special Needs. Cambridge: Cambridge University Press.

Becker, H.
1963   Outsiders: Studies in the Sociology of Deviance. New York: Free
Press.

Bogdan, R. and Biklen, D.
1981   "Handicapism." Pp. 15-26 in A.D. Spiegel and S. Podair (eds.)
Rehabilitating People with Disabilities into the Mainstream of
Society. Park Ridge, N.J.: Noyes Medical Publications.

Bowe, F.
1978   Handicapping America: Barriers for Disabled People. New York:
Harper and Row.

Buell, C.E.
1973   Physical Education and Recreation for the Visually Handicapped.
Washington, D.C.: AAHPER.

Coakley, J.J.
1982   Sport in Society: issues and controversies. St. Louis: C.V. Mosby,
2nd ed.

DHEW (Department of Health, Education, and Welfare)
1973   Current Estimates from the Health Interview Survey United States—1971. Rockville, Md.: National Center for Health Statistics.
1977a Section 504. U.S. Department of H.E.W. Rehabilitation Act of 1973 (P.L. 93-112), Federal Register, May 4, pp. 22676-22702.
1977b U.S. Department of H.E.W. The Education for All Handicapped Children Act of 1975, Federal Register, August 23.

Erikson, K.
1964   "Notes on the sociology of deviance." Pp. 9-21 in H. Becker (ed.) The Other Side. New York: Free Press.

Fait, H.F.
1978   Special Physical Education: Adapted, Corrective, Developmental. Philadelphia: W.B. Saunders, 4th ed.

Freidson, E.
1965   "Disability as social deviance." Pp. 71-99 in M. Sussman (ed.) Sociology and Rehabilitation. Washington, D.C.: American Sociological Association.

Gliedman, J. and Roth, W.
1980   The Unexpected Minority: Handicapped Children in America. New York: Harcourt Brace Jovanovich.

Goffman, E.
1963   Stigma: Notes on the Management of Spoiled Identity. Englewood Cliffs, N.J.: Prentice-Hall.

Gove, W.R.
1975   The Labeling of Deviance. New York: Wiley.
1976   "Societal reaction theory and disability." Pp. 57-71 in G.L. Albrecht (ed.) The Sociology of Physical Disability and Rehabilitation. Pittsburgh: University of Pittsburgh Press.

Groves, L.
1979   "Physical education as part of the total education of handicapped children." Pp. 3-19 in L. Groves (ed.) Physical Education for Special Needs. Cambridge: Cambridge University Press.

Jackson, R.W. and Fredrickson, A.
1981   "Sports for the physically disabled." Pp. 328-336 in A.D. Spiegel and S. Podair (eds.) Rehabilitating People with Disabilities into the Mainstream of Society. Park Ridge, N.J.: Noyes Medical Publications.

Jansma, P. and Krasnavage, R.
1982   "Progressive inclusion of the handicapped into community youth football." The Physical Educator 39: 30-35.

Josephson, E.
1968   The Social Life of Blind People. Research Series no. 19. New York: American Foundation for the Blind.

Katz, I.
1981   Stigma: A Social Psychological Analysis. Hillsdale, N.J.: Lawrence Erlbaum Associates.

McClenaghan, B.A.
1981   "Normalization in physical education: a reflective review." The Physical Educator 38: 3-7.

Nagi, S.Z.
1969   Disability and Rehabilitation. Columbus: Ohio State University Press.

Nixon, H.L. II
1982   "Overcoming handicapism in and through sport: a new focus for sport sociology." Paper Presented at the Third Annual Meetings of the NASSS, Toronto, November.

Orr, R.E.
1979   "Sport, myth, and the handicapped athlete." Journal of Physical Education and Recreation 50: 33-34.
1981   "Changing attitudes toward wheelchair athletes." Journal of Health, Physical Education, Recreation, and Dance 52: 40-41.

Owens, M.F.
1981   "Mainstreaming in the Every Child a Winner Program." Journal of Physical Education, Recreation, and Dance 52: 16-18.

Peterson, C.A.
1978   "The right to risk." Journal of Physical Education and Recreation 49: 47-48.

Safilios-Rothschild, C.
1970   The Sociology and Social Psychology of Disability and Rehabilitation. New York: Random House.
1976   "Disabled persons' self-definitions and their implications for rehabilitation." Pp. 39-56 in G.L. Albrecht (ed.) The Sociology of Physical Disability and Rehabilitation. Pittsburgh: University of Pittsburgh Press.

Scott, R.A.
1969   The Making of Blind Men. New York: Russell Sage Foundation.

Sherrill, C.
1976   Adapted Physical Education and Recreation: A Multidisciplinary Approach. Dubuque, Iowa: W.C. Brown.

Sonka, J.J. and Bina, M.J.
1978   "Coming out ahead in the long run." Journal of Physical Education and Recreation 49: 24-25.

Vannier, M.H.
1977   Physical Activities for the Handicapped. Englewood Cliffs, N.J.: Prentice-Hall.

Weisman, M. and Godfrey, J.
1976   So Get On With It: A Celebration of Wheelchair Sports. Toronto and Garden City, N.Y.: Doubleday.

Williamson, D.
1979   "Some methods of integrating handicapped children into physical education and recreation with other young people." Pp. 137-145 in L. Groves (ed.) Physical Education for Special Needs. Cambridge: Cambridge University Press.

Winnick, J.P.
1978   "Techniques for integration." Journal of Physical Education and Recreation 49:22.

SOCIAL JUSTICE IN SPORT: THE NORM OF EXPECTED INEQUITY

Mary E. Duquin
University of Pittsburgh

CONCEPTS OF SOCIAL JUSTICE arise from learning and internalizing societal norms. According to Lerner (1974), our belief in a just world comes from a desire to believe that we deserve our own outcomes, that the world is so constructed that if we make the required effort and self deprivation, we will receive the appropriate benefits. Witnessing injustice results in a conflict with our need to believe in a just world and thus threatens our security. Perceptions of justice in any given situation are based upon the socially normative form of justice considered appropriate to the situation and specific belief patterns associated with the event and the people involved.

For example, "competition" is a commonly employed form of justice in sport where performance decides what person or group is deserving. Just behavior under competition is based upon recognizing with special treatment or reward the best or winning person or group. In contrast, the "parity" form of justice assumes each person or group deserves equal treatment, the same reward or outcome, or equal access to resources. Justice as "parity" is reflected in much of the legislation concerning equal rights in school sport programs. "Equity" justice requires that a person or group be rewarded in proportion to their investments or costs, promoting the notion of fair exchange. The Marxian "need" form of justice requires that resources be distributed to meet the most pressing needs of people without regard to individual investments. In sport, distribution of medical services could be seen to function under the need form of justice. A fifth form of justice is "legal." This form appeals to the law or rules governing a situation or interaction. Legal justice is usually based on one or more of the other forms of justice and is more likely employed in an interpersonal settlement of differences between parties with a clear conflict of interest.

Judgments about justice are dependent not only on the form of justice one chooses to employ in a given situation but on the specific beliefs one holds about the context of the injustice, the perpetrator, and the victim. Previous research (Lerner, 1974) has identified a number of variables which have been found to affect peoples' judgments about whether an injustice has occurred, the seriousness of an injustice, and the assignment of blame to the victim or to the perpetrator. The purpose of the research was to test a number of these variables in a sport context. Specifically, the author hypothesized that injustice in a sport context would be rated less serious, the perpetrator blamed less or the victim more if:

1) the victim was seen as receiving some compensation for the injustice (Lerner and Simmons, 1966; Lerner, 1970);
2) the consequences of the injustice were viewed as minor as opposed to major (Kaufmann, 1970; Lerner, 1970);
3) the injustice did not break a formal law or rule (Kaufmann, 1970);
4) the victim was seen as responsible for bringing on the injustice (Lerner, 1974; Scholper and Matthews, 1965; Tannenbaum and Gaer, 1965);
5) the victim was perceived as low as opposed to high status or was viewed stereotypically as a class (Bandura, Ross and Ross, 1963; Baxter, Lerner, and Miller, 1965);
6) the victim was perceived as innocent or unknowing (Lerner, 1974);
7) the victim was viewed as dissimilar to the observer or the observer did not identify with the victim (Chaikin and Darley, 1971; Novak and Lerner, 1968).

METHODOLOGY

The subjects in this study were 128 middle class Pittsburgh area high school students ages 14 to 18. The sample consisted of equal numbers of male and female athletes and non-athletes. All athletes were members of varsity teams while non-athletes had not participated on a high school varsity team.

Each subject read six sport scenarios in which a conflict arose between a member of the athletic department and an athlete. The majority of the scenarios were constructed from details of actual sport incidences related to the author by coaches and college athletes.

Each scenario had four forms, a "high" serious form A with a male victim, form A with a female victim, a "low" serious form B with a male victim and form B with a female victim (See Tables 1 and 2). According to the hypotheses, scenario A was expected to elicit a greater seriousness of injustice rating and higher perpetrator blame than the less serious scenario B.

Subjects read one of the four forms of each of the six scenarios. After reading each scenario, subjects completed a questionnaire on which they judged whether any injustice to the athlete occurred in the situation described. Subjects used a rating scale of 0 to 10 with 0 = "no injustice," 1 = "slight injustice" up to 10 = "great injustice." A subject who judged that an injustice had occurred, was then asked to decide what percentage of blame to place on the perpetrator and what percentage of blame, if any, to put on the athlete. The sum of these percentages was to add to one hundred percent. Although no written comments were required, many subjects felt motivated to give rationales for their judgments. Such comments were helpful in interpreting the statistical analysis of the data.

The experimental design consisted of a two between, two within ANOVA with repeated measures. The between variable included sex of subject and subjects' athletic status. The within variables included seriousness of the scenario and sex of victim (athlete). Significance was set at the $p < .05$ level.

RESULTS

Variable 1: Victim Compensation

Scenario A in which the basketball freshman was not compensated was not viewed as significantly more unjust than scenario B, although the means were in the predicted direction. The compensation manipulation was not effective in this situation, possibly because the compensation was not seen as valuable enough or because it was not perceived as compensation.

In comparison to the other scenarios, subjects did not rate this situation as a very serious miscarriage of justice. On a scale of 0-10 the athlete's situation was rated as moderately unjust with a majority of blame going to the recruiter but a hefty amount of responsibility (36%) being placed on the athlete in both the compensated and noncompensated scenarios.

TABLE 1. High Serious Sport Scenarios by Variable: Form A

V1:   Victim Compensation

Larry (Linda), an excellent basketball player, was heavily recruited by many universities. He finally signed with a large and prestigious university and was told by the recruiter that he had a good chance of making the first string on the basketball team. After sitting on the bench for most of the first season, Larry realized that he was misled by the recruiter about how much he would be played. Larry knows that he could have gone to a smaller college and made the first string. Larry feels he was deceived by the recruiter and thus treated unjustly.

V2:   Seriousness of the Consequences

Barb (Bill), a sophomore on a basketball scholarship at a large university, broke an ankle in the third game of the season. The trainer told the coach that Barb would be out for seven weeks. Barb thinks that she can come back just as good as ever. The coach, however, decides to drop Barb from the team. The coach then speaks to Barb about giving up her scholarship to a player who will be able to help the team. Barb feels that she has been treated unjustly by the coach by not being given a chance to come back and by being pressured to give up her scholarship without which she can not afford to finish out the school year.

V3:   Law or Rule Violation

The volleyball team has been plagued with major and minor injuries from the beginning of the season. In the fifth game of the season, the coach must decide whether to default for lack of six fit players or to play with an injured player. John (Jane), who is the team's best server, is recovering from a bad knee injury and so is usually only substituted for serves. The doctor told the coach that John's knee required two more weeks of rest. In direct violation of university policy regarding doctor's recommendations, the coach decides to play John rather than default. In the second game John seriously reinjures his knee. The doctor reports that John's volleyball career is over.

V4:   Victim Responsibility

Joan (Mike) was unable to participate in the national collegiate gymnastic championships when her university was banned from all national competitions for one year because the athletic department was found guilty of serious recruiting violations. Joan feels that the athletic department's illegal behavior caused her harm by depriving her of the opportunity to participate in the national championships.

V5: Victim Status
     After four years of playing varsity basketball at a big time university, Anne (Steve) discovers that she doesn't have enough credits to graduate with her class. Anne, a B+ student, feels that she was treated unjustly because her advisor in the athletic department, with whom she was required to register each term, never told her she'd have to go a fifth year in order to fulfill graduation requirements.

V6: Victim Knowledge
     Chuck (Carol) is on the university track team. According to a decision made by the athletic director, he and his team are sent *by bus 500 miles* to the eastern track championships. Each member of the track team is given *$50* to cover food and miscellaneous expenses for the three-day trip. Chuck and his team are not aware of it, but each member of the basketball team, which *flew 300 miles* to an away game was given *$150* spending money for the same three-day period.

TABLE 2: Low Serious Sport Scenarios by Variable: Form B

V1: Victim Compensation
     Larry (Linda), an excellent basketball player, was heavily recruited by many universities. He finally signed with a large and prestigious university and was told by the recruiter that he had a good chance for making the first string on the basketball team. After sitting on the bench for most of the first season, Larry realized that he was misled by the recruiter about how much he would be played. Larry knows he could have gone to a smaller college and made the first string. Larry feels he was deceived by the recruiter and thus treated unjustly. When Larry talked to the coach about his complaint the coach reminded Larry of the advantages of attending a large prestigious university, as opposed to a small college, namely, an excellent academic education and the opportunity to be a member of a high quality winning team.

V2: Seriousness of the Consequences
     Barb (Bill), a sophomore on a basketball scholarship at a large university, broke an ankle in the third game of the season. The

trainer told the coach that Barb would be out for seven weeks. Barb thinks that she can come back just as good as ever. The coach, however, decides to drop Barb from the team. Barb feels that she has been treated unjustly by the coach by not being given a chance to come back.

V3:   Law or Rule Violation

The volleyball team has been plagued with major and minor injuries from the beginning of the season. In the fifth game of the season the coach must decide whether to default for lack of six fit players or to play with an injured player. John (Jane), who is the team's best server, is recovering from a bad knee injury and so is usually only substituted for serves. The coach decides to play John rather than default. In the second game John seriously reinjures his knee. The doctor reports that John's volleyball career is over.

V4:   Victim Responsibility

Joan (Mike) was unable to participate in the national collegiate gymnastic championships when her university was banned from all national competitions for one year because the athletic department was found guilty of serious recruiting violations in recruiting Joan to their school. Joan feels that the athletic department's illegal behavior caused her harm by depriving her of the opportunity to participate in the national championships.

V5:   Victim Status

After four years of playing varsity basketball at a big-time university, Anne (Steve) discovers that she doesn't have enough credits to graduate with her class. Anne, a C− student, feels that she was treated unjustly because her advisor in the athletic department, with whom she was required to register each term, never told her she'd have to go a fifth year in order to fulfill graduation requirements.

V6:   Victim Knowledge

Chuck (Carol) is on the university track team. According to a decision made by the athletic director he and his team are sent *by bus 500 miles* to the eastern track championships. Each member of the track team is given $50 to cover food and miscellaneous expenses for the three-day trip. When he returns from the weekend meet he discovers that each member of the basketball team which *flew 300 miles* to an away game was given $150 spending money for the same three-day period. Chuck feels that this difference in treatment is unfair.

TABLE 3. Ratings on Seriousness of Injustice by Variable

Variable	High Serious Scenario A X	Low Serious Scenario B X	F	f
V1: Victim Compensation	5.48	4.93	1.75	.19
V2: Seriousness of the Consequences	8.15	6.98	6.31	.01
V3: Law or Rule Violation	7.96	6.99	6.08	.02
V4: Victim Responsibility	7.04	6.58	.79	.37
V5: Victim Status	6.87	5.18	15.15	.0002
V6: Victim Knowledge	6.23	6.06	.12	.73

Written comments made by the subjects revealed that many felt the athlete in this situation was naive and responsible. The athlete was seen as responsible not only for the decision to go to University A but for sitting on the bench. Some said that the athlete was "probably not good enough," suggesting the use of the competition notion of justice. Other subjects rationalized the recruiter's role in the scenario by noting that "a chance is not a guarantee," "the recruiter never *promised* him," and "you can never believe what recruiters say." Some subjects, mostly male athletes, responded with a "let the buyer beware" attitude. This attitude may help explain the sex-by-athlete interaction (p<.01.) found in the data. Male athletes rated this situation far less seriously and tended to blame the recruiter less than non-athletes or females, suggesting that male athletes may have different expectations of the sport establishment and of athletic responsibility due in part to their different competitive sport experiences (Allison, 1982; Theberge, Curtis and Brown, 1982).

Variable 2: Seriousness of the Consequences

In comparing scenarios A and B, being pressured to give up one's scholarship in addition to being dropped from the team was viewed as more unjust. Of all the athletic situations, this one was rated one of the most serious, and a significant difference (p <.01) was found between the two scenarios (see Table 3). Not being given a chance to come back was seen by some subjects as violating the norm of fair competition, that is, "give her a chance to prove she's good enough after she's well." In addition some subjects saw being pressured to give up a financially necessary scholarship as violating the need form of justice. Blame on the coach was greater in scenario A (x 84%) than B (x 74%); this difference approached significance, p <.06.

Rationales for those who did not see any injustice in these scenarios came in two main forms. Some subjects saw this situation as part of "the breaks of the game." Other subjects saw this action as the coach's prerogative to play the best players, reflecting the competition notion of justice with the coach being able to legitimately call an injured player "out" of the competition.

Variable 3: Violating a Rule or Law

Subjects' ratings of injustice were high for both scenarios A and B. In both situations the seriousness of the consequences of the coach's action in playing a hurt player were the same—the end of the athlete's career. However, scenario A made clear that the coach's action violated a specific formal policy. Thus, a significant difference (p <.02) was found on the rating of the seriousness of the injustice in scenario A (x 7.96) over B (x 6.99). Blame on the coach was also greater in the "policy violating" scenario A (x 78%) than in B (x 70%; p <.03).

Some subjects commented that the athlete should have taken responsibility for his or her own health and should not have gone into the game. Such perceptions of responsibility on the part of the athlete may exist independent of rules or policies governing the coach's behavior. However, it is evident that athletic structure does influence perceptions of rights, responsibilities, and unjust behavior in sport. These results point out the importance of structuring and publicizing formal rules and policies governing both athlete and coach.

Variable 4: Victim Responsibility

The ratings of seriousness of injustice were high in both scenarios and did not change significantly with the manipulation of victim responsibility. However, the percent of blame attributed to the athlete in scenario A (x 9%) versus B (x 20%) was significantly greater (p<.002).

Although scenario A is ambiguous as regards the athlete's knowledge or compliance in the recruiting violation, it was enough merely to tie the athlete to the violation in order to change an observer's assessment of victim blame. Again this result suggests the need for athletes to be aware of all rules and regulations which might affect their athletic participation.

Variable 5: Victim Status

Status was manipulated by making the victim either a B+ or a C- student-athlete. Of all the situations this manipulation was surprisingly the most successful. Not only was it viewed as more unjust that a B+ athlete not graduate but significantly more blame was placed on the C- student (p<.0001). The B+ student's mean blame was 41% compared to the C- student's blame of 58%. Despite what one might think about the ability of the B+ versus the C- student to see to it that they make it through in four years, the fact is that the advisor was blamed less and the athlete more when the victim was a C- student. Besides the obvious status

differential, the C- and B+ information may have been interpreted as a reflection of the athlete's effort and interest, or lack
thereof, in academic endeavors.

Variable 6: Victim Knowledge

Although the athletic director was heavily blamed for this
moderately unjust situation, it made no difference in perception of justice or blame if the victim was aware or unaware of
the injustice being done. The athlete's ignorance of the injustice
did not have a positive effect on the subjects' ratings of the
seriousness of this injustice.

Variable 7: Identification with the Victim

Observers are more likely to see an injustice if they identify
with the victim or less likely if they view the victim as dissimilar
to themselves. One way this was tested was to look for a sex
of subject, sex of victim interaction. An analysis of the data found
no such interaction. Since no overall sex-of-victim main effect
nor interaction was found, the results suggest that sex of victim
may not be considered of primary importance when making
judgments of injustice in certain sport situations.

A second test of the identification hypothesis compared the
ratings of athletes and non-athletes. Although the hypothesis
states that athletes should identify more with the victim than
non-athletes and thus view sport injustice more seriously, no
significant differences were found between the two groups. One
possible reason for the lack of identification on the part of the
high school athletes is that the victims in each sport scenario
were college athletes.

A second possibility is that the athlete-subjects did experience
identification with the athletes in the scenarios but that in making judgments about injustice in sport, the athletes tended to
use a norm of expected inequity, which acted to offset their identification bias. That is, given the structural basis and ideological
perception of athletics as a benevolent dictatorship (Rafferty, 1971),
athletes learn to expect less in sport than what would be considered equitable treatment in other contexts. The decidedly
asymmetrical power relationship between athletes and the athletic
establishment comes to be accepted by athletes as the norm, thus
moderating their perceptions and judgments of injustice in sport.

One unexpected result which may lend some support to the
suggestion of an inequity norm is the finding that, overall, female
subjects were more sensitive to injustice (x 6.85) than males

(x 6.23, F = 7.60, p<.007). Females also placed more blame on the athletic establishment (x 74%) than did males (x 68%, F = 7.10, p<.009). The lower scores of the males may be a reflection of their longer and stronger socialization into sport with an accompanying realization and acceptance of a certain amount of inequity in the athletic life.

IMPLICATIONS

The results of this research point to some important factors governing perceptions of injustice in sport.

1) Injustice in sport is denied, ignored, or perceived as less serious if an athlete is viewed as a willing participant, as low status, as suffering only minor consequences, as acting irresponsibly, or as associated with the cause of the negative outcome.

2) Injustice in sport is viewed more seriously if a formal law or rule is violated. Thus it is in the interest of athletes to be aware of all rules governing their participation and to engage in the establishment and implementation of fair athletic policies and practices.

3) The established power structure and tradition of athletics supported by the ideology of a benevolent dictatorship serves to reduce awareness of the possibility of a potential conflict of interest between athletes and the athletic establishment. The establishment of a more balanced power relationship encourages the adoption of a norm of expected inequity. Thus, when an athlete encounters injustice in sport, both the seriousness of the situation and the degree of blame placed on the perpetrator are modified.

Some evidence suggests that the hierarchical structure and control pattern of athletics is endorsed by both coaches and athletes and that athletes are less sensitive than non-athletes to individual rights (Carron, 1980; Petrie, 1976; Puretz, 1969). While it is true that not all athletes are "falsely conscious" or willingly compliant in their role as athletes (Ingham, 1976), many athletes appear unaware of the factors influencing perceptions of injustice in sport under the present sport structure. Knowledge of these factors may encourage athletes to take a greater responsibility in redefining and securing fair and just treatment in sport.

Further research underway in this area compares the social justice judgments of fans, coaches, and athletes and the underlying forms of justice or rationales used by each in deciding issues of social justice in sport.

REFERENCES

Allison, M. T.
1982 "Sportsmanship: variations based on sex and degree of competitive experience." Pp. 153-166 in A. O. Dunleavy, A. W. Miracle, and C. R. Rees (eds.), Studies in the Sociology of Sport. Fort Worth: Texas Christian University Press.

Bandura, A., D. Ross, and S. A. Ross
1963 "Vicarious reinforcement and imitative learning." Journal of Abnormal and Social Psychology 67: 601-607.

Baxter, J. C., M. Lerner, and J. S. Miller
1965 "Identification as a function of the reinforcing quality of the model and the socialization background of the subject." Journal of Personality and Social Psychology 2: 692-697.

Chaikin, A. L. and J. M. Darley
1971 "Victim or perpetrator: defensive attribution of responsibility and the need for order and justice." Unpublished manuscript. Princeton University.

Carron, A. V.
1980 Social Psychology of Sport. Ithaca, New York: Movement Publications.

Ingham, A.
1976 "Sport and the new left: some reflections upon opposition without praxis." Pp. 238-248 in D. Landers (ed.), Social Problems in Athletics. Chicago: University of Illinois Press.

Kaufmann, H.
1970 "Legality and harmfulness of a bystander's failure to intervene as determinants of moral judgement." In J. Macaulay and L. Berkowitz (eds.), Altruism and Helping Behavior. New York: Academic Press.

Lerner, M. J.
1970 "The desire for justice and reaction to victim." In J. Macaulay and L. Berkowitz (eds.), Altruism and Helping Behavior. New York: Academic Press.

Lerner, M. J.
1974 "Social psychology of justice and interpersonal attraction." In J. Macaulay and L. Berkowitz (eds.), Altruism and Helping Behavior. New York: Academic Press.

Lerner, M. J. and C. Simmons
1966   "Observer's reaction to the innocent victim: compassion or rejection?" Journal of Personality and Social Psychology 4: 203-310.

Novak, D. and M. J. Lerner
1968   "Rejection as a consequence of perceived similarity." Journal of Personality and Social Psychology 9: 147-152.

Petrie, B. M.
1976   "The athletic group as an emerging deviant subculture." Pp. 224-237 in D. Landers (ed.), Social Problems in Athletics. Chicago: University of Illinois Press.

Puretz, D. H.
1969   "Athletics and the development of values." Paper presented at the American Alliance for Health, Physical Education and Recreation National Convention. Boston.

Rafferty, M.
1971   "Interscholastic athletics: the gathering storm." In J. Scott (ed.), The Athletic Revolution. New York: Free Press.

Scholper, J. and M. Matthews
1965   "The influence of the perceived cause focus of partners' dependency on the use of interpersonal power." Journal of Personality and Social Psychology 4: 609-612.

Tannenbaum, P. H. and E. P. Gaer
1965   "Mood changes as a function of stress of protagonist and degree of identification in a film viewing situation." Journal of Personality and Social Psychology 2: 612-616.

Theberge, N., J. Curtis, and B. Brown
1982   "Sex differences in orientations toward games: tests of the sport involvement hypothesis." Pp. 285-308 in A. O. Dunleavy, A. W. Miracle, and C. R. Rees (eds.), Studies in the Sociology of Sport. Fort Worth: Texas Christian University Press.

SECTION IV

SPORT AND SOCIAL POLICY

THE INSTITUTIONALIZATION OF SPORT in North America has been profoundly affected by the policies of a variety of public institutions and agencies. These include governments at all levels, national and international sport governing bodies and educational institutions. Policies developed in these settings have had a significant impact both on the character of sport in our society and the availability of sporting opportunities to different segments of the population.

The three papers in this section deal with the impact on sport of policies developed in three settings. The first paper is Ian Franks and Donald Macintosh's comparative analysis of the development of Canadian governmental policies toward sport and culture. In this case, culture refers to artistic or "high" culture, as opposed to sport, which ranks as "popular" culture. Government involvement in both sport and culture was motivated by a concern for the development of a Canadian national identity and an improvement in the well-being of citizens. In the case of sport, government interest was triggered by widespread concern for the declining performance of Canadian teams in international ice hockey and other sports. Allied to concerns for the development of elite sport were concerns for mass fitness and recreation. As Franks and Macintosh show, however, the goals of excellence and mass participation were ultimately incompatible. Since the government receives far more prestige from athletes' success in international sport than it receives from providing opportunities for recreational involvement, elite sport programs have received a larger share of government revenues than mass participation programs.

In the second paper, Arthur Johnson is concerned with the development of municipal government policies that have resulted in the subsidization of professional sports teams in the majority of the 49 North American cities that host such teams. Since cities stand to profit from hosting a professional franchise, if not financially then in terms of enhanced prestige, there has been a growing tendency to compete for franchises by making attractive subsidy offers to the owners of sport teams. Johnson describes the relationship that is established as a partnership, but an uneasy or unequal one in which the professional team has frequently become the dominant partner, occasionally blackmailing city officials into providing increasingly greater subsidies lest they risk incurring electoral disapproval over the loss of the franchise. The author calls for a greater understanding of the established partnership and offers suggestions for creating a more equal relationship.

In the final paper in this section, Jay Coakley and Patricia Pacey assess the effects of the implementation of Title IX regulations on involvement in women's intercollegiate sport at National Collegiate Athletic Association institutions. Less than half of their sample of women athletes were receiving any form of scholarship aid, but Coakley and Pacey are able to document quite clearly that the introduction of athletic scholarships into women's programs has led to the adoption of the model established by men's programs. Specifically, the highest proportion of scholarships is provided to athletes in revenue-producing sports, and financial need is not a criterion for the provision of scholarship aid to athletes. Another similarity to practices in men's programs concerns the proportion of scholarships that are awarded to black athletes. Coakley and Pacey show that the underrepresentation of blacks is even more pronounced among female scholarship athletes than it is among male scholarship athletes. Thus, the often cited rationale for the provision of athletic scholarships— that they enhance the educational opportunities of minority groups—is called into question by these data.

THE EVOLUTION OF FEDERAL GOVERNMENT POLICIES TOWARD SPORT AND CULTURE IN CANADA: A COMPARISON

C. E. S. Franks and Donald Macintosh
Queen's University

MOST OF THE POLITICAL HISTORY of Canada is a chronicle of nation-building by an interventionist government rather than a history of struggles between varying philosophies or economic classes. Part of this effort at nation-building has been a continuing effort to foster and encourage national institutions, to reduce dependence on outside powers (in particular Britain and the United States), and to promote national unity and a sense of national identity among the disparate English, French, and other cultural groups that inhabit the second largest country in the world. Government in the post-World War II period has been active in both culture and sport, and policies have been directed towards this end of nation-building. The programs have been elitist in orientation and closely related to and supportive of the existing, powerful, and stable structure of economic and political power in Canada. This is perhaps the operational meaning of "nation-building."

Active government intervention in culture began earlier than in sport. Nevertheless, there is a marked similarity between the arguments for, the issues faced in, and the instruments of administration used for federal policies in culture and sport. This paper will compare and contrast the initiatives and early development of federal government policies in the two areas.

Both "culture" and "sport" are difficult terms to define, culture perhaps the more so. The area in which government has intervened is "high culture" or "the fine arts," and not "low," "mass" or "popular" culture. High culture is much like the Oxford English

Dictionary definition of culture as "the training and refinement of mind, tastes, and manners; the condition of being thus trained and refined; the intellectual side of civilization," or as Matthew Arnold said, "the acquainting ourselves with the best that has been known and said in the world." This sort of culture is, by definition, elitist and asserts a set of social, ethical, and artistic values. Among other things, it serves a function in asserting the legitimacy of the dominant elite. It is also expensive, and wherever a tradition of high as opposed to popular culture has existed, it has relied for support on wealthy patrons, whether merchants, barons, ecclesiastics, or government. The distinction between high and low culture is often uncertain, and in spheres such as mass media and film appears to be shifting so that there is some overlap; the distinctions between which areas need government support and which can be self-supporting in the open market is also blurred. Modern technology's advances in information handling, pay television, and multi-channel television reception are creating even more overlap in activities and intensifying the need for new government policies regarding allocation of resources between public and private sectors and control over content, especially the proportion of materials made in Canada to those from abroad.

Sport, according to the Oxford English Dictionary is a "pleasant pastime; amusement; diversion." This would seem to place it squarely in the area of low culture, without edifying or political content or ends apart from the utility of amusing and diverting the populace. This is an elitist view of sport, however, and government involvement in Canada has been based on a much broader view of its meaning and functions. The development of the federal government sports program included refinement of three distinctions: first, competition as opposed to recreation; second, elite as opposed to mass participation; and third, that requiring support from that which is self-supporting (in large part distinguishing amateur from professional). The resulting definition of sport for the federal government was competitive, elitist, and amateur, with a mass television audience. Sport programs were directly related to national goals, especially nation-building.

The following sections will examine and compare first, the arguments that were put forward for government involvement in culture and sport, and second, the policies and administrative instruments and the evolution and development of the programs. A final section will consider conclusions which can be drawn from this as to the role of government in Canada and the functions and evolution of sport and culture.

ARGUMENTS FOR GOVERNMENT INTERVENTION

Culture

In 1967, the centenary of confederation, the Government of Canada published a 500-page volume entitled *Canada: One Hundred; 1867-1967*, which described the people, economy, society, and history of Canada. In it, the sections on broadcasting and the National Film Board were placed just after the sections on the press and news agencies and just before the sections on the post office, telephones, and the Department of Transport. Hidden within this description of business enterprises and hardware is the curious story of how Canada in the 1930's created two national organizations involved in the mass media and commerce but also involved in sponsoring and communicating culture: The Canadian Broadcasting Corporation and the National Film Board. The CBC, which had its origins within the Canadian National Railways (railways were the first vital government-sponsored link joining East to West in Canada) was described in 1965 as ". . . the *essential* element of the Canadian broadcasting system and the most important single instrument available for the development and maintenance of the unity of Canada" (Canada Royal Commission on Broadcasting, 1957:32). Like the British Broadcasting Corporation, the CBC has tried to appeal to high as well as popular taste. Its most popular television program has always been Hockey Night in Canada, and the interest aroused within its mass audience helped to create the climate which encouraged government intervention in sport.

The National Film Board has not been so prominent. Its birth coincided with the beginning of World War II. During the war, it was harnessed to national goals and played a substantial role in encouraging unity and the war effort through documentaries on Canada and Canadians. Its films have not enjoyed success in the commercial market, which in both English and French Canada has been dominated by American products. The NFB has defined for itself a non-commercial role in interpreting Canada to Canadians and abroad. Its activities in the post-war period have been supported by government and have become increasingly directed towards education and elite culture.

Both the CBC and the NFB were created to provide a Canadian alternative to domination by American media. Government involvement directly in high culture had similar motives. Walter B. Herbert (Canada, 1967) has described the evolution of Canada's cultural development:

> . . . Most of its stimuli and main influences have come not from within but from without and the general pattern of the arts has been notably imitative. . . . Only since the early 1950's have there been country-wide signs of the emergence of vigorous, ambitious, and original powers within the community of Canadian creative and performing artists; a development which has prospered in an atmosphere of public approval and support hitherto unknown in Canada. To generalize: prior to 1950 Canada's cultural development was a long, dull, earnest, and imitative business, whereas the succeeding years have brought forth a cultural explosion of genuine validity and far-reaching promise (p. 394).

This quasi-official description of the contrast between the earlier "long, dull, earnest, and imitative business," and the "vigorous, ambitious, and original. . . cultural explosion of genuine validity and far-reaching promise" nicely and not coincidentally coincides with the emergence of strong, overt, active government involvement in the arts.

The origins of this change were in the report of the Massey Commission of 1951, which noted that, "In most modern states, there are ministries of 'fine arts' or of 'cultural affairs.' Some measure of official responsibility is now accepted in all civilized countries whatever political philosophy may prevail" (Ostry, 1978:63). This argument for imitation as a path to autonomy was the commissioners' way of skirting gingerly around the issue of government involvement in the arts and education. This issue has always been particularly problematic in Canada because of the mistrust within Quebec of federal cultural initiatives and the fear that their initiation reflected the imperialism of English Canada. Arthur Lower, the noted historian, saw more clearly the motives of the commissioners:

> How can we maintain a Canadian community in any vital sense of the term against the unparalleled strength—in every aspect of life—of our great neighbour? . . . The Canadian state now turns to the highest function of a state, building the spiritual structure (the word is not used in the religious

sense) of a civilization, the material foundations of which it has already sturdily laid. (Ostry, 1978:73).

Government at the time of the Massey Commission was more concerned with the infrastructure of nation-building—the construction of pipelines, seaways, radio and television networks, and industries—rather than with the development of intellectual and cultural components. Nevertheless, by 1957, the Canada Council had been formed, financed by massive tax windfalls from the succession duties on the huge estates of two tycoons. The Canada Council gave the federal government for the first time a strong and active role in fostering and encouraging high culture. Curiously, this encouragement of the fine arts does not appear to have been seen as a means of providing material and content for the new telecommunications infrastructure; it was remote from the broadcasting, film, and commercial publishing industries. This gap between the producers of high culture and media and the consumers of artistic products continues to cause problems in Canada.

Later arguments for government intervention in high culture continue to be couched in terms of national development:

The fact that public goods cannot pass the market test has never been sufficient justification for not providing them. It is recognized that, while consumers cannot be made to purchase them individually, it does not follow that public goods are unwanted by individuals. Clean air and national defence are obvious examples. The market mechanism is not geared to handle this type of commodity and the public is usually content to pay for it collectively through government subventions.

In regard to the arts, there are many people who, though they may never buy concert tickets in their lives because of lack of interest or lack of access, would be saddened by the prospect of the total absence of live performances in their country. They are content to let government support such enterprises.

. . . Leaving aside such intangible concepts as the inherent value of beauty or the civilizing influence of aesthetic activity, there are a number of rather materialistic and mundane considerations which support these assumptions. One of these is the prestige which accrues to a country from its performing arts and the international recognition and acclaim which it receives. In a world in which we are concerned with the image we project, it is not illogical or unreasonable to spend public funds on aesthetic pursuits.

Moreover, the spin-off from artistic activity has important material and economic value. The multiplier effect of the Stratford Theatre or the Shaw Festival is significant for the communities in which they are located as well as for the province as a whole. They generate employment in the food and beverage industry, in transportation, hotels and restaurants, and in the service industries generally. Tax receipts from all the expenditures and purchases made by visitors and tourists to these attractions are significant. (Samlalsingh, 1982:50)

The arguments are and were a mixture of national unity and prestige, economic benefits, and a civilizing and educational role for government, supporting an intellectual and artistic elite.

Sport

Government involvement in sport, which followed the formation of the Canada Council by four years in 1961, also was in part a product of nation-building and the assertion of national identity. And, like culture, sport was also seen as a means for improving the well-being of the populace. International competition in hockey was a key factor. By 1960, Canada's supremacy in this "national" sport had been usurped by the Soviet Union, and Canadians were aware of the active government involvement in the sports programs of Russia and other Eastern European countries. Consternation at the lack of success of Canada's teams was widely expressed in both the press and Parliament. The advent and rapid growth of television in the late 1950's had contributed to deepening this concern at the same time that it encouraged broader interest in professional hockey and football through nation-wide exposure to a mass audience.

Professional sport became a large-scale commercial industry with appeal to both elites and masses. It also came to be seen less as a "pleasant pastime; amusement; diversion" and more as, on the one hand, a profit-making activity, and on the other hand, a focus for national pride and a vehicle through which the Canadian image could be extended abroad.

Before 1961 amateur sports organizations in Canada had never been strong at the national, provincial and local levels. In the 1950's, these organizations faced problems in staging national championships and financing teams to attend national events. There was an apparent need for government support and funding.

At the same time, physical educators, recreation leaders, and health professionals were concerned about the fitness of Canadians. They enlisted the aid of sports organizations and influential patrons, in particular the Duke of Edinburgh, to lobby the federal government to initiate mass sport and fitness programs. Failure in earlier efforts led them now to marry their interests with the interests of others who were concerned about Canada's declining fortune in international sports events.

Thus two concerns encouraged government intervention in sport: a concern about national prestige and the success of elite athletes, and a concern about mass fitness and recreation. The development of a mass audience through television provided a receptive climate for encouragement of elite athletes, but, at the same time, contributed to the sedentary lifestyle which gave cause for mass fitness programs. Prime Minister John Diefenbaker believed that sport was important for national unity and international prestige. But in general, government intervention in sport was a motherhood issue that was uncontentious, widely supported, and of little importance to most members of the government, parliamentarians, and senior public servants. There was no public examination or discussion of sport comparable to the Massey Commission and the ensuing debate in press and Parliament.

In 1961, Bill C-131, An Act to Encourage Fitness and Amateur Sport, was enacted by Parliament. It committed the federal government "to encourage, promote, and develop fitness and amateur sport in Canada." According to speeches by Prime Minister Diefenbaker and the Minister of National Health and Welfare, Waldo Monteith, the act was intended to encourage mass participation as well as to improve international sport performances. Sports leaders and physical educators hoped for improvement in physical fitness levels of Canadians and an increase in the number of sports participants (West, 1973). The media, supported by a substantial portion of the public, however, looked primarily for increased successes by Canadian amateur athletes (Paraschak, 1978). The two different programs, motives, and goals were married within one bill.

The program established by this act was not large; the maximum expenditure proposed to fulfill the legislation was $5 million *per annum*, and this amount was not reached for several years. In comparison, the Canada Council in 1960-61 spent $1.15 million on grants to organizations in the arts, some $143,000 on grants for the humanities, $127,000 in the social sciences, and $1.2 million on scholarships and fellowships for a total of some $2.6 million. St. Laurent noted that these programs of the Canada Council were intended to support:

> . . . the study and, I hope as a result of this study, the acquired knowledge of the treasures that have been provided by the experience, studies, and philosophies of past generations. When I say "past generations" I mean the generations that have succeeded each other for many thousands of years in the world. I mean that general knowledge of proper human behaviour that results from the accumulated experience of mankind since history has commenced to be written and not those special things that prepare for the exercise of a special avocation or profession. I mean the general broadening and training of the human mind so that the human individual whose mind it is may have as great benefit as one can derive from the accumulation of lore and knowledge over the centuries (Canada House of Commons, 1957:394)

It is apparent that sport fared well in comparison.

By the early sixties Canada was committed to active intervention and support of both culture and sport. The programs in both areas were established largely for reasons of nation-building and national prestige, coupled with concern over the development and well-being of individual Canadians. Financed at roughly comparable levels, these programs were not entered into on the basis of any deep analysis of their effect on the structures of political and social power in Canada, nor on an analysis of their costs and benefits, nor the distribution of costs and return between groups and classes in society. Rather, the program in sport was an outgrowth of Diefenbaker's personal interest and of public concern over international competition, while the establishment of the Canada Council was due to pressure from an intellectual elite combined with a timely financial windfall.

POLICIES AND ADMINISTRATION

Culture

The Canada Council was created as an autonomous, non-departmental agency, although its members, its director and associate director are appointed by the government. The council reports annually to Parliament, and its accounts are audited by the Auditor General. But it does not come under the Public Service Act, nor under the financial guidelines of the Treasury Board. The council invests and manages its own funds, and unlike government departments, is permitted to carry unspent revenues from one year to another (Milligan, 1979).

The Canada Council was originally intended to support itself by income from its original endowment, but since 1965, a growing proportion of its revenues has been provided by parliamentary appropriations—in 1977-78, these amounted to more than 85% of its budget. This, in turn, made it subject to annual budget review by the Treasury Board, which includes examinations of the purposes and goals towards which programs are directed, the efficiency of administration, and the effectiveness with which programs achieve their stated ends.

The contradiction that faces a cultural agency in a liberal democracy is that on the one hand a fundamental political and social value is independent and free inquiry, teaching, and expression, but on the other hand, the agency will inevitably limit, encourage, and distort the practice of these freedoms through support of some activities at the expense of others. The Canada Council resolved this contradiction in two ways: first by being independent and autonomous in policies and administration; and second, within the broad areas of its grants programs, by inviting proposals independently developed by applicants and subjecting them to a review by peers, rather than by initiating, directing, and commissioning research and artistic creations. As long as its independent sources of funds were adequate to support its activities, this autonomy and reactive rather than initiating mode of funding were acceptable. Not infrequently, however, the council was criticized for supporting apparently irrelevant and useless research and art. It was also criticized for not giving adequate support to Canadian studies, as opposed to research without direct reference or relevance to Canada.

Public briefs to the Massey Commission had seen the most urgent priority as being the promotion of Canadian culture (meaning 'high' culture) among the masses and the support of community level activities. But by 1962, the council had established a policy whereby support for the arts was to be directed only to professional arts groups. The council's second chairman, Claude Bissell, enunciated this policy as follows: "We believe that our revenues should go to the support of fulltime professional artists and organizations that are likely to achieve some degree of national prominence and to efforts to create an audience for first class performance" (Quoted in Ostry, 1978:75). This bias was evident in the Massey Report itself, and according to Crean (1976: 135-136), this "few but roses" theory of excellence was adopted on the assumption that Canadians would benefit more from concentrated excellence than from widespread competence.

Since 1968, there has been a concentrated effort by the Government of Canada to change its policy-making from a largely reactive and somewhat haphazard process, which decentralized much of the responsibility for initiating and refining policies within agencies, to a centralized, "rational" process in which the programs of all agencies are directed towards and evaluated in light of stated national goals. Much of the refining and initiating of policies comes from the center—the Prime Minister's office and the Cabinet Secretariat. The council has not been left unscathed by this process. In 1978, its responsibilities for the humanities and social sciences were diverted to a new Social Sciences and Humanities Research Council. This body is much more active than its predecessor in directing scholarly work towards approved national goals and issues—a policy developed in order to sustain government funding and approval. So far, criticism of this policy has been muted and largely confined to academic circles, but a lingering question remains as to whether this sort of direction and this utilitarian evaluation are appropriate for the well-being of the humanities and social sciences.

Sport

From the beginning, government programs for sport were less autonomous than for culture. The Minister of National Health and Welfare, not an independent council, was charged with the responsibility for carrying out the objects of the act To Encourage Fitness and Amateur Sport, including the establishment of federal-provincial cost-sharing agreements. Federal-provincial relations can, without much exaggeration, be described as the heart and soul of Canadian politics. The Canada Council in its early years was fortunate in not being involved in the traditional disputes. Education, and by inference culture, were provincial rather than federal responsibilities. The fledgling sports program was not so fortunate.

The act provided for the establishment of a National Advisory Council to advise the minister on matters referred to it and on other matters relating to the objects of the act. The advisory council was given the authority to make rules for regulating its own administration, but, unlike the Canada Council, was not given any executive power, program funds, or an independent secretariat. Finally, the act provided for the appointment of public servants for its administration, but the relationships between these public servants and the advisory council were not set down in the act.

The creation of the National Fitness and Amateur Sport Advisory Council was a compromise response to pressures from interest groups and politicians to create an independent agency similar in nature and function to the Canada Council. On the one hand, the federal government was not prepared to create such an independent council, because of an unfortunate experience with the Bank of Canada and because of public criticism of the Canada Council. On the other hand, it was not willing to take direct responsibility for implementing the provisions of the act by establishing a regular division and bureaucracy within a federal government department. In establishing a national advisory council, the federal government created a buffer group which would protect it from criticism, and, at the same time, would provide advice from various regions and from different program biases.

The council took over the role of policy development and assumed an executive function, except in federal-provincial cost-sharing agreements where policies and directions were determined by the minister. The federal government did not want to be seen to be interfering with the autonomy of national sport and related governing bodies and agencies. It was not very interested in the sports program and used the council to protect itself from the anticipated flood of supplicants and petitions for support (West, 1973:10). The public service at the time contained only one qualified sports administrator. This delegation of policy-making authority worked reasonably well for the first few years until the scope and complexity of the tasks which the advisory council had assumed became overwhelming (Canada Department of National Health and Welfare, 1968: Appendix 7 to the Minutes of the 19th Meeting, 25 and 26 November).

The advisory council membership represented diverse backgrounds and widely different views on key issues. As a result, the council's decisions were often based on bargain and compromise rather than agreement upon policies and directions. As the directorate staff grew in size and maturity, it became increasingly opposed to this style of policy-making. As a result, the minister was often confronted with two different sets of recommendations—one from the advisory council and a second from the directorate staff. Consequently, the minister began to listen more closely to the public servants, a change that was, not surprisingly, resented by the advisory council (Westland, 1979:40-41).

At first, federal government involvement in the program was indirect and consisted mainly of distributing funds to sports governing bodies and to the provinces in the form of federal-provincial cost-sharing agreements. These funds went largely to support mass fitness and sports programs which were favoured by the provincial governments of the day. But by 1968, conflicting views of the federal government role in the promotion of sport and physical fitness had become crystalized. The combination of mass programs and the development of elite athletes made in the original act in 1961 was increasingly difficult to maintain. The federal government was having little success in promoting and developing mass fitness and sports programs. Provincial directors of recreation felt that increased funding of their "grass roots" programs needed highest priority. Federal government efforts in the development of elite sport were not effective. Spurred on by the press and the Canadian public, sports governing bodies clamored for more money to improve international performance. Added to these frustrations was the realization that the federal government was receiving very little political acclaim for joint federal-provincial programs.

Sport had become important enough to Canadians to be used as an antidote to the divisive forces of greater provincial autonomy and Francophone nationalism in Quebec. As a result of extensive television exposure in the late fifties and sixties, sport became an integral part of the mass culture of the country. The federal government saw sport as a potential "master symbol" in its campaign for national unity. For sport to fill this role, however, a much higher profile and success level on the part of government-sponsored elite athletes was essential. International sport also experienced a tremendous growth in importance and exposure. Television gave it both wide coverage around the world and the monies with which to stage mammoth "sports spectacles." The growing importance of hockey in Europe and the Soviet Union and the success of these countries in international hockey competitions harmed Canada's international image and reputation; Canadians clamored for redress.

In 1968, Prime Minister Trudeau fulfilled a campaign promise by appointing a Task Force on Sport. The report of this three-person commission focused largely on elite sport, especially on hockey and the manner in which Canada might regain international hockey supremacy. In response, the National Advisory Council convinced federal officials to appoint P. S. Ross, a managerial and consultant firm, to study the wider aspects of sports and fitness in Canada. The broader scope and concerns expressed in their report helped to modify the impact of the Task Force Report.

Thus there was an increased emphasis on the development of elite athletes in the new sports policy statement made public in 1970. The federal government indicated its intention to establish new agencies and programs which would give it more direct influence over the development of sport and greater control over sport governing bodies and related agencies. Among the most important of these developments were the establishment of a national sports administration center in Ottawa, a grant-in-aid program to assist athletes in meeting training and competition costs, the establishment of a National Coaches' Association and Hockey Canada, and the initiation of a "Game Plan" in preparation for the Montreal Olympics. At the same time, the federal government attempted to maintain a commitment to the area of mass participation and physical fitness with the establishment of a Recreation Canada division in the Fitness and Amateur Sport Branch. An important part of the mandate of this division was the well-known "Participaction" program. But the incompatibility of mass participation and elite sport development was apparent in the new policy statement and later in program implementation.

The new policy statement commited the government to a direct and greater role in the development of sport. Elite sport became an instrument employed by the federal government and then by provincial governments for political ends. The great growth of government-sponsored sport extravaganzas in the 1970's was highlighted by the 1976 Olympic Games in Montreal. Sports governing bodies and elite athletes became dependent upon governmental support, and the relative autonomy from government which sport had enjoyed for 100 years in Canada was lost. The nature of sport and its meaning to Canadians was irrevocably changed. Elite amateur sport became professionalized and success in international competition a matter of national prestige and active government involvement. The federal government's choice of this role was a logical end to the path it had begun to follow in the 1960's.

CONCLUSIONS

This discussion of the comparative development of sport and cultural programs in Canada has emphasized several points. First, sport and culture were similar because government was involved actively in both spheres. The motives for government involvement included benefits to community well-being and nation-building and were based on the assumption that success and activity in both spheres encouraged legitimacy and support for the regime. A second motive was to provide cultural and personal benefits to individual Canadians.

Second, culture has developed as the more autonomous sphere. The reasons advanced for this distinction are that freedom of inquiry and expression is an essential political right; in comparison, the struggles within the sports sphere are often seen more as struggles for power without important content. Many people in sport are content with this contrast. But there are some who argue that sport has the potential for transformation in society, and is equally in need of autonomy from government involvement. The dominant form of sport in Canada, with its emphasis on performance, record, and spectacle is more and more being shaped by commercial interests and television, and by government intervention in its efforts to develop elite athletes. This development poses a serious threat to the existence of alternative forms of sport in our country. A strong autonomous voice is needed if these other forms of sport are to flourish.

Third, both programs, despite an expressed concern with mass culture and community development, are oriented towards elites and elite development. In culture, this took the form of supporting "high" culture and professional artists and scholars. In sport, this took the form of supporting the development and training of international caliber amateur athletes. Broader programs encouraging participation by the general public in sport and culture were relegated to the provinces, in part as an attempt to resolve federal-provincial rivalry.

Fourth, there has been a problem in relating the benefits of high culture to the "needs of society." High culture finds its roots in the broad western international tradition, and its relationship to the Canadian experience is not always apparent. In fact, on many occasions, the two are contrasted and opposed. The question of what the individual who has benefited from high culture does with these benefits is not one that can be resolved by economic analysis. As a result, there is a tendency to play down this benefit, and to stress those aspects which lead to a further end, such as Canadian unity, or resolution of problems such as aging or multiculturalism. Successful support of elite athletes by contrast has direct benefit and return to government in enhanced national pride.

Fifth, if the distinction between high and low culture has any validity, then sport is part of low culture. Sport has a large mass audience which includes a high proportion of the elite. Unlike much of high culture, sport is commercially successful. Competitions between elite athletes, even amateurs, are readily consumed by the mass audience.

Sixth, high culture, unlike elite sport competition, has not found ready access to the media. The relationships among audience, mass media, and performers are much weaker in culture than in sport. The audience for high culture is small. Nevertheless, it is a powerful elite. Mass culture in English-speaking Canada (music, writing, television drama, and film) remains dominated by American rather than Canadian products. Support of high culture has not translated into indigenous Canadian products for mass culture. There is, however, a greater linkage of the two and reliance on domestic products in French Canada. In sport, in comparison, there is a successful link between elite Canadian performers and the mass audience through the media.

Seventh, changes in television technology, including cable, pay television, and satellites will give most of the people of Canada access to ten, twenty, perhaps hundreds of different and competing channels. This will divide the audience so that, probably, the present mass market will no longer exist. Canadian, American, local, regional, foreign, and other sources will compete for small shares of a huge and varied market. The commercial market for television will be more like the book or magazine market rather than the present film and television market. This will make the difference between "high" and "mass" culture and market inappropriate and irrelevant. The need to assert and preserve a Canadian identity and industry in this diffuse market will be both an opportunity for Canadian sport and culture and a challenge to governments.

Finally, the roles of both sport and "high" culture in modern society and politics are not well understood. Government became involved in both areas in order to respond to stated demands and to meet stated needs, and through its involvement it has substantially changed both the sport and cultural domains. What the outcomes of these changes are and will be in terms of nation-building, individual well-being and the development of mass or elite culture, is still far from clear. The stated demands and needs, and the outcomes, are perhaps only tenuously related.

REFERENCES

Canada
1967   Canada: One Hundred, 1867-1967. Queen's Printer.

Canada Department of National Health and Welfare
1961-68 Annual Reports of the Fitness and Amateur Sport Program.
1962-68 Minutes of the National Advisory Council Meetings.

Canada House of Commons
        Debates.

Canada Royal Commission on Broadcasting (The Fowler Commission)
1957   Report of the Royal Commission on Broadcasting. Ottawa: Queen's Printer.

Crean, S. M.
1976   Who's Afraid of Canadian Culture. Don Mills: General Publishing.

Milligan, Frank
1979   The Canada Council as a public body. Canadian Public Administration, summer 1979, volume 22, number 2.

Ostry, Bernard
1978   The Cultural Connection. Toronto: McClelland and Stewart.

Paraschak, V.
1978   "Selected Factors Associated With the Enactment of the 1961 Fitness and Amateur Sport Act. Unpublished Master's thesis," University of Windsor.

Samlalsingh, R.
1982   Market Forces and the Arts. Policy Options, III, 5, (September/October).

West, J.
1973   Fitness, Sport and the Canadian Government. Ottawa: Fitness and Amateur Sport Branch.

Westland, C.
1979   Fitness and Amateur Sport in Canada. Ottawa: Canadian Parks and Recreation Association.

THE UNEASY PARTNERSHIP OF CITIES AND PROFESSIONAL SPORT: PUBLIC POLICY CONSIDERATIONS

Arthur Johnson
University of Maryland, Baltimore County

FORTY-TWO AMERICAN AND SEVEN CANADIAN cities host professional sports franchises in baseball, basketball, football and hockey. With few exceptions, if any, these professional sports franchises receive public subsidies in some form, e.g., below-market rents for use of publicly-owned stadiums and arenas. At least 13 of the 42 American communities hosting sports franchises have been confronted with demands for increased sports subsidies (such as stadium improvements and tax breaks) in the period from 1980 to 1982. Almost without exception, removal of the franchise from the host community was an implied, if not explicit, threat underlying negotiations.

The interaction between sports entrepreneurs and municipal governments has been little studied by students of urban public policy. The recent abandonment of Oakland by the National Football League Raiders is an exception that has attracted some attention. However, academics as well as journalists have focused upon the motives of team owners and have ignored the socio-political-economic environment of the conflict.

This paper reviews professional sports franchises since 1950, identifies trends related to franchise instability, and analyzes the franchise-city relationship in its political context. It concludes with an examination of the public policy options that have been suggested to resolve the problem of franchise instability.

TEAM MOVEMENT AND PUBLIC SUBSIDY

Attention focuses on the relationship between municipalities and sports franchises when a city without a franchise in a particular sport seeks to acquire one, either by convincing a league to expand to its environs or by persuading an existing franchise in another community to relocate. The courtship of a city's sports franchise by another forces the host city to commit resources to convince the franchise not to move.

In the past, league rules ultimately have determined the suitor city's success. Each league has specific rules governing the creation and location of new franchises as well as the movement of existing franchises. History suggests that although only a small number of owners are needed to veto a move, rejection of a proposed relocation is rare unless the owner proposing to move is a maverick who has been at odds with other team owners (see Quirk, 1973: 46-60). It also should be noted that each franchise has exclusive rights over a "home territory," usually a 25-50 mile radius from the team's home stadium or arena, and must give its approval before another team in the same league can operate within that territory.

Obviously, these rules raise anti-trust questions. Leagues find themselves attacked by rival leagues for expanding into new cities as well as for not expanding.[1] Similarly, leagues have been sued by a municipality for disapproving a move by an existing franchise as well as for permitting relocation (Rozelle, 1982: 3; Ziegler, 1982; Stern, 1982)[2]. This dilemma is related directly to the unsettled anti-trust question concerning the legal nature of sports leagues (are they joint ventures or separate business entities?) and the fact that the demand for sports franchises by communities outstrips supply due to the league's conscious control of the number of franchises. In their attempts to resolve this dilemma, the leagues have focused their attention on the anti-trust issue and argued that they are joint ventures. Their critics reject that position and cite the second factor as the principal source of the dilemma.

The case of Oakland and the National Football League (NFL) Raiders, illustrative of the leagues' dilemma and the complexity of the anti-trust issue, threatens to invalidate league rules governing relocation. The NFL (at this writing) appears to have lost on the anti-trust question (its rules governing relocation are unreasonable and, therefore, cannot be applied in preventing an owner from relocating his franchise) in an apparent reversal of case law.[3] As a result of the Raiders' challenge to league rules, the NFL sought passage in 1981 of legislation that would have defined a sports league as a "*de facto* single economic entity" and in 1982 of legislation (S. 2784) that will (1) allow leagues to keep a team in its existing location even if the owner desires to move, (2) establish rules for the division of league revenues (revenue sharing), and (3) apply to pending actions (i.e., the Oakland Raiders). The 1982 legislation, called the Sports Community Protection Act, ostensibly would resolve the anti-trust question in the leagues' favor and allow them to protect community interests against *ownership* relocation desires but would permit *league* decisions to relocate teams. In fact, much of the testimony during four days of hearings before the Senate Judiciary Committee was concerned with league revenue sharing and the future impact of pay television on revenues. A narrower bill (S. 2821), confined only to franchise movement, was not endorsed by the sports leagues but did receive the qualified support of the football and baseball player associations and representatives of the Los Angeles Coliseum and the Raiders (U.S. Congress, 1982).

Although the anti-trust issue is most complex (see Weistart and Lowell, 1979: 687-759), it is relatively easy to understand how the law of supply and demand has affected city-sport relationship. Simply put, the control of the number and location of franchises has given sports entrepreneurs leverage to exact concessions from those cities desirous of attracting a franchise as well as from those desperate to retain an existing franchise. The imbalance of supply and demand leads cities to attempt to outbid one another for franchises. This increases the public subsidy required to attract and retain a sports franchise and presumably contributes to the instability of franchise location.

The instability of sports franchise location is not a new phenomenon. While baseball and hockey franchises were stable in the years before 1950, such was not the case in professional basketball and football. Cities won and lost teams as rival leagues in those sports warred. Large and medium-size cities such as Boston, Chicago, Cleveland, Denver, St. Louis and Toronto were affected as were smaller communities such as Anderson, Oshkosh, Sheboygan and Waterloo.

The extent of the problem since 1950 can be documented by tracing the number of franchise creations, relocations and failures for each sport. Table I reports the number of new franchises, relocations and failures in the four sports since 1950. A total of 78 sports franchise relocations occurred in sports leagues that existed two years or longer. Numerous changes in location, team name and ownership occurred in the American Basketball League and the World Football League.

Before 1957-58, franchise relocation primarily was due to the inability to succeed financially in a specific location and was perceived as a sign of league weakness. Such a view had to be qualified in 1958 with baseball's abandonment of Brooklyn and New York for the West Coast (parroted by the NBA in 1960 and 1962). Financial distress was no longer a justification for relocation. Once league expansion was initiated in the early 1960's, mainly in attempts to abort rival leagues, factors other than a team's gate performance, especially civic inducements, became most important variables in a franchise owner's relocation decisions. Thus, 95 acres of prime real estate led the Rams to leave the Los Angeles Coliseum. The potential pay television wealth of the Los Angeles market attracted the Raiders from Oakland, as the size of the Atlanta television market attracted the Braves from Milwaukee. The inducements that municipalities are willing to offer, while most often taking the form of playing facilities built with public funds and tax abatements for those that are not, have included land, broadcasting arrangements, and assumption of past debts (see especially Rosentraub and Nunn, 1978).

Stability of franchises in a particular league may be deceiving. The NFL, for example, recognizes only one approved franchise shift (Chicago to St. Louis) in the last two decades (U.S. Congress, Sept. 20, 1982: 20). However, 19 of 28 NFL clubs have changed stadiums during that time. Several teams have moved from one jurisdiction to another, usually from the central city to the suburbs, although one team has actually relocated in a different state. Yet these teams remain within their home territories. These moves, including that of the Rams from Los Angeles to Anaheim, are not considered a relocation by the NFL. Clearly, however, cities do suffer from such moves in the loss of economic benefits and/or by having continued responsibility for the costs of a playing facility with one less tenant or without its sole tenant (see Foschio, 1976).[4] In several areas, Boston for example, a virtual war is being fought between central cities and their suburbs over sports franchises.

Relocation decisions have been justified in terms of the public interest by referring to geographical balance, or, in other words, bringing professional sports to all regions of the nation. Congress voiced concern about the geographical pattern of franchise location as early as 1952 (U.S. Congress, 1952), but it was unable to force baseball to expand until the Continental League was proposed in 1959-60. Congress was able to insure that the NFL would not reduce the number of football franchises in existence (and would not relocate the Oakland Raiders or the San Francisco Forty-Niners, or the New York Giants or Jets) after the AFL-NFL merger in 1966. At that time, it extracted a promise to expand to four new cities. Similar concern for franchise location was voiced when basketball and hockey league mergers were proposed. Yet, significant league expansion seems more directly related to rival leagues than Congressional pressure.

In sum, franchise instability in each sport has been the rule. Each league has experienced at least one period of some form of franchise relocation affecting municipalities. Franchise relocation can be attributed to financial losses of the team owner and league weakness as well as to factors relating to the short term profit potential of an alternative location. The significant conclusion is that as long as franchises are able to relocate and leagues control the expansion process, sports entrepreneurs will be at an advantage in their dealings with local governments, and cities will continue to compete with one another for new or existing franchises by offering publicly funded inducements. These public subsidies are likely to escalate in the future as cities compete more intensely for a limited number of sports franchises. NFL commissioner Pete Rozelle (U.S. Congress, 1982) has testified:

> . . . if we have a state of law that a club can go whenever it wants to if its lease [for a stadium] is up. . . you are going to have auction of a franchise. I assure you you will have auctioning of franchises (p. 47).

THE UNIQUENESS OF PROFESSIONAL SPORTS

Municipalities have sought to prevent franchise moves by utilizing the anti-trust laws against team owners and league officials. Sports entrepreneurs have sought anti-trust immunity consistently since 1951 (Johnson, 1979). A basic premise in their presentations before Congressional committees is that professional sports are unique. They argue that their uniqueness derives from the

Statistical Summary of Professional Sports Franchise Creation, Movement, and Demise

	Baseball[a]			Basketball[b]			Hockey[c]			Football[d]		
	cr	mov	de	cr	mov	de	cr	mov	de	cr	mov	de
1950-60	-	5	-	-	4	11	-	-	-	8	3	6
1961-70	8	5	-	17	12	-	8	-	-	5	2	-
1971-82	2	1	-	6	14	8	22	14	15	2	8	-
Totals	10	11	-	23	30	19	30	14	15	15	13	6

Legend:
cr = franchises created (usually through expansion)
mov = franchise relocations
de = franchise failures

a - In 1950 Major League Baseball was represented in 10 cities by 16 teams. In 1960, 16 teams were located in 15 cities; in 1970, 24 teams were located in 22 cities; and today, 26 teams are located in 24 cities.

b - In 1950, 19 National Basketball Association teams were located in 19 cities. In 1960, eight teams were located in 8 cities; in 1970, 25 teams were located in 24 cities and in 1982, 23 teams were located in 23 cities. The American Basketball League, which was created in 1962 and survived one year, is not included in this summary. The American Basketball Association was created in 1968 and merged with the NBA in 1977.

c - The National Hockey League was represented in six cities by six teams in 1950 and 1960. In 1970, 14 teams were in 14 cities. In 1982, 21 teams were in 21 cities. The World Hockey Association was created in 1972 and absorbed by the NHL in 1979.

d - The National Football League was represented in 11 cities by 13 teams in 1950. In 1960, 21 teams (eight from the newly-created American Football League), were in 18 cities. The AFL and NFL merged in 1966, and in 1970, 26 teams were in 25 cities. In 1982, 28 teams were in 27 cities. The new United States Football League promises to add 12 teams and two cities. The World Football League, which was created in 1974 and survived for one year, is not included in this summary.

nature of sports leagues; although each team is an independent economic unit, each is dependent upon the others for its ability to produce a product (the game). The nature of sport is emphasized as opposed to its economic aspects. Bowie Kuhn, Commissioner of Baseball, testifying before the House Select Committee on Professional Sports (1976), made the case for all sports.

> . . . when you are in a team sport you can't compete the way you can if you are in the steel industry or the bread business or something else where you can put your competitor out of business and if he is gone that is the system and the system will work without him, whereas if you put your competitor out of business by outcompeting him in professional sports you destroy your league and when you destroy your league you destroy the business you operate in (p. 30).

On the other hand league officials speak as businessmen when opposing tax legislation, broadcasting regulations, or other potentially injurious government action. This is the case especially when team owners wish to justify franchise relocation. They argue that it is unjust "to force the owner of a business to continue to sustain financial losses operating in one location when he believes he could do much better elsewhere" (Noll, 1974: 412). This especially is unjust when no other business is so treated.

In sum, sports entrepreneurs when arguing for favorable treatment emphasize the uniqueness of their activity and downplay its business aspects. On the other hand, when defending themselves against regulatory or other limiting government action they emphasize the economics of their operations and compare themselves to other businesses. Indeed, each sport has claimed to be experiencing financial problems and each has predicted ruin as the likely result of each oversight proposal considered.

It is desirable therefore to determine the nature of professional sport and to decide if professional sport in some way is unique. To that end, it appears fruitless to deny either its sport or business aspects. It possesses both, and that fact becomes important in the question of franchise relocation.

It is not unusual for industries to attempt to convince legislative bodies of their uniqueness (Sims, 1976: 288). It is not the nature of sports leagues that attracts our attention, but the enthusiasm, interest and identity that a team provokes within its locale. Many fans do view a team as theirs, and owners encourage that. Thus, the Mayor of Kansas City (Berkeley, 1982: 145) is correct when he asserts, "On the one hand they [sports franchises] sell entertainment, but they also sell civic identity, emotion and community involvement."

This aspect of sport, which the sports entrepreneurs themselves promote, makes sport akin to a cultural resource of a community or region. Indeed, Congress has spoken to the issue of a right to access for fans (Johnson, 1979: 113-114).

Sport also is a business. It does not matter for our purposes whether it is big business or small. The fact that sports franchises are profit oriented, however, becomes most important when we recognize sport as a cultural resource. That combination of cultural resources with a profit goal is unique. That is, if sport were solely a cultural enterprise without a profit motive one set of public actions (i.e., subsidy, permanent location) might be appropriate. That is not the case. If sport were solely a profit making venture, the admonition that "a businessman cannot be forced to do business when he does not want to" could be accepted without a second thought. That is not the case either. It is the combined cultural-business character of sport that creates dilemmas when subsidies and team relocation are debated.

No widespread excitement occurs in a city when a medium-size factory shuts down and relocates. That which does arise usually originates from those who directly suffer—the employees. Even large-scale shutdowns evoke only limited negotiations and small increments of social services from city governments. The public concern in these cases usually is the loss of jobs, not the loss of the specific company. With sport, of course, the public concern (at least in the short run) is for the loss of the team due to its symbolic importance and the fact that a facility with few alternative uses is the city's liability.

If it is valid to view professional sports as a cultural resource as well as a business, new questions about the city-sport relationship emerge and the notion of partnership suggests itself. Baltimore's Mayor Donald Schaeffer (1982: 17) has quoted Edward Bennett Williams, owner of the Washington Redskins and Baltimore Orioles, as acknowledging that "teams are held in trust for the cities where they function." If so, permanence is implied.

If our view is valid, the legal questions shift from those of antitrust to those of rights—ownership rights versus those of the public to maintain a recognized cultural resource. In that case, subsidies to attract and retain a franchise may be justified even if economic costs outweigh benefits; teams can be expected to contribute something to their host community in return for patronage and subsidies; and communities may have a legal as well as a moral right to prevent a team from relocating. Ultimately, these become questions of public policy for local officials to decide within the political and economic context of their communities.

THE POLITICAL CONTEXT

This section of the paper is concerned with two types of communities—those without a sports franchise and desirous of obtaining one, and those possessing a sports franchise and desirous of retaining it. It places the policy decisions related to the attraction and retention of a sports franchise in the context of urban politics, a context which the literature ignores. In doing so, the analysis offers an alternative to those that describe such decisions in terms of an elite conspiracy (see, for example, Lowenfish, 1978: 80; Bogarsky and Bogarsky, 1974: 178-179).

Yates (1982) characterizes urban decisionmaking as fragmented, unstable and reactive. While there are many types of decision games, Yates argues that officials' ability to treat problems is often constrained. He (1982) concludes that:

> the greater the number of participants and/or the more that participants are not controlled by city hall, the more likely it is that the demands will require zero-sum decisions, and the more likely, too, that symbolic politics of a highly polarizing nature will arise (p. 120).

Thus, local officials will welcome the rare issue that promises community consensus and will allow them to demonstrate leadership. If the issue also permits them to manipulate political symbols and promotes economic development, it will be even more attractive. The pursuit of a sports franchise is just such a policy for cities without one. It is nearly impossible for any official to resist.

The decision to seek a sports franchise for one's community, therefore, is primarily a political rather than an economic decision, regardless of the economic data generated to justify franchise pursuit and subsidy. The likelihood of opposition to the decision at this stage is miniscule since most groups will not perceive the possibility of specific costs. The support of the media is likely to keep public support high. Thus, although an unusual sight, it should not have been surprising to hear 50,000 fans chanting in unison "we want the Colts" during an exhibition game in Jacksonville played by the Colts after the team's owner had made it known he wished to leave Baltimore.

Opposition is likely to erupt when it is understood a playing facility must be provided by that city. Groups will oppose the selected location of the stadium and its cost. The former will impose specific costs (i.e., relocation or disruption of neighborhood lifestyle) upon those in the stadium neighborhood, while the latter can create general fear of higher taxes or opportunity for symbolic protest (Johnson, 1982). Activists are likely to argue that the money used to build the playing facility could be better spent on food for the hungry, housing, education, etc.

This type of argument, however, is misdirected. Funds spent for franchise subsidy, such as stadium construction, most often are obtained through long term loans (bonded indebtedness) and categorical grants from state and federal sources. They appear in a city's capital budget. The policy areas for which opponents demand increased funding are not likely to be eligible for funding from such categorical grants. Furthermore, no city is willing to borrow long term to attack social problems. Funding for these policy areas appears in the operational budget, which often is not very flexible. The point is that despite obvious need to attack specific urban problems, no city is going to increase its operational expenditures by millions of dollars to do so (see Peterson 1981: 46-50). There are obvious political limits to which tax rates can be raised to address such issues. The expenditure of funds for a sports facility is spread out over a long period of time and, therefore, does not have the same impact upon tax rates. This type of subsidy expenditure, therefore, does not take money from the poor directly nor is it available to address different types of urban problems. Such debates, however, often become ideological and are beyond the control of public officials.

Officials must be careful not to oversell the benefits of acquiring a franchise or building a sports facility. If this occurs citizens may believe they were deceived and their subsequent political alienation may defeat future projects. As Burck (1973: 182) concluded from his analyses of stadium campaigns in Seattle and New Orleans, "civic pride can take a terrible battering when the voters feel they've been had."

A frequent promise is that the arrival of a new sports franchise will somehow allow taxes to be lowered. Even if new tax revenues are in excess of new expenditures related to the franchise, it is unlikely that taxes will be lowered. The demand for new or improved services is so insatiable that new revenues are laid claim to as rapidly as they are collected. Thus, the lowering of the tax rate also is a political decision and an unlikely one today in urban centers because of its implications for service delivery.[5]

Once a city obtains a franchise it must then work at retaining it. Due to the symbolic importance of the franchise to a city, no official will want to take responsibility for losing it to another city. Officials may still face a dilemma, however. Although few citizens will wish to lose their team, there may be substantial opposition to meeting an owner's demands for additional public funding. The officials' dilemma is clear when we realize that as a fan, a citizen may be opposed to having the team move, but that same individual as a taxpayer may be adamantly against additional subsidies.

The dilemma is further complicated by the fact that, similar to the demands for subsidy from other business interests in the city, those of the sports entrepreneurs are likely to emerge when the city is most vulnerable—that is, when it can least afford to lose revenue producing enterprises but also when it can least afford to subsidize them. Thus, Prince George's County, Maryland, in fiscal difficulty due to a voter imposed tax limitation, granted tax abatement to arena and franchise owner Abe Pollin in the face of his threats to relocate the NHL Washington Capitals. Boston, in similar difficulty, in part due to voter-mandated reductions in property taxes, granted tax relief and subsidies to the owners of Fenway Park and Boston Garden to quiet their discontent and threats to move franchises from Boston.

The irony is that obtaining a sports franchise, which once was an ideal issue for public officials, has now become one of many potentially harmful issues over which they have little control. The team owner is no longer bearing new idealized gifts to the city but has now been reduced to one of many interests scrambling for scarce public monies. The publicity that originally helped obtain subsidies may now be harmful.

To avoid political harm, it appears that elected officials in some cities have been content to allow their stadium authorities to negotiate with team owners over the conditions necessary to keep them from moving. Their entry at the last hour into these negotiations appears to be without effect. Such a strategy has proven disastrous for Los Angeles and Oakland. On the other hand, where elected officials, usually the mayor, have taken the lead in negotiating with team owners (Pittsburgh and Baltimore, for example), it appears they have been successful, at least in the short run.

Nevertheless, it is clear that public officials, whether seeking a new franchise or attempting to retain an existing one, are at a disadvantage in their dealings with sports entrepreneurs. The concluding section speaks to policy options.

SUMMARY AND CONCLUSIONS

In sum, city officials seek to attract and retain sports franchises in cooperation with other community interests in order to maintain a city's economic and psychological health. Public subsidy is the means for doing this. League officials and team owners are at an advantage in their negotiations with cities due to the scarcity of available franchises. Franchises appear to have complete freedom of movement and may choose to relocate whenever it suits their financial interest to do so regardless of a community's history of support.

To prevent widespread relocation, various proposals have been put forth to make it more difficult to relocate or to make franchise creation and league entry easier. These proposals range from absolute prohibition of franchise relocation to complete freedom of movement and from a government regulatory body for sports to continuation of the present system of self-regulation.

It is unlikely that Congress will choose to resolve the problem. Congress historically has preferred to "remain in the grandstand" rather than intervene in the affairs of professional sports (Johnson, 1979). It found little merit in a proposal to provide federal assistance to cities negotiating with sports leagues and teams (Foschio, 1976), and it failed to create a sports commission when it was proposed in 1972.

More recently, Congress has chosen not to act on tax legislation (HR 2557) that would penalize team owners involved in a "prohibited move" (i.e., more than 50 miles from former home stadium with certain exceptions). Legislation proposing criteria under which a financially troubled franchise would be allowed to relocate has met NFL opposition, on the grounds it would generate excessive litigation over criteria definition and that owners could easily doctor their books. This opposition likely will prove fatal. The NFL attempt to gain an anti-trust exemption so that it may control relocations without judicial interference is not likely to succeed. The complicating variable is the promise of new franchises to the districts of the bill's sponsors. If that is a serious consideration surprise passage could occur.[6]

Judicial administration of relocation issues is also unlikely. "The judicial process is unsuited for the type of regulation necessary where public control of a private firm is desired" (Weistart and Lowell, 1979: 743). Abuse of the "home court advantage," much discussed in the cases of the Oakland Raiders and Milwaukee Braves, also appears to make judicial oversight undesirable.

The decision, however, to consider Oakland's right under California law to use eminent domain to prevent the Raiders' relocation makes real the suggestion that sports franchises are analogous to public utilities. While California law may permit such a taking (see City of Oakland, 1980: 7-13), Weistart and Lowell (1979: 742-743) suggest general principles of law would reject the sport-as-public utility argument.

> It would be difficult to argue that a local sports franchise has the characteristics of a public utility as that term has been historically applied. While the services it offers may be of economic importance, that fact alone has not traditionally provided a reason for judicial control. Any firm with a large payroll or significant sales may be important to the local economy. The element missing from a sports operation, and from most other significant local enterprises, is the presence of an activity affecting the basic public need for food, shelter, and sanitation. Even if the concept of "public welfare" were expanded to include emotional well-being, it would require a quantum leap to find that privately-run forms of entertainment were of vital importance. In short, there is little law to support the application of public utility concepts to sports enterprises.

The argument that sports franchises represent community cultural resources has not been attempted yet, but it too may strain judicial interpretation. Remaining options include adjusting league rules and self-help on the part of franchise cities.

The court which found against the NFL in the Raiders case implied that a more reasonable vote requirement than unanimity or three-fourths on relocation might be acceptable. However, any movement to reach such voting criteria will only make it easier to relocate, something the cities do not want. On the other

hand, history suggests that it is rare when a league denies relocation requests. Thus, it is questionable what impact new vote requirements may have.

Noll (1974: 414-415) suggests that leagues be forced to expand
whenever someone is willing to put up a reasonable amount
of money for a franchise. While this speaks to the franchise scarcity issue, it is doubtful if it would resolve the relocation problem. Cities prefer an established franchise to an expansion team.
Thus, Oakland reportedly refused an expansion team, and instead demanded return of the Raiders. Cities would continue
to bid for each other's franchises rather than host a new team.
The fact that many of the teams in the new leagues of the 1960's
and 1970's were denied use of public facilities attests to the cities'
support of existing leagues and teams.

If proposals for change are not likely to be adopted or, if
adopted, have little impact, self-help remains the last option.
A union of sports cities, suggested by one commentator, is unlikely
to be effective since it could exercise no control over members
or non-members who desired a sports franchise. Officials must
learn to negotiate better and more aggressively, to be willing to
take risks, and to seek alternatives to sports as economic projects and objects of city pride. They must not believe they have
no option but to grant all that the franchise owner demands.
Nearly every sports city has a market and facilities that are desired
by the owner.

Teams appear to be short-term profit oriented. If that is the
case a lease that is generous early but seeks to recoup costs during the middle and late years may be salable to an owner. A short-
term lease that gives the city but not the team options of renewal
may be negotiable under certain conditions.

Perhaps an agreement whereby the team purchases the
stadium with a city leaseback agreement will meet an owner's
need for tax shelter. Such an arrangement not only meets the
short term financial needs, but gives him or her a financial stake
in remaining in the city.

The city's officials must work hard at involving the team's players
and owners with the city itself. Their psychological attachment
to the city is as important as the fans' identity with the team.
Markham and Teplitz (1981: 28) report that Detroit Tigers owner
John Fetzer turned down an opportunity to move to the suburbs
because "it would be the end of midtown Detroit." When this
commitment occurs, it is the beginning of partnership.

A true partnership may emerge in Baltimore between the city and the Orioles. As rental payment for stadium usage, the city shared equally, on a one-year trial basis, the team's profits. The more fans the team drew, the more revenue the city earned. Whether such an arrangement will continue on a long-term basis is questionable, but its symbolic significance should not be dismissed.

As long as franchise scarcity exists, officials will be at a bargaining disadvantage. They must decide to what limits they are willing and able to go to meet ownership demands. Satisfying those demands may lead to similar demands from others, especially those who can claim to attract tourists to the city. Too large a subsidy package may be demoralizing to the community and lead to political costs greater than losing a team. Instead, officials might think of other images, aside from sport, that they might foster for their city. If successful, it will be more to the team owner's benefit to be associated with the city than the reverse. At this point, of course, the leverage shifts.

Finally, assuming the status quo will remain, officials need to consider cost sharing with neighboring jurisdictions and higher levels of government. In most cases a sufficient number of citizens from surrounding jurisdictions attend games and relate to a team to justify their government's participation in the subsidy of the team. Similarly, the state benefits from a team's presence, and might be persuaded to help support the costs of hosting it. To achieve cost sharing, the city's officials must lobby their counterparts and perhaps use the threat of relocation to their advantage.

Public subsidy of sports franchises creates a partnership between city and team. It is a partnership that is not understood well and one that is often misrepresented in the literature. It is an economic partnership based upon local politics. It is, at present, a most uneasy partnership.

NOTES

1.   An example of the former is American Football League v. National Football League 205 F. Supp. 60 (D. Md. 1962), affirmed 323 F. 2d 124 (4th cir. 1963). An example of the latter is Mid-South Grizzlies, et al. v. National Football League et al., E.D. Pa. Civ. No. 79 4373JLM.
2.   An example of the former is the on-going Los Angeles Coliseum case. An example of the latter is San Diego v. National League of Pro-

fessional Baseball Clubs, Civil No. 73-529 (S.D. Cal. filed Dec. 12, 1973) which was eventually withdrawn.

3. Until the Los Angeles Coliseum case, the precedent had been San Francisco Seals Ltd. v. National Hockey League, 379 F. Supp. 966 (Cent. D. Cal. 1974), which confirmed the right of the NHL to determine that a club should remain in its present location.

4. Representatives of the Los Angeles Coliseum estimate an annual loss of $750,000 from its net revenues due to the Rams' departure (Robertson, 1982: 5).

5. Rosentraub and Nunn (1978) have demonstrated that it is unlikely that smaller suburban communities will sufficiently capture the economic benefits of a franchise to offset the costs of subsidies due to the fact that benefits will spill over into the center city and neighboring jurisdictions.

6. The other aspect of this is Commissioner Rozelle's firm assertion that there will be no expansion of the NFL during the present state of confusion. Thus, unless this legislation is adopted, the NFL will not consider expansion plans (U.S. Congress, 1982).

REFERENCES

Berkeley, Richard L.
1982   "Statement" on the Major League Sports Community Protection Act of 1982 before the Committee on the Judiciary, United States Senate.

Bogarsky, Nancy and William Bogarsky
1974   Back Room Politics. Los Angeles: J. P. Tarcher.

Burck, Charles
1973   "Superstadium game." Fortune 87 (March): 103 ff.

City of Oakland
1980   "Points and authorities in opposition to motion for judgment on the pleadings and summary judgment," City of Oakland v. The Oakland Raiders, Ltd. et al. Superior Court of California, County of Monterey (May 21), No. 76044.

Foschio, Leslie
1976   "Statement." pp. 507-524 in U.S. Congress, House Select Committee on Professional Sports, Inquiry Into Professional Sports, Part 1: Hearings Ninety-Fourth Congress, Second Session. Washington, D.C.: Government Printing Office.

Johnson, Arthur
1979 "Congress and Professional Sports: 1951-1978." ANNALS (September): 102-115.
1982 "Government, opposition and sport: the role of domestic sports policy in generating political support." Journal of Sport and Social Issues (Fall/Winter): 22-34.

Kuhn, Bowie
1976 "Statement." pp. 17-51 in U.S. Congress, House Select Committee on Professional Sports, Inquiry Into Professional Sports, Part 1: Hearings Ninety-Fourth Congress, Second Session. Washington, D.C.: Government Printing Office.

Lowenfish, Lee
1978 "A tale of many cities." Journal of the West (July): 71-82.

Markham, John and Paul Teplitz
1981 Baseball Economics and Public Policy. Lexington, Mass.: Lexington Books.

Noll, Roger
1974 "Alternatives in sports policy," pp. 411-428 in R. Noll (ed.) Government and the Sports Business. Washington, D.C.: Brookings Institution.

Okner, Benjamin
1974 "Subsidies of stadiums and arenas," pp. 325-347 in R. Noll (ed.) Government and the Sports Business. Washington, D.C.: Brookings Institution.

Peterson, Paul
1981 City Limits. Chicago: University of Chicago Press.

Quirk, James
1973 "An economic analysis of team movements in professional sports." Law and Contemporary Problems 38 (Winter/Spring): 42-66.

Robertson, William
1982 "Statement" on The Major League Sports Community Protection Act of 1982 before the Committee on the Judiciary, United States Senate.

Rosentraub, Mark and S. R. Nunn
1978 "Suburban city investment in professional sports: estimating the fiscal returns of the Dallas Cowboys and Texas Rangers to in-

vestor communities." American Behavioral Scientist 21 (January/February): 393-414.

Rozelle, Pete
1982   "Statement" on The Major League Sports Community Protection Act of 1982 before the Committee on the Judiciary, United States Senate.

Schaeffer, Donald
1982   "Statement" on Professional Sports Anti-Trust Immunity. Hearing before the Committee on the Judiciary, United States Senate, Ninety-Seventh Congress, Second Session.

Sims, Joseph
1976   "Statement" pp. 285-302 in U.S. Congress, House Select Committee on Professional Sports, Inquiry Into Professional Sports, Part 2: Hearings Ninety-Fourth Congress, Second Session. Washington, D.C.: Government Printing Office.

Stern, David
1982   "Statement" on The Major League Sports Community Protection Act of 1982 before the Committee on the Judiciary, United States Senate.

U.S. Congress
1952   Organized Baseball. Report on the Subcommittee on Study of Monopoly Power. House Report 2002. Eighty Second Congress, Second Session. Washington, D.C.: Government Printing Office.

U.S. Congress
1982   Transcripts of Hearings on S. 2784 The Major League Sports Community Protection Act of 1982 before the Committee on the Judiciary, United States Senate, August 16, September 16, September 20.

Weistart, John and Cyn Lowell
1979   The Law of Sports. Charlottesville, Va.: Bobbs Merrill Co.

Yates, Douglas
1982   The Ungovernable City. Cambridge, Mass.: MIT Press.

Ziegler, John
1982   "Statement" on The Major League Sports Community Protection Act of 1982 before the Committee on the Judiciary, United States Senate.

THE DISTRIBUTION OF ATHLETIC SCHOLARSHIPS AMONG WOMEN IN INTERCOLLEGIATE SPORT

Jay J. Coakely, University of Colorado, Colorado Springs
Patricia L. Pacey, University of Colorado, Boulder

APART FROM ISSUES related to Title IX, such as per capita expenditures and general budget matters, very little is known about intercollegiate women's athletes. In order to learn more about their biographies, current experiences, and future goals we attempted to contact as many of them as possible from a sample of 146 NCAA institutions. The schools were selected to provide a representative cross section of programs from all regions of the country at each of the three division levels.

During the fall semester of 1979 the athletic directors at each of the schools were sent letters informing them that they were to be part of an NCAA-funded study of "The Factors Affecting the Participation of Females in Intercollegiate Athletics."[1] As one phase of this study each of the athletic departments received a package of questionnaires to be distributed to as many female athletes as possible. The distribution process was to be supervised by the coaches of the various women's teams. The athletes were instructed to complete the questionnaires in private and return them to the athletic departments in sealed envelopes.[2] After the questionnaires were returned to the athletic departments, the athletic directors returned them to us at the University of Colorado at Colorado Springs. Completed questionnaires were received from 2272 athletes at forty percent of the Division I and Division II schools in the sample.

Although the information in the questionnaires covered a wide range of topics, the purpose of this paper is to explore the relationship between the distribution of athletic scholarships and the status-related variables of race and father's occupation. Since sport participation rates among females have traditionally been limited by factors such as lack of opportunities and constraints related to family structure, it was suspected that the vast majority of intercollegiate women athletes would come from high status backgrounds where families had the resources to encourage involvement and take advantage of existing participation opportunities. In comparison with their higher status counterparts, girls growing up in middle- and lower-income families would be more likely to have homemaking and childrearing chores assigned to them at a young age. This would interfere with their sport participation and inhibit the development of their athletic skills. Girls in higher status families would have had a higher degree of freedom to participate, and they would have had greater access to programs in which athletic skills and motivation could be nurtured.

The existence of differential family constraints was expected to influence the distribution of athletic scholarships among the women in the sample. If young women from higher status families grew up with fewer constraints on involvement as well as more opportunities than young women from lower status families, they would be more likely to have top level skills and therefore receive the vast majority of the scholarship aid offered by Division I and Division II schools. Furthermore, to the extent that race and socioeconomic status have been related in the United States, the participation patterns and the distribution of athletic scholarships were expected to reflect an underrepresentation of black athletes.

Before taking a look at the data, some of the methodological weaknesses of the study should be explained. Unfortunately, the data provide a rather poor basis for making generalizations about the proportion of women athletes receiving scholarships in Division I and II schools. The data collection procedures were set up so that respondents were most likely those women who were known members of teams and in regular contact with their coaches or the staffs of their athletic departments. Since the teams not actively practicing or playing during the fall semester did not have full rosters when the questionnaires were distributed, we did not receive any responses from the "walk-ons" who would try out and make teams during the last half of the academic year. Coaches did not know in advance who these walk-ons would be, but the coaches did know the athletes who were on athletic scholarships, especially those on full scholarships. Therefore, the sample from which these data were collected contained an overrepresentation of athletes receiving some form of aid. However, it is likely that the data do present a relatively accurate picture of the characteristics of those who were on athletic scholarships in the major schools and conferences around the country during the fall of 1979.

FINDINGS AND DISCUSSION

General Patterns

In spite of the fact that scholarship athletes are overrepresented among the respondents, the data indicated that the majority (52%) of the athletes participating in Division I and II programs received no aid in conjunction with their involvement in sport.[3] Only 18.6% of the respondents were receiving full scholarships, 20.4% had partial scholarships, and 9% had tuition waivers. Table 1 shows the distribution of aid among athletes at both division levels. Full scholarships were proportionately more common in Division I schools while a higher proportion of athletes who received no aid was greater in Division II schools. These differences correspond to the program philosophies and budgets in the respective divisions.

When the distribution of aid was viewed for each sport it was found that basketball players received proportionately more full scholarships than players in any other sport. This was true for schools in both divisions. As can be seen in Table 2, nearly half the basketball players in Division I schools were receiving full scholarships; in Division II schools it was about 18%. In Division I, the athletes least likely to receive any compensation for their sport involvement were those in track and field and in the minor team sports (i.e., all team sports except basketball and volleyball). The athletes least likely to receive any aid in Division II schools were tennis players, gymnasts, swimmers, and those in minor team sports. At the Division II level it seems that the major commitment to the women's programs in terms of scholarship aid was focused on basketball and volleyball. At the Division I level, this commitment was more evenly distributed with over half of the respondents in all sports except track and field and the minor team sports receiving some form of aid.

Scholarships, Race, and Socioeconomic Status.

The question of who receives athletic scholarships has remained

TABLE 1

The Distribution of Athletic Scholarships in Division I and Division II of the NCAA.

Division	Full Scholarships	Type of Aid Partial Scholarships	Tuition Waivers	No Aid	Total
Division I	23.3 (369)	19.4 (308)	7.4 (118)	49.9 (791)	100 (1586)
Division II	7.5 (50)	22.6 (151)	12.9 (86)	57.0 (381)	100 (668)
Total	18.6 (419)	20.4 (459)	9.0 (204)	52.0 (1172)	100 (2254)

TABLE 2
Percentage Distribution of Scholarships by Sport in Division I and Division II (N=2241).

Sport	Full Scholarships	Type of Aid Partial Scholarships	Tuition Waivers	No Aid	(Total N)
Division I					
Basketball	48.6	16.5	5.7	29.2	(212)
Volleyball	30.9	23.6	8.9	36.6	(191)
Other team	11.3	15.6	6.9	66.2	(348)
Track/field	10.6	19.0	5.5	64.9	(274)
Tennis	25.2	25.2	6.1	43.5	(131)
Gymnastics	28.1	19.0	8.3	44.6	(121)
Swimming	25.3	21.6	9.3	43.8	(162)
Other ind.	18.2	22.6	11.7	47.5	(137)
Division II					
Basketball	18.2	18.6	13.6	49.7	(177)
Volleyball	5.6	33.6	17.6	43.2	(125)
Other team	3.7	18.4	9.7	68.2	(125)
Track/field	2.5	25.0	13.7	58.8	(80)
Tennis	—	20.0	—	80.0	(5)
Gymnastics	5.2	10.3	1.7	82.8	(58)
Swimming	—	18.9	9.5	71.6	(74)
Other ind.	9.5	23.8	19.0	47.7	(21)

TABLE 3

Percentage Distribution of Scholarships by the Occupational Status of Athletes' Fathers (N = 2092).*

Father's Occupation	Type of Aid				
	Full Scholarship	Partial Scholarship	Tuition Waiver	No Aid	Total (N)
Professionals & Top Executives	16.4 (135)	21.3 (175)	8.2 (67)	54.1 (444)	100 (821)
Mid-level Managers and Officials	20.3 (170)	20.1 (169)	9.2 (77)	50.4 (423)	100 (839)
Skilled/Clerical Workers	17.9 (56)	20.8 (65)	9.9 (31)	51.4 (161)	100 (313)
Minimum Wage/Semi-Skilled Workers	18.5 (22)	15.1 (18)	11.8 (14)	54.6 (65)	100 (119)

*The occupations of the athletes' fathers were broken down into four categories corresponding to their respective socioeconomic status scores as designated by the U.S. Bureau of the Census. The Census Bureau developed these scores as summary measures for the prestige, education, and income associated with 297 different job categories. In this table, each of the four occupation labels were chosen to generally represent the types of jobs in the respective categories.

unanswered for years. There are no good sources of information on the characteristics of scholarship athletes in either men's or women's programs. However, the data in this study provide some tentative answers about who receives aid in women's programs.

Using information on the occupations of the respondents' fathers we were able to look at the relationship between the socioeconomic status of female athletes and the distribution of scholarships. Analysis showed that the distribution of aid did not vary with the occupational status of the respondents' fathers. In fact, the proportion of athletes receiving no aid was 54.1% for the daughters of top level executives and professionals and 54.6% for the daughters of minimum wage and semi-skilled workers. Scholarships, full and partial, were also evenly distributed. This suggests that female athletes received financial awards strictly because of their athletic skills; financial need did not seem to be a factor influencing who received scholarships. In fact, about 80% of all the scholarships were awarded to women whose fathers had high status occupations.

The conclusion that athletic scholarships do not reflect financial need should be qualified in one respect. The coaches in men's programs have been known to supplement their own scholarship budgets by helping low income student-athletes obtain financial assistance through special programs outside athletic departments. When they do this successfully, they are able to recruit and "provide support" for athletes without using funds from their own budgets. The extent to which this practice occurs in women's programs is unknown. If it was occurring in 1979-80, low income student-athletes may have received more financial assistance than is shown in these data, but that assistance would be only indirectly tied to their sport participation. The data in Table 4 do indicate that athletes from lower status family backgrounds were more likely than their high status counterparts to have received nonsport financial aid.

In exploring status-related issues we were also concerned with the distribution of scholarships among blacks and whites. As expected, the proportion of black athletes in our sample was significantly lower than the proportion of blacks in the population as a whole. In fact, black women constituted only 4.7% of the respondents. Women from other minority groups and Anglo women made up 2.8% and 92.6% of the sample, respectively.[4] Table 5 shows the distribution of scholarships for whites, blacks

TABLE 4

Athletes' Primary Source of Financial Support for Living Expenses by the Occupational Status of Their Fathers (N = 2059).

Father's Occupation	Source of Support				
	Parents/ Relatives	Savings/ Job	Athletic Scholarship	Student $ Aid	Total (N)
Professionals and Top Executives	53.9 (440)	12.8 (104)	21.9 (179)	11.4 (93)	100 (816)
Mid-level Managers and Officials	47.5 (392)	11.4 (94)	26.3 (217)	14.8 (122)	100 (825)
Skilled/Clerical Workers	39.3 (120)	14.7 (45)	22.5 (69)	23.5 (72)	100 (306)
Minimum Wage/Semi- Skilled Workers	25.9 (29)	20.5 (23)	24.1 (27)	29.5 (33)	100 (112)

and "other minorities" in both divisions as well as a comparison of blacks and whites at each of the division levels.

The data show that black athletes were more likely to have had the benefit of full scholarships than either whites or other minority athletes. However, it must be emphasized that only 34 black women had full scholarships. This means that, at most, about 1.5% of all women intercollegiate athletes during 1979-80 were black women with full scholarships. Whites received 89.2% of all full scholarships given compared to 8.2% for blacks and 2.6% for other minority group members. It should also be noted that 30% of the white athletes received some form of partial aid or tuition waivers while only 24.7% of the black athletes received such assistance. Relatively few athletes from other minority groups received partial aid (19.4%), and they were most likely to be playing without any form of aid (62.9%).

When the data for blacks and whites were broken down for each division, there were some slight variations on the pattern shown for the total sample. The direction of the pattern did not change but in Division II, the proportion of black athletes who were receiving full scholarships (33.3%) was much greater than the proportion of whites receiving them (6.3%). However, a far greater proportion of whites were receiving partial scholarships and tuition waivers than were black athletes (37.4% vs. 16.6%). The fact that a greater proportion of black athletes had full scholarships may have been due to the size of the budgets in the sports in which they were most likely to participate. Table 6 shows the proportions of blacks and whites in various sports for each division. Compared to whites, a greater proportion of black athletes were basketball players. Since basketball has been the sport most likely to generate revenue in women's programs, it has often had the largest budget of any single sport, and it has had a higher proportion of athletes receiving full scholarships. (Refer to Table 2.) However, before making any conclusions about the opportunities provided minority athletes who can dribble and shoot jump shots, it must be remembered that about 88% of the basketball players in this sample were whites; only about 10% were blacks.

The data in Table 6 also indicate that if minority athletes did not play basketball they were most likely to be on track and field teams. This was especially the case in Division I schools where nearly 52% of all the black athletes were members of track and field teams. Black athletes were least likely to participate in in-

TABLE 5

Percentage Distribution of Scholarships by Racial Background in Both Divisions and Percentage Distribution of Scholarships for Blacks and Whites in Division I and Division II.

Race	Type of Aid				
	Full Scholarship	Partial Scholarship	Tuition Waiver	No Aid	Total (N)
Whites (92.6%)	17.8	21.0	9.0	52.2	100
	(371)	(437)	(187)	(1086)	(2081)
Blacks (4.7%)	32.4	15.2	9.5	42.9	100
	(34)	(16)	(10)	(45)	(105)
Other Minority (2.8%)	17.7	8.1	11.3	62.9	100
	(11)	(5)	(7)	(39)	(62)
Division I					
Whites	22.7	19.8	7.1	50.4	100
	(332)	(290)	(104)	(739)	(1465)
Blacks	32.1	17.3	9.9	40.7	100
	(26)	(14)	(8)	(33)	(81)
Division II					
Whites	6.3	23.9	13.5	56.3	100
	(39)	(147)	(83)	(347)	(616)
Blacks	33.3	8.3	8.3	50.0	99.9
	(8)	(2)	(2)	(12)	(24)

dividual sports such as tennis, gymnastics, swimming, etc. This was due to a variety of social and cultural factors which have shaped both opportunities and motivation for developing specific skills. The fact that over 80% of the black athletes in our study were members of either basketball or track and field teams indicates that black women (1) may not have access to opportunities to develop skills in other sports or (2) they may not be motivated to do so or (3) if they do develop skills, they are not recruited to play on intercollegiate teams. Research on black males suggests that these explanations are presented in the order of their explanatory power (i.e., (1) access, (2) motivation, and (3) recruiting biases), but more research is needed to discover if the same dynamics are at work among women and in women's programs. At the time of this study there seemed to be considerable segregation existing within women's intercollegiate sport.

SUMMARY AND CONCLUSIONS

As we expected when we initiated the study, the majority of athletes on Division I and II teams received no form of scholarship aid in conjunction with their sport participation. This was in spite of the fact that our data were collected in a manner that overrepresented the number of scholarship athletes in the sample. If we had included Division III respondents the data would have shown that well over 60% of all women intercollegiate athletes received no scholarship aid and less than 15% received full scholarships. Of course, the proportion of women athletes who receive scholarships is growing as conformity with Title IX becomes more complete, but for the foreseeable future it seems that women with athletic scholarships will be in the minority among women intercollegiate athletes in general. This means that parents with visions of their daughters saving them money for college expenses by landing athletic scholarships should not let their expectations get too high lest they and their daughters be disappointed.

As in men's programs, the major revenue-producing team sports accounted for a relatively large segment of the scholarship athletes in women's programs. In fact, basketball accounted for one third of the full scholarships awarded to athletes at both division levels in our sample. As women's volleyball grows in popularity among spectators, it will also continue to capture more than its share of scholarship aid for its players. However, changes

TABLE 6

Athletes' Primary Sport by Race within Division I and Division II (N = 2199).

Race	Primary Sport				
	Basketball	Other Team	Track Field	Other Individ.	Total (N)
Division I					
Blacks	25.9	18.5	51.8	3.7	100
	(21)	(15)	(42)	(3)	(81)
Whites	13.0	34.5	15.5	37.0	100
	(192)	(508)	(227)	(545)	(1472)
Division II					
Blacks	76.0	12.0	12.0	0.0	100
	(19)	(3)	(3)	(0)	(25)
Whites	25.1	38.7	11.9	24.3	100
	(156)	(240)	(74)	(151)	(621)
Total					
Blacks	37.7	17.0	42.5	2.8	100
	(40)	(18)	(45)	(3)	(106)
Whites	16.6	35.7	14.4	33.3	100
	(348)	(748)	(301)	(696)	(2093)

in the proportions of scholarships awarded to athletes in other sports can be expected to be slight. Increases will be scarce, and with cutbacks in minor sports being made in many men's programs, there may even be a decline in the proportion of women in minor sports who receive scholarship aid of any type.

Also in line with our expectations, the data showed that scholarships were not awarded to women on the basis of financial need. In fact, over 80% of all athletic aid was received by athletes whose fathers were in relatively high status, upper- and upper-middle-income occupations. Although this pattern can be expected to prevail long into the future, the fact that local community and high school programs are now offering publicly funded sport opportunities for girls and young women will tend to give lower income athletes a better chance to develop their skills and be noticed by recruiters. However, if there are significant cutbacks of programs in the communities and school districts serving low-income segments of the population, the existing patterns can be expected to change very little. In either case, intercollegiate programs for women are not going to be very helpful in "opening doors" and providing "free" educational opportunities for many young women who would not otherwise have the chance to attend college. Of course, this is also the case in men's programs, but because women experience gender-related constraints to a greater degree in low-income groups, low-income females are at an even greater disadvantage than low-income males when it comes to scholarship prospects.

The data also indicated that very few minority athletes were benefitting from the scholarships offered in women's programs. Black athletes in particular constituted less than 5% of the total sample. Relative to white athletes, they received a proportionately greater number of full scholarships and proportionately fewer partial scholarships and tuition waivers. However, in absolute terms, whites received nearly 17 times as many scholarship awards as were received by black athletes. Furthermore, over half the black athletes receiving scholarship aid had fathers in relatively high status, high income occupations. This emphatically reinforces the notion that sport is not a significant mobility catalyst within the black population. And it is less likely to be such a catalyst for black women than for black men.

Finally, the pattern of segregation that has existed in men's programs was also characteristic in women's programs. Few black women were participating on intercollegiate teams other than those in basketball and track and field. The existence of such a pattern is hardly encouraging for those who would like to credit sport with a potential for changing negative racial attitudes and stereotypes among whites.

In conclusion, our data showed that women's intercollegiate sport was characterized by many of the same patterns found in men's programs. Such a finding is not surprising but it empirically documents the notion that as conformity with Title IX increases among NCAA member institutions, the programs for women will not be much different than those for men. Social structural factors rather than gender seem to be the major determinants shaping programs for both males and females.

NOTES

1. This survey is part of a larger study conducted by Dr. Patricia L. Pacey and partially funded by the National Collegiate Athletic Association.

2. Although anonymity was insured by the researchers it may have been that some of the athletes doubted the trustworthiness of members of the athletic department; these doubts could have influenced the number of athletes responding to the questionnaire as well as responses to questions related to program evaluations. However, none of the material on program evaluation is included in this paper.

3. In the questionnaire the respondents were asked to indicate what kind of financial aid they were receiving in conjunction with their participation in the school's athletic program. The response categories were: full athletic scholarship (tuition, books, room, board), partial scholarship, tuition waiver, or no aid.

4. "Other minorities" included American Indians, Hispanics and Orientals.

SECTION V

SPORT AND CAREERS: SPORT IN THE LIFE CYCLE

THE THREE PAPERS in this section are concerned with a specific stage in the life of an athlete—the end or presumed end of an individual's playing career. The study of desocialization from sport has become increasingly popular in recent years, probably as a reaction to the mass of research devoted to socialization into sport. But there are other reasons for focusing upon this particular stage in the sporting life cycle. First, there is an increasing tendency to employ the career model to investigate sport involvement and it is inevitable that the issue of retirement will be dealt with as a consequence of the use of this model. Second, because of the rapidly rising mean age of the North American population, the field of gerontology has begun to expand and to receive greater research funding. Sport sociologists have contributed to this expansion by turning their attention to retired and aging athletes. Finally, there has been a growing awareness of the difficulties faced by many retired professional athletes in adjusting to their career terminations and pursuing new careers. Thus, research in this area may have an applied component in the provision of athletic counseling programs.

The first two papers in this section employ the concept of social death as a model for understanding the difficulties associated with retirement from a career in sport. Social death refers to the condition of being treated as if one were dead even though still biologically alive and may be applied to a range of situations from being comatose to being "sent to Coventry." Edwin Rosenberg provides a discussion of the relevance of the model to the analysis of retirement from sport and notes that the analogy to death has frequently been employed by sportswriters and athletes. Stephen Lerch develops the analogy in the context of two thanatological models: Glaser and Strauss's "awareness contexts" and Kubler-Ross's "stages of dying." Rosenberg and Lerch clearly recognize

243

that the concept of death is an analogy and that there is a world of difference between actual death and retirement from sport. However, the concept of social death is perceived to be useful, and the thanatological models discussed by Lerch have some utility for athletic counseling programs.

James Curtis and Phillip White take a different approach to the study of sport in the life cycle by questioning the assumptions of disengagement theory. This widely accepted theory suggests that there is declining participation in sport and physical activity with increasing age. Employing data from the Canada Labour Force Survey of 50,000 adults, they find support for disengagement theory when the entire sample is considered. When only those who participate in physical activity are considered, a different interpretation is warranted and support is found for continuity and activity theories. That is, among the still active they found a pattern of greater specialization in activities with increasing age. While these findings have obvious implications for interpretations of the aging process, they will also be of interest to practitioners concerned with the promotion of sport and recreation programs.

ATHLETIC RETIREMENT AS SOCIAL DEATH: CONCEPTS AND PERSPECTIVES

Edwin Rosenberg
University of Pittsburgh at Bradford

THERE IS NOW QUITE A BODY of literature on desocialization from sport, i.e., the processes by which an athlete disengages from his or her sport involvement and the adjustment necessitated by this disengagement. While many desocialization studies are empirically sound and theoretically grounded, the same cannot be said of early studies of one particular form of sport desocialization, athletic retirement. In this paper athletic retirement means disengagement from active sport involvement by a college, elite amateur (e.g., Olympic), or professional athlete.

Early ideas about athletic retirement were discovered through and based upon non-representative studies (e.g., Mihovilovic, 1968) and occasional gleanings from popular sport literature (e.g., Bouton, 1970; Kahn, 1971; Kramer, 1969; Plimpton, 1973). More recently, sophisticated empirical and theoretical attempts have been made to place athletic retirement within an analytical framework which might predict problems to be faced by retiring athletes and propose solutions to those problems (e.g., Arviko, 1976; Haerle, 1975; Lerch, 1981; McPherson, 1980; Reynolds, 1981; Rosenberg, 1981a, b). These studies have often relied upon gerontological theories which address the adjustment to retirement of older workers.

This led to a recognition in sport sociology that "identity, status and occupation are inextricably bound together in the human psyche. Thus, adjustment to the social and psychological changes involved in retirement becomes more pressing than facing up to the biological effects of aging" (Hill and Lowe, 1974: 12). One might add that, at least in some cases, social and psychological adjustment is more problematic than economic adjustment.

Sport sociologists are not alone in this new awareness. In some sports one now finds vocational counseling programs to help players plan for their inevitable post-playing careers. Similar programs have appeared in the private sector as well (Rosenberg, 1981a: 8).

These developments acknowledge both the sport structure's disinterest in preparing the athlete for his or her post-playing days and the additional social pressures which create adjustment obstacles. The rise of vocational counseling and training programs for athletes is evidence that these social pressures create psychological adjustment problems which often transcend economic security.

This article maintains a focus on social structural and individual psychological forces. The topic is the treatment of an athlete when it becomes known he or she is retiring, or cut, or irrevocably waived, and the effect of these dynamics on the athlete's self-image.

Anticipatory adjustment to retirement, or pre-retirement planning, is under-utilized by older workers and athletes alike. Both nonsport business and the professional sport structure have begun to endorse and/or offer pre-retirement counseling, but these efforts barely scratch the surface. Mandatory retirement for older workers and athletic retirement are both involuntary. It is true that, on occasion, athletic retirement is voluntary or has an element of volition and autonomy; this usually depends on the availability of attractive, plausible second-career options. Upon retirement, even in the best scenario, the athlete is deprived for the first time of the rewards his or her sport has showered on him or her since childhood. For the first time he or she is fully saddled with such adult responsibilities as managing finances, arranging travel, or doing laundry. He or she is now likely to perceive him or herself a decade or so behind nonsport age peers in career development. Thus, regardless of economic status, retirement is a status transition of considerable social and psychological stress for the athlete.

The popular press has featured an increasing number of articles on former athletes and their adjustment to non-playing status. Yet these have not been collated in any systematic way, and academic studies of athletic retirement remain few in number. (For representative bibliographies see Loy *et al.*, 1978: 244-248; Rosenberg, 1981a; Williams, 1981.) And, though several sport sociology texts have been published in the last half-decade, it is hard to find any which devote even a page to athletic retirement. (Exceptions include Loy et al., 1978; Coakley, 1982.)

This article is an attempt to shed new light on disengagement from sport. The analytical perspective taken here is that since athletic retirement signals the termination of one career, of one stage of life, insight can be gained from the application of concepts and conceptual frameworks from thanatology, the study of death and dying. If extant knowledge about psychological adjustment to dying and death can be adapted to professional and elite amateur sport retirement, counseling strategies can be adapted as well. Thus a major criterion of evaluation is applicability.

SOCIAL DEATH: THANATOLOGY

America is known as a death-denying society. Rather than hush up sex while making death a public event, as was the case in Victorian England, Americans have reversed the process and made death "the new pornography" (Gorer, 1965). We have also developed the belief that science and technology are omnipotent, and that death is merely another technological problem to be conquered by man's ever-increasing knowledge. Thus "we have become ashamed of death, and we try to hide it, or hide ourselves away from it. It is, to our way of thinking, failure" (Thomas, 1980: 4). It is not unusual to find physicians avoiding contact with terminal patients, who are visible and vivid proof that medicine is not all-powerful.

As the science of thanatology grew, an awareness of different modes of conceptualizing death developed. This was important because, with the advent of life-support equipment, the medical and legal professions began demanding statutory definitions of death. The leading contenders were (and remain) cardiopulmonary death, which centers on the ability of the circulatory and respiratory systems to function without artificial support, and brain (or decerebrate) death, which defines life in terms of measurable brain activity. These two definitions represent philosophies of life which place primary importance on, respectively, physiological and intellectual functioning.

Another way of looking at death is socially. Social death does not refer to the biological death of an individual, but rather to social isolation and ostracism from another individual or group. It may but need not contribute to or result in actual death. Kastenbaum (1981a: 25), describing the feeling of social death, writes, "You are there, part of a situation. But nobody is paying attention to you. Nobody addresses remarks to you, or looks you in the eye. You might as well not be there."

Each of us can probably recall at least one such incident in our own lives. Often the social death syndrome is found in hospitals, for example, in the case of a comatose patient. The staff then "tend to act in the patient's presence as if he were a 'non-person,' talking freely even about things that would matter to him if he were sentient, just as if he were not there. . . . Socially he is already dead, though his body remains biologically alive" (Glaser and Strauss, 1965: 108).

Gerontologist Richard Kalish (1966: 73) states that "social death occurs when an individual is thought of as dead, although he remains medically and legally alive. Any given person may be socially dead to one individual, to many individuals, or to virtually everyone."

Another gerontologist, Robert Kastenbaum (1981a: 25), adds that social death is context-specific. "Social death must be defined situationally. In particular, it is a situation in which there is absence of those behaviors we would expect to be directed toward a living person, and the presence of behaviors we would expect when dealing with a deceased or nonexistent person."

Kastenbaum (1981a: 25) adds that: "Social death is read by observing how others treat and fail to treat the person with whom we are concerned. The individual himself may be animated enough and potentially responsive. As a matter of fact, the individual may be desperately seeking recognition, attention, interaction." Thus social death reminds us that we have a social not just a biological and psychological identity. The importance and relevance of such basic sociological concepts as consensual validation and "the looking-glass self" in promoting successful adjustment among retiring athletes is obvious.

There are different manifestations of social death (Kastenbaum, 1981a: 25-26). An individual may violate a group taboo so seriously that he or she is "cut dead." An example is being written out of a will. Or the offending individual may be ritualistically expelled from the group or killed. An example of this process is religious excommunication. One remains alive, even acknowledged, but is considered a "subperson." More relevant for the athlete are Kastenbaum's (1981a) other categories.

3) There is an intrinsic change in the individual that results in loss of live person status. [For example,] growing old in

the United States still represents a decrement in social value. . . . The individual has broken no taboos and committed no crimes, unless it be an implicit sin against a youth-glorifying culture to grow old. . . .

4) The terminally ill or dying person may be treated as though already dead. . . . an elaborate pattern of aversive and person-denying behavior can be generated around a living individual whose demise is, correctly or incorrectly, anticipated (p. 25).

These types of behaviors protect group members from having to admit their own fallibility or mortality or deterioration. If I ignore (your) failure, they seem to be saying, perhaps it will go away, or at least pass me by.

Another practical result of the phenomenon of social death which has relevance for athletes is "posting." David Sudnow (1967: 72) has described posting in a hospital. "When, in the course of a patient's illness his condition is considered such that he is 'dying' or 'terminally ill,' his name is 'posted' on the 'critical patients' list. . . . Posting also serves as an internally relevant message, notifying certain key hospital personnel that a death may be forthcoming and that appropriate preparations for that possibility are tentatively warranted." At one hospital Sudnow studied, a Catholic chaplain checked the posted list in each ward prior to his daily rounds. He would then administer last rites to Catholics whose names appeared on the list. The analogy to sport is strong here. Cut sheets posted by team staff let everyone know which players have been declared "terminal." And how's this for the athlete's last rites: "Coach wants to see you. Bring your playbook."?

The presence of social death in the hospital setting is well documented and the similarities to sport situations easy to discern. Charmaz (1980: 128) writes, "Social death is. . . intimately connected with issues of professional and moral accountability. Social death permits doctors to turn away from their 'failures.' It legitimizes staff treating patients as nonpersons without human qualities. Most strikingly, social death serves to rationalize abandonment of the aged dying through banishing them to organizational repositories for terminal patients." To see the relevance of the concept of social death in studying the psychological adjustment of the athlete to retirement, merely substitute "managers" for doctors, "coaches" for staff, "athletes" for patients, "older or injured players" for aged dying, "minor or semi-pro leagues" for organizational repositories, and "over the hill jocks" for terminal patients.

SOCIAL DEATH: ATHLETICS

The late Don Ball (1976) laid the foundation for the bridge joining thanatology and sport sociology in his article, "Failure In Sport." Ball's study concluded that the group's reaction to a player who has "failed" is either degradation (ignoring the player, which corresponds to the concept of social death) or cooling out (comfort and sympathy are extended and accepted). The individual's reaction is usually embarrassment or humiliation, loss of face, and anxiety over the incongruity between his self-image and the image of himself being presented by his reference group.

The preceding section attempted to focus on social death solely as a thanatological concept. Nonetheless there are instances where the parallel to athletic retirement events is too strong to ignore. The practice of "posting," for example, is found in sport as well as in the hospital. And Rashad (1982: 84-85) recently described his efforts to "cool out" a rookie who had just been cut from the team. Contrary to Ball's framework, the rookie did not graciously accept Rashad's sympathies. Rather, there was some antagonism because Rashad, a veteran and star, could not possibly understand how the rookie felt. Uneasy, Rashad left.

Rashad (1982: 85) also describes the aspect of failure in sport called degradation:

> Most times, no matter who's cut, it's like the guy died. No, it's worse than dying because when you die people sit around and talk about you, eulogize you. When you're cut from a football team, it's more like you never existed at all. The ship sails every day, and if you're not on it, it's like you never were.
>
> It's even that way when you're injured. You could score 16 touchdowns in the first half, but if you get hurt at the start of the second, you're forgotten. Your teammates walk right by you. There's nothing more shameful than to be an injured football player on the sidelines during a game.

Note that in sport being injured is often regarded as temporary failure and the injured player becomes an object of degradation.

The degradation reaction occurs in other sports as well. Jim Bouton (cited in Ball, 1976: 731), former pro baseball player, recalls,

"As I started throwing stuff in my bag, I could feel the wall, invisible but real, forming around me. I was suddenly an outsider, a different person, someone to be shunned, a leper."

OTHER THANATOLOGICAL TOOLS

The remainder of this article discusses other concepts and analytical frameworks from thanatology which might be beneficially applied to an understanding of the psychodynamics of athletic retirement.

Thanatology first came to the public eye with the 1969 publication of Elizabeth Kubler-Ross' book, *On Death and Dying*. In this book Kubler-Ross presents her stage theory of dying, a model which, in fact, has proven popular to the point of blanket acceptance and occasional misinterpretation (for details see Kastenbaum, 1981b). Based on her observations of and interviews with terminal patients, Kubler-Ross writes that the dying patient seems to progress through a series of psychological stages. First comes shock and denial, followed by anger, bargaining, depression, and finally acceptance. The serious analyst of sport retirement can perceive these stages in the athlete's reaction to the news of his impending "sport career death." (For a fine example of such an analysis, see the article in this volume by gerontologist and sport sociologist Stephen Lerch.) Despite the lack of empirical testing of Kubler-Ross' theory, there seems to be much there which can be of use in helping the counselor and athlete understand the retiring athlete's feelings and dilemmas.

A second useful perspective comes from the work of Glaser and Strauss (1965). They noted that, in the interaction between a terminal patient and the patient's family and medical staff, various states of "awareness" of the terminal condition may exist. The state of awareness dictates the amount and type of communication which occur between the patient and family or staff. Certain awareness states seem to promote acceptance of death by both patient and family or staff. Glaser and Strauss described four "awareness contexts": closed; suspicion; mutual pretense; and open.

An open awareness context, in which all involved parties are aware of the true nature of the patient's condition and thus communication can be frank and to the point, seems best for effecting positive adjustments to the termination of life. In the same sense, it should bring about optimal adjustment for the athlete in the transition from player to non-player status. In practice, however, it seems that one is far more likely to find relations between players and management characterized by closed or suspicion awareness. (For an illustrative elaboration of awareness contexts and their applicability to athletic retirement, again see the article in this volume by Stephen Lerch.)

Another related concept is that of "appropriate death." An appropriate death is one we would design for ourselves if we had the opportunity and means. This idea might be used in guiding the development of pre-retirement counseling for players, and perhaps players and management might agree on standard procedures to be followed in notifying a player that his or her athletic condition is "terminal." If professional teams have no knowledge of the fates of their former players (Rosenberg, 1981a), we can infer they have no interest either. Thus it is incumbent upon the players or their representatives to approach management with an "appropriate death" proposal. Management, however, might well have its own reasons for refusing to grant such proposals or, for that matter, discussing a player's prospects in an open awareness context.

The nature and timing of one's death are relevant concerns, as shown in the discussion of appropriate death, and the nature and timing of the athlete's disengagement from sport are, too. Here we can consider the differences between voluntary and involuntary retirement, and the possibility of applying the concept of euthanasia to athletic retirement. In regard to the former, Loy *et al.* (1978: 244-245) wrote:

> Inevitably, at some stage of the life cycle, individuals cease to be involved in institutionalized sport as competitors. For some this occurs voluntarily early in life. . . for others it occurs later in life when they decide to retire from a full- or part-time career as an elite amateur or professional athlete; and for others it can occur quite suddenly and unvoluntarily [sic] when they are seriously injured or "fired" from a team. . . . The reaction or adjustment to this state can range from satisfaction, if the process is voluntary or planned for in advance, to traumatic psychological or life-style adjustment problems, if the process is involuntary.

It seems safe to say, first, that the voluntaristic trait of retirement is a continuum, rather than a dichotomy. As with old-age retirement, athletic retirement may be partly forced and partly chosen. Often, faced with certain retirement, one will rationalize it into a self-selected option. Nevertheless, given the intense and long-standing involvement of athletes in their sport, and given the comparatively high frequency of retirement due to injury, it seems safe to say that a large portion of athletic retirements are of a largely involuntary nature.

To what extent is athletic retirement congruent with euthanasia? Euthanasia, which literally means "a good death" and which is popularly referred to as "mercy killing," has two basic categories. One, called "passive euthanasia," involves bringing about a death by "pulling the plug"; that is, allowing someone to die naturally rather than prolonging life artificially. The other category, called "active euthanasia," involves hastening someone's death through deliberate action, such as providing poison, so that the person dies before he naturally would. Each form has its advocates and detractors. The distinction between active and passive euthanasia is often referred to as the distinction between "killing and letting die."

The concept of active euthanasia seems to have little applicability to athletic retirement, since the athlete usually plays until his abilities give out, and management is happy to have him until that time. Thus neither is likely to do anything intentionally to bring about the premature termination of an athletic career.

Nor does passive euthanasia have a clear-cut role here. Rather, it appears that the player and management will argue over a player's forced retirement. The player sees it as active euthanasia; he feels he still has the necessary abilities and accuses management of arbitrarily foreshortening his career, of "killing" his athletic life. Management, on the other hand, may see their action as a merciful gesture. "Retire," they may be saying, "before you wind up looking like a fool on the field."

A more pertinent issue is that of the relationship between social status and social death. A major finding of Sudnow's (1967) study was that one's social status has much to do with the application of the "dead" label. Sudnow found in the hospital that the higher the patient's social status, the slower others would be to begin treating the patient as socially dead. Also, the higher the social status, the more likely the patient would be treated as if there were a real chance of recovery. Finally, the greater the patient's social status, the harder others would work to actualize the belief in recovery. This may explain why star athletes are allowed to remain with a team when their skills have deteriorated to a level which would banish a lesser-known player from the team. But this also shows, given the inevitability of retirement, that star athletes may be encouraged to indulge in more illusions about career longevity than would their less-skilled counterparts. When retirement does come to the star, it may thus be more of a psychological shock, even though the star should be better prepared financially.

CONCLUSION

There is still much uncharted territory in the exploration of athletic retirement. It is obvious now: 1) that this phenomenon, a result of functional rather than chronological aging, was initially overlooked by gerontologists and sport sociologists alike; 2) that economic security does not guarantee successful adjustment to post-playing life, and; 3) that vocational aptitude and career counseling programs can have beneficial results for athletes. There are many former athletes who had difficulty making the transition and, despite recent developments, many current athletes will likely have problems, too. As Loy *et al.* (1978: 245) noted, "In many cases the reaction depends on age, the options of alternative lifestyles available, the degree of sport involvement, the amount of preplanning or socialization for alternative roles, and the available mechanisms for desocialization from the role."

While we are a long way from being able accurately to predict successful adjustment to athletic retirement in a quantitative fashion, we can transform the relationships stated above into research hypotheses for future investigations:

1. There is an inverse relationship between post-playing options and athletic retirement adjustment problems.

2. There is a positive relationship between the degree of sport involvement (which could be operationalized as either competitive level or personal intensity) and athletic retirement adjustment problems.

3. There is an inverse relationship between anticipatory socialization for athletic retirement and athletic retirement adjustment problems.

4. There is an inverse relationship between utilization of desocialization mechanisms and athletic retirement adjustment problems.

5. For amateur athletes, there is a positive relationship be-

tween perceived likelihood of a professional career and athletic retirement adjustment problems.

It seems obvious that social death, a thanatological concept, describes several aspects associated with the end of a college, elite amateur, or professional athletic career. In the poem "To An Athlete Dying Young," A. E. Houseman wrote:

The time you won your town the race
We chaired you through the market-place;
Man and boy stood cheering by,
And home we brought you shoulder-high.

To-day, the road all runners come,
Shoulder-high we bring you home,
And set you at your threshold down,
Townsman of a stiller town.

Smart lad, to slip betimes away
From fields where glory does not stay
And early though the laurel grows
It withers quicker than the rose. . . .

Now you will not swell the rout
Of lads that wore their honours out,
Runners whom renown outran
And the name died before the man. . . .

Houseman wrote of biological death, of course, and argued in his poem that fame is fleeting, fans fickle, and glory transitory. The athlete who dies young, who predeceases his fame, is fortunate indeed. Macabre reasoning, perhaps, to prefer a legendary death to a life of disappointing oblivion, but perhaps not.

Compared to athletes of the past, today's athletes are better educated and more conscious of the need to prepare for a second career. They tend to invest, rather than frivolously spend, their salaries. They choose off-season jobs which will develop into full-time positions when they retire from sport.

But the athlete can't always pre-plan and socialize himself for the transition on his own. In some sports, such as pro football, players associations have set up counseling programs. Also, a few private-sector vocational counseling programs oriented toward professional athletes have sprung up. The combination of athletic vocational counseling programs and recent studies of athletic retirement are evidence that there are social and psychological adjustments to be made, regardless of financial status, for nearly all athletes.

The point is that money, health, and relative youthfulness do not entirely prepare the athlete for the future. In fact, their latent function is often to obscure his vision of it. The psychological problems of adjustment loom larger the more they are studied. The social death and the accompanying stigma of failure experienced by the athlete as his career comes to an end hardly help the transition.

The goal of social research involves more than just explanation and understanding. It involves the application of research-derived knowledge toward the solution of real-life problems. If concepts and theoretical models from gerontology and thanatology can shed light on problematic aspects of athletic retirement, and if this knowledge is integrated into athletic counseling programs, then the goal of this line of investigation will have been reached.

REFERENCES

Arviko, I.
1976   Factors Influencing the Job and Life Satisfaction of Retired Baseball Players. Unpublished Master's thesis, University of ' Waterloo, Ontario.

Ball, D.
1976   "Failure in sport." American Sociological Review 41 (August): 726-739.

Bouton, J.
1970   Ball Four. New York: World.

Charmaz, K.
1980   The Social Reality of Death. Reading, Ma.: Addison-Wesley.

Coakley, J.
1982   Sport In Society. Second edition. St. Louis: Mosby.

Glaser, B. and A. Strauss.
1965   Awareness of Dying. New York: Aldine.

Gorer, G.
1965   Death, Grief and Mourning. New York: Doubleday.

Haerle, R.
1975   "Career patterns and career contingencies of professional
        baseball players." Pp. 457-519 in Ball and Loy (eds.), Sport and
        Social Order. Reading, Ma.: Addison-Wesley.

Hill, P. and B. Lowe.
1974   "The inevitable metathesis of the retiring athlete." International
        Review of Sport Sociology 9 (3-4): 5-29.

Kahn, R.
1971   The Boys of Summer. New York: Harper and Row.

Kalish, R.
1966   "A continuum of subjectively perceived death." The Geron-
        tologist 6(2):73-76.

Kastenbaum, R.
1981a   Death, Society, and Human Experience. Second edition. St.
        Louis: Mosby.
1981b   "Do we die in stages?" Pp. 109-117 in Wilcox and Sutton (eds.),
        Understanding Death and Dying. Sherman Oaks, Ca.: Alfred.

Kramer, J.
1969   Farewell to Football. New York: World.

Kubler-Ross, E.
1969   On Death and Dying. New York: Macmillan.

Lerch, S.
1981   "The adjustment to retirement of professional baseball players."
        Pp. 138-148 in Greendorfer and Yiannakis (eds.), Sociology of
        Sport: Diverse Perspectives. West Point, N.Y.: Leisure Press.

Loy, J., B. McPherson and G. Kenyon.
1978   Sport and Social Systems. Reading, Ma.: Addison-Wesley.

McPherson, B.
1980   "Retirement from professional sport: the process and problems
        of occupational and psychological adjustment." Sociological
        Symposium 30: 126-143.

Mihovilovic, M.
1968   "The status of former sportsmen." International Review of Sport
        Sociology 3: 73-96.

Plimpton, G.
1973   Mad Ducks and Bears. New York: Random House.

Rashad, A.
1982   "Journal of a Plagued Year." Sports Illustrated (Oct. 25): 82-96.

Reynolds, M.
1981   "The effects of sports retirement on the job satisfaction of the
        former football player." Pp. 127-137 in Greendorfer and Yian-
        nakis (eds.), Sociology of Sport: Diverse Perspectives. West
        Point, N.Y.: Leisure Press.

Rosenberg, E.
1981a   "Professional athletic retirement." Arena Review 5(2): 1-11.
1981b   "Gerontological theory and athletic retirement." Pp. 118-126 in
        Greendorfer and Yiannakis (eds.), Sociology of Sport: Diverse
        Perspectives. West Point, N.Y.: Leisure Press.

Sudnow, D.
1967   Passing On: The Social Organization of Dying. Englewood
        Cliffs, N.J.: Prentice-Hall.

Thomas, L.
1980   "Dying as failure." Annals of the American Academy of Political
        and Social Sciences 447 (January): 1-4.

Williams, J.
1981   "Focus on: desocialization from sport." NASSS Newsletter 3(2):
        2.

ATHLETIC RETIREMENT AS SOCIAL DEATH: AN OVERVIEW

Stephen Lerch
Radford University

BOTH FICTIONAL AND NON-FICTIONAL accounts of disengagement from an active career in sport have utilized the analogy of death to describe the phenomenon. The assumption seems to be that "life" for the athlete is dependent upon continued active involvement in the game or, at a minimum, a close and direct association with the game as coach, manager, or front-office executive. The skills required to maintain the consistently excellent performance which is the *sine qua non* of sports involvement at elite amateur and professional levels require a commitment to training and preparation which is unusual among most life pursuits. For this reason, it is not uncommon to hear dedicated athletes say "The game [baseball, football, etc.] *is* my life." If this is the athlete's perception, it is understandable that he or she also feels that life ends when the game ends. As former pitcher Jim Bouton said (1971: 231): "You can't give all your adult attention and striving to a single purpose and walk away from it without feeling a great deal of emptiness and even more sinking feeling."

In this vein, two highly acclaimed American sportswriters have recently written novels which discuss the social deaths of sports heroes facing the termination of their careers. In Frank Deford's (1981) *Everybody's All American*, the protagonist, Gavin Grey, is in the process of making the transition from his collegiate football career at North Carolina to his professional career. His mentor brings up the topic of social death of athletes:

"There's an expression I heard long ago—that an athlete dies twice. . . . You're going to die three times, Gavin Grey. It can't be helped. . . . All athletes die when they have to leave the game. That's their first death. But you're going to have an earlier one too, because what you achieved at Carolina cannot be continued or duplicated wherever you play next. . . . But I hasten to amend that, to add that it has nothing whatsoever to do with football. . . . Do you know what you've been? You've been playing a role. . . . Gavin Grey was a football player. But the Grey Ghost was a character. . . ."

"And The Ghost is dead," Gavin said softly, a calm smile crossing his face (p. 115).

Similarly, the hero of Roger Kahn's (1982) *The Seventh Game*, 41-year-old pitcher Johnny Longboat, discusses his dying pitching arm. Before the big game, the pitching coach asks "How is the arm?" and Johnny replies "One-hundred-forty-five years old" (1982: 64). Later, after finding out that the radar gun has recorded his fastest pitch has lost 8.4 miles per hour over the past three years, Johnny says, "Goddamn. You hate to die, and that's what my pitching arm is doing on me. It's dying" (1982: 66).

The analogy to death is by no means limited to fictional accounts of retirement from sport. Indeed, it is undoubtedly in non-fictional works that we find the most compelling depictions of the consequences of disengagement from sport, especially since empirical studies have been lacking until recently. Although there may be some question of the scientific validity of such accounts, it is argued that the writings of sportswriters and other journalists are those of field researchers acting in the role of complete observers (Gold, 1969): those who record their impressions of social processes (in this case, the final years of sports careers) without interacting in any way in these processes. Thus, in his classic *The Boys of Summer*, Kahn (1973) related that:

Unlike most, a ball player must confront two deaths. First, between the ages of thirty and forty he perishes as an athlete. Although he looks trim and feels vigorous and retains unusual coordination, the superlative reflexes, the major league reflexes, pass on. At a point when many of his classmates are newly confident and rising in other fields, he finds that he can no longer hit a very good fastball or reach a grounder a few strides to his right. At thirty-five he is experiencing the truth of finality. As his major league career is ending, all things will end. However he sprang, he was always earthbound. Mortality embraces him. The golden age has passed as in a moment. So will all things. So will all moments (p. xviii).

First-person accounts by athletes involved in the activities about which they are reporting provide even greater insight into their perceptions as they approach the termination of their careers. These athletes are acting in the role of either participant-as-observer or observer-as-participant (Gold, 1969). In the former, research intentions are made clear at the outset, and the research-er participates fully in the group; in the latter, the researcher does not pretend to be a full participant. Ball (1976: 729) suggests that such works may be treated *ala* anthropology's "key informant," allowing for a sociological examination of a member's reality, if not the members' realities, rather than the approximation of member-reality constructed by a non-member, i.e., the typically detached scientist.

One of the most noteworthy of these key informants is Bill Bradley, former All American, Rhodes scholar, and professional basketball player, presently U.S. Senator from New Jersey. In noting the social death of the athlete at retirement, Bradley (1977) remarked:

> For the athlete who reaches thirty-five, something in him dies; not a peripheral activity but a fundamental passion. It necessarily dies. The athlete rarely recuperates. He ap-proaches the end of his playing days the way old people approach death. He puts his finances in order. He reminisces easily. He offers advice to the young. But, the athlete differs from an old person in that he must continue living. Behind all the years of practice and all the hours of glory waits that inexorable terror of living without the game (p. 204).

Jim Bouton is undoubtedly the most famous (or, from the point of view of the baseball establishment, infamous) of the first-person commentators upon professional athletics. Bouton's remarks con-cerning career termination are particularly compelling because they were written during his final full season in major league baseball, during a time when he was literally attempting to hang onto his career by his fingertips as he made the transition from a fastball pitcher to a knuckleballer. As Ball (1976: 729) noted, Bouton's own marginality is a recurrent theme. Since his account includes a wealth of detailed information, his comments will form the basis for much of the analysis of sports retirement as social death below.

Bouton (1971) pointed out that the ballplayers themselves frequently utilized the imagery of death in discussing the separation of players from the active roster:

> Now that the cut-down season is here we'll soon be talking about deaths in the family. At least that's what we did with the Yankees. When a guy got cut we'd say he died. Fritz Peterson would come over to me and say, "Guess who died today." And he'd look very downcast and in the tones of an undertaker read the roll of the dead.
>
> A player who wasn't going well was said to be sick, very sick, in a coma, or on his deathbed, depending on how bad he was going. Last year when I was sent to Seattle, Fritz asked me what happened and I said I died.
>
> "You can't die," Fritz said. "You're too good to die" (p. 56).

The messenger of this social death is known as the "Grim Reaper." In football, such duties are performed by a more benevolent "Turk." Ball (1976: 734) suggested this is due to the organizational features of the two sports. Failure in baseball's major leagues almost invariably results in a stint in the despised minor leagues, whereas failure in professional football usually signals the end of one's career. Therefore, reactions to failure in football are more sympathetic and less degrading. At any rate, Bouton (1971) discussed the position of the Grim Reaper:

> On the Yankees the Grim Reaper was Big Pete [the equipment manager]. Once he whispered in your ear that the manager wanted to see you, you were clinically dead (p. 56).

Apparently, the status of the Grim Reaper is as unsavory as the title implies, for the death message was sometimes delivered symbolically (1971):

> Another way Big Pete would let you know you had died was by not packing your equipment for a road trip. There would be a packed bag in front of every locker except yours. Rest in peace. It's kind of like, "All those who are going to New York City, please step forward. Not so fast, Johnson" (p. 57).

SOCIAL DEATH IN SPORT: THE RELATIONSHIP TO TWO THANATOLOGICAL CONSTRUCTS

It has been documented that the imagery of death is commonly utilized to depict the experience of the disengaging athlete. However, we have not yet fully developed the relationship between social death and its "real life" counterpart. What similarities are there between social and "real" death? In an attempt to provide some preliminary answers to this question, we will examine two "theories" prominent in the study of death and dying; the awareness contexts notion of Glaser and Strauss (1965), and the better known "stages of dying" of Kubler-Ross (1969). Such an examination reveals interesting parallels between the socially dying athlete and the physically dying hospital patient.

Awareness Contexts

When a non-comatose patient is hospitalized, there is invariably some question about his or her condition among patient, family, and hospital staff. In broad terms, all interactants make some assessment as to whether the patient's condition is terminal or not. Glaser and Strauss (1965: 10) say that what each interacting person knows of the patient's defined status, along with recognition of the others' awareness of this definition—the total picture as a sociologist might construct it—is an awareness context. Since there are a number of persons involved in the interaction, there are different types of awareness context. Glaser and Strauss suggest four types: closed awareness, suspicion awareness, mutual pretense awareness, and open awareness.

In the first type, the closed awareness context, the patient does not recognize that he or she is dying, but the attending hospital personnel are cognizant of the fact. Closed awareness is common due to five structural conditions: patients are not experienced at recognizing the signs of death; physicians usually do not tell patients of impending death; families guard the secret; medical information is hidden from patients; and the patients have no allies to assist them in gathering pertinent information about their condition (Glaser and Strauss, 1965).

Closed awareness is suggested by the case of athletes who are unaware that their teams plan to cut, release, or trade them. When the demotion does occur, individuals involved are surprised; their teammates, however, may have been able to see management's "ax" approaching. The structural conditions bringing about this awareness (or, in this case, unawareness) of social death may be very similar to those for physical death. For example, athletes may be unfamiliar with the signs of social death (or they may rationalize instances of failure as the results of injuries, playing conditions, distractions, bad breaks, etc.); neither management nor teammates will discuss a player's failures with him or her; and it is difficult for athletes to find allies to honestly assess their situations. Although the "medical information" of sport—voluminous statistical data—is always available, such information may be deceptive because of variable interpretations.

Bouton (1970) provided an example of closed awareness:

> Brandon has taken being sent down pretty hard, *although he did have a poor spring.* [Emphasis added.] He took a long time packing his bag and after we were through with our workout he was still in the clubhouse, just sitting there in front of his locker, looking as though he hoped Schultz [the manager] might change his mind and tell him it was all a mistake. No one went over to talk to him. It was sad and strange (p. 91).

The second awareness context, suspicion awareness, is more complicated than the first. In this context, the patient suspects that he or she is dying. The hospital staff and others recognize the suspicion, so they try to negate it. Glaser and Strauss (1965: 47) utilize the metaphor of the fencing match: the patient is on the offensive, trying to confirm his or her suspicions; the staff is on the defensive, trying to negate them. As the structural conditions sustaining closed awareness change, patients may begin to suspect that their condition is terminal. For example, the physician may hint at the truth, or use terms like "cancer" which are inherently frightening. Similarly, movement of a patient to a new room or changing his or her treatments may, along with increasingly severe symptoms, arouse suspicions that death is inevitable.

Thus, when the equipment manager packs everyone's bags for a road trip save one person's, that person may suspect that a demotion is forthcoming. Suspicions may also be aroused by the tone of interaction with managers and coaches. Bouton (1970: 17-18) related that he evaluated his standing by the way the pitching coach said good morning to him. When he was performing very well, he was greeted with "Well now, good morning, Jimsie boy." If he was only pitching moderately well, the coach nodded at him and said "Jimbo, how are you doin', How are you doin'?" If he was struggling, the greeting was "Mornin'. " If the team had lost confidence in him, the coach would nod and say nothing. However,

> . . . if he looked past you, over your shoulder as if you didn't exist, it was all over and you might as well pack your bag because you could be traded or sent down at any moment.

Bouton (1970: 68) also described a spring training situation in which a group of players is called into the manager's office and informed that because of space limitations, they will have to work out with the team's minor league affiliate—an alteration in treatment that is greeted with suspicion by the players involved. The manager tries to negate their suspicions by insisting:

> "You're not cut. Your stuff is still in your locker and you're still on the team. Don't draw any conclusions from this."
> It wasn't really death. It was just the priest coming to your bedside to say a few choice Latin words. . . . One of the guys who got the call, Lou Piniella, didn't go into Joe's office, but sort of sulked outside. "Come on in, Lou," Joe said. "It's not going to be anything bad." Lou knew better.

The third awareness context, mutual pretense, is analogous to a grown-up form of make-believe. It occurs when both patient and staff know that the patient is dying but pretend otherwise. Both agree to act as if he or she were going to live (Glaser and Strauss, 1965: 66). It is imperative that staff members avoid talking about death with the patient in order to maintain the charade that death is not inevitable. In effect, all parties involved maintain false fronts, pretending that the condition is not terminal even though they know full well that it is.

Although specific examples are lacking, this seems analogous to the case of athletes who are ostensibly given every chance to make the team. They receive encouragement from teammates, managers, coaches, and front-office personnel. However, all concerned know that no matter how well these players perform, they will not make the team. Interestingly, this probably happens most frequently to those at the far ends of the age spectrum. Young players are "farmed out" (sent to the minor leagues) to obtain more "seasoning" (experience). Older athletes, on the other hand, are demoted so that teams may "go with youth."

A mutual pretense context that is not sustained can only change to an open awareness context. In this final context, both patients and those around them know that death is inevitable and openly acknowledge the fact. Many athletes come to training camp realizing that it will be impossible for them to attain a position on a major league roster, and all concerned acknowledge this fact. Examples would include the late round draft choice or free agent in basketball, football or hockey as well as the athlete with modest skills who is trying to earn the position presently held by a superstar. The latter is depicted in the following example, in which the athlete is able to make light of his plight (Bouton, 1970):

> I remember toward the end of one spring training Don Lock, an outfielder with a pretty good sense of humor (he needed it, having spent a lot of years in the Yankee chain trying to break into an outfield of Tom Tresh, Mantle, and Maris), barricaded his locker. He hung sweatshirts across the top, crossed out his name, piled up his gloves and shoes in front to form a barrier, then snuggled inside the locker holding a bat like it was a rifle, and fired it at anyone who came near. It was good for a few laughs, but in the end, the Grim Reaper got him anyway (p. 56).

Stages of Death

In her landmark study *On Death and Dying* (1969), Elisabeth Kubler-Ross deals at length with the reactions of terminal patients as they attempt to deal with impending death. Since death has traditionally been a taboo topic for discussion in American society, Americans have an almost perverse fear of death. When it is our own death that is being considered, we become especially afraid. In her interviews with terminal patients, Kubler-Ross found that patients utilize a variety of coping mechanisms to deal with death. Furthermore, these coping mechanisms appear to be inevitable. Patients (and their families) universally pass through them, albeit at different rates. Kubler-Ross's work has been criticized on a variety of grounds; hospital staff, for example, have sometimes been found attempting to "coax" terminal patients through the stages. However, in this preliminary analysis of retirement from sport as social death, an interesting parallel can be drawn between the Kubler-Ross stages of coping with terminal illness and coping with social death, particularly utilizing Bouton's experience in being demoted to the minor leagues.

The first stage of coping with terminal illness is denial: "No, not me, it cannot be true" (Kubler-Ross, 1969: 38). Patients sometimes develop rituals to support the denial: doctor gave mistaken diagnosis, charts were mixed-up, etc. Thus, when Bouton is sent to the minor leagues ("I died tonight. I got sent to Vancouver."), he first attempts denial (Bouton, 1970):

> We'd lost a 2-1 game in Kansas City when Sal [the pitching coach] came over and said "Joe wants to see you in his office."
>
> My heart started racing. I mean Joe never wants to see me anywhere. So I knew. At the same time I thought "Nah. It's too early. I've really only pitched the once. How can they tell anything from that? Maybe it's a trade? Or maybe he's just sore at something I've done. Let's see, what have I done lately?" (p. 105).

The second stage is anger. If our first reaction to catastrophic news is, "No it's not true, no, it cannot involve me," it gives way to a new reaction when it finally dawns on us: "Oh, yes, it is me, it was not a mistake" (Kubler-Ross, 1969: 50). We then ask: Why me? What did I do to deserve this? Why can't this happen to somebody else?

In Bouton's (1970: 105) experience, anger does not only occur after denial, but it is interspersed throughout the entire coping experience. He describes his first reaction to the bad news as "outrage." After talking to the manager about the demotion, he visited the general manager, who justified the demotion by telling Bouton (1970):

> . . ."Well you didn't show us much all spring." If I had shown much more I wouldn't be getting sent down. I felt like kicking him in the shins, but I said, "Hell, I had a better spring than four or five guys. In fact, I'm healthy, which is more than you can say for at least two of the guys." What I didn't say, but what I thought, was: "What about Steve Barber? He hasn't been able to pick up a baseball. He had a brutal spring. What's this love affair with Barber? Why can't he go on the disabled list? Ah, the hell with it." (p. 106).

One of the first of the journalist-athletes, Jim Brosnan (1960), similarly related the anger of ball players on cut-down day:

. . .[the clubhouse man's] spoken word, "Skip wants to
see you in his office," can unleash the torment of harassed,
frustrated ambition. "I won't go. I'll quit first. To hell with
this goddamn club! And baseball! I've had it. I quit!" (p. 53-54)

The third coping mechanism is bargaining. The terminal patient attempts to strike a bargain with God so that death may
be postponed, e.g., "I'll dedicate my life to God" or "I'll do something to aid the unfortunate" for a reprieve from the death
sentence.

Bouton (1970), too, tried to bargain about his trip to Vancouver:

I told [the manager] I would have done anything to help
the club and I really felt bad about having to leave it.
"I know," Joe Schultz said. . .
So I said, "Well, if I do real good down there, I'd like to
come back."
. . . Joe Schultz said, "Well, if you do good down there,
there's a lot of teams that need pitchers."
Good grief. If I ever heard a see you later, that was it.
So I said thanks a lot and left (p. 105).

The fourth stage is depression. Eventually, the patient realizes
that he or she is dying, and all the denials, rage, and bargaining
are ineffective. They are replaced by a profound sense of loss
(Kubler-Ross, 1969: 85). This occurs not only because of the
devastating effect the imminent loss of one's life has upon the
individual, but also due to the concomitants of illness—high costs
of hospitalization and treatment, failure to perform roles as parent,
spouse, worker, etc.

Bouton (1970) said that after his outrage, his second reaction
was:

Omigod! How am I going to tell [my wife]? The *problems.*
Where to live? How to get rid of the place we'd already signed
a lease on in Seattle? What would happen to the $650
deposit? Moving again. *Again.* And we just got here (p. 105).

Later:

. . . I packed up my bag and walked out. It felt lousy
(p. 106).

And still later:

One of the worst things about getting sent down is the

feeling you get that you've broken faith with so many people. I know my mother and father were rooting real hard for me, and all my friends back home, and they'll all feel bad. . . (p. 107).

Eventually, the patient reaches the final stage: acceptance. This is ". . . not a happy stage. It is almost void of feelings" (Kubler-Ross, 1969: 113). Affairs have been put in order, the imminent end is recognized, and the patient waits with a sense of quiet expectation (1969: 112).

It is at this stage that natural death differs most from the social death of the athlete. There is, to be sure, an element of acceptance involved in athletic failure; if one has been demoted or cut, he or she has little choice but resignation to the fact. Thus, former minor leaguer Pat Jordan (1975) related reactions to being cut:

They fingered their unconditional release, stared at it, their day ruined, possibly the week, *forced* [emphasis added] now to abandon the false spring of their new lives and begin again (p. 119).

After the unleashing of the "torment of harassed, frustrated ambition" discussed earlier, Brosnan said ". . . you go, quietly" (1960: 53-54).

However, social death differs from real death in that the individual continues to live; there is a recovery—a resurrection, if you will—from social death. When athletes are cut, demoted, or released from a team in professional sport, a part of them may die, but *only* a part. For all his lamentations about "dying" socially in *Ball Four*, Bouton (1971) himself noted in his sequel:

You can't, you *don't* believe your life ends when you stop playing a game. Baseball isn't the only way of life. It's a game you play for fun and money and when the time comes you have to be able to walk away from it (p. 231).

Professional athletes—other than those who earn enough to avoid subsequent careers—tend to move on to new pursuits.

Furthermore, there is often the hope of "resurrection" in the sport. This is particularly true for those who are sent to the minor leagues from the majors. Most undoubtedly see the demotion as temporary, believing it will only be a matter of time before they are recalled. Bouton (1970) eventually came to accept his demotion to Vancouver, but only because he harbored the hope for an eventual return to Seattle:

Quitting altogether crosses my mind. But I won't. I'm convinced I can still get out big league hitters with my knuckleball. I *know* I can. I know this is crazy, but I can see the end of the season and I've just won a pennant for some team, just won the final game, and everybody is clamoring around and I tell them, "Everybody have a seat. It's a long story."

I could be kidding myself. Maybe I'm so close to the situation that I can't make an objective judgment of whatever ability I have left. Maybe I just *think* I can do it. Maybe everybody who doesn't make it and who gets shunted to the minors feels exactly the way I do. Maybe, too, the great cross of man is to repeat the mistakes of all men (p. 107).

DISCUSSION

Before concluding this overview of the analogy of athletic retirement to death, there are a number of points that should be made. First, the comparison of the circumstances surrounding the cessation of physical life to those surrounding the end of of social life rests on somewhat tenuous theoretical grounds, due primarily to the fact that the event outcomes are drastically different. Physical death is final and absolute; social life goes on, albeit in a different form. It is obvious, then, that reactions to social death will be less serious. Indeed, whereas relatives and friends are the mourners when one dies physically, it is athletes themselves who mourn at the death of their beloved careers.

Acknowledging that the analogy itself may be tenuous, certain other shortcomings should be noted. For example, the analogy is not well documented. First-person retirement accounts often discuss social death; obviously, Bouton's work is foremost in this regard, primarily because of his perspective as a marginal athlete. However, empirical studies of retirement—themselves lacking until recently—have for the most part either not noted the analogy or not discussed it in any detail. In the author's 1979 study of 511 retired baseball players, the former athletes made not one mention of death, social or otherwise. Such revelations lead one to question the extent to which Bouton and others have utilized the analogy as a literary device. It is suggested that forthcoming studies of athletic retirement pursue the analogy in greater detail.

One of the consistent criticisms of Kubler-Ross is that her stages of dying may not have the universality she insists they do. Similarly, although Bouton fits the denial-anger-bargaining-depression-acceptance pattern almost perfectly, we must question the extent to which his experiences represent only a case study. The author's (Lerch, 1979) earlier study indicates that although most athletes do eventually accept the termination of their active careers, some become emotionally fixated in one of the other of Kubler-Ross's stages, especially anger, as for example the comment:

> I was very bitter and still am. . . every time I pick the papers up and see a lot of these guys managing in the majors that can't carry my jock strap into the ball park when it comes to managerial ability, it makes me sick (p. 99).

Similarly, Jordan (1975) indicated that his minor league teammates varied in the coping mechanisms utilized upon the release notification, but he provided no evidence that they moved through a series of stages:

> Some refused [to sign the formal release], as if they could retain their career by simply refusing to sign the document that ended it [denial]. Some signed in stunned silence [acceptance]; others cried [depression], begged, pleaded for another chance [bargaining]; and still others departed like the father of Dylan Thomas, cursing, raging, and, in a final act of defiance, crumpling their release and flinging it back into [the team executive's] face [anger] (p. 118).

Finally, we should note that the analogy is much more applicable to involuntary rather than voluntary retirement. This, of course, is because physical death is almost universally not voluntary; on the contrary, we fear impending physical death, much in the same way that athletes fear the demotion, cut, or release. Thus, the reaction to being socially terminated may be the same as that to awareness of impending physical death: anger, depression, bargaining, etc. The consequences of voluntary retirement, on the other hand, would be far less severe because the subject is retaining control over his own fate rather than having another's will imposed upon him. Further studies of the relationship of death to athletic retirement should take into account the qualitative differences between voluntary and involuntary retirement.

REFERENCES

Ball, D.W.
1976   "Failure in sport." American Sociological Review 41 (August): 726-739.

Bouton, J. (L. Shecter, ed.)
1970   Ball Four. New York: Dell Publishing Co., Inc.
1971   I'm Glad You Didn't Take It Personally. New York: Dell Publishing Co., Inc.

Bradley, B.
1977   Life on the Run. New York: Bantam Books, Inc.

Brosnan, J.
1960   The Long Season. New York: Harper and Brothers.

Deford, F.
1981   Everybody's All American. New York: The Viking Press.

Glaser, B.G. and A. Strauss
1965   Awareness of Dying. Chicago: Aldine Press.

Gold, R.L.
1969   "Roles in sociological field observation." In G.L. McCall and J.L. Simmons (eds.), Issues in Participant Observation. Reading, Mass.: Addison-Wesley.

Jordan, P.
1975   A False Spring. New York: Bantam Books, Inc.

Kahn, R.
1973   The Boys of Summer. New York: Signet.
1982   The Seventh Game. New York: New American Library.

Kubler-Ross, E.
1969   On Death and Dying. New York: MacMillan Publishing Co., Inc.

Lerch, S.H.
1979   "Adjustment to early retirement: the case of professional baseball players." Unpublished Doctoral Dissertation, Purdue University.

AGE AND SPORT PARTICIPATION: DECLINE IN PARTICIPATION OR INCREASED SPECIALIZATION WITH AGE?[1]

James E. Curtis and Philip G. White
University of Waterloo

A COMMON FINDING in cross-sectional survey research on the sport and physical activities of adults is that there are lower levels of participation in the older age categories (cf., e.g., Kenyon, 1966; Robinson, 1967; Dumazedier, 1973; Milton, 1973; Hobart, 1975; McPherson and Kozlik, 1980; White, 1980: chapters v and vi; and Smith *et al.*, 1980: chapter 7 and 8). This pattern of apparent "disengagement" with age is not surprising in light of results from studies of other forms of leisure activity; studies of political participation, voluntary association activity, and participation at cultural events, for example, are consistent in demonstrating that there are lower levels of involvement for older age categories (cf. Smith and Foner, 1980; Curtis, 1971; Hausknecht, 1962: chapter 4; Milton, 1975: chapter 4ff; and Riley and Foner, 1968: part iv). This paper presents some relevant findings on patterns of sport participation by age from a national sample of adult Canadians. The findings are of interest for two reasons. First, many of the results are consistent with the common pattern of findings and provide further confirmation of it. Second, and most importantly, some of the results are not consistent with the common pattern; they are more suggestive of the "continuity" and "activity" interpretations of aging. Thus far, results from studies of age and sport participation have given little support for these latter interpretations. As we will suggest, though, previous studies have not been designed in a manner which might easily uncover evidence of continuity and activity processes. We present an alternative type of analysis.

THEORETICAL PERSPECTIVES ON AGING AND SPORT PARTICIPATION

As Loy, McPherson and Kenyon (1978: 357-364) have suggested, one or more of three theoretical approaches used in the literature on leisure social participation may be applicable to age differences in sport and physical recreation. The most often mentioned interpretation of previous results on age and sport and physical activity, because of its apparent consonance with the common inverse relationship, is the disengagement theory (see especially Cumming and Henry, 1961). This theory argues that there is an increased withdrawal from social participation with greater age.

It is argued that this may occur in two ways. First, "societal disengagement" is the process whereby, either consciously or inadvertently, society members make fewer roles available for persons of advancing age. As Atchley (1977) says:

> Older people may no longer be sought out for leadership in organizations, their labor may no longer be desired by their employers, their children may no longer want them to become involved in their decisions, their unions may no longer be interested in their financial problems, and their government may no longer be responsive to their needs (p. 227).

Our casual observations of sport and physical recreation organizations give us some suggestions of this process, beyond the common survey findings. Older people appear to have more limited access to sport facilities than younger people. Organized opportunities for participation and for instruction in many sport and physical recreation activities seem to be more often geared to the young. A subcultural variant of the disengagement theory (cf. Rose, 1965) would argue that the lack of encouragement of participation by the wider society leads to older people developing their own unique norms in response. These norms include acceptance of the definition of themselves as not active in sport and physical activities and, perhaps, as not capable of being active.

This process of acceptance is involved in the second type of disengagement, "individual disengagement." This refers to the situation where individuals voluntarily withdraw from the wider society and spend more time on other activities, such as in passive leisure activities, rest, recuperation and introspection (Atchley, 1977: 26). As Atchley (1977) has emphasized, the two components of disengagement may be causally related:

> Most voluntary individual disengagement has resulted from the fact that people see disengagement as inevitable by the rules of the institution they participated in. That is voluntary disengagement is really the result of societal disengagement (p. 231).

A good example of this process is contained in the phenomena of different sport and physical activity roles being defined age-specifically. For example, cultural beliefs about the appropriate ages for participants in lawn bowling are quite different from those for the ages of football players. Such age-specific definitions of sport are probably influenced by the amount of speed, strength and endurance required for good performance and the supposed characteristics of the different age categories.

Loy, McPherson and Kenyon (1978: 362ff) have cautioned, though, that there are problems involved in any simple extrapolation of the disengagement theory to participation in sport and physical recreation. First, participation in many sport and physical activities is not totally dependent upon social interaction with others, except as a source of motivation to be active. Therefore, social pressure for disengagement for older persons may not always be strong. Some forms of participation such as bicycling, jogging or cross-country skiing can easily be engaged in entirely alone. Second, even those older people who are moved to disengage from roles in sport and physical recreation may seek to adopt new rules in related activities but in ones that are deemed appropriate for their age by societal definitions.

The alternative activity interpretation of aging emphasizes that maintaining the activity level of middle age is one way that old people have of coping with getting older (see, for example, Friedman and Havighurst, 1954). It is argued that the pursuit of high levels of activity is common among many middle-aged and older persons and that this may stem from a need to postpone an evaluation of the significance of passing life. It is argued that when persons lose active roles they will likely assume others in order to maintain an acceptable and reasonably constant activity level. This perspective suggests, then, that individuals who are active should attempt to change the sport and physical recreation roles that they occupy over the life cycle by dropping those roles that they cannot easily perform any longer or those that are defined as socially inappropriate and by adding others. Presumably they might also increase their activity levels in some roles when others must be dropped. Thus far, though, there has been no clear evidence that these processes occur for sport and physical recreation involvement.

The continuity theory of aging (see, for example, Atchley, 1977) is similar to activity theory. It focuses on the fact that, through the socialization process, young adults develop patterns of behavior and commitments to lifestyles which often are so thoroughly ingrained that they are followed for the entire life cycle. Applied to sport and physical activities the argument would be that, if physiologically able and allowed by opportunities, the individual will continue to satisfy predispositions for activity and habits that were acquired in earlier stages of the life cycle. Studies of socialization into sport which have used retrospective questioning about the past have yielded some results that may be interpreted as consistent with this view (see Kelly, 1977; Spreitzer and Snyder, 1976; and McPherson, 1978). These studies show that childhood involvement in sport is positively associated with sport participation during the adult years.

WORKING HYPOTHESES

The consistent findings of inverse relationships between age and sport participation in previous studies led us to expect that similar relationships would obtain for our subsamples of adult males and adult females. Beyond this, we began with the view that each of the different sets of aging processes described above may well occur simultaneously, for different respondents, or as alternative effects impacting the same individuals. Therefore, we chose to ask how the available data might best be brought to bear on each set of theoretical interpretations.

We noted, first, that information on reasons for non-participation might lend some further credence to disengagement theory. If the processes implied by this theory were operating, and respondents perceived them to occur, then the elderly should be comparatively high in saying that they lacked facilities for participation, had no opportunity to participate, and had no one to participate with. We explore these possibilities in available data on the respondents' reasons for non-participation in activities. We further expected that the elderly would most frequently give physical problems as their reasons for non-participation or for limited participation because (a) there should be such problems for some older people and (b) this is part of the social definition of the aged.

As far as the processes discussed in the continuity and activity interpretations are concerned, we noted that the common approach to survey data on age and sport and physical recreation participation is not very appropriate for even indirect tests of these processes. The previous studies that we are aware of looked only at participation among all respondents, participants and non-participants taken together. Yet the interpretations in continuity and activity theory have especially to do with what occurs for those who have become participants at some time. Thus, we decided to look, separately, at age-involvement patterns for those with some minimal involvement or more. We wondered, for example, if there would be any evidence to suggest that older people drop some roles that they can no longer do but continue to focus on a few types of activity. We thought that the mean frequency of involvement per sport and physical activity might remain constant, or might even increase, across age levels among participants. We also expected older participants to be involved in fewer sports than young participants.

The common strategy of making age comparisons for all respondents cannot be expected to show a pattern of greater specialization in some sport and physical recreation activities. This is the case because participation of any kind is characteristic of only a small minority of older people. Given a strong overall pattern of declining participation with age this is what would be most manifest in any analyses for total samples. Of course, the alternative strategy of comparing age levels among participants only must be approached cautiously, as well, for other methodological reasons. In these comparisons, we do not have direct evidence of the extent to which respondents have moved into and out of sport and physical recreation over their lives. All we know is that they all had some involvement at the time of the survey. For example, we do not know the extent to which some middle-aged and older persons have moved into sport and physical recreation, after not having been involved earlier. Nonetheless, using caution in our interpretations, we can ask if older people who participate appear to have fewer activities, but participate in them as much, compared with their younger counterparts.[2]

DATA SOURCE AND PROCEDURES
We present secondary analyses of data from a Canadian Labour Force Survey of some 50,000 adults. This survey of employment/unemployment and worker characteristics is conducted monthly using a sample chosen to be representative of the adult Canadian population (see Statistics Canada, 1971). The particular survey that we employ involved a supplemental set of questions on various aspects of sport and physical recreation. Respondents completed a nine-page self-administered questionnaire during October, 1976.

A working sub-sample was selected which was comprised of native-born Canadians who were 20 years of age and older (N=33, 762). Native-born respondents were selected to limit the analysis to persons who, clearly, had been socialized into the Canadian culture and its age roles. Respondents who were younger than 20 years of age were not included in order to exclude students whose sport involvement might be school-related rather than voluntary leisure activities. Our analyses were conducted separately for males and females to check on the possibility of differences in the age-participation relationships by sex and because we expected the sexes to differ markedly in levels of participation, with women being less active (see, for example, Milton, 1973).

Five measures of sport and physical recreation participation were employed as dependent variables. In these we wished to cover as many aspects of participation as allowed by the data source[3] The dependent variables were as follows (with the range of values indicated in parentheses): Involvement/noninvolvement was defined as participation in one or more sports one or more times in the preceding year, or not. Sustained involvement was measured as participation in one or more sports more than ten times during the preceding year, or not. Number of activities (range of 0 to 4+ for phase 1 of the analyses for the total sample, and 1 to 5+ for phase 2, for sport participants only) was the total number of different activities participated in during the year. An index of mean frequency by activity (range of 0 to 3+ for phase 1 and 1 to 4+ for the second phase) was defined as the mean number of times respondents said they had participated in their different sport and physical activities in the year. Respondents were given these forced choice responses for each activity that they cited: none, 1-10 times, 11-20 times, 21-30 times, and over 30 times. These levels were assigned scores of 0, 1, 2, 3, and 4 respectively. These frequency scores were then summed and divided by the number of activities. Finally, an index of overall involvement was defined as the sum of the frequency scores for each activity reported. Since a few respondents reported on as many as 10 different types of sport and physical recreation, the potential range for this variable was 30 for the first phase of the analysis and 40 for the second phase. However, because this variable was highly skewed (with only a few respondents reporting several activities with high frequency of involvement) this measure was collapsed so that its highest category was 9 for the first phase of the analysis and 10 for the second phase.[4]

As we have indicated, participation reasons were also examined as dependent variables. Respondents were asked if they would like to participate more in sport and physical recreation, and, if so, why they were not participating more. The reasons provided in a list were: "it's difficult to find others to participate with," "not enough time because of other leisure activities," "not enough time because of work," "there is no opportunity to participate near my home," "it costs too much to participate," "the available facilities/areas are of poor quality, are inadequate and are not challenging," "I am physically unable to participate," and "I don't know how to do it well enough." Unfortunately, no questions were asked on recent changes in involvement or planned changes for the future.

Our independent variable, age, was coded into these categories: 20-29; 30-39; 40-49; 50-59; and 60 and older. The following control variables were also employed: language (English or French spoken most often at home); education (less than high school; high school; some post secondary; university degree); income (<$4,000; 4,000-6,999; 7,000-9,999; 10,000-14,999; $15,000 and over); and community size (100,000 and over; 30,000-99,999; 15,000-29,999; 1,000-14,999; rural and less than 1,000). Our rationale for using the control factors was based, in part, on preliminary analyses showing that each factor was related to age and to one or more of our dependent variables and that their effects confounded some of the age-participation relationships (for details see White, 1980: chapters v and vi). Controls were made, given this, because the theoretical perspectives from which we drew our hypotheses clearly refer to age effects on participation which are supposed to be independent of the effects of the control variables.

Our statistical procedure was Multiple Classification Analysis, or MCA (see Nie et al., 1975: 409ff). This procedure assesses the effects of a predictor variable on a dependent variable while simultaneously controlling for the effects of other variables. MCA yields an adjusted mean score for the dependent variable for each category of the predictor after controlling statistically for the effects of each of the other predictors. An F-test for statistical significance is reported for each relationship after controls.

FINDINGS

Table 1 reports findings for sport and physical recreation by age, before and after controls, for all males and all females. Each of the five measures of sport and physical recreation was inversely related to age before controls for each sex. For example, 70 per cent of the youngest male age category had at least one activity in which they were involved for one or more times per year compared with 15 per cent of the oldest age category. The comparable figures for females were 60 per cent and 10 per cent.

The controlled relationships were also in the same direction, and they were statistically significant for all dependent variables for both the male and female subsamples (p <.001 in each instance). The relationships tended to be less marked after controls, however. The latter occurred, especially, because education was positively related to participation and the aged were low in education. For one or more activities done one or more times a year there was a decrease in adjusted proportions from 66 per cent to 27 per cent for the youngest to the oldest male categories. The comparable figures for females were 56 per cent and 16 per cent. The adjusted proportions of those who reported involvement of more than ten times a year was 54 per cent for the youngest male age level compared with 22 per cent for the oldest male category. The females showed 40 per cent and 13 per cent respectively for these age levels. The mean frequency of activities varied from 1.17 to 0.54 from the youngest to the oldest age categories for males, and the figures for females varied from 0.90 to 0.33.

TABLE 1

Unadjusted and Adjusted Means (via MCA) For Five Measures Of Participation In Sport And Physical Recreation By Age, For Male And Female Subsamples Of Native-Born Adult Canadians, 1976.[1]

Subsamples and Age Levels		Sport and Physical Recreation Measures[2]				
		Involv. (%)	Sustain. (%)	Number (0-3+)	Freq. (0-3+)	Overall (0-9+)
Males	(N)					
20-29 years	4319	66 (70)	54 (57)	1.90 (1.99)	1.17 (1.23)	3.83 (4.03)
30-39 years	3134	54 (60)	42 (49)	1.37 (1.54)	0.97 (1.06)	2.79 (3.12)
40-49 years	2482	43 (45)	33 (34)	1.00 (1.04)	0.78 (0.81)	2.03 (2.12)
50-59 years	2203	33 (31)	26 (24)	0.72 (0.65)	0.64 (0.60)	1.54 (1.39)
60 and over	2551	27 (15)	22 (12)	0.59 (0.25)	0.54 (0.32)	1.29 (0.59)
Stat. Sig.[3]		***	***	***	***	***
Females						
20-29 years	4761	56 (60)	40 (43)	1.38 (1.51)	0.90 (0.97)	2.56 (2.80)
30-39 years	3439	50 (52)	37 (38)	1.12 (1.18)	0.88 (0.91)	2.21 (2.31)
40-49 years	2608	40 (28)	29 (29)	0.80 (0.78)	0.74 (0.73)	1.67 (1.64)
50-59 years	2380	29 (26)	22 (19)	0.55 (0.45)	0.58 (0.52)	1.20 (1.01)
60 and over	2849	16 (10)	13 (8)	0.31 (0.14)	0.33 (0.22)	0.71 (0.37)
Stat. Sig.[3]		***	***	***	***	***

[1] Statistical controls were made for education level, income, language and community size. The results before controls are presented in parentheses.

[2] The dependent variables for sport and physical recreation participation are: percent with some involvement; percent with sustained activity in one or more activity; number of activities; frequency of involvement per activity; and overall level of involvement. The range of values for each variable appears in parentheses. See the text for further details on the definition and measurement of these variables.

[3] Statistical significance levels: *** <.001; ** <.01; * <.05; ns=not significant.

The controlled relationships of involvement and age for only those who reported some participation are reported in Table
2. The age differences were not as consistent as in Table 1,
although age was significantly related to each of the participation measures in each subsample (p <.001). Among males, the
adjusted proportions of those who participate in a sport more
than 10 times a year show a slightly curvilinear relationship with
age. Those in the middle age ranges were slightly less involved than those in the youngest and oldest categories. There was
only a 1 per cent difference in the proportions who were involved comparing the youngest and oldest male age categories.
Among the females, the adjusted proportions of those who
showed sustained involvement was highest for the oldest age
category; 12 per cent more of the oldest age category than the
youngest age category were this highly involved among females.
Also, there were minimal differences between the youngest and
the middle age categories among females. The index of number
of sports and the measure of overall involvement both showed
roughly linear declines in participation as the age levels increased, both for males and females.

Perhaps the most interesting finding in Table 2, though, is
one consistent with our hypothesis drawn from continuity and
activity theory. Among sport participants, whether male or
female, the mean frequency of involvement per activity
showed an inverse relationship with age level. The adjusted
average frequency of involvement for males rose from 1.83 to
2.37 from the youngest to the oldest age categories. The older
females also reported participating more frequently per type
of activity than their younger counterparts, with an increase
of 1.68 to 2.57 from the youngest to the oldest age levels. At
the older age levels, then, males and females participate in fewer
activities but participate more per activity.

Table 3 gives the percentages of non-participants who reported
each of eight reasons for their non-involvement. Only those
who wished to have more participation answered these questions. Because controlled analyses showed the same patterns
as those that were uncontrolled, only the latter are presented
in Table 3.

The following findings seem noteworthy: As expected, the
older the age category the more likely physical inability was
reported as a problem for participation, both for males and
females. For males, the reason for non-participation that was

TABLE 2

Adjusted Means (via MCA) For Four Measures Of Participation In Sport and Physical Recreation By Age, For Those With Some Participation In The Subsamples Of Male And Female Native-Born Adult Canadians, 1976.[1]

Subsamples and Age Levels		Sport and Physical Recreation Measures[2]			
		Sustain. (%)	Number (1-5+)	Freq. (1-4+)	Overall (1-10+)
Males	(N)				
20-29 years	3006	81	3.12	1.83	6.05
30-39 years	1873	78	2.67	1.91	5.30
40-49 years	1105	76	2.42	1.95	4.88
50-59 years	691	76	2.15	2.13	4.58
60 and over	378	80	1.83	2.37	4.37
Stat. Sig.[3]		***	***	***	***
Females					
20-29 years	2875	70	2.36	1.68	4.68
30-39 years	1776	73	2.36	1.84	4.56
40-49 years	1019	72	2.10	2.01	4.32
50-59 years	607	74	1.88	2.19	4.14
60 and over	274	82	1.64	2.57	4.13
Stat. Sig.[3]		***	***	***	***

[1] Statistical controls were made for education level, income, language and community size.

[2] The dependent variables for sport and physical recreation participation are: percent with sustained activity in one or more activity; number of activities; frequency of involvement per activity; and overall level of involvement. The range of values for each variable appears in parentheses. See the text for further details on the definition and measurement of these variables.

[3] Statistical significance levels: *** <.001; ** <.01; * <.05; ns=not significant.

most often given was the lack of time due to work commitments. As might be expected this constraint on participation was cited more often from early adulthood to middle-age and declined in importance thereafter (p <.001). While 51 per cent of males in the 40-49 age category reported that they had not participated for this reason, only 21 per cent of their counterparts in the oldest age category did. A comparatively high proportion of females also gave this reason for their non-participation; the 40-49 age category gave this reason most often while the oldest age level reported it least often (p <.001). A lack of opportunity to participate was given as a reason for non-participation by a large proportion at all ages for both sexes. Among males, the frequency with which this reason was given declined with age until the oldest age category where it increased in importance (p <.05). Nevertheless, the oldest age group did not report this reason as often as the youngest age group. Problems with finding others to participate with declined in importance with age for both males and females except, again, for the oldest age level which found it a relatively important reason. Among males, the youngest respondents cited this reason most often (p <.05). The youngest females also gave this reason a lot of weight, although those who were 60 years of age and over found this factor to be an even greater obstacle to participation.

Findings on reasons for non-involvement for sport participants only are reported in Table 4. Insufficient time to participate because of work was the most frequently given reason by each sex. This reason was related in a curvilinear manner to age; the middle age levels were most constrained by this factor. The lack of coparticipants and opportunities were related to age as reasons for non-involvement for both males and females. The proportions of those who reported that they did not have someone to participate with declined with age for males even to the oldest age level. Among females this reason was found to be the most important at the youngest and the oldest ends of the age scale. The proportions who indicated that a lack of opportunity prevented them from participating declined slowly with age until the oldest category where this reason was most often cited, for both males and females.[5]

TABLE 3

Percentage Giving Different Reasons For Non-Involvement In A Sport Or Physical Recreation Activity That They Would Like To Participate In, For Male and Female Non-Participants In Sport.

		Age Levels					
		20–29	30–39	40–49	50–59	60+	
Reasons for	M[1]	(381)	(255)	(181)	(144)	(94)	Stat.
Non-Participation	F	(664)	(415)	(277)	(220)	(103)	Sig.[2]
		%	%	%	%	%	
No Others to	M	15.2	11.4	7.7	5.6	10.6	*
Participate with	F	18.7	16.9	16.6	11.8	21.4	ns
Physically	M	1.3	1.6	4.4	4.2	10.6	ns
Unable	F	1.8	2.2	1.8	5.5	12.6	ns
Time: Competing	M	17.1	17.6	13.3	12.5	17.0	ns
Activities	F	15.7	16.6	13.4	12.7	7.8	ns
Time: Because	M	38.6	47.5	51.4	45.1	21.3	***
of Work	F	28.2	28.9	32.5	24.1	14.6	***
No	M	29.7	25.5	20.4	17.4	27.7	*
Opportunity	F	31.3	28.7	26.7	25.9	25.9	ns
Too	M	16.8	17.6	18.8	17.4	12.8	ns
Costly	F	17.2	17.6	19.5	14.5	10.7	ns
No	M	5.5	5.5	4.4	4.9	5.3	ns
Facilities	F	5.6	4.8	3.2	1.8	1.0	ns
Don't	M	6.0	6.3	10.5	7.6	6.4	ns
Know How	F	15.1	15.7	19.5	11.8	6.8	*

[1] M=Male; F=Female.

[2] Statistical significance levels: *** <.001; ** <.01; * <.05; ns=not significant.

SUMMARY AND DISCUSSION

Disengagement theory leads us to expect that with greater age there is an increased withdrawal from sport and physical recreation because roles become normatively inappropriate. The continuity and activity theories suggest that sport and physical activity roles, once acquired, will be maintained or replaced if possible, as long as physical disability does not dictate otherwise. Our results on sport and physical recreation participation and on reasons for non-participation allow some inferences about these different processes. There are findings consistent with each theoretical approach.

There was an important difference when we compared the results on age and involvement for all males and females with those for male and female sport participants only. The findings for all men and all women are consonant with disengagement theory in that involvement levels were lower the older the age level for each measure of involvement. In the analyses for sport participants only, the findings differed sharply from those that might be expected from disengagement theory. There was not clear evidence of decreased involvement levels for the older age categories. The results suggested that sport participants do not relinquish their inclinations to participate with greater age. They may change the nature of their involvement, however. One adjustment suggested by the results is that as age increases participants reduce the number of different activities that they are involved with and intensify their involvement in these (fewer) activities.

Our findings on the mean frequency of involvement among sport participants may result from dynamics specified by the continuity and activity theories of age and participation. It may be that older individuals who have participated must, and do, adjust the nature of their sport and physical recreation participation to what they feel is appropriate and what they are able to do. There may be forced or voluntary disengagement from some roles coupled with greater attachment to others which are defined as age-appropriate. The selection of fewer activities with greater age may also be a reflection of physical inability to perform some activities well. At the same time, there is perhaps a large majority among each sex who have not had much involvement, for reasons of socialization and such, at any point in their adult lives.

The disengagement theory of aging suggests that older in-

TABLE 4

Percentage Giving Different Reasons For Non-Involvement In Another Sport Or Physical Recreation Activity That They Would Like To Participate In, For Male And Female Participants In Sport.

Reasons for Non-Participation	M[1] F	Age Levels					
		20–29 (1558) (1707)	30–39 (888) (887)	40–49 (373) (408)	50–59 (226) (191)	60+ (81) (52)	Stat. Sig.[2]
		%	%	%	%	%	
No Others to	M	17.7	11.6	10.2	10.2	7.4	***
Participate with	F	22.6	15.4	13.0	17.3	21.2	***
Physically	M	0.4	2.3	2.4	5.3	7.4	ns
Unable	F	1.6	2.0	2.2	5.6	3.8	ns
Time: Competing	M	18.7	20.0	19.6	19.9	12.3	ns
Activities	F	14.6	16.7	17.6	20.3	7.7	ns
Time: Because	M	37.9	41.6	46.9	42.5	34.6	*
of Work	F	30.1	29.7	35.0	24.9	15.4	*
No	M	29.3	25.1	26.0	17.3	27.3	***
Opportunity	F	30.2	25.1	24.5	22.3	40.4	**
Too	M	24.1	22.3	21.4	18.6	22.2	ns
Costly	F	22.7	24.6	20.3	21.8	23.1	ns
No	M	8.8	8.3	5.6	7.5	6.2	ns
Facilities	F	7.4	6.8	4.2	3.6	3.8	ns
Don't	M	11.0	8.3	11.5	7.1	3.7	ns
Know How	F	18.0	19.3	16.7	16.2	26.9	ns

[1] M=Male; F=Female.

[2] Statistical significance levels: *** <.001; ** <.01; * <.05; ns=not significant.

dividuals will report the lack of opportunities, coparticipants and facilities as the reasons for their non-participation in sport. There is some evidence of this, although the findings are somewhat inconsistent. First, there is evidence that, for participants and non-participants alike, problems with the availability of facilities, opportunities and coparticipants are seen as less important by middle-aged persons than by the young. One interpretation of this pattern would be that the young and the old have different reference points. For the older cohorts, the recent growth in the popularity of sport and exercise and the development of commercial and municipal facilities may have yielded an increase in facilities compared with those available during their earlier lives. Younger persons would not have experienced such a change in facilities over their lives. Also the middle-aged may have lower expectations for participation than the young and, therefore, see fewer problems with available resources for participation. The findings do suggest, however, that those who are 60 years of age and older are more likely to feel that the lack of opportunities to participate and of people to participate with are constraints on their participation.

As we have said, it would take detailed longitudinal data to test conclusively the alternative interpretations discussed here. The expense involved in such research is so great that few long-term projects may ever be undertaken. In any event, longitudinal research cannot be used for the older cohort that we have described because they have already lived most of their lives. We could get some additional information on this cohort by asking people to recall activities at different points in their lives but the accuracy of retrospective reports is questionable.

Forced to draw conclusions based only on the available information we would have to say that there remain good reasons to pursue each of the disengagement and continuity and activity theories further. One or the other cannot be discarded on the basis of the data. It may be the case that the processes specified by each theory operate simultaneously in society. We would recommend that the theories each be pursued further in "manageable" longitudinal designs where the researcher closely followed the sport and physical recreation activities of small samples of young adults, middle-aged adults, and those near retirement for five or ten-year periods. Such studies would allow direct tests of the major interpretations of aging.

There are also possible interpretations in terms of generational effects which should be tested in such studies. We shall conclude by mentioning some of these. The lower participation levels for older compared with younger cohorts for all males and females may result, in part, because the different cohorts were socialized differently to sport and physical recreation. For example, the young may have been taught activities, and their importance, and may have had opportunities to participate in them in ways not available to currently older people when they were young. The lack of impetus and opportunity to participate in early life may have kept the level of participation low for those who are now older.

Generational differences may help account, as well, for the high frequency of involvement per activity for older sport participants. The older cohorts may have had available to them opportunities to participate in fewer sports and physical activities compared to the experiences of cohorts which followed. If so, given sport involvement, the older people may be participating more intensely in the fewer activities that they know, while their younger counterparts are involved in the broader range of activities that they learned about. It seems unlikely, though, that this would result in a linear inverse relationship of age and mean frequency, as obtained in the data for sport participants.

It may also be that those most specialized in given activities are most committed to the activity and are most likely to continue involvement into older age. Those who involve themselves minimally in several activities may drop out of participation in some of them with age, because of the lack of commitment. This, too, may help explain why, among participants, we find that the aged are more likely to be "specialists" than their younger counterparts who have a higher proportion of "generalists."

NOTES

1.   We gratefully acknowledge that this project received support from the Small Research Grants Programme of the Social Sciences and Humanities Research Council. We would also like to acknowledge that support in computer time was generously provided by the University of Waterloo. The data utilized in this study were obtained from a supplement (in 1976) to Statistics Canada's monthly Labour Force Survey. The data were made available through the Leisure Studies Data Bank at the University of Waterloo. These agencies bear

no responsibility for the analyses and interpretations reported here, however. We should also thank Terry Stewart of the Leisure Studies Data Bank for his assistance in preparing the data for our analyses and Barry McPherson who gave helpful comments on an earlier draft of this paper.

2.   We should emphasize that cross-sectional data, because they are gathered at one point in time for the different age categories, allow us only to make inferences about life cycle changes. They do not provide conclusive evidence of changes with aging, nor do they necessarily provide accurate predictions for changes in the future for younger and middle-aged cohorts. First, persons who are now older differ from present young persons in their education, income and wealth, both currently and for comparisons of the situations when they were the same age. Second, they differ in experiences unique to their generation. For these reasons, the sport and physical recreation participation of present young adults may differ from that of older persons when they were young. Also, the participation of older people may not accurately predict the participation of currently young people when they are older. We can control our studies for factors such as education and income (as done in our analyses here) to improve the probable accuracy of inferences of life cycle differences, but we cannot control for the effects of generational experiences. Nevertheless, our data source allows us cautiously to make inferences about life cycle changes, and it provides some very detailed baseline data on the sport and physical recreation participation patterns of the different age categories of Canadian adults. Short of pursuing very expensive and long-term longitudinal studies, of a sort that have yet to be conducted, we could not improve on the type of data presented here.

3.   The respondents were provided with a list of types of activities and write-in options for other activities and they were asked to check off their involvement/non-involvement and frequency of involvement in the preceding twelve months, for each activity. The following list of activities was given before space was provided for citing other activities: swimming, ice hockey, golf, ice skating, tennis, alpine/downhill skiing, cross-country skiing, curling.

4.   Our multivariate analysis technique, Multiple Classification Analysis, required a normally distributed or dichotomous dependent variable. Coding decisions for the various dependent variables were made in light of this requirement.

5.   The survey also asked why respondents were not more heavily involved in their favorite activity, if they wished to be more involved. The patterns of findings for responses on this question by age were essentially the same as those in Table 4. The relationships between

reasons of lack of facilities and age were statistically significant (p<.01) for each sex, however. Younger respondents were more likely to see the lack of facilities as a problem.

REFERENCES

Atchley, R.
1977   The Social Forces of Later Life. Belmont, Calif.: Wadsworth.

Cumming, E. and W.E. Henry
1961   Growing Old: The Process of Disengagement. New York: Basic Books.

Curtis, J.
1971   "Voluntary association joining: a cross-national comparative note." American Sociological Review 36: 872-880.

Dumazedier, J.
1973   "Report to a symposium on sport and age." Pp. 198-199 in Grupe, O. et al. (eds.), Sport in the Modern World—Chances and Problems. New York: Springer Verlage.

Friedman, E. and R. Havighurst
1954   The Meaning of Work and Retirement. Chicago: University of Chicago Press.

Hausknecht, M.
1962   The Joiners. New York: Bedminster Press.

Hobart, C.W.
1975   "Active sports participation among the young, the middle-aged and the elderly." International Review of Sport Sociology 10, 3-4; 27-40.

Kelly, J.R.
1977   "Leisure socialization: replication and extension." Journal of Leisure Research 9,2: 121-132.

Kenyon, G.S.
1966   "The significance of physical activity as a function of age, sex, education and socio-economic status of northern U.S. adults." International Review of Sport Sociology 1: 47-57.

Loy, J.W., McPherson, B.D. and G.S. Kenyon
1978   Sport and Social Systems. Don Mills, Ontario: Addison-Wesley.

McPherson, B.D.
1978   "Aging and involvement in physical activity: a sociological perspective." Pp. 111-128 in F. Landry and W. Orban (eds.), Physical Activity and Human Well-Being. Vol. 1, Miami: Symposium Specialists.

McPherson, B.D. and C.A. Kozlik
1980   "Canadian leisure patterns by age." Pp. 113-122 in V.W. Marshall (ed.). Aging in Canada. Don Mills: Fitzhenry and Whiteside.

Milton, B.G.
1973   Social Status and Leisure Time Activities: National Survey Findings for Adult Canadians. Unpublished Master's thesis, University of Waterloo.
1975   Social Status and Leisure Activities: National Survey Findings for Adult Canadians. Monograph 3 in Canadian Sociology and Anthropology Association Monograph Series, Montreal.

Nie, N.H., C.H. Hull and others
1975   Statistical Package for the Social Sciences. New York: McGraw-Hill Inc.

Riley, M.W. and A. Foner
1968   Aging and Society: Volume I. New York: Russell Sage.

Robinson, J.
1967   "Time expenditures in sport across ten countries." International Review of Sport Sociology 2: 67-84.

Rose, A.
1965   "The subculture of aging: a framework for research in social gerontology." Pp. 3-16 in A. Rose and W. Peterson (eds.), Older People in Their Social World. Philadelphia: F.A. Davis.

Smith, D. H., J. Macaulay and others
1980   Participation in Social and Political Activities. San Francisco: Jossey-Bass.

Spreitzer, E. and E. Snyder
1976   "Socialization into sport: an exploratory path analysis." Research Quarterly 47, 2: 238-245.

Statistics Canada
1971   Methodology of the Canadian Labour Force Survey. Ottawa:
        Statistics Canada, Publication No. 71-526.

White, P.G.
1980   Sport Participation Among Anglophones and Francophones In
        Canada. Unpublished Master's thesis, University of Waterloo.

SECTION VI

SPORT AND CAREERS: CONTINGENCIES AND EFFECTS OF SPORT PARTICIPATION

THE SELECTIONS IN THIS SECTION present two additional approaches to the study of sport and careers. The articles by Robert Prus and Edward Albert are concerned with the analysis of careers within a sport subculture and with the career contingencies that influence membership. Norman Okihiro's paper addresses a well-researched area in the sociology of sport, namely, the effects of high school athletic participation upon occupational attainments.

Prus provides an extensive review of ethnographic research in order to provide an overview of issues related to career contingencies and patterns of involvement. His article presents a model of career contingencies based on four stages ("processes") of a career: initial involvements, continuities, disinvolvements, and reinvolvements. Suggestions are made for the applicability of the model to the study of sport and leisure subcultures.

Albert is concerned with a specific sport subculture, that of racing cyclists, and with the "gatekeeping" function of equipment in that subculture. Attaining membership in all subcultures involves the acquisition of special knowledge; in many sport and leisure subcultures that knowledge frequently involves equipment—which models are best, proper use, correct terminology, etc. One of the better ways in which to determine legitimate membership, to determine the status of another member, to verify the achievements of another member, and to reduce the risk of accident in the more dangerous sports is to determine by observation or interrogation the extent of an individual's knowledge of equipment used by members of the subculture. Albert explores in detail the special place of equipment in the subculture of racing cyclists and its usefulness for distinguishing better competitors from equipment freaks, reckless riders, and novices.

Although there has been considerable research on the correlates and effects of high school sport participation, much of this work suffers from the methodological limitations of cross-sectional studies. Utilizing longitudinal data from a six-year study of male Canadian high school students, Okihiro traces the effects of involvement in athletic and other extracurricular activities upon educational and occupational attainments. Fortunately, Okihiro has avoided the tendency to isolate athletic participation from other forms of extracurricular social activity and has situated sport in its proper place as part of a student's total choice of extracurricular involvement rather than as a magical means by which to build character, improve grades and insure a successful future. Okihiro's interpretation of his sophisticated statistical analysis suggests that the benefits of these activities "have something to do with a facility and preference for dealing with people." That is, his data provide indirect evidence that extracurricular activities differentially attract persons who are extraverted and prefer group activities. As Okihiro notes, the implications of this pattern of selective recruitment are significant, for characteristics such as extraversion and group orientation are valued occupational skills in our corporate economy. While further research on this issue is needed, particularly research directed at separating selection and socialization effects of athletic participation and research on females, Okihiro's analysis provides an important contribution to the literature on sport and socio-economic attainment.

CAREER CONTINGENCIES: EXAMINING PATTERNS OF INVOLVEMENT[1]

Robert Prus
University of Waterloo

THIS PAPER EXAMINES THE CONCEPT of "career contingencies" within the context of sport and leisure activity. Following a brief introduction of the forerunners and tradition this concept reflects, an abstracted version of the model entailed is presented. While reflecting my own research, this statement is very much a synthesis of the work of other researchers in this tradition. Specific references to many sources will be made later in the paper, but the works of the following scholars have been particularly basic to the present formulation: Sutherland (1937); Lemert (1951, 1953, 1962, 1967); Goffman (1959, 1961, 1963); Klapp (1962, 1969); Becker (1963); Matza (1964, 1969), Lofland and Stark (1965), and Blumer (1969). The concept of career contingencies did not have its origins in the sociology of sport or leisure, but there seems little doubt about the viability of the concept for these realms of inquiry. Thus, numerous sport/leisure applications of this concept and its components will be suggested as the discussion unfolds. And, as the works of Faulkner (1973; 1974a, b), Scott (1982), Stevenson (1982), McKeown (1982) vividly indicate, the areas of sport and leisure provide exciting testing grounds for this concept.

EARLY ROOTS

The concept of "career contingencies" has its roots in the Chicago School of symbolic interactionism. Focusing on the processes by which interaction unfolds, the meaning experiences have for the participants, and the problematic and negotiable aspects of group life, the interactionists have long been concerned with how people become involved in activities, how they work out these activities with others, and how they become disengaged from these activities. While the Chicago school also reflects the contributions of other scholars such as Herbert Blumer, Ernest Burgess, George Herbert Mead, Robert Park, and Frederick Thrasher, the following are some of the early works of particular relevance for the concept of career contingencies: Thomas and Znaniecki's (1958-reprinted) account of the Polish peasant; Anderson's (1923) depiction of the "hobo"; Shaw's (1930) portrayal of the "jack-roller"; Cressey's (1932) analysis of the "taxi-dance hall"; Sutherland's (1937) statement on the "professional thief"; and Hughes' (1971) writings on the sociology of work. Some of these researchers make explicit reference to the concept of "career," while others use terms such as "natural history" and "life history" in a similar manner.

In contrast to those in a "positivist tradition," these early scholars recognized that the "world" could have multiple meaning to people,[2] that people act towards "objects" in terms of the meanings they have for these objects, and that these meanings are shaped by people's interactions with others (Blumer, 1969). Instead of viewing people's involvements as a function of various forces acting upon them ("billiard ball determinism"), the interactionists examine people's behavior as a minded, self-reflective, emergent aspect of group life. Involvements are explained in reference to the group contexts in which they occur, and as "objects unto themselves" (Mead, 1934). Actors can assess situations (not necessarily "wisely" or with "foresight" by the definitions of others) and can endeavor to work out their interests through interaction with other (minded, self-reflective) people. The interactionists ask not "why has someone done such and such?" (thereby eliciting "motives"), but rather examine the processes (when and how) by which involvements take place. While most of their research has an ethnographic flavor, focusing on the way of life of a particular group, the interactionists are concerned with developing concepts applicable to any group situation. Thus, concepts such as "identities," "conflict," "cooperation," "recruitment," and "world views" are examined generically in an attempt to arrive at a more comprehensive understanding of (any/all) group life.

MULTIPLE INVOLVEMENTS

If we are to comprehend involvements in any phenomenon more adequately, it is essential to recognize (1) that actors are apt to have multiple involvements on a simultaneous and/or sequential basis; and (2) that each involvement may interfere with an actor's other involvements. Thus, for instance, disinvolvement from A may be significantly related to involvement in B. Although simultaneous multiple involvements are both commonplace and inevitable, it is important to consider the broader involvement contexts in which actors find themselves. Figure 1 denotes the sorts of involvement competition and fluctuations actors are apt to experience over time. Without dwelling on this aspect of involvements, a recognition of multiple involvements (and the options they represent) signifies a vital backdrop to the understanding of participation.

FIGURE I: Multiple Involvements by Intensity and Over Time

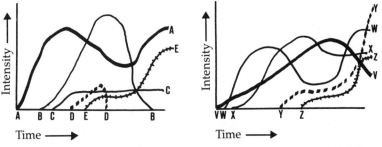

Any Involvement A,B,C,D,E,   Any Involvement V,W,X,Y,Z

ROLE CAREERS

In discussing career contingencies, most interactionists have focused on "careers of role participation," how one becomes and remains a doctor, thief, drug user, entertainer, cultist, etc. Regardless of whether people are "recruited," "seek out," or are "closed into" involvements, researchers examine the ways in which novices come to terms with the sets of perspectives their new roles entail, learn techniques, become more intensively involved in these roles, and become disinvolved from them. This is the most common use and is reflected in: Shaw's (1930) portrayal of jackrollers; Cressey's (1932) depiction of taxi-dance girls; Sutherland's (1937) analysis of professional thieves; Karsh, *et al*'s (1953) discussion of union recruitment tactics; Lemert's (1953) statement on "naive check forgers" and his (1962) analysis of paranoia; Reiss' (1961) study of adolescent involvement in male prostitution; Becker's (1963) research on drug users and jazz musicians; Lofland and Stark's (1965) inquiry into cult recruiting tactics; Faulkner's (1974a) discussion of hockey players and musicians; Lesieur's (1977) investigation of involvement in gambling; Prus and Sharper's (1977) statement on card and dice hustlers; and Prus and Irini's (1980) analysis of the participants of the hotel community (hookers, strippers, desk clerks, bar staff, thieves, and patrons).

Using these works (and others indicated later) as a base, we will consider the ways in which people become involved in roles, continue these involvements, and become disinvolved and/or reinvolved in these pursuits.

INITIAL INVOLVEMENTS

Interactionist research suggests that there are three major routings by which people may become involved in roles. These are "seekership," "recruitment," and "closure." These three routings are not mutually exclusive; any involvement may entail multiple routings. All involvement reflects existing opportunity contexts and is qualified by a fourth element, "drift."

Seekership

Seekership assumes a self-defined attraction towards, or fascination with, a particular phenomenon. While one might ask how these interests develop, once actors recognize themselves as having certain kinds of interests, a general concern is one of seeking out ways of realizing these interests.[3] Thus, people wanting to become doctors, teachers, and football players illustrate this notion as do people who want to go swimming, hang around gyms, make pottery, and collect stamps.

While seekership is affected by a person's existing frame of reference, the nature and intensity of one's interests can also be shaped by contact with others. Others not only denote a "reference group" (Shibutani, 1961), influencing one's interests but may also actively promote certain interests. Self-defined interests may be sufficient to prompt seeking activity, but their realization depends on acceptance by others in all cases in which two or more people are involved. Self-defined interests, likewise, are not necessary for involvement (people do many things they do not want to do). Interests may also develop over time, so that one may develop an "aesthetic" interest while doing an activity (e.g., running) after having been initially involved in other ways (e.g., to lose weight). In addition to the questions of (1) origins and extensiveness of interests and (2) the ways in which people with pre-existing interests seek out particular phenomena and their success (and obstacles) in doing so, we can ask (3) to what extent (and ways in which) people presently involved in particular situations "sought these out," as opposed to being "recruited" or "closed" into them.

Recruitment

Referring to attempts on the part of others to encourage or facilitate one's involvement in particular situations, recruitment endeavors may develop in a number of ways. But, regardless of whether recruitment efforts are extensively prepared in advance or on the spot, we may distinguish three general forms of recruitment: solicited recruitment, sponsored recruitment, and consensual recruitment. "Solicited recruitment" reflects the deliberate efforts of others to involve a person in a context. These "promotions" may vary in intensity, explicitness, persistence, and basis of appeal. This might be noted in a college's outreach program, wherein coaches and/or others encourage persons to come to their school for athletics. Reflecting the more obvious definitional power of others (in contrast to seekership), solicited recruitment seems most effective when the target is disenchanted with a situation and encounters someone seemingly able (from the target's perspective) and willing to assist the target develop a new line of involvement.[4]

"Sponsored recruitment" denotes a willingness to support someone's involvements. This may be combined with solicitation to become involved, but need not. Consider the case of a parent supporting a child's participation in sports (e.g., purchasing equipment, arranging travel) but not otherwise encouraging that involvement over the child's other options.

Signifying a willingness to accept someone's participation, "consensual recruitment" denotes the least obvious form of recruitment. It can, however, be critical to people's involvements. Unless prospects are able to find others willing to acknowledge their personal acceptability, interests, capabilities, etc., group based involvements become impossible. Thus, for instance, people unable to meet the coach's expectations (i.e., be accepted) may not play on a given team, regardless of whether they were "recruited" or had "sought out" the team on their own.

A classification of the forms of recruitment does not tell when and how people are recruited to involvement. Clearly, however, recruiting agents can play major roles in determining people's life-chances. This is not limited to their "veto powers" but also reflects the definitional encouragement and other support they provide. Concerns with strategies, counter-strategies and competing involvements are especially noteworthy in this context as all parties endeavor to realize their interests.

Closure

The concept of closure denotes involvements which come about in attempts to obtain goals and/or meet obligations thought unattainable by more desirable means.[5] As such, one experiences limited options relative to one's self-imposed responsibilities or those imposed by others and so may become involved in an activity by "necessity" rather than by preference. As the "necessity of fulfilling specific obligations appears more acute," and "as the options for doing so become more limited," one's sense of closure becomes more intense. Persons may experience closure in conjunction with seekership, but may also find themselves pursuing involvements they ordinarily would not seek out. For example, people may experience "role" closure when they find themselves taking a job in an unwanted line of work "to make ends meet," "finance their schooling," etc. Persons may also become involved in activities they did not prefer in order not to be left alone or face derision. Likewise, people may find themselves closed into relationships when they are thrown together with others by some unavoidable quirk of fate.

Drift

The concept of "drift" refers to the (greater) sense of freedom one experiences with reference to one's usual obligations.[6] Thus, people who perceive fewer moral restraints or concerns with personal safety, financial well-being, and the like, in reference to a particular involvement have less reason for avoiding that activity. By contrast, people experiencing greater reservations in reference to any external concern may avoid involvements they might otherwise eagerly seek out.

While differing from closure (sense of obligation to act), drift (a sense of freedom to act) is also apt to vary in intensity over time, subject in part to definitions from others. Thus, in addition to noting the sorts of personal reservations people may have in reference to involvement, we might ask what others do or have done to affect the levels of drift that persons experience.

Multiple Routings

Although we have discussed each of these four elements separately, it is abundantly clear that any involvement may reflect a combination of these elements. Thus, for instance, a college athlete may have an interest in becoming a professional athlete and take his/her sport seriously but not actively seek out a professional team. A professional team may draft (recruit) this prospect and offer him/her so much money that he/she feels obligated (to be financially independent and help out at home) to forego his/her prospective career in the sociology of leisure. Although concerned about his/her long-term future, the athlete surmises (with a little help from his/her friends) that one "can get an education anytime" and that chances for professional sports are a once in a life-time opportunity. He/she signs two days later.

It should also be noted that the significance of any of these elements for particular involvements is likely to vary over time for any given actor. Thus, while one may speak of the shifting opportunities of which persons are aware via recruitment, chance encounters, etc., one can also consider the critical timing of these options relative to persons' interests, obligations, and reservations.

CONTINUITY

Having examined the routings by which people may become involved in roles, the emphasis shifts to concerns with continuity and intensification of involvement. The ways in which initial involvement occurs can have important implications for continuity (e.g., seekership combined with recruitment seems more likely to result in long term continuation than recruitment alone), but it is also important to recognize that "roles" are rather encompassing concepts.

Part of the difficulty one encounters in coming to terms with the concept of "career contingencies" as commonly used is that it involves not one but five components. Attention to each generates greater depth and facilitates understanding of role involvement more generally. These components are: ideology; identity; commitment; activity; and relationships. Although each merits analysis in its own right, and while each can also be seen in career-process terms, together these elements are critical in explaining the career contingencies of "role participation."

These elements are interrelated, but each is unique and can operate somewhat independently of the others. For example, one may acquire an "ideology" prior to acquiring an "identity" in some cases and vice-versa in others. The following graphics (Figure 2) indicate the relativity of each over a time-frame. Clearly one may be involved in one or another aspect of role prior to the others.

These graphs assume interchangeability of A,B,C,D, and E, relative to ideology, identity, commitment, activity, and relationships (i.e. any component could precede and/or be more intense than the others).

FIGURE 2: Components of Role Careers by Intensity Over Time

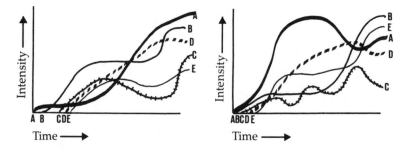

One may discuss "careers" of each component, examining initial involvements, continuities (and intensifications), disinvolvements, and reinvolvements. Thus, although the present focus is on the career contingencies of roles, similar models could be developed for each of these components. However, as the concept of "role" lends some continuity across these other components, each of these is presently examined in career terms within the broader concept of role career.

Careers of Ideologies

Referring to "perspectives," "frames of reference," "world views," or "belief systems" (Shibutani, 1961; Lofland and Stark, 1965; Berger and Luckmann, 1966; and Blumer, 1969), one can also examine the processes by which persons come to acquire ideology, sustain (and intensify) these viewpoints, and become disinvolved from and/or reinvolved in these orientational frames. Examining ideology in process terms, one can ask when and how viewpoints become accepted, intensified, challenged, devalued, and regained.

Shifts in perspectives are discussed in one form or other in most of the literature on role careers. This topic is, however, especially evident in: Lofland and Stark's (1965) analysis of conversion to a doomsday cult; Klapp's (1969) depiction of cults and crusaders; Simmons' (1969) discussion of "Espers" (an ESP cult); Prus' (1976) statement on religious recruitment; and Haas and Shaffir's (1982) discussion of medical students. It may not be common to think of sports and leisure activities as denoting ideologies, but orientations towards "fitness," "performance," "challenge," and "winning" denote perspectives for involvement, as do justifications for time and monetary expenses, playing while hurt, and neglecting other obligations (e.g., school, work, family). One may also ask how these orientations are acquired, maintained, and when and how they are likely to diminish, be replaced, or reinstituted in reference to both group and individual involvements.

Careers of Identities

Denoting self (and other) definitions of self, identities can also be seen as having careers. One may wish to delineate self definitions from a target's reputation (views others are perceived to hold and/or those others actually hold), but one can ask how any particular target (actor) definitions come about, when they become more intense and/or widespread, and when they are likely to dissipate. Likewise, although identities may influence and be influenced by one's activities (for example), they may also transcend particular activities and may last longer than or not as long as one's involvement in particular activities. As with the other components of role careers, actors may find their identities reflecting definitions proposed by others as well as those they initiate themselves.

Materials particularly relevant to the emergence, maintenance, or dissipation of identities (and reputations) include: Lemert's (1951, 1967) notion of "secondary deviation"; Goffman's (1959) statement on "impression management"; his (1961) analysis of the "moral careers" of mental patients, and his (1963) depiction of "stigma"; Klapp's (1962) portrayal of "heroes, villains, and fools," his (1964) discussion of "symbolic leaders," and his (1969) depiction of the "collective search for identity"; Gross and Stone's (1964) study of "embarrassment"; Garfinkel's (1964) analysis of "degradation ceremonies"; Scott and Lyman's (1968) statement on "accounts"; Emerson's (1969) material on "judging juveniles"; Daniels' (1970) examination of "military psychiatric diagnoses"; Hewitt and Stokes' (1975) inquiry into "disclaimers"; Prus' (1975a, b; 1982) statements on typing, designating, and resisting labels; Haas and Shaffir's (1977) discussion of "cloaks of competence" in medical school; and Cullen and Cullen's (1978) survey of labeling theory. The study of identities and reputations denotes another area in which sport and leisure involvements have much to offer in rich data for analysis. The pressure, competition and drama of sport readily lend themselves to a multiplicity of self and other assessments, and have important implications for continuity in involvements. Scott's (1982) depiction of women's basketball players and Stevenson's (1982) analysis of involvements in national team sports amply illustrate the relevance of identity for the involvements and life-styles of the participants. A setting offering immediacy and intensity of identity definition, sport involvements provide valuable contrasts with some other settings. Presuming to offer relaxation, leisure activities suggest sharp and insightful comparisons to the definitions that emerge "in the fast lanes."[7]

Careers of Commitments

As with ideology and identity, commitment is problematic and best understood in process terms. Commitment may be defined in many ways, but an actor's own sense of commitment may be most viable. Thus, commitments may be defined by total resources (e.g., time, money, energy, etc.) expended, proportions of resources expended, options eliminated, availability of enjoyable involvement-related practices, and securities unavailable elsewhere. We may also define commitments by the actors' perceptions of their sacrifices, costs of leaving, lack of alternatives and the like.

The impact of commitment for role continuity and its variability are examined in: Stebbins' (1970) discussion of commitment; Hearn and Stoll's (1975) statement on waitressing, Prus and Sharper's (1977) analysis of card and dice hustlers, and Prus and Irini's (1980) analysis of the hotel community. The sport and leisure settings provide interesting contrasts in reference to commitments. In the competitive sport setting, it is often a matter of, "If you're serious, show it!" and performance is rated according to one's willingness to make the sacrifices necessary to excel. People in the leisure world, by contrast, may become as committed as any others, but generally under less externally demanding conditions. It is interesting and worthwhile to ask when and how commitments come about in these settings and when prior commitments lose their relevance as elements promoting continuity.

Careers of Activities

While a role career may be seen as the stringing together of certain activities by particular actors and while identities can affect the ways in which people do activities, one may also look at the ways in which activities unfold. Activities may be of a solitary or a group nature, but an examination of activity brings to focus a more immediate sense of uncertainty, definition, excitement, frustration and the like.

Focusing on the processes by which participants work out their interests with others, the study of activities lends great insight to our understanding of all the elements entailed in the concept of role career. Especially pertinent in this respect are discussions of: "hustling techniques" (Sutherland, 1937; Prus and Sharper, 1977); "student fritters" (Bernstein, 1972); the emergence of violence (Faulkner, 1973 and 1974b; Prus, 1978); the management of trouble (Bittner, 1967; Rubinstein, 1973; Prus and Stratton, 1976; Emerson and Messinger, 1978); drinking activity (Rubington, 1968; Prus, 1983); the resolution of insurance claims settlements (Ross, 1970); and the management of respectability (Weinberg, 1970).

Whether one considers solitary activities or those involving multiple participants ("joint activity"—Blumer, 1969), activities take place over time periods. Thus, one may ask how activities begin, intensify, dissipate, and become reconstituted. Engulfing a wide range of activities conducted at a variety of paces, the sport/leisure context provides powerful settings in which to examine activity as a social process. Whether one is studying the problematics of coordinating team sports, the "doing" of competitive events, or focusing on people watching "soaps," going shopping, or playing video games, researchers can ex-

amine "ongoing action." In all cases, one can look at the perspectives of the involved parties, their objectives, the dilemmas and
obstacles they encounter, their sense of frustration and excitement, and the role that other persons play in defining and otherwise shaping their experiences.

Careers of Relationships

As with the other components of roles, one can also examine
relationships in process terms, asking how relationships begin,
intensify, dissipate, and become reconstituted. Thus, while we
may speak of the role career of a marathoner, we may also ask
about the relationships that runner has with others, each relationship having a career of its own. And while one may focus
on careers of specific relationships, one may also delineate the
elements affecting the careers of relationships in particular settings. Illustrative of the research on careers of relationships are
analyses of: heavy drinkers' relationships with others (Jackson,
1954; Wiseman, 1970); tuberculosis patient-doctor encounters
(Roth, 1962); cab drivers and their fares (Davis, 1959; Henslin,
1968); relationships among groups of hustlers (Prus and Sharper,
1977); and relationships emerging within the hotel community (Prus and Irini, 1980). Applications of relationship careers
within sport and leisure sociology might have foci such as these:
the coach-athlete relationship in individual and team sports;
the emergence of friendship in team sports/ leisure pursuits;
the effects of intense sports careers and/or leisure involvements
on pre-existing friendship and family relations; and the
team/leisure event as a basis of community (e.g., basketball community, weaving community). In all cases, one examines the
ways in which people become involved in the lives of others
and the ways in which they work out their overlapping interests
relative to the other relationships in which they are involved.

DISINVOLVEMENT

Given the integral connection of "role" to each of the five components discussed in reference to continuity, it becomes evident that disenchantment with any component may be an
element contributing to eventual disinvolvement. Thus, in
reference to particular roles, as persons (1) shift frames of
reference, (2) redefine and/or experience alternative definitions
of self, (3) question the value or cost of their commitments, (4)
find activities disappointing, or (5) find relationships inadequate,

they are more likely to contemplate disengagement from those roles. However, to the extent persons are more fully involved in the other components, they are more likely to remain in that role. An actor's more extensive involvement in a role, thus, constitutes a barrier to disengagement. As Lemert (1951, 1967) suggests, the same patterns facilitating adjustment, once established, deter disinvolvement. And, as persons become more extensively embedded in the role, more effort and planning may be required for successful disentanglement.

Just as seekership, closure, recruitment, and drift may have played a role in initial involvements, these elements are critical in reference to new (alternative) involvements. Although people may become disinvolved to face a void, a perceived lack of options ("What else can I do?") can be an effective deterrent. Hence, disinvolvements often develop as a consequence of opportunities and contacts existing prior to a more complete disinvolvement. Each person may be seen to face an ongoing, shifting set of actual and potential role involvements. Each role has its own contingencies in the situation, but each role also has the potential to affect the person's other role involvements.

The literature on disinvolvement is considerably more limited than that on involvements. Particularly valuable in this sense are: Ray's (1961) analysis of drug users; Becker's (1963: 101-119) discussion of musicians; Lofland and Stark's (1965) material on the doomsday cult; Wiseman's (1970) account of the treatment of skid row alcoholics; DellaCava's (1976) study of Catholic priests; and Prus and Irini's (1980) statement on hotel life. In general, disinvolvement seems most likely when (1) the actor is disenchanted/having problems with his present situation and at that time makes (or has) contact with a person who (a) seems trustworthy and accepting, (b) introduces the actor to the new phenomenon, (c) reduces any reservations the actor may have, (d) indicates the relevance of the new involvement in terms of the actor's present difficulties, and (e) promotes the actor's participation in ideology, identities, commitments, activities and relationships relative to the new role involvement.

Depicting another aspect of participation, the notion of disinvolvement merits considerable attention in the areas of sport and leisure. While some disinvolvement in sport may be imposed by injury, many athletes "retire before their time." Although it tends to be more difficult to locate former players than active practitioners, there is little doubt that further study of the disinvolvement process could add greatly to our overall understanding of participation not only in sport and leisure contexts, but in group life more generally.

REINVOLVEMENT

Although very little research has been done on reinvolvements, it appears that some definite vacillation of participants between two or more competing involvements is not uncommon. New roles may seem to offer elements thought desirable and unobtainable in one's present roles, thus suggesting options to one's present involvements. As "success" in any role is problematic, however, actors encountering difficulty in new roles may pursue still other new involvements, but they may also elect to return to former involvements. A return to former roles tends to be easier than "breaking into" new roles. Not only are actors more familiar with the activities the old role entails and anticipate greater receptivity by people in that setting (former relationships), but they may still have some commitments, ideological persuasion, and identities consistent with that (former) role. As with initial involvements, individuals may seek out their former role, be recruited into it by former associates, or define it as a means of meeting their present obligations (closure). They also seem to experience fewer reservations the second (or more) time around. Although the literature on this phenomenon is quite limited, Popenoe's (1938) discussion of remarriages among divorcees, Ray's (1961) analysis of relapse among drug users, and Wiseman's (1970) portrayal of skid row "drunks" denotes the relevance of this aspect of involvement.

Although people may have only one or a few chances to become involved in certain pursuits, the opportunities for (re)-involvement are unlimited in many areas of amateur sport and leisure. Participants may find themselves excluded from certain levels of play, but most sports offer a variety of "levels of competition" and many leisure activities are "always available." To the extent these inferences are valid, the notion of reinvolvement may denote a particularly viable concept for subsequent research.

IN PERSPECTIVE

Recognizing the necessity of examining group life as it "unfolds", this paper has focused on the contingencies affecting initial involvements, continuities, and disinvolvements of people within roles. The model developed has its roots in symbolic interaction and was developed from research on a variety of "conventional" and "deviant" pursuits. While the focus was on careers of "roles," it is hoped that the value of examining "ideology," "identity," "commitment," "activity," and "relationships" in process-career terms has also been indicated. Insofar as this paper was intended to provide a theoretical outline of the concept of career contigencies, it does not provide much illustrative contextual material. Thus, the reader is referred to the many sources cited in the paper to obtain a better appreciation of the viability of this concept for analyzing group life.

In contrast to correlational analyses which largely "flatten process" and rely heavily on researcher interpretations of participants experiences from a distance, the career contigency model developed herein emphasizes process, participant meanings, and the negotiable aspects of group life. It enables researchers to examine group life as it unfolds. In Goffman's (1967) terms, it allows us to study "where the action is."

Focusing on process, the career contingency model has a generic base, one which lends itself to a variety of sport and leisure applications. As one of a number of relatively untapped areas of group life, sport and leisure involvements represent rich settings in which to assess and qualify models such as this, thus generating a stimulating, more germane sociology.

NOTES

1. I would like to thank Ian Hall for his comments on an earlier version of this paper.
2. From an interactionist perspective (Mead, 1934; Becker, 1963; Blumer, 1969), meaning is a quality attributed to some (object). "Objects" do not have inherent meanings (e.g., no "thing" is "good" or "bad," except as defined as such by some audience).
3. See Lofland and Stark (1965), Klapp (1969), and Prus and Irini (1980) for more extensive and illustrated discussions of the concept of "seekership."
4. Lofland and Stark (1965), Prus (1976), Prus and Sharper (1977), and Prus and Irini (1980) provide more detailed, contextualized statements on recruitment as a social phenomenon.
5. See Lemert (1967: 99-108), Lesieur (1977), Prus (1978), and Prus and Irini (1980) for more elaborate, illustrated material on closure.

6. Matza (1964), Prus (1978), and Prus and Irini (1980) develop this concept in reference to involvements in deliquency, violence, and hotel life, respectively.

7. Reflecting a combination of "sport," "leisure," and "work" involvements, McKeown's (1982) analysis of gamblers' typifications of one another illustrates some other aspects of identity within the subculture of race-track betting. Also see Hayano's (1982) monograph on "professional card players."

REFERENCES

Anderson, Nels
1923   The Hobo. Chicago: University of Chicago Press.

Becker, Howard S.
1963   Outsiders: Studies in the Sociology of Deviance. New York: Free Press.

Berger, Peter and Thomas Luckmann
1966   The Social Construction of Reality. New York: Anchor.

Bernstein, Stan
1972   "Getting it done: notes on student fritters." Urban Life and Culture 1:275-292.

Bittner, Egon
1967   "The police on Skid Row." American Sociological Review 32: 699-715.

Blumer, Herbert
1969   Symbolic Interaction. Englewood Cliffs, N.J.: Prentice-Hall.

Cressey, Paul
1932   The Taxi-Dance Hall. Chicago: University of Chicago Press.

Cullen, Francis T. and John B. Cullen
1978   Towards a Paradigm of Labeling Theory. Lincoln, Nebraska: University of Nebraska Series (no. 58).

Daniels, Arlene Kaplan
1970   "The social construction of military diagnoses." Pp. 181-208 in H.P. Dreitzel (ed.), Recent Sociology No. 2. New York: Macmillan.

Davis, Fred
1959   "The cab driver and his fare." American Journal of Sociology (65): 158-165.

DellaCava, Frances A.
1976   "Becoming an ex-priest: the process of leaving a high commitment status." Sociological Inquiry 45 (4): 41-49.

Emerson, Robert M.
1969   Judging Delinquents. Chicago: Aldine.

Emerson, Robert M. and Sheldon L. Messinger
1978   "The micro-politics of trouble." Social Problems 25:121-134.

Faulkner, Robert
1973   "On respect and retribution: towards an ethnography of violence." Sociological Symposium 9:17-35.
1974a   "Coming of age in organizations: a comparative study of career contingencies and adult socialization." Sociology of Work and Occupations 1:131-173.
1974b   "Making violence by doing work: selves, situations, and the world of professional hockey." Sociology of Work and Occupations 1:288-312.

Garfinkel, Harold
1964   "Conditions of successful degradation ceremonies." American Journal of Sociology 61: 420-424.

Goffman, Erving
1959   Presentation of Self in Everyday Life. New York: Anchor.
1961   Asylums. New York: Anchor.
1963   Stigma: Notes on the Management of Spoiled Identity. Englewood Cliffs, N.J.: Prentice-Hall.
1967   Interaction Ritual. New York: Anchor.

Gross, Edward and Gregory P. Stone
1964   "Embarrassment and the analysis of role requirements." American Journal of Sociology 70:1-15.

Haas, Jack and William Shaffir
1977   "The professionalization of medical students: developing and maintaining a cloak of competence." Symbolic Interaction 1:71-88.
1982   "The Fate of Idealism Revisited." Unpublished manuscript.

Hayano, David
1982   Poker Faces. Berkeley, Cal.: University of California Press.

Henslin, James
1968   "Trust and the Cab Driver." Pp. 138-155 in Marcello Truzzi (ed.), Sociology and Everyday Life. Englewood Cliffs, N.J.: Prentice-Hall.

Hewitt, John P. and Randall Stokes
1975   "Disclaimers." American Sociological Review 40: 1-11.

Jackson, Joan
1954   "The adjustment of the family to the crises of alcoholism." Quarterly Journal of Studies on Alcohol 15: 564-586.

Karsh, Bernard, Joel Seidman, and D.M. Lilienthal
1953   "The union organizer and his tactics." American Journal of Sociology 59: 113-122.

Klapp, Orrin
1962   Heroes, Villains, and Fools. Englewood Cliffs, N.J.: Prentice-Hall.
1964   Symbolic Leaders. Minerva Press (USA).
1969   Collective Search for Identity. New York: Holt, Rinehart and Winston.

Lemert, Edwin
1951   Social Pathology. New York: McGraw-Hill.
1953   "An isolation and closure theory of naive check forgery." The Journal of Criminal Law, Criminology and Police Science 44: 296-307.
1962   "Paranoia and the dynamics of exclusion." Sociometry 25: 2-25.
1967   Human Deviance, Social Problems and Social Control. Englewood Cliffs, N.J.: Prentice-Hall.

Lofland, John and Rodney Stark
1965   "Becoming a world saver: a theory of conversion to a deviant perspective." American Sociological Review 30: 862-875.

Matza, David
1964   Delinquency and Drift. New York: Wiley.

McKeown, Brent M.
1982   "Horseplayers: some key elements in identity construction." North American Society for the Sociology of Sport Meetings. November 4-7. Toronto, Ontario.

Mead, George H.
1934 Mind, Self and Society. Chicago: University of Chicago Press.

Popenoe, Paul
1938 "The remarriage of divorcees to one another." American Sociological Review 3: 695-699.

Prus, Robert
1975a "Labeling theory: a reconceptualization and a propositional statement on typing." Sociological Focus 8: 79-96.
1975
b   "Resisting designations: an extension of attribution theory into a negotiated context." Sociological Inquiry 45: 31-14.
1976 "Religious recruitment and the management of dissonance: a sociological perspective." Sociological Inquiry 46: 127-134.
1978 "From barrooms to bedrooms: towards a theory of interpersonal violence." Pp. 51-73 in M.A.B. Gammon (ed.) Violence in Canada. Toronto: Methuen.
1982 "Designating discretion and openness: the problematics of truthfulness in everyday life." Canadian Review of Sociology and Anthropology 19: 70-91.
1983 "Drinking as activity: an interactionist analysis." Journal of Studies on Alcohol. 44: 460-475.

Prus, Robert and Styllianoss Irini
1980 Hookers, Rounders, and Desk Clerks: The Social Organization of the Hotel Community. Toronto: Gage.

Prus, Robert and C.R.D. Sharper
1977 Road Hustler: The Career Contingencies of Professional Card and Dice Hustlers. Lexington, Mass: Lexington Books.

Prus, Robert and John Stratton
1976 "Parole revocation related decision making: private typings and official designations." Federal Probation 40: 48-53.

Ray, Marsh B.
1961 "Abstinence cycles and heroin addicts." Social Problems 9:132-140.

Reiss, Albert J., Jr.
1961 "The social integration of queers and peers." Social Problems 9: 102-120.

Ross, H. Lawrence
1970 Settled Out of Court. Chicago: Aldine.

Roth, Julius
1962 "The treatment of tuberculosis as a bargaining process." Pp. 575-588 in A. Rose (ed.), Human Behavior and Social Process. Boston: Houghton-Mifflin.

Rubinstein, Jonathon
1973 City Police. New York: Ballantine.

Rubington, Earl
1968 "Variations in bottle-gang controls." Pp. 308-316 in E. Rubington and M. Weinberg (eds.), Deviance: The Interactionist Perspective. New York: Macmillan.

Scott, Lois
1982 "Career contingencies: The social construction of continuing involvements in women's intercollegiate basketball." North American Society for the Sociology of Sport Meetings. November 4-7. Toronto, Ontario.

Scott, Marvin B., and Stanford M. Lyman
1968 "Accounts." American Sociological Review 33: 46-62.

Shaw, Clifford
1930 The Jack-Roller. Chicago: University of Chicago Press.

Shibutani, Tamotsu
1961 Society and Personality. Englewood Cliffs, New Jersey: Prentice-Hall.

Simmons, J. L.
1969 Deviants. Berkeley, California: Glendessary Press.

Stevenson, Christopher
1982 "Career contingencies: Involvement at the National Team Level." North American Society for the Sociology of Sport Meetings. November 4-7. Toronto, Ontario.

Sutherland, Edwin
1937 The Professional Thief. Chicago: University of Chicago Press.

Thomas, W.I. and Florian Znaniecki
1958 The Polish Peasant in Europe and America. (Reprinted, five volume works, 1918-1920). New York: Dover.

Weinberg, Martin
1970 "The nudist management of respectability: strategy for, and the

consequences of, the construction of a situated morality." Pp. 375-403 in J. D. Douglas (ed.) Deviance and Respectability. New York: Basic Books.

Wiseman, Jacqueline
1978 Stations of the Lost: The Treatment of Skid Row Alcoholics. Englewood Cliffs, N.J.: Prentice-Hall.

EQUIPMENT AS A FEATURE OF SOCIAL CONTROL IN THE SPORT OF BICYCLE RACING

Edward Albert
Hofstra University

THE CENTRALITY OF EQUIPMENT to the sport of competitive cycling cannot be overstated. It goes without saying that the bicycle serves as a means to a competitive goal, but, as importantly, it takes on a life of its own in the world of the bicycle racer. As an orienting feature of conversation, a focus for community activities, an object of endless investment, and an instrumental sign of competence and warrant, it serves considerably more than its ostensive purpose. In fact, for those involved, the bicycle might be seen as the sport itself, for it is in the embodying of the bicycle that they create that involvement.

Using materials collected from the cycling press, extensive participation and observation, and informal interviews, this paper explores the relationship of bike racers to their equipment. Specifically, I will address three items of a related character: first, the way in which equipment—its acquisition, care, and use—provides the rider with a warrant for claiming acceptance into the sport; second, the relationship of equipment to competitors' perceptions of their sport; and third, a brief exploration of the role of equipment in maintaining an elitist cast to North American bicycle racing.

Cycling is a sport in which success depends primarily on physical condition and strength, tactical acumen, and riding skill. All of these require riders to spend many hours each day riding. "Serious" competitors, whether world class or beginner, might ride between 150 and 400 miles per week, some doing considerably more. Given the time spent "in the saddle," it is not surprising that much significance is attached to the relationship between bike and rider. The rider's world is dominated by the bicycle and the perceived need to acquire the best available technology. Such technology serves not only in fact and belief as inseparable from riding and racing success but also works to warrant claims of community membership.

Even cursory observations of cycle racing by outsiders are often dominated by the hardware. The literature of the racing scene—newspapers, magazines, technical and how-to books—is laden with talk about equipment: how or what to buy, how to use it, how to fix it, etc. Regularly this technology does the work of providing for status and membership, stands as a necessary but insufficient element in racing success, and serves as a topic of interest and conversation. Vanderzwaag (1972: 101) notes:

> . . . Equipment may be viewed as more than just a means of participating in sport. Similar to the automobile, the kind of sport equipment (including the clothing) may become a symbol of prosperity. Thus it becomes important not only to ski, but also to own a certain make of skis.

Unlike the world of skiing or auto racing, however, the equipment of cycling carries little weight as a status conferring object outside of the community. In fact, the very opposite is understood to be the case. Outsiders are perceived to view the bicycle as child's play. A status cost is seen to be involved in bicycling; a status offense is committed if it is engaged in by those over a certain state of development. As one enthusiast noted in a letter to a racing publication (Velo-News, May 14, 1982):

> In our culture bikes have been equated with kids. They were something to be ridden until driving age was reached and then discarded. Toys, you know. Those in their post teens who took them up again or who never really left them were begging to be branded as a juvenile or some kind of nut (p. 16).

In this light, the bicycle's status and membership-conferring qualities are internal to those who are oriented to it, and although equipment may confer a certain status on the owner it is not indicative of a more generalized position.

WARRANTING MEMBERSHIP

Within this specialized community equipment is used to judge rights of access. By access we mean such things as riding rights or the right to ride along with others in informal groups; conversational rights or the right to stop and chat; and racing rights or the right to acceptance as competent in the field of a race.

Although equipment per se is its own justification, its possession in the hands of those not subsequently validated to have a right to its use can become an occasion for sanction. Equipment awaits the test of use; its recognition by others serves as preliminary validation of the right to its use but is contingent on forthcoming evidence of the user's competence. Although the bike is a first focus in encounters with strangers, attention can shift from bike to rider if validation occurs or remain with the bike if validation is not forthcoming, e.g., "That's a nice machine—do you race?" is an invitation to justify the claim which an expensive bike makes for its rider. If the equipment, however, appears to be the only attraction, then the possessor is open to categorization as an "equipment freak," a stigmatized label applied to those preoccupied with hardware to the detriment or even the exclusion of use. On the other hand, if validation occurs, the label "bikie" may be understood to have been applied.

In such preliminary assessments considerable detail is available for identification purposes. Items of apparel, make and type of bicycle, make and type of accessories, the presence of shaved legs—all are indicative of a claim. The community is watchful of such claims and perceived misuse of equipment may subject the misuser to sanction. By misuse we are not referring to maltreatment in a physical sense, i.e., rough, careless, or even indifferent handling. In fact, there is a limited respect granted to those who act with a careless disregard for their equipment. Rather, misuse is a consequence of warrantlessness, of owning equipment for which one has no right, no appreciation, or no functional knowledge. As noted, those judged guilty of such misuse may be lumped into categories such as "turkey" or "nobody," both terms of derision.

Membership, however, can be and is established through a show of competence. Conversance with such esoteric issues as the weight of components (lightness has a positive value), the geometry of frame design, the relative merits of brands of equipment, the intricacies of position on the bicycle, the appearance of the bicycle and, recently, the aerodynamics of both frames and components comprise such a show. Competence might be seen to serve as a first line of defense against unwarranted intrusion.

This abiding concern with membership and boundary maintenance functions in such a way as to provide a degree of protection against the unskilled. The "tourist," "turkey" or "nobody" is assumed to be lacking in basic skills associated with bike racing, lacking in bike handling ability. This ability, although not spoken of as embodiment, carries a similar meaning.

Like many other sports bike racing can be dangerous. Although fatalities are few, crashes which result in bad abrasions, broken bones, and minor concussions are common, and their complete absence from a race and/or a season of training is more surprising than their occurrence. Bike handling, the ability to control the bike as one controls the body, is a valued and required skill which is provisionally granted to a rider through the bicycle he or she rides and the conversational competence evidenced in talk about equipment. To find, initially, an absence of either is to be alerted to potential disaster. This provisional acceptance of riding ability has a retrospective-prospective quality. One is willing to wait for some future moment at which time the promise of the equipment and the talk will be kept. On the other hand, in the face of contradictory revelations, what was putative competence is reinterpreted as having been, all along, an unwarranted claim, the claimant now being seen to have never been more than what he or she was from the outset, a "turkey".

Among those who know better, the presence of a poor bike handler within a group is cause for consternation and derision. Good bike handlers, on the other hand, are the subject of storied accounts and cause for awe. Between the two lies a zone of assumed competence within which an element of trust prevails insofar as one is only minimally in control of possible mishaps and, in large measure, dependent on the skills of others. In this way the importance of equipment skill looms large. It is the prerequisite for the cooperative effort that is the race among competitors.

As in other racing sports "drafting," the sharing of effort expended in overcoming wind resistance, creates a system of cooperation within a competitive structure. So dependent is this sport on the benefits derived from drafting that the cooperation induced must be seen as constitutive of the sport itself. For drafting to be beneficial, however, riders must ride in close proximity over long periods of time. The ability to exist and to trust others' ability in such a context is part and parcel of racing. Apparently incompetent bike riders may be pushed aside because their presence places in question the very possibility of competition. If a dangerous bike handler is identified within a racing group, riders will take this as a topic and will be given to "watch out for this guy." The offender will be singled out with a comment like "hey, number XX, ride straight." One story related to me concerned a top ranked Canadian cyclist who "hooked" a fellow rider into a ditch because this rider was so bad a bike rider as to be a danger to the rest. (Hooking is an intentional move wherein a rider in front moves the rear wheel into a following rider's front wheel thus destabilizing him or her.)

THE COGNITIVE EXPERIENCE OF THE SPORT

We noted earlier that equipment plays a critical role in structuring the experience of the sport. Technical talk serves more than a gatekeeping function. It is valued for its own sake and is frequently unrelated to the manifest goals of competition. One feature of racers' conversational practice is that both bicycle and equipment are understood as organic in the sense that change and alteration are ongoing activities.

> . . . The distinguishing feature of the champion is that he brings to his equipment a knowledge of its use. On the basis of experience he modifies, tunes, adapts, and in other senses assures himself that the equipment will work perfectly for him. Perfect response in the equipment to his total satisfaction will bring him his sense of aesthetic accomplishment, whether it be in a "win" or in "self-expression" (Lowe, 1977: 208).

This observation need not be limited to the champion nor to performance. Within this sport a high level of equipment perfecting and discussion occurs at all levels and for multiple reasons. Discussions over the merits of various brakes or brake pads, the relative advantage of differing handlebar widths, the strength to lightness ratio of saddle rails or wheel rims, the advantages provided by differing spoking patterns or numbers are seemingly endless. Much of the time such talk is understood to be just that; it has a life of its own frequently with little practical significance. Such discussions might be seen as displays of insider's knowledge. The novice, in fact, may on occasion be castigated for taking such discussions seriously. The novice follows such discussions for the information they might convey concerning racing success while the old hand sees in them nothing more nor less than their symbolic importance. Thus, for example, asking if lighter tires or wider handlebars might help, the novice is told not to worry about such things, just train harder.

Further, we see such talk as a display of athletes' interest in the embodiment discussed earlier, in maximizing the elusive unity of bike and rider as having performance as well as aesthetic value. Barbara Lockhart, an Olympic speed skater (cited in Lowe, 1977), seemed to catch the experience as follows:

> Achieving speed in speed skating is a phenomenon that is hard to compare with any other feeling. . . . For instance, there is a real exuberance, a real feeling of joy, or lightness, at one with yourself. . . . it's a really ecstatic feeling (p. 205).

Referring to the bicycle, one speaks of characteristics like smooth, positive, response, or tight to describe what should be present to maximize this elusive unity. Of riders possessing this characteristic, one speaks of "looking good on the bike," "smooth as silk," or "at home on the bike." An accolade given by technical writers in the specialized cycling press when speaking of a newly-tested bicycle is that one forgets that it is there when one is riding. For example, in describing a "state of the art" Italian bicycle one writer (Schubert, 1982) noted:

> Completely neutral in handling and steering, it felt so natural that it seemed to disappear underneath the rider (p. 83).

In another road test similar comments were made:

> A good road racing bike is said to disappear underneath you, to handle so predictably and maneuver so effortlessly that you forget it's there. (Fisher and Schubert, 1981: 113)

A supply industry servicing this environment of equipment perfecting exists in a symbiotic relationship to the sport. The industry both meets the needs of participants and, at the same time, is complicit in the creation of those needs. Advertisers of bicycles and equipment are quick to reference those characteristics which speak to the rider's quest for the unification of body and machine. The following are illustrative:

> . . . so we've kept the weight and rolling resistance low, the handling quick and responsive. (Bicycling, July, 1982: 2)

> . . . so every Trek is designed for maximum response and control. . . . Trek offers a synthesis of frame performance characteristics to enhance your style of riding. (Bicycling, July, 1982: 19)

or:

> The bike is a tool. . . a means to an end. Its fundamental purpose is to extend the range and speed which man can travel under his own power. Bike and rider are an ergonomic system, and it is vital to this system that the mechanical components which support it work in complete harmony with the realities of the human component's needs and behavior. (Bicycling, July, 1982: 163)

Such text is frequently accompanied by pictures which represent visually what speed and the unity of bike, equipment, and rider might look like.

The elusiveness of embodiment as an achievable phenomenon may, in part, be due to the inability to gauge empirically its contribution to performance and/or its actual presence or absence in the experience of the rider. In part, it is a feeling that may be understood to lack a one-to-one relationship with technical achievement. Although not strictly equipment related, the act of shaving one's legs is parallel. Justified in functional language, it is, at the same time, understood to heighten the process of embodiment: it looks fast.

It is worth noting how the cycling industry conveys the potential presence of embodiment to possible customers. Not, as we have said, accountable through technical achievement alone, its presence must be artfully referenced. Alongside a colorful photo of a cyclist rounding a corner—speed simulated by blurring—the copy reads:

> RESPONSE. It doesn't just happen in a high performance bicycle. It takes engineering, experience, dedication and a touch of inspiration. . . . (Bicycling, February, 1982: 5)

or:

> Before you buy your next bike, compare. Windsor—When you buy with your head and your heart. (Bicycling, July, 1978: 30-31)

or:

> A New Exciting Bicycle. . . MATSURI! Thoroughly Custom-Crafted with professional expertise and vivid imagination. (Bicycling, August, 1979: 6)

Of equal importance is that this experience of rider and bicycle has a somewhat paradoxical side. As we noted, on the one hand, much energy, talk, and time is devoted to one's equipment. Yet, on the other hand, one can credit riding success or failure to that equipment only within definable and limited bounds; within a set of tacit agreements concerning the relationship of mechanical advantage and success. The preoccupation with equipment finds warrant in the advantage it confers while at the same time that advantage is known to be insufficient to make the difference.

Esoteric issues of a technical nature serve as a common ground in and out of print and the competitor is understood to be conversant with these issues. However, racers know that "at a certain level" none of this matters in performance terms. What does matter is physical and tactical ability. This is not to say something like "in their hearts they know" but rather as a feature of their knowledge it is understood that although these issues are conversationally and presentationally important, in a practical sense, once a certain level of quality is achieved, equipment does not make the difference. The sometimes-heard maxim that "a good rider can win on almost any bike" speaks to this understanding.

In this vein, cycling columnists comment on buying a bicycle:

> One of the wrong reasons is the belief that a new bike will help you go faster. This is almost never true. Some racers are always shopping for a frame that is stiffer, or has tighter angles, or sports components that are lighter or more aerodynamic. In most cases, the new bike won't outperform the old one. . . . Racing bikes are pretty much alike. (Matheny, June 11, 1982: 6)

or:

> Don't make the all-American mistake of worrying too much about what kind of bike you ride. Many great racing careers have been launched on ordinary bicycles. (Mulholland, May, 1981: 37)

This notwithstanding, the bike/rider relation upholds an idea not identical with winning or losing a race. In fact, we might see the sport as espousing two themes which can be understood to be at the same time both complementary and contradictory: cognitive-aesthetic themes on the one hand, performance themes on the other. Under the former such intrinsically valued equipment-related items as equipment loyalties, craftsmanship and personal attention, lightness, and design elements all reference an idea which finds its locus in that almost mystical unity of bike and rider at speed. As an idea it contains no impediments to its accomplishment; as a reality it comes up against the obdurateness of the physical world. Under the latter theme are included elements specifically serving the value of success: technological innovation and reliability, training regimens, and utilitarian considerations.

The following are by way of example of cognitive-aesthetic themes. Product loyalty frequently surmounts cost and even efficiency. One product line manufactured by an Italian firm named Campagnolo is known for quality, sometimes for design innovation, reliability, and for high cost, and occupies a religious place among bike racers. Comments like "these classic Campagnolo designs have a 'right' look about them," (Berto, October, 1982: 82) are common. The presence of the Campagnolo-equipped bicycle is indicative of the owner's appreciation of the sport. Dealers post decals on their doors proclaiming "Campagnolo spoken here." The sign is interesting insofar as it infers more than the fact that the store has such and such a brand; if the sign is to be taken seriously, it opens up a world of possible talk for which Campagnolo stands as an important expression.

The idea of craftsmanship is, in its own right, thematic. References to "custom-made," "hand built," and "handmade" frames signify value regardless of the presence or absence of technological superiority. Repetition of the craftsman's custom work theme is routine for advertisers of bicycles:

> Finished by hand in the custom frame builders tradition.

> If you could custom build your own bike you would build
> a Kabuki. The Richard Sacks frame is handmade and fine-
> ly crafted. One on One. [Referring to craftsman and bicycle]

Further, the theme is played out aesthetically in the machinery
itself. Insofar as builders are relatively limited in what can be
done by way of "marking" their work as their own given the
engineering criteria of good frame design, conventions have
arisen allowing for such personalization. The engraving of the
builder's name on parts not of his or her manufacture is common, valued, and requested at considerable extra expense.
Handlebar stems, chain wheels, seat posts frequently are so
engraved although manufactured by others.

The notion of the master craftsman rooted in old ways can
be paradoxical when winning is the ostensible game. In an article on a prominent frame builder comments such as the following were laudatory in spite of the observation that the builder
used none of the accepted quality control methods which insure reliable frame construction.

> . . . few concessions to the industrial age. . . virtually all
> his work is done by hand. . . this kind of precision, and
> an Old World passion for detail. . . artistic spirit and at-
> tention to detail.

Equally paradoxical is the fact that radical frame design which
breaks with tradition, although the sine qua non of performance and control, is suspect. There is a sense that the most
radical of frames, the newly introduced Japanese aerodynamics
with oval or flat wind "slippery" tubes rather than round ones,
are seen to be somehow devoid of the craftsman's touch.
Although performance may be enhanced, the frame violates
not only the aesthetic values of "what a bike should look like,"
but the theme of the individually crafted machine is also placed
in question.

A related issue, that of popularity and dispersion, is relevant.
One Italian builder, Ernesto Colnago, was for years *the* premier
frame builder. As more and more frames began to appear,
rumors were heard to the effect that the bicycle was no longer
built by Ernesto, was being mass produced, and had declined
in quality. The large number of frames seemed to belie the
mythology of the craftsman's attention. Not only is craftsmanship placed in question by dispersion of a frame but individuali-

ty also becomes an issue. A pervasive topic of discussion between riders (especially while riding) is the issue of one's next frame purchase. As with an automobile, what one rides says something about who one is. Although much can be said in this context, it is sufficient here to note that the dispersion of a particular frame is related to its favored status; a brand new frame is slow to gain acceptance, but as more appear it becomes a trustworthy possible choice, and, finally, as the frame proliferates riders will comment to the effect "an X? . . no, everybody is riding them."

The theme of the craftsman and the individual buyer glosses several notions central to the experience of the *aficionado*. First, although concretely a team and/or collectively-oriented sport much of the time, the myth of the long distance rider maintains currency. The notion of unifying with the bicycle for long periods of solitary training is enhanced in the idea that the machine is tailored, has at the outset the characteristics of a proper fit. One builder of custom frames comments:

> In two and one-half years of building I have never built two identical frames because I have never met two identical people. My building philosophy is simple: individual design and attention. (Heilman, May, 1977: 31)

The individual attention speaks to the archetypical success fantasies of the bike racer. Such scenarios revolve around ideas of the "lone breakaway," the "solo effort," the rider who "solos to victory," or the rider who "explodes" out of the "screaming pack" to win the sprint finish. Such successes often are accounted for by reference to the place that mental factors occupy in victory. Equipment is often discussed in terms of the "complete confidence" one must have in it so as to permit the all-out effort. Such confidence is tied to the theme of the craftsman whose attention to detail ensures the perfect performance.

Secondarily, the bicycle provides for the individuality of the rider. It is common for a rider to be identified by the bike he rides.

"Do you know Fish?"

"No, I don't think I do."

"You know, he rides a Gios."

"Oh yea, I know who you mean."

In such a case the bike does not extend individuality but creates the identifiable individual. It is perhaps not warranted to hypothesize that actors are not unaware of such typification, selecting machines, in part, on the basis of their identity conferring properties.

The preoccupation with weight which, in a practical sense, is an attempt to deal with the problems of overcoming inertia and gravity is also thematic. Technical discussions among the initiated rage, often centering around the delicate balance between lightness, strength, and reliability. Apart from its utilitarian merit lightness has an aesthetic value. Weight is both observable and notable to those who know how to see it in the drilling or milling out of various components and/or frame parts, in the color of metal, i.e., black parts may be seen to be of the lighter titanium as opposed to steel, and in the presence of nonmetallic components, e.g., plastic.

Again, the practical benefits of ultralight components and frames are ambiguous—more breakage and less rigidity—and understood in that way. The aesthetic value, however, can be considerable, enhancing the experience of embodiment. The paradoxical demands of aesthetics and utility were nowhere more evident than in a technical article describing a very light bicycle made with a somewhat exotic tubing material.

> The handling of this bike was a pleasant surprise. . . . I feared that the light 753 frame might be whippy. . . . But the 753 combines ultralight weight with the handling of a top quality racing frame. . . . Some bottom bracket sway was evident during sprinting, but the frame tracked true and was easy to control. The light weight, of course, gives the bike a noticeably light, fast "feel." (Kolin, 1980: 124)

It is often commented in discussions of lightness that the best way to achieve this goal is to lose a few pounds of excess fat. Although meant as a joke, it is a practical criticism of riders' talk insofar as when components and frames are lightened the improvement is measured in grams.

Under the rubric of the aesthetics of design we must include the obvious elements of paint, decals, and generally the area of "finish." In this context, however, perhaps the most interesting issue concerns the way performance items acquire an aesthetic theme sometimes in conflict with ostensible goals. The design aesthetic of the bicycle frame is structured around a set of codes which reflect cultural values of speed, elegance, balance, etc. Capitalizing on such values, a radical design was advertised by treating the ideal design aesthetic in bold letters as follows:

A BETTER FRAME
BECAUSE *STIFF* IS BETTER
BECAUSE *LIGHT* IS BETTER
BECAUSE *SHORT* IS BETTER (Bicycling, October, 1981: 87)

Stiff, light, and short equal a frame with geometry emphasizing torsional rigidity, low weight, and a short wheelbase. As with component lightness, these design values are visually available and notable in such esoteric considerations as the clearance between tires and frame tubes or the degree of bend in a front fork. At a glance the initiated can make judgments concerning these items. In choosing a frame riders will often seek to maximize these characteristics insofar as they play out the themes of speed and precise handling; they incarnate these themes.

The clash of the aesthetic and the utilitarian is, in this context, the most glaring. Although small, short, stiff, light add up to responsive, quick, lively, etc., at the same time, the list of qualities might include rough, hard, harsh, twitchy, touchy, squirrelly. As with the theme of lightness, insiders understand this value in this way, as paradoxical. The valued equipment is understood to be set by practical contradictions.

EQUIPMENT, ELITISM, AND CYCLING

Within the sport the question of elitism is usually an issue only in the context of superior athletic performance and the support that it does or does not merit. The complaint is often heard that the national federations give too much emphasis and money to national and international class riders and ignore the rest who are the backbone of the sport. This situation is one which is not unique to cycling. Cycling does, however, present some problems of a relatively unique nature due to its dependence on high cost equipment. The initial investment in a bicycle runs well over $1,000; added to this are the costs of a racing license, clothing, helmet, tools, the weekly expense of transportation to and from races, entry fees, and a supply of training and racing tires.

The sport itself, through clubs and sponsorships, is organized in such a way as to help soften the impact of such costs. Riders join clubs which frequently are associated with local bike shops. Members get discounts of varying amounts on bikes and equipment. Riders of some standing, on the other hand, frequently find sponsorship which can amount to the payment of all expenses associated with the sport plus a small "salary." This type of aid, however, is available only to a small elite. For example, of the 1981 total of 6734 licensed U.S. senior men riders, only 107 were listed as Category I. It is not an unwarranted generalization to say that such sponsorships are, in the main, available to these few riders.

Unlike other sports, considerable monetary investment is required prior to participation. Although an investment of perhaps $50 is sufficient to outfit one for a running race this is certainly not the case in cycling. If one is fit, the runner's $50 investment will establish a competitive picture; if one is fit, perhaps ten times that would be needed to even approach such a picture in cycling. Only the incipient superstar could manage a first sanctioned race on a "shit bike." (The expression is not mine but the parlance of the sport.) It is no wonder then that the characteristics of the bicycle racer paint a general picture of affluence. If we can, as is done in other estimates, take race as a broad indicator of social status, then it is interesting that at the top of North American bicycle racing only one black appears. Further, a 1978 readers' poll by the key racing publication showed that of those who responded (450) 46% had household incomes of $20,000 or more, 48% were college graduates, and 54% were employed in managerial or professional occupations. (Velo-News, March 9, 1979: 2)

If we add to this picture the observation that, like other minor sports in North America, cycling provides little or no opportunity to rise above the amateur ranks and that in cycling status is internal to the sport and not generalizable to external social roles, then we seem to have a set of conditions which cater to an elite able to make a significant investment without concern for its potential payoff as an agent of social mobility. Such an attitude is, practically speaking, a luxury.

It might be argued that such a situation is ideal in a Huizingian (1950) sense in that it provides a clearly demarcated arena of activity having no raison d' etre other than itself. However, such a contention might be irrelevant to the reality of contemporary sport. The de facto restrictions placed on entrance to the sport retard its development by discouraging broad-based participation. Further, the realities of contemporary life are such that to devote one's time and thus one's future to an activity like sport requires that it provide both intrinsic and extrinsic rewards. At this time North American cycling provides no practical extrinsic benefits.

In bicycle racing the coherence of a course of action is discernible for athletes in the ongoing elaboration of relationships to equipment. This relationship is so paramount as to overshadow most other aspects of the experience or participants. The role of equipment is both to structure the day-to-day activity of the sport and to create an atmosphere of community which enables the race to go on as an accountably safe environment.

REFERENCES

Berto, Frank
1982   "Campagnolo VS. Shimano VS. SunTour." Bicycling October: 80-105.

Bicycling
1978-1982.

Fisher, Gary and John Schubert
1981   "Italy's Ciocc." Bicycling. December: 113-115.

Heilman, Gail
1977   "Introducing 21 American framebuilders." Bicycling May: 30-73.

Huizinga, Johan
1950   Homo Ludens. Boston: Beacon.

Kolin, Michael
1980   "What is strong, light and begs to be ridden?" Bicycling December: 124-126.

Lowe, Benjamin
1977   The Beauty of Sport. Englewood Cliffs: Prentice Hall.

Matheny, Fred
1982   "Think before you buy that dream machine." Velo-News June 11: 6.

Mulholland, Owen
1981   "Hankering for a crack at racing." Bicycling May: 37-39.

Schubert, John
1982 "Italy VS. Japan." Bicycling July: 79-94.

Vanderzwaag, Harold J.
1972 Toward a Philosophy of Sport. Reading, Mass: Addison-Wesley.

EXTRACURRICULAR PARTICIPATION, EDUCATIONAL DESTINIES AND EARLY JOB OUTCOMES

Norman R. Okihiro
Mount Saint Vincent University

IN SPITE OF EARLY ARGUMENTS to the contrary (e.g., Coleman, 1961), a plethora of research has shown that athletic involvement in high school has a net beneficial influence on subsequent high school grades and college aspirations, controlling for other pertinent factors such as I.Q. and social class (Schafer and Armer, 1968; Snyder and Spreitzer, 1976). Investigation of high school athletic effects on actual attainments beyond high school, however, has been more controversial. Spady (1970) found that much of the effect of high school athletics on educational attainments was mediated by peer status perceptions. This psychological model has received some support (Spreitzer and Pugh, 1973) but has also been refuted (Otto and Alwin, 1977). Spady also found, however, that without the development of skills and attitudes that can sustain one in college, including leadership and service activities in high school, athletes were less likely than non-athletes to fulfill their educational plans. Thus, along with Otto (1976a), Spady argued that participation in non-athletic or social extra-curricular activities provides a sounder basis for future success than athletics.

Assessment of the effects of high school athletic and social activities on eventual occupational outcomes has been rare. Otto and Alwin (1977) found that high school athletics have a salutary effect on occupational prestige and income among Michigan high school students followed up in 1972, 15 years after the first interview. Using the same data set, Otto (1976b) found that an index of extra-curricular activity (incorporating both athletic and social items) exerted significant effects on income and prestige, *net* of family background, intelligence, academic performance and educational and occupational expectations. He concluded that extracurricular participation has an important role in the status attainment process, and this role was not limited to the learning of success orientations.

If educational or occupational aspirations, perceptions of peer status, or other social psychological variables such as significant others' influence or self-concept of ability do not mediate much of the relationship between activities (athletic and social) and subsequent attainments, what is at the crux of the extra-curricular effect? One line of reasoning is that extra-curricular activities are an indicator of existing or learned preferences for certain sorts of group-oriented activities and interaction. Indeed, Coleman (1961) argued that one of the reasons for the popularity of interschool athletics was that it allowed students to work together with other people to achieve common goals, in contradistinction to the individual competition ethos of the academic curriculum. A preference for social or group activities has its own intrinsic rewards, not just those associated with instrumentalities like raised visibility and peer status. This reasoning is congruent with the observation that the relationship between extracurricular participation and attainments may be due to a common, unspecified antecedent variable such as a personality trait (Otto, 1976b), and research which shows that stable extraverts are highly represented among those engaged in sporting activities (Hendry and Douglass, 1975: 229).

This paper has several objectives. The first is to examine the effect of high school athletic and social participation on a number of life outcomes. In the absence of a direct measure of extraversion, preferences for group interaction or interpersonal skills, only indirect inferences can be made. To the extent that extracurricular activities affect educational and occupational outcomes *net* of a number of variables associated with competing explanations, we can have confidence in the effect being due to an intrinsic element of such participation. This requires detailed specification of a model of status attainment.

The second objective of this paper is to examine the antecedents and effects of post-secondary athletic and social involvement, an area where there is little empirical research of note (Hanks and Eckland, 1976). In addition to assessing the persistence of preferences for voluntary activities, the extent to which post-secondary extra-curricular activities directly and indirectly affect occupational outcomes and mediate the influence of prior variables will be looked at.

Thirdly, this paper extends the dependent variables considered beyond the usual income and occupational prestige. Two additional variables have been selected. One is related to the nature of the current job. Other things being equal, one would expect that extraverts would prefer to obtain jobs in which there is a possibility of dealing with people on a sustained basis. The percentage of time spent in the current job dealing with people (as opposed to working with one's hands or processing information) is thus included in the model. The second variable is a more general measure of activity, taken from a factor analysis of a number of dimensions of self-evaluation and labelled as an active orientation. If part of the reason for extra-curricular activity involvement entails preferences for social activities as an intrinsic end, and this preference is durable, one would expect this to be reflected in one's current lifestyle and self-concept.

DATA AND METHODS

The original study was based on a representative sample (N = 2555) of Ontario Grade 12 students, contacted in 1973 as part of an examination of educational intentions. This sample was re-contacted in 1979, employing both mailed questionnaires and a back-up telephone survey, with the purpose of obtaining detailed information on educational and occupational histories. The completion rate was 69 percent for the follow-up, and males comprised 727 of the 1522 persons successfully contacted. Six years after Grade 12, they averaged 24 years of age, just over half were still single, and four in five were employed full-time in the labor force.

The working sample for this study included only the 460 who responded by mail, since some of the variables pertinent to this paper were not included in the truncated telephone instrument. Those answering by mail differed from telephone respondents primarily in coming from more educationally advantaged sectors of the population (see Anisef et al., 1980). Thus, care should be taken in generalizing from the results.

Information on the operational definitions used is available from Okihiro (1981) and Anisef et al. (1980). Both high school and post-secondary extra-curricular participation were derived from factor analysis of responses concerning the frequency of participation in athletic, social, service and academic organizations, measured retrospectively in 1979. These dimensions were orthogonal.

The order of variables in the structural equation model is depicted in Figure 1. The causal order is based on both the assumed temporal order of events in the normal life cycle (cf., Blau and Duncan, 1967) and on the general scheme of the Wisconsin models of status attainment (e.g., Sewell and Hauser, 1975), with the exception of the variable representing high school program. This variable is associated with a conflict perspective in sociology (see Okihiro, 1981). Socioeconomic status and urban-rural location are exogenous since their causal order is not clear. High school program selection is assumed to take place early in high school, usually before Grade 11 grades are received. High school athletic and social participation and family encouragement measured in Grade 12 were blocked since both refer to later high school experiences generally, and there was no clear causal ordering between them. Leading crowd membership, however, is dependent on high school experiences like athletic and social involvement, according to the adolescent subculture literature (e.g., Coleman, 1961). The relationships among the remaining variables are discussed in detail in MacKinnon and Anisef (1979) and Turrittin et al. (1980), with sets of variables blocked when their internal order is not clear. The individual, in forming educational and occupational expectations, forms a self-concept which is affected by prior academic performance, track, and others' encouragement. Expectations precede actual post-secondary experiences which in turn precede current job outcomes. Self-evaluation in 1979 along the active dimension is the ultimate dependent variable.

Following usual procedures, a just-identified model was estimated, using ordinary least squares regression. Paths not significant at the .05 level were deleted and the over-identified paths were re-estimated. To aid in interpreting the causal scheme, the effects of athletic and social involvement on selected later variables were decomposed, using the Alwin-Hauser (1976) method on the just-identified model. Pairwise deletion was employed. Table 1 shows the means, standard deviations and cases for each variable. Table 2 displays the standardized regression coefficients for each endogenous variable in the over-identified model, and Table 3 shows selected effect decompositions.

FINDINGS

The findings are presented as they relate to educational and occupational expectations, post-secondary educational and extra curricular outcomes, current job outcomes, and finally, self-evaluations. We are particularly interested in the role that athletic and social participation in high school plays in the attainment process and the mechanisms by which effects operate. First, though, a note on antecedents of high school extracurricular involvement.

No variable exerted a significant direct effect on high school athletic participation, a finding which substantiates the democratic nature of such involvement for males (Coleman, 1961). The fact that GRADES did not exert any effect indicates that the relationship between GRADES and sports is weak at best, when other variables are held constant (cf., Buhrmann, 1972). On the other hand, both SES and TRACK exert moderate direct effects on extracurricular social activities, accounting for eight percent of the variance explained. These results confirm Otto's (1976b) observation that youth organizational memberships are related to social class background. Clearly, some of the effect of SES is indirect, operating through TRACK and GRADES. The effect of TRACK strongly suggests that there are social as well as well-documented educational costs of non-academic program selection.

Educational and Occupational Expectations

The model explains 40 percent of the variance in educational expectations and 43 percent of the variance in occupational expectations. Examination of the total (direct plus indirect) effects of high school social activity on expectations (not shown) showed no significant influence. However, high school athletic participation strongly affects educational expectations. How does this occur? Table 3(1) shows the total direct and indirect effects, employing the Alwin-Hauser method. Note, first of all, that the total effect of athletics excludes the effects of prior and contemporaneous variables in the model, notably significant others' encouragement. Otto and Alwin (1977) state that such social psychological variables mediate a substantial proportion of the total effect of athletics on educational outcomes. At this point,

Figure 1: The Causal Order of Variables in Model

SES URBAN	TRACK	GRADES	FAMENC NFMENC HSATH HSACT	LCROWD	SCA	EDEXP OCCEXP	EDATT PSATH PSACT	BLISHEN EARNINGS PEOPLE	ACT

Legend:

SES	—socioeconomic status
URBAN	—urban-rural location
TRACK	—high school program
GRADES	—grade 11 grades
FAMENC	—family educational encouragement
NFMENC	—non-family educational encouragement
HSATH	—high school athletic participation
HSACT	—high school non-athletic activity participation
LCROWD	—membership in leading crowd
SCA	—self-concept of ability
EDEXP	—educational expectations
OCCEXP	—occupational expectations
EDATT	—highest level of education attained
PSATH	—post-secondary athletic participation
PSACT	—post-secondary non-athletic activity participation
BLISHEN	—prestige of current job
EARNINGS	—yearly current job earnings
PEOPLE	—percent of time in current job spent dealing with people
ACT	—activity dimension of self-evaluation inventory

we can only point out that athletics exerts a total effect over and above significant others' encouragement, and for the most part, the effect is direct. It does not operate primarily through perceived leading crowd membership, as Spady (1970) argued. These results substantiate research by Otto and Alwin (1977).

Post-secondary Educational Outcomes

The over-identified model was successful in explaining 53 percent of the variance in educational attainment, with educational expectations having by far the largest direct effect. Since high school athletic participation has no antecedents and exerts a direct effect only on educational expectations in this model, the latter mediate all of the clearly small effect of athletics on attainment. Examination of paths to and from high school social activities shows that the effect on educational attainment is spurious, with the common antecedents being SES and TRACK.

Post-secondary social participation is directly affected by social participation in high school, high school athletics and educational expectations. The latter is no doubt partly due to the fact that post-secondary enrollment is a necessary condition for post-secondary extra-curricular activity. Examining the decomposition of the total effect of high school social activity, almost all of the effect is direct, indicating perhaps that there is a carry-over of preferences for this type of behavior which is not due to raised perceptions of status, self-concept of ability, or expectations.

The total effect of high school athletic activity on post-secondary social activity is negative. The fact that the total effect is smaller in absolute magnitude than the direct effect (Table 3(2)) indicates that conflicting processes are taking place. The decomposition of effects shows that athletic involvement in high school raises educational and occupational expectations which increases social participation at the tertiary level. Controlling for such intervening variables, however, results in a stronger negative direct effect, an effect which is suppressed by the intervening variables. One plausible explanation takes into consideration the limited non-academic time available for students of post-secondary institutions. Students with preferences for athletic involvement (as evidenced by high school sport participation) may be hard pressed to find time to become involved in social activities and still carry a regular academic course load, especially if they are in-

TABLE 1

Means, Standard Deviations And Number Of Cases
For All Variables In The Model

	Mean	Standard Dev	Cases
SES	.0076	.2192	472
URBAN	2.3039	1.1415	489
GRADES	3.4005	.9245	488
TRACK	.6637	.4729	486
FAMENC	.1095	.9780	489
NFMENC	−.1158	.9801	489
LCROWD	.3265	.4694	486
HSATH	−3.0531	1.3600	479
HSACT	−4.3627	.6898	453
SCA	.0158	.1415	489
EDEXP	2.1083	.8828	442
OCCEXP	52.6609	17.5680	392
EDATT	3.0615	1.8464	489
PSACT	−.0787	.1185	482
PSATH	−.0627	.1362	482
BLISHEN	48.8715	13.4994	387
EARNINGS	14555.7840	5551.1015	368
PEOPLE	29.1060	22.0678	385
ACT	.0022	.0629	480

volved in college or university sport. This explanation is buttressed by the next finding.

Post-secondary athletic participation is directly affected by high school athletic participation and educational and occupational expectations. Breakdown of the total effect of high school athletics (Table 3(3)) shows that about two-thirds (.139/.188) of the total effect is direct, with most of the rest operating through expectations. This finding suggests that, like social participation, a preference for athletic activities in high school carries over into the post-secondary sphere and that this carryover effect is not due to perceptions of peer status with its implications of status maintenance.

TABLE 2

Standardized Regression Coefficients (Betas) In Over-Identified Model And Variance Explained By Just- And Over-identified Models

Dependent Variable	Independent Variable	Variance Explained		
		Beta	Just-identified Model	Over-identified Model
TRACK	SES	.259	.158	.158
	Urban	.233		
GRADES	SES	.148	.074	.074
	Track	.184		
FAMENC	SES	.198	.047	.039
NFMENC	—		.009	0
HSATH	—		.003	0
HSACT	SES	.185	.080	.077
	Track	.154		
LCROWD	SES	.147	.215	.207
	HSATH	.262		
	HSACT	.272		
SCA	Track	.370	.357	.329
	GRADES	.286		
	FAMENC	.157		
	NFMENC	.096		

EDEXP	Track	.289	.408	.401
	Grades	.231		
	FAMENC	.170		
	HSATH	.174		
	SCA	.221		
OCCEXP	SES	.117	.432	.430
	Track	.168		
	Grades	.251		
	FAMENC	.137		
	SCA	.306		
EDATT	SES	.168	.536	.527
	Track	.160		
	Grades	.169		
	EDEXP	.361		
	OCCEXP	.156		
PSACT	HSATH	−.159	.371	.330
	HSACT	.455		
	EDEXP	.295		
PSATH	HSATH	.148	.326	.304
	OCCEXP	.240		
	EDEXP	.349		
BLISHEN	OCCEXP	.437	.279	.191
EARNINGS	—		.061	0
PEOPLE	LCROWD	.190	.119	.082
	PSACT	.197		
ACT	HSATH	.310	.187	.096

Current Job Outcomes

The over-identified model explains approximately 19 percent of the variance in occupational prestige of the current job, substantially below that explained in other studies (e.g., 71 percent in Otto, 1976b). In addition, the key role of educational attainment in mediating the effect of exogenous and intervening social psychological variables in most status attainment research (e.g., Sewell and Hauser, 1975) does not occur in the present data. Instead, most of the effect of prior variables is mediated by educational expectations. This is no doubt partly due to the rather short six-year follow-up period, as many of those with high educational levels were either still in school or had been working for only a short period. It may also be partly due to the depressed economic picture in recent years. Clearly athletic participation in high school plays a part in occupational attainment since it exerts a direct effect on educational expectations, and high school social activity has indirect effects, but the size of these effects is small.

Unlike Otto and Alwin (1977) or Otto (1976b), the present study found no significant direct paths (and hence no indirect ones) to income. Indeed, in the just-identified model, only six percent of the variance in current job earnings is explained, compared to 14 percent for Otto and Alwin. The inability to explain income has been reported elsewhere (Jencks *et al.*, 1972, Sewell and Hauser, 1975).

While the model is poor at predicting earnings and occupational attainment, it fares moderately well in explaining about 10 percent of the variance in time spent dealing with people in the current job. Both leading crowd membership and post-secondary social participation exerted significant direct effects, with high school athletics exerting direct effects and indirect ones through leading crowd. That leading crowd membership, high school athletic participation and post-secondary social participation should all significantly influence time spent dealing with people supports the view that an underlying dimension, possibly the preference for social activity or extraversion, results in consistent choices for voluntary behavior.

Self-concept as Active

Table 2 shows that only high school athletics exerted a significant causal path to self-concept as an active person. Decomposition of the total effects of high school athletic and social

TABLE 3   345

Decomposition Of Effects In The Just-identified
Model For Selected Variables

Dependent Variable	Independent Variable		
1. EDEXP	HSACT	Total Effect	.153
		Through LCROWD	−.003
		Through SCA	−.019
		Direct	.175
2. PSACT	HSATH	Total Effect	−.081
		Through LCROWD	−.009
		Through SCA	−.013
		Through EDEXP, OCCEXP	.058
		Direct	−.117
	HSACT	Total Effect	.261
		Through LCROWD	−.010
		Through SCA	.008
		Through EDEXP, OCCEXP	.004
		Direct	.259
3. PSATH	HSATH	Total Effect	.188
		Through LCROWD	.001
		Through SCA	−.013
		Through EDEXP, OCCEXP	.061
		Direct	.139
4. PEOPLE	HSATH	Total Effect	.148
		Through LCROWD	.042
		Through SCA	−.001
		Through EDEXP, OCCEXP	.011
		Through EDATT, PSATH, PSACT	0
		Direct	.114
5. ACT	HSATH	Total Effect	.297
		Through LCROWD	.029
		Through SCA	.010
		Through EDEXP, OCCEXP	.013
		Through EDATT, PSATH, PSACT	0
		Through Job Outcomes	.016
		Direct	.229
	HSACT	Total Effect	.097
		Through LCROWD	.030
		Through SCA	−.006
		Through EDEXP, OCCEXP	0
		Through EDATT, PSATH, PSACT	.005
		Through Job Outcomes	−.001
		Direct	.069

participation, however, indicated that both variables were influential, with membership in leading crowd mediating significant proportions of the indirect effects. These findings once again suggest that selection of social activities or a preference for group interaction contexts is a stable individual response.

SUMMARY AND DISCUSSION

The study revealed that athletic and social involvement in extracurricular activities play an important role in the process of educational and early job attainment. High school involvement, particularly athletic involvement, raises college expectations and does so independently of perceived peer status and achievement orientations, confirming Otto and Alwin's (1977) findings. No evidence indicated that perceived peer status had a negative effect on educational attainment when athletic and social participation were held constant, refuting Spady's (1970) suggestion that inflated self-perceptions of status were detrimental to the successful completion of higher education.

In terms of post-secondary extra-curricular involvement, participation in high school activity, whether athletic or social, predicted similar post-secondary involvement *net* of all other variables. This was so especially for social activity. Frequent high school sport involvement, however, had a negative cross-over effect on post-secondary social participation, suggesting that the tendency to enjoy athletics ruled out other involvement, given the limited time available for such pursuits.

There was not much support for Spady's (1970) view that athletic participation was less efficacious than service or social participation in the attainment process. Indeed, six years after Grade 12, comparatively little variance in occupational prestige or income was explained. However, extracurricular involvement strongly affected the task nature of the job selected (i.e. percent of time spent dealing with people) and respondents' self-concept as active persons.

The results summarized above support the idea that the major influence of athletic and social involvement on educational and occupational outcomes has something to do with a facility and preference for dealing with people. The fact that the effect of extra-curricular activities is largely unmediated by any of a large number of variables associated with perceived peer status, occupational and educational expectations and other social psychological variables, family background, or high school academic factors provides strong indirect support for this view. It was impossible in the present study directly to measure personality traits, such as extraversion, or to separate selection effects, the differential attraction of athletics for people with preferences for group activity, from socialization effects of extra-curricular activities. This is an area where further research is indicated.

The question of whether extra-curricular participation provides economic or prestige payoffs further down the career road (cf., Otto and Alwin, 1977) is central. In an increasingly complex world, where supply exceeds demand for nearly every desirable position, a propensity for and facility in dealing with people would seem to be a competitive advantage. People who have such qualities and others working alongside them may find working in our corporate economy more satisfying and less tension-producing. Such activity is clearly rewarded in adolescent society, and there is no reason to suppose that adults value such orientations less.

It should be noted that the present data do not specify exactly what is at the crux of the extra-curricular effect. The preference for dealing with people or solving group problems or extraversion are no more than educated guesses. Research needs to pinpoint the crucial underlying dimensions. At a minimum, we should attempt to distinguish between qualities of co-operation and dependability associated with working with others, and abilities to take the initiative and direct others. Bowles and Gintis (1976) argue that traits such as dependability and acquiescence may be required and desired at middle level technical and managerial jobs, but decision-making and the ability to influence others may be required for upper level jobs in the corporate hierarchy.

To the extent that high school athletic and social participation carry over into adult activities, add enjoyment to our lives, and constitute potential occupational career assets, the prognosis on their value is favourable. This study suggests that the saying, "It's not the winning that counts, but playing the game," may have more sociological significance than one might expect.

REFERENCES

Alwin, D.F. and R.M. Hauser
1976   "The decomposition of effects in path analysis." American Sociological Review 40: 294-303.

Anisef, P., J.G. Raasche and A.H. Turrittin
1980   Is the Die Cast? Toronto: Ontario Ministry of Colleges and Universities.

Blau, P. and O.D. Duncan
1967   The American Occupational Structure. New York: John Wiley and Sons.

Bowles, S. and H. Gintis
1976   Schooling in Capitalist America. New York: Basic Books.

Buhrmann, H.G.
1972   "Scholarship and athletics in junior high school." International Review of Sport Sociology 7: 119-132.

Coleman, J.S.
1961   The Adolescent Society. Glencoe: The Free Press.

Hendry, L.B. and L. Douglass
1975   "University students: attainment and sport." British Journal of Educational Psychology 45: 299-306.

Jencks, C., et al.
1975   Inequality: A Reassessment of the Effects of Family and Schooling in America. New York: Basic Books.

MacKinnon, N.J. and P. Anisef
1979   "Self-assessment in the early educational attainment process." Canadian Review of Sociology and Anthropology 16(3): 305-319.

Okihiro, N.R.
1981   Community Colleges and Early Job Outcomes. Unpublished Doctoral Dissertation. York University, Toronto.

Otto, L.B.
1976a "Social integration and the status attainment process." American Journal of Sociology 81: 1260-1283.
1976b "Extracurricular activities and aspirations in the status attainment process." Rural Sociology 41: 217-233.

Otto, L.B. and D.F. Alwin
1977   "Athletics, aspirations and attainments." Sociology of Education
        42: 201-213.

Schafer, W.E. and J.M. Armer
1968   "Athletes are not inferior students." Transaction 5: 21-26, 61-62.

Sewell, W.H. and R.M. Hauser
1975   Education, Occupation and Earnings. New York: Academic
        Press.

Snyder, E.E. and Spreitzer, E.
1976   "Participation in sport as related to educational expectations
        among high school girls." Sociology of Education 50: 47-55.

Spady, W.
1970   "Lament for the letterman: effects of peer status and extracur-
        ricular activities on goals and achievement." American Journal
        of Sociology 75: 680-702.

Spreitzer, E. and M. Pugh
1973   "Interscholastic athletics and educational expectations." Sociology
        of Education 46: 171-182.

Turrittin, A.H., P. Anisef and W.J. MacKinnon
1980   "Social Inequality, Gender Roles and Educational Achievement."
        Paper presented at Annual Meeting of Canadian Sociology and
        Anthropology Association, Montreal, P.Q.

SECTION VII

THE CHARACTERISTICS OF SPORT PARTICIPANTS: TWO STUDIES OF RUNNERS

THE TWO PAPERS in this section provide profiles of two types of runners. William McTeer and James Curtis present data on the social backgrounds of marathoners, while Barbara Brown and James Curtis present profiles of recreational runners. The analyses show that in both cases runners are predominantly male, young, single and high in social status. It is interesting to note that patterns of social stratification evident in other sports are also present in running.[1] Thus, even in an inexpensive and accessible sport such as this one there are social and cultural barriers that prevent proportional representation from all social class, age and gender groups.

Brown and Curtis also address the question of why married persons are underrepresented among runners. Through carefully controlled statistical analyses, they show that this pattern is not a function of differences in age, education or commitment to running among married and single persons. That is, the pattern persists with very few exceptions across all categories of these variables and holds for men and women alike. Brown and Curtis suggest that the underrepresentation of married persons among runners is due to the incompatibility between family responsibilities and the time and emotional commitment often exacted by involvement in the sport.

1. For overviews of the stratification research, see any one of the several texts in the sociology of sport.

DOES RUNNING GO AGAINST THE FAMILY GRAIN? NATIONAL SURVEY RESULTS ON MARITAL STATUS AND RUNNING[1]

Barbara A. Brown, University of Western Ontario
James E. Curtis, University of Waterloo

THE LAST DECADE HAS WITNESSED a phenomenal increase in participation in running as a form of leisure activity in North America. Estimates from the 1976 Survey of Fitness, Physical Recreation and Sport indicate that 2,575,000 Canadians fourteen years of age and over had participated in jogging or running at least once in the month prior to the survey (Statistics Canada, 1980). This represented fifteen percent of the Canadian population. Jogging or running was the third most frequently reported exercise activity in this study, and temporal analyses suggested that it was continuing to grow in popularity (Statistics Canada, 1980). In addition, recent years have witnessed an upsurge in fitness promotion campaigns (e.g., *Participaction*) which support and encourage involvement in physical activity and more often than not include jogging or running among the suggested activities.

Despite the apparent popularity of running, little research effort has been directed towards understanding this activity as a social phenomenon. We know little concerning such basic sociological issues as the social backgrounds and recruitment patterns of runners (see McTeer and Curtis, in this volume). Our purpose in this paper is to present survey data on running activities in the general adult population which provide some accurate estimates of the types of people, sociologically speaking, who are involved. We will focus, for the reasons given below, on the relationship between marital status and running.

THE MARITAL STATUS-RUNNING RELATIONSHIP

The popular media have given us information which suggests the presence of a marriage-running relationship. This takes the form of reports on case study marriages. Runners who are married to non-runners and non-running spouses of runners have reported on how difficult it has been for them to carry on a "normal" family life of leisure, home-making and child-rearing when one spouse is investing so much time and emotion elsewhere. Other frequent themes in these reports have to do with problems in coming to grips with the life style and personality changes of the running partner and with his or her different schedule, different eating pattern, and different friends. Husband non-runners have emphasized how difficult it is to accept a more fit, more accomplished, and often absent running wife. Many testimonials along these lines have appeared in the press over recent years under such titles as: "Can Marriage Survive the Running Craze?" (Hoover, 1980); "The Loneliness of a Long-Distance Runner's Wife" (Los Angeles Times, 1980); "Marathon Mania: Running Against the Family Grain" (Plunkett, 1979); and "What Do You Do When Your Wife Is Always Running Around with the Boys?" (Schwartz, 1979).

Pursuing these issues in research that goes somewhat beyond the case study approach, Shipman (1980) surveyed about 200 runners at a local marathon. She found that marathoning appeared to have the effect of crystallizing what was already happening in the marriage relationship before the activity began or was intensified. Running seemed to act as a catalyst which accentuated or exposed differences in personalities and interests between the spouses. This had the possibility of therapeutic value for the couples, if the differences were adequately addressed by the couple. If the differences were not addressed, their accentuation spelled greater trouble for the marriages.

Shipman's report and the other evidence from the media give us valuable insights into how running affects family life, but they do not tell us how much of a relationship there is between marital status and running. Since the evidence is from couples or individual runners or spouses and does not involve representative samples of runners and non-runners, it cannot tell us if married people are actually less involved in running.

In the only survey studies of representative samples of runners that we are aware of, McTeer and Curtis (in this volume) found, consistent with the conventional wisdom, that married persons were under-represented among female runners in comparison to their proportions in the general female population. Male runners did not show a pattern of under- or over-representation for the married. In addition, and also consistent with conventional wisdom, marathoners were found to be overwhelmingly male, young, highly educated and of higher social status.

McTeer and Curtis (in this volume) interpreted their results on marital status by emphasizing that running is an activity which, by its nature, demands a fairly high level of time and emotional commitment, especially as participation increases in intensity or frequency. They argued that, for women especially and sometimes for men, the time and emotional commitments of running can become incompatible with other strong demands for time and emotions which follow from having a spouse, children and a job (cf. Blood, 1969, 1972). They further argued that, given a finite amount of time and energy, it may not be possible to reconcile all three commitments. In our society a job is virtually a necessity. Thus, if sacrifices are to be made in remaining areas, it may well be that either family or running is given precedence. For this reason, they argued, it is reasonable to expect an under-representation of married persons among runners.

The McTeer and Curtis study indicates that the married are under-represented among marathoners, an elite group of runners. Their results, however, may not extrapolate to recreational runners, where the demands on time and energy from running would be far less than for marathoners. For recreational runners, the conflicts with the demands from marriage may be far less evident. Moreover, because of limited sample size, McTeer and Curtis were unable to make marital status comparisons which were controlled in detail for sex, social class and age. This is important if marathoners are largely from the upper middle class and younger age groups. Comparing the proportions married among all marathoners, a homogeneous group, with the proportion married in the adult population, as they did, gives us only a very rough estimate of the representation of the married among marathoners because marital status differs by age and social class. The young are less likely to be married than the middle aged (or average aged) and, at some young age levels, those higher in social status are less likely to be married than those lower in status.

It is desirable for us to seek detailed controlled comparisons of runners and others in the adult population to establish accurate benchmarks for the marital status-running relationship. Comparisons for different intensities of running activity would be useful as well to determine if, extrapolating from the arguments of McTeer and Curtis, being married seems more problematic for those who are heavily involved in running. We now have available the requisite data for these types of analyses, and we present the results here.

Our working hypothesis, extrapolated from the arguments and findings in the McTeer and Curtis study, was that married persons would be under-represented among runners. Also, it was expected that the marital status distribution for runners would most closely approximate that of the general population at low intensity and frequency of participation in running and would be more similar to that of the marathoners at high intensity and frequency of participation. We also expected that runners would be disproportionately male, young, highly educated and of higher social status.

DATA SOURCE AND PROCEDURES

Our findings are taken from secondary analyses of the data derived in the 1976 Survey of Fitness, Physical Recreation and Sport. This study was conducted by Statistics Canada for Health and Welfare Canada using a supplement to the monthly Labour Force Survey. The survey, designed to provide comprehensive data on Canadian participation in fitness, sport and physical recreation activities, was administered to a sample of some 50,000 individuals aged fourteen years and over. The data are representative of Canadian residents fourteen years of age and over (see Statistics Canada, 1980 for further details). Only respondents aged twenty years and over were included in our analyses, to limit the sample to adults. The data from the survey were used to provide information on both individuals who reported involvement in running and the general adult population from which the runners were recruited.

The respondents were asked if they had participated in jogging or running during the month prior to the survey and, if so, how often and for what average amount of time. The answers to these questions provided our operational definitions of runners and frequency and intensity of running. Runners were defined as anyone who had participated in running in the past month (N=3481). Our other running measures are described below.

FINDINGS

Background Characteristics of Runners

Table 1 shows the social background characteristics of runners by sex and includes comparable figures for the general Canadian adult population. The respondents who participated in jogging or running during the month prior to the data collection were disproportionately male (61% were males and 39% were females), as expected. Also, the runners were concentrated in the lower age levels with over 50 percent less than 30 years of age and almost 80 percent reporting their ages as under 40 years. This pattern held for both males and females. The analysis also showed that overall and among both males and females, the runners were an elite group in comparison to the general adult population. They were highly educated, with over 30 percent being post-secondary graduates; this compared to 19 percent in the general adult population. Similarly, the proportion of runners in the upper income categories was greater than that for the general adult population. Over 20 percent of runners reported personal incomes in the upper ranges ($15,000 or more) compared to 12 percent of the general population. The status advantage of runners over the general population was also reflected in occupational status information. Greater proportions of runners compared to the general population were active in the labor force (77% compared with 61%) and reported being employed (72% versus 58%). Almost 18% of runners reported that they held positions at the professional or managerial level and another 50% had other white collar positions. Only 10% of the general population held managerial or professional positions with another 44% being employed in other white collar jobs. Each of these patterns of over-representation held in comparisons for both males and females.

In summary, the runners were concentrated in the younger age levels, and they were more highly educated and of higher status than their counterparts in the general population. In addition, running appears to be a male dominated activity with significantly fewer females participating. These results are as expected from the conventional wisdom and from the McTeer and Curtis study. They also reinforce our argument that con-

TABLE 1
Comparison Of Background Characteristics
Of Runners And The Adult General Population By Sex

	Runners			General Population		
	Male N=(2133) 61.3%	Female (1348) 38.7%	Total (3481)	Male (20380) 48.0%	Female (22047) 52.0%	Total (42427)
Age						
20-29 years	52.0%	52.9%	52.3%	26.7%	27.1%	26.9%
30-39	25.2	26.5	25.7	21.4	21.4	21.4
40-49	13.3	11.5	12.6	17.6	16.5	17.1
50-59	7.0	6.8	6.9	15.6	15.1	15.4
60-69	1.8	1.6	1.7	11.5	10.9	11.2
70 and older	.8	.8	.8	7.2	8.9	8.1
Education						
none or elementary	8.7	8.8	8.8	31.6	27.7	29.6
high school	38.7	44.0	40.7	40.1	45.9	43.1
some post secondary	16.4	13.2	15.1	8.7	7.3	7.9
post secondary graduate	14.3	20.4	16.7	9.9	13.8	11.9
university degree	21.9	13.6	18.7	9.7	5.4	7.5
Labor Force Status						
employed	84.9	51.7	72.0	77.2	39.6	57.7
unemployed	4.9	6.2	5.4	4.0	3.4	3.7
not in labor force	10.2	42.1	22.6	18.8	57.0	38.6
Occupation						
manager-professional	23.0	8.5	17.8	14.7	4.9	10.0
other white collar	35.9	74.0	49.5	28.5	61.5	44.3
blue collar	40.7	10.9	30.1	56.2	13.4	35.5
never worked	.3	6.7	2.6	.8	20.2	10.2
Personal Income						
none	3.0	17.7	8.6	3.1	24.8	14.4
<$9,999	37.1	65.4	47.9	47.4	65.4	56.7
$10,000-$14,999	29.3	11.6	22.6	26.7	7.1	16.5
$15,000-$19,999	16.2	3.9	11.5	13.2	2.0	7.4
>$20,000	14.4	1.3	9.4	9.6	.7	4.9

TABLE 2

Marital Status Of Runners
And The Adult General Population

| | Runners | | | | General Population | | |
	Male N=(2133).	Female (1348)	Total (3481)	Male (20380)	Female (22047)	Total (42427)
Married	66.8%	70.4%	68.2%	79.3%	74.5%	76.8%
Single	30.1	21.9	26.9	16.1	11.1	13.5
Other	3.1	7.7	4.9	4.6	14.4	9.7

TABLE 3

Percent Married By Sex And Age
For Runners And The Adult General Population

Age	Runners			General Population		
	Male	Female	Total	Male	Female	Total
20-24	29.1%	46.3%	35.7%	38.6%	58.9%	49.2%
25-29	73.2	76.5	74.5	77.3	82.4	80.0
30-34	85.9	87.4	86.5	87.7	87.2	87.4
35-39	86.6	87.4	87.0	91.6	88.6	90.0
40-44	87.7	85.7	87.0	91.0	87.1	89.1

trols are required in any accurate assessment of the relationship of running to marital status.

Marital Status and Running

Among the runners, 68% were married, 27% were single and 5% had "other" marital statuses. This compared with 77% married, 13% single and 10% other in the general population (see Table 2). Thus, consistent with the predictions based on conventional wisdom, runners were more likely to be unmarried than were members of the general population. However, unlike the findings of McTeer and Curtis, when marital status patterns were examined by sex, the same pattern was evident for each sex. Both males and females were more likely to report being married than any other marital status, but when compared with figures for the general population, the proportions of married runners were smaller than would be expected. 67% of male runners reported being married, and for female runners the proportion married was 70%. These figures compare with general population proportions of 79% married for males and 75% married for females.

Marital Status and Running with Controls for Age

Table 3 presents the results of an analysis of marital status patterns for males and females with age held constant. Sufficient numbers of cases were available for marital status comparisons at five age levels: 20-24 years; 25-29 years; 30-34 years; 35-39 years; and 40-44 years. Among male runners aged 20 to 24 years, 29% were married versus 39% in the general population. 46% of the female runners in the same age category were married compared to 59% of females in the national sample. 73% of male runners in the 25 to 29 year age group were married while 77% of those in the general population were married. For female runners, 77% were married versus 82% among their age counterparts in the general population. The proportion of married runners in the 30-34 year age group differed little from the proportion in the general population for both males and females. Slight differences were evident among those 35 to 39 years of age. Both male and female runners were 87% married compared to 92% and 89% for males and females, respectively, in the general population. In the oldest age category, 88% of male runners were married compared to 91%

in the national sample; 86% of female runners compared to 87% of females in the general population were married.

Thus, within nearly every age category considered, the proportion of married persons was smaller among runners than was true in the general population. This pattern held for both males and females (except in the 30-34 age category). The most marked differences between runners and their age counterparts in the general population occurred for women in the younger age levels.

Marital Status and Running Controlling for Education

We used education level as a social status control because this variable was more applicable to both women and men than were the personal income and occupation measures. When education was held constant the pattern of findings was somewhat different from those just described. Among those with no post-secondary education, 69% of the male runners were married, a substantially smaller proportion than their educational counterparts in the general population; 80% of the latter reported being married. Surprisingly, married persons were not under-represented among female runners in this educational category in comparison to their proportions in the general population. Among those who had at least some educational training beyond secondary school, the pattern expected on the basis of conventional wisdom was observed. Runners, in comparison to their educational counterparts in the general population, were less likely to be married (65% for runners compared to 74% in the general population). This pattern held for each of the sexes. Sixty-five percent of male runners were married versus 77% for males in the general population; 64% of female runners were married compared to 72% married for women in the general population. It is interesting to note that the difference in proportion of married runners compared to those married in the general population is higher among males (12%) than among females (8%).

Similar patterns were observed when comparisons were made for university degree holders among whom 76% of male runners and 64% of female runners were married compared with 81% of males and 68% of females in the general population. Further analyses which controlled for age and education simultaneously showed the same patterns of under-representation of married persons. The same was true of analyses using income or occupation as controls.

Thus, regardless of the sub-categories considered (in an age-, education- or sex-specific fashion) the analyses provided strong support for the conventional wisdom. Married people were under-represented among joggers and runners overall and for both males and females. This suggests that commitments to job and family leave little time for involvement in a recreational pastime which can demand a major time commitment on the part of participants. As the intensity or frequency of involvement in this activity increases, the demands on the finite amount of time available to individuals increases as well and they may impinge on other commitments. If this is so, it is reasonable to expect that the marital status patterns for those more heavily involved in running would show greater differences in comparison to those less involved in running and those in the general population. We turn, next, to analyses bearing on this issue.

Marital Status and Running Controlling for Intensity and Frequency of Running

Runners were categorized in terms of commitment to running in two ways. First, intensity of participation was used as a measure of commitment. Those runners who reported that they regularly spent more than 60 minutes running on each occasion were classified as high intensity runners; those who spent less than 60 minutes per run were classified as low intensity runners. By this definition, only 200 respondents, or .47% of the overall working sample fell into the high intensity category (.76% of all males and .20% of all females); 5.75% of all runners were high in intensity (7.27% for male runners and 3.34% for female runners.) As might be expected from the results presented above, the high intensity runners were younger and higher in education and socio-economic status than other runners.

Table 4 presents the percent married for runners in each category, by sex, and includes a panel with comparable figures for the general population. Among both low intensity and high intensity runners, married persons are under-represented in comparison to the population figures—68.6% of low intensity and 61% of high intensity runners were married compared to almost 77% in the general

TABLE 4

Percent Married By Sex Controlling For Running Intensity
For Runners And Comparisons For The Adult General Population

	Runners		General Population
	Low Intensity	High Intensity	
Male	67.2%	61.9%	79.3%
Female	70.8	57.8	74.5
Total	68.6	61.0	76.8

population. When marital status differences are examined for each of the sexes, it is evident that with increasing intensity of participation, both male and female runners are less likely to be married. At the low level of intensity, 67% of male runners reported being married, some 12% lower than the figure for males in the general population. At the high level of intensity the proportion of married males dropped to 62% or over 17% lower than the 79.3% of the general male population who were married. For females the differences related to participation intensity were even more striking. At the low level of intensity, 71% of female runners were married. This was only 3% lower than the 74% of females in the general population who were married. At the high level of intensity, however, only 58% of female runners were married, and this was 16% lower than the comparable figure for the general population.

Frequency of participation was used as a second indicator of commitment to running. Runners who reported participating 28 times or more in the month prior to the survey (i.e., almost daily) were classed as high frequency runners while those running less than 28 times were considered low frequency participants. Three hundred and five respondents were high frequency runners. This represented .72% of the overall sample (.92% for males and .53% for females) and

8.76% of the runners (8.81% of the male runners and 8.76% of the female runners). The high frequency runners were somewhat younger and higher in education and socio-economic status than other runners.

TABLE 5

Percent Married By Sex Controlling For Running Frequency For Runners And Comparisons For The Adult General Population

	Runners		General Population
	Low Frequency	High Frequency	
Male	66.5%	70.2%	79.3%
Female	70.7	67.5	74.5
Total	68.1	69.2	76.8

Similar to the findings reported with regard to intensity of participation, both runners classed as low and high frequency participants were less likely than individuals in the general population to be married (see Table 5). Unlike the findings related to intensity, however, a slightly higher proportion of those classed as high frequency participants were married (68.1% for low frequency and 69.2% for high frequency). These proportions compared with almost 77% of the general population who were married. However, breakdowns by sex revealed different marital status patterns for males and females with regard to frequency of participation. Although married persons were under-represented in comparison to the general population among males and females at both the low and high frequency levels, a greater proportion of males at the high frequency level were married (70.2%) compared with low frequency male participants (66.5%). For females, however, the pattern was reversed. A smaller proportion of females in the high frequency participants was married (67.5%) compared to the proportion of married women among the low frequency participants (70.7%). The proportion of married females in the high frequency category was almost 7% lower than their proportion in the general population. Further analyses controlling for age (not reported here) showed that the apparent anomaly of a higher married rate for frequent versus other participants among males resulted because the former were older on average.

SUMMARY AND DISCUSSION

The results of the present study provide support for conventional wisdom concerning the marital status and other characteristics of individuals participating in jogging or running. Runners were more likely to be unmarried, younger, more highly educated and of higher status than the general population and were more likely to be male than female. These patterns probably result, in large part, because flexible free time, a prerequisite for participation in leisure activities demanding some degree of time and emotional commitment, is more characteristic of young, unmarried and higher socio-economic status individuals. In addition, the more highly educated members of society are probably more likely to be health conscious and to be among the first to be aware of and affected by the media campaigns promoting health and fitness which have become more numerous in recent years. Also, through their higher status, they are more able to afford any financial costs involved in undertaking and maintaining participation in such activities. Male dominance in running should come as no surprise given, first, the sex-role socialization in our society which defines sport and physical activity as masculine territory and, second, the literature which suggests that females, especially married females with children, have less unobligated time available to them for participation in leisure activities because of multiple role responsibilities.

Our results show a consistent pattern of differences in the marital status of runners versus the general population in comparisons across appropriate subgroups. With very few exceptions (in no case did the proportion of married persons among runners exceed the proportion in the general population) married persons were under-represented among runners. Although the under-representation of the married was not as great as in the findings for marathoners reported by McTeer and Curtis (in this volume), the results are marked and consistent enough to indicate that there is a strong relationship between marital status and running, irrespective of the social subgroups studied. Unlike the results of the McTeer and Curtis survey, the under-representation of the married reported here clearly holds for males as well as for females. We, therefore, suspect that further detailed studies of marathoners will show an under-representation of married males.

The marital status findings for those runners with a high commitment to running showed even more marked under-representation of the married, as we expected. Again, this was true of both males and females. These findings suggest support for the interpretation that the time and emotional commitments involved in long distance running are incompatible with the responsibilities to spouse, home and others which married life entails.

Future research efforts should be directed towards examination of the various factors related to marital status which influence running behavior. There probably are several influences—children, the running involvement or non-involvement of the spouse, the amount of leisure time available, the flexibility of free time, and the type, range, number and intensity of other activity involvements. It will be important for future research efforts to focus on the separate influences of such factors on the running behavior of both males and females. There are likely to be sex-specific influences, meaning that the appropriate theoretical interpretations of the marital status relationship are somewhat different for males and females. Our data source did not allow us to pursue such issues very far, of course. However, these will be easily researchable in further in-depth comparisons of runners, ex-runners and non-runners of both sexes.

NOTES

1. Thanks are due Barry McPherson, William McTeer and Nancy Theberge for helpful comments on an earlier draft of this paper. We also gratefully acknowledge that the University of Waterloo made available computing funds for our analyses and that our data were provided by Statistics Canada through the Leisure Studies Data Bank at the University of Waterloo. Neither of these organizations is responsible for our analyses or interpretations.

REFERENCES

Blood, R.
1969 Marriage, 2nd Edition. New York: The Free Press.
1972 The Family. New York: The Free Press.

Hoover, E.
1980 "Can marriage survive the running craze?" People, January 16:33-34.

Los Angeles Times
1980 "Loneliness of the long distance runner's wife." June 16:14.

Plunkett, B.
1979 "Marathon mania: running against the family grain." Running, Winter: 11-15.

Schwartz, S.
1979 "What do you do when your wife is always running around with the boys?" Running Times, May: 11-12.

Shipman, C.
1980 "The effects of long distance running on the marriage relationship." Unpublished Master's thesis, LaVerne College.

Statistics Canada.
1980 "Participation in Jogging or Running, and Bicycling, October 1976." Statistics Canada: Education, Science and Culture, Division; Travel, Tourism and Recreation Section. Ottawa.

SOCIOLOGICAL PROFILES OF MARATHONERS[1]

William McTeer, Wilfrid Laurier University
James Curtis, University of Waterloo

THE RECENT POPULARITY OF MARATHONING is one of the more significant changes in the North American sport scene. It has been estimated that there are 350 certified marathons per year in North America, with about 50 of these taking place in Canada. One of the most popular, the New York City Marathon, has 16,000 entrants annually, and there are at least that many persons again who have their entries rejected because the race committee is unable to handle more than 16,000 participants. Because of the great number of applications for this race, entrants are accepted on a lottery basis. The most prestigious marathon, the Boston, uses specified qualifying times to limit the number of eligible entrants, and even with stringent requirements approximately 7,000 runners have entered this race in each of the past two years. The National Capital Marathon run in Ottawa, Canada has drawn between 3000 and 5000 runners in each of the last four years.

Despite the numbers involved in marathoning, we do not have answers yet to even very basic sociological questions about the marathoning phenomenon. For example, we do not have details on the social backgrounds of marathoners. Researchers have begun to gather some social psychological information on personality characteristics and reasons for running (see, e.g., Carmack and Martens, 1979; Glasser, 1976; Henderson, 1976; Kostrubala, 1977; Sachs and Pargman, 1979).

Our recent surveys of finishers (in 1979) and entrants (in 1981) in the Canadian National Capital Marathon allow us to begin to provide a sociological profile of marathoners, and our purpose in this paper is to supply this profile. We surveyed finishers once and entrants once in different years to determine whether the two categories of marathoners were particularly different in their sociological profiles. To anticipate our findings, differences were negligible between the two categories. Each sample showed the same patterns of over-and under-representation of social status backgrounds.

WORKING HYPOTHESES

Our working hypotheses were drawn from casual observations. These hypotheses involved the notions that a disproportionate number of marathoners are (1) male (2) young, (3) unmarried, and (4) from higher status jobs. We do, in fact, see large numbers of these types in marathons. But, it is still another issue to develop careful comparisons of marathoners and persons in the general population. These hypotheses are also suggested by one of the key aspects of the training of all marathoners—the large amount of time required. For example, to anticipate one of our findings, over 80 percent of our respondents in 1979 ran 40 miles or more per week in season; about a quarter of them ran 70 miles or more per week. It seemed clear that this type of time commitment could be made only by those with very flexible hours and great amounts of spare time. Flexible free time is probably more characteristic of those who are young, unmarried, and from higher socioeconomic statuses.

We also wanted to explore the current sport involvement and sport backgrounds of marathoners. We wondered if marathoners participated in other sports regularly, or if they were specialized in distance running. The heavy time commitment required for training for running might dictate the latter. We wondered if marathoners were encouraged to run following their participation in other similar sports. We thought that they might be largely from backgrounds in individual sports as opposed to team sports, i.e., from sports which have a high degree of affinity with competitive running.

DATA SOURCES AND PROCEDURES

Our surveys involved entrants and participants in the National Capital Marathon which is run in the spring in Ottawa, Canada. This is one of the most prestigious races in the country. The 1981 National Capital Marathon was the 7th annual running of the race, and it had about 4,500 entrants (about 4,100 completed the race). The 1981 survey was conducted using a questionnaire inserted into the National Capital Marathon entry package. About 50% of all race entrants (2,205) completed and returned the questionnaire with their race entry forms. The 1979 survey involved the mailing of a questionnaire to a random sample of one-half of the some 3,000 finishers in that year's National Capital Marathon. About 50% of the sample of finishers (or 773 of 1,500) returned completed questionnaires in 1979.

Data on the general adult population in Canada are also provided where these are relevant for comparative purposes. This information is taken from a Labour Force Survey conducted by Statistics Canada in 1978. The regular Labour Force surveys provide details on selected characteristics of a large (30,000 plus) representative sample of the nation's adults in order to monitor employment patterns and the characteristics of workers/non-workers (see Statistics Canada, 1971). This survey deals with persons aged 15 and older. We chose the 1978 survey for comparative purposes because, of those available, it was conducted closest in time to our marathoner surveys. We make the assumption that this sample is representative of the population of adults from which marathoners might be recruited.

FINDINGS ON SOCIAL STATUS BACKGROUNDS

Sex and Age Distributions

In each survey, only nine percent of the respondents were female. This is a slightly lower figure than the 11 percent of the entrants in 1981 who were females and slightly higher than the seven percent of finishers who were females in 1979. These figures may be compared with the slightly over 50 percent of the general adult population who are women. Obviously, women have a long way to go before representative participation is reached here. In information supplied by race organizers there was no evidence to suggest that women entrants finished the race at a greater or lesser rate than their male counterparts.

Because there was such a marked difference in the proportions of male and female respondents we will report our other results for each sex separately and will make note of any statistically significant male-female differences. The sexes could well differ on some characteristics. Where this is the case, the male patterns, only, would be reflected in the findings for males and females combined because of the far larger number of males among the respondents.

The results on the ages of the marathoners are presented in Table 1. The ages of the 1981 sample ranged from 10 years to 70 years with the average age being 34.9 years, while the 1979 sample ranged from 15 years to 75 years with the average age being, again, 34.9 years. There were significant differences in the ages of men and women, with women being younger on average. Over 70 percent of the women were under 35 years old in the 1981 survey and over 75 percent were under this age in the 1979 survey. Only 49 percent of the males were under 35 in 1981 while 55 percent were in 1979. Thus, the average age of about 35 in each sample was especially influenced by the involvement of males over 35.

To put the figures on age in some comparative perspective, we looked at the ages of elite marathoners listed in the *Canadian Marathon Annual* (Thomas, 1980). We defined the top marathoners by the best marathon times reported in this source. The average age of the top 50 Canadian male marathoners in 1979 was 28.12 years. The average age of the next best 50 males was 29.38. The top 50 women had an average age of 26.23. The next best 50 women had an average age of 26.66. Here, again, the women are younger than the men, and the average ages are somewhat younger than in our sample. Further computations from the data on the elite marathoners showed, as might be expected, that as performance declined (as times increased) the average age increased to figures over 30 years for both men and women, closer to the average age of our sample.

We wondered if the race finishers might be older on average than race participants in general: that is, younger participants might have dropped out of the race in larger proportions. However, when our sample of finishers (1979) is compared with our sample of entrants (1981), with the latter presumably containing both finishers and non-finishers, there is little difference in age. As we have shown, the 1981 sample has a smaller proportion under 35, but this may have less to do with younger persons not completing marathons and more to do with the aging of marathon participants.

The male and female finishers and entrants were young, however, compared to the age profile of the national sample (p<.001 for each sex for comparisons using 10-year age groups of marathoners and the same age groups in the national sample). In the general adult population the average age falls in the 40-44 range for both men and women; 49 percent of the male general population is under 35, while 46 percent of females are under this age.

Socio-economic Status

Information on the socio-economic status levels of the marathoners was supplied according to three criteria—personal income, occupational status (available for 1979 only), and educational level. The results are presented in Table 2.

Starting with income, Table 2 shows that about 75% of the 1981 sample reported that they had a yearly income of $20,000 or more; 31% reported $20-30,000; 22% reported $30-40,000; and 23% reported $40,000 or more yearly. The comparable figures for the 1979 sample were 63% at $20,000 or more and 12% at $40,000 or more. The greater income levels of the 1981 sample may be attributed to inflation and the general increase in salaries between 1979 and 1981. The females and males differed in income, with the latter having the advantage as might be expected from the patterns of earnings by sex in the society. For example, in 1979, 18% and 13% respectively of males were in the $30-40,000 and $40,000 plus categories compared to 4% and 3% of women in those categories. The findings by sex for 1981 show that a larger portion of the males are found in both the $30-$40,000 and $40,000 plus categories, 23% for each case. The females showed a large increase in their representation in these two income levels: 10% in the $30-40,000 range and 21% in the $40,000 plus category. Only about 4% of the national sample were in the $20,000 and over category, with about 8% of males and under 1% of females being at this level. By the income measure, then, the marathoners were overwhelmingly from higher socio-ecomic status levels (p<.001 for both men and women when comparing the marathoners and the general population, each with five income levels).

The findings on occupational status for 1979 show the same patterns as for income, as would be expected. As Table 2 indicates, 47% of the respondents reported that they held professional or managerial positions; another 34% had other white collar jobs. Again there was the same pattern of sex differences with 48% of the males as opposed to 31% of the females being at professional and managerial levels. Our national sample data did not have similar findings on occupations to allow comparisons.

High education was also the norm for each sample of marathoners; 68% in 1981 and 72% in 1979 had some university

TABLE 1

Age Distribution by Sex for Samples Of Marathoners from the
1979 and 1981 National Capital Marathons

Age Levels	Sample of Finishers in 1979			Sample of Entrants in 1981		
	Total Sample (767) %	Male (698) %	Female (69) %	Total Sample (2191) %	Male (1985) %	Female (206) %
10-14	0.0	0.0	0.0	0.2	0.2	0.5
15-19	4.5	4.5	4.5	3.1	2.7	6.8
20-24	8.4	7.2	20.9	8.5	7.9	14.6
25-29	18.5	17.7	26.9	14.3	13.3	24.3
30-34	24.4	24.5	23.9	25.6	25.6	24.8
35-40	21.6	22.5	11.9	25.4	26.0	19.4
41-45	10.6	11.4	6.0	11.1	11.7	4.9
46-50	7.2	7.3	6.0	6.4	6.7	3.9
51-75	4.5	4.9	0.0	5.6	6.0	1.0
			p=<.001[1]			p=<.001[1]

[1] The p values are for chi squares for the differences between the sexes.

TABLE 2

Socio-Economic Status and Marital Status of Marathoners by Sex for 1979 and 1981
Samples of National Capital Marathoners

Socio-economic and Marital Status	Sample of Finishers in 1979			Sample of Entrants in 1981		
	Total Sample (767) %	Male (698) %	Female (69) %	Total Sample (2154) %	Male (1953) %	Female (201) %
Current Yearly Income						
Less than $10,000	14.1	11.7	37.1	7.1	6.1	16.4
10,000 to 19,000	23.7	22.7	33.3	17.6	16.3	29.9
20,000 to 29,000	33.6	34.7	21.7	30.6	31.4	22.4
30,000 to 39,000	16.8	18.1	4.3	21.9	23.0	10.0
40,000 and over	11.8	12.7	2.9	22.9	23.0	21.4
			p=<.001			p=<.001
Education Level Completed						
Some Secondary	7.7	7.9	5.9	7.5	7.6	6.8
Completed Secondary	12.2	12.1	13.2	12.8	12.7	13.7

Some Community College	3.8	3.7	4.4	5.4	5.3	7.3
Completed Community College	4.6	4.6	4.4	6.8	6.6	8.3
Some University	13.8	13.8	14.7	12.4	12.5	10.7
Completed University	27.1	26.4	33.8	30.1	29.9	31.7
Graduate Studies	30.8	31.5	23.5	25.0	25.4	21.5
			p=n.s.			p=n.s.
Occupational Status						
Professional and Managerial	46.8	48.3	31.3	*	*	*
Other White Collar	34.0	34.9	37.3			
Blue Collar	5.7	5.8	4.5			
Farmer	0.4	0.4	0.0			
Housewife	0.8	0.0	9.0			
Retired	0.7	0.7	0.0			
Student	10.6	9.8	17.9			
			p<.001			
Marital Status						
Single	28.3	26.5	49.3	23.8	22.5	36.3
Married	64.7	66.5	46.4	68.2	69.8	53.0
Divorced or Separated	5.2	5.5	2.9	7.7	7.4	10.3
Divorced and Remarried	1.8	1.9	1.4	*	*	*
Widow/Widower	*	*	*	0.2	0.2	0.5
			p<.001[1]			p<.001[1]

* Data are not available from this study.
[1] The p values are for chi squares for differences between the sexes.

training, and 12% in 1981 and 14% in 1979 were working toward a university degree; 25% in 1981 and 31% in 1979 had an advanced university degree. Only about 20% in each survey, for each sex, had secondary school education or less. There was no appreciable difference between men and women in these respects. These figures show a marked over-representation of the highly educated when compared with the national data (p<.001 for both men and women comparing marathoners and the general population and using four education levels). The latter indicate that 9% of the population has university-level training, with 11% for males and 6% for females.

Marital Status

Table 2 shows that 68% in 1981 and 67% in 1979 were married, 24% in 1981 and 28% in 1979 were single, and 8% in 1981 and 5% in 1979 were divorced or separated. There were significant male-female differences in this regard for both surveys; 23% of males and 36% of females were single in 1981 and there are comparable figures of 27% and 49% in 1979. 70% percent of males and 53% of females were married in 1981 as were 67% and 46% of males and females in 1979. These figures compare with 65% of the national sample who are married; 64% of females and 67% of males are married. Therefore, married persons were under-represented among the marathoner females (p<.001), but not among the males.

FINDINGS ON SPORT BACKGROUNDS

Earlier Involvement in Sport

The marathoners seemed to have been very active in sport in their earlier years, and they appeared not to have been highly specialized in individual sports. In the 1979 survey the respondents were asked to report on their involvement in organized sporting activities in the school and community during the school years. About 79% reported that they were involved in one or more sports, and males and females differed very little (79% vs. 75%); 58% and 61% respectively of men and women were involved with one or more team sports. About 64% reported being involved with one or more team sports; 58% reported playing one or more individual sports; females were similar to males in both respects. Only 12% of men and 23% of women reported that they played only individual sports in the school years; 28% of men and 16% of women reported doing only team sports; 39% of men and 31% of women had done at least one sport of each type.

Track and field were the sports that most marathoners reported on for both males and females (42% of all respondents cited these), followed by football, hockey and basketball for men and basketball and volleyball for women. Other sports which received fairly frequent mention (i.e., were reported by more than 10% of the respondents) were soccer, cross-country running, volleyball and baseball/softball for men and badminton, cross-country running, field hockey, gymnastics and swimming for women.

Current Sport Involvement

About 76% of the 1979 respondents said that they currently participated in one or more other sports on a regular basis; 76% of men and 80% of women reported this. About one-half of the men and women (49% vs. 54%) were involved in multiple sports; 27% and 41% respectively played three or more sports. About 70% reported being involved in one or more individual sports and 31% reported playing one or more team sports. There were no female-male differences. About 44% of men and 49% of women reported that they played only individual sports; 9% of men and 1% of women reported doing only team sports; 24% and 17% said they did one or more of each. Thus, the marathoners do appear to be active in other sports; they are not highly specialized in running. They also appear to be specialized now in individual sports. There was more concentration of this type among women, probably reflecting the lesser availability of female team sport activities in the community. The most popular other activities for men were cross-country skiing followed closely by downhill skiing, tennis, squash, hockey and golf. For women they were squash and tennis, followed by cross-country skiing, cycling, swimming and downhill skiing.

The 1979 sample was also asked if they were members of a track club. Less than one-half (42%) said they were members, with no female-male differences. The average training miles per week were slightly higher for men than for women; 62% and 75% respectively did from 40-69 miles per week in season while 25% of the men and 10% of the women did 70 miles or more per week in season. During the off-season the weekly mileage dropped to the point where over one-half of the marathoners were running less than 40 miles per week, for both males and females.

The runners in each sample were asked how long they had been running regularly and how long they had been running marathons. The results by sex are presented in Table 3. As might be expected from the heavy training requirements of marathoning, most of the marathoners had considerable experience. About 70% of the males and 60% of the females in each survey had been running regularly for three years or more. Seventy to 75% of the males (depending on the survey) and 75 to 85% of the females had been running marathons for more than one year. A large majority of the males in each instance, but fewer of the females, had completed more than one marathon. Few males (about 4%) or females (about 2%) had run marathons for over five years, in either sample.

FINDINGS WITH CONTROLS
FOR PLACE OF RESIDENCE

It occurred to us that we should consider controls for place of residence in our analyses. We wondered if some of our patterns of findings on social status and sport backgrounds might result because the vast majority of our respondents had to travel some distance from their home towns to participate in the marathons. They might, for this reason, be selected from those with higher status backgrounds and more intense involvement levels of marathoning. The cost and effort required for travel might dictate the heavier participation of higher status and highly committed individuals in these marathons. If this were the case, we might expect local marathon participants to be somewhat different from travellers in their social and sport backgrounds.

We checked on these possibilities by replicating each of our analyses for the 1981 data with two controls for place of residence (place of residence was not asked in the 1979 survey). In one set of analyses we controlled for residence in Ottawa vs. residence elsewhere. In the other set of analyses we looked at the effects of place of residence measured as within 100 miles of Ottawa vs. 101-500 miles from Ottawa vs. a greater distance from Ottawa. Eighteen percent of the respondents were residents of Ottawa. Of those from outside Ottawa, 6% came

TABLE 3

Running Experience of Marathoners by Sex for the 1979 and 1981
Samples of National Capital Marathoners

Running Experience	Sample of Finishers in 1979			Sample of Entrants in 1981		
	Total Sample (767) %	Male (698) %	Female (69) %	Total Sample (2191) %	Male (1985) %	Female (206) %
Number of Years Running Regularly						
Less than 3	31.1	30.6	37.7	31.6	29.7	40.6
3 to 5	36.4	35.6	46.4	39.4	39.5	38.6
6 or more	32.5	33.8	15.9	29.0	30.2	20.2
			$p=<.01$			$p=<.01$
Number of Years Running Marathons						
Less than 3	82.4	81.4	94.1	66.0	64.5	81.8
3 to 5	13.8	14.7	4.4	29.6	30.8	16.5
6 or more	3.8	3.9	1.5	4.4	4.7	1.7
			$p=<.05$			$p=<.001$
Number of Marathons Completed						
0	*			15.3	13.2	36.4
1 to 2	65.7	64.0	81.1	42.4	42.6	44.6
3 to 5	23.6	24.8	14.5	26.4	27.5	14.7
6 or more	10.7	11.2	4.4	15.5	16.7	4.3
			$p=<.02$			$p=<.001$

[1] The p values are for chi square for differences between the sexes.
* All respondents in the 1979 sample had completed at least one marathon because the survey was for race finishers.

from within 100 miles of Ottawa; 75% were from 100-500 miles away; and 19% were from over 500 miles away.

The patterns of findings for social and sport backgrounds were essentially the same regardless of the distance of the runner's place of residence from the marathon site. For example, using the second three-level measure of distance, and considering analyses for the total sample and for each sex, there was only one statistically significant relationship between a social status variable and distance from Ottawa. For males, those living near-by were more likely to be married (84%) than those living at either of the two categories of greater distance (64% and 64% respectively) (p<.05). The only other statistically significant relationship showed that persons living nearby were less likely to have been doing some running for several years (p<.05 in analyses for the total sample) and less likely to have run several marathons (p<.005 for the total sample and p<.005 for the sample of males).

The findings with controls for place of residence suggest, then, that those who travel to marathons are more likely to be well experienced than local participants and that both locals and travellers show the same marked over- and under-representation by social status, marital status, sex and age.

CONCLUSIONS

Each of our studies show that marathoning is a sport of males, the young, the unmarried, the highly educated, and those with higher incomes. Comparisons with statistics on Canadian adults in general show these categories of people to be markedly over-represented among marathoners.

The over-representation of men among marathoners may be caused, in large part, by differences in time availability for the sexes. Married women, especially, may not have the time required for running after responsibilities to children, spouse and work are met. Our findings for marital status are consistent with this interpretation. Non-married persons were over-represented among marathoners for females, but contrary to our expectations this was not the case for males. This suggests that if there is a conflict between family responsibilities and training time it affects women most. This issue of timetable conflicts may help account for the female-male differences in participation, among married persons anyway. It is also possible that women find it difficult to get involved in marathoning partially because those who do participate now, and who could provide necessary guidance and information, are mostly men. These men may prefer to run with men.

While the marathoners were young, comparatively speaking, the average age of about 35 years old for all marathoners is probably not what we would expect from the image of the youthful marathoner who is relatively free of other responsibilities and able to devote time to running. This average age figure is also surprising judged against other findings showing that the practice of heavy physical activity in leisure time declines markedly with age from the late teens and early twenties on (see, for example, White, 1980). Probably these age findings bespeak a sport where extensive training and high level commitment is required. Normally, a year or more of training is required before one can successfully enter competition. Therefore, only the very committed are likely to endure this period of training. Because this amount of training is required, most marathoners probably try to persist in the activity for some time if they can. The women may show a younger age profile because they have entered the sport more recently.

Higher involvement in marathoning by the higher status groups is probably to be expected when one considers who has the large amounts of time which are required for proper training for this sport. Also, of course, higher status individuals have greater financial resources with which to facilitate their participation in running. And, those with higher education may be more aware of the health benefits of running.

Advocates of running and its benefits will wish that the findings on representation were otherwise. They will hope that things are changing in the direction of more widespread involvement in running and marathoning. They will prefer a more popular distribution of the sport across the social divisions of class, education, sex, age and marital status. Our results bear on changes over a brief time period if we can make two assumptions which seem reasonable: (1) that our research procedures for the two survey years are near-equivalent and (2) that the National Capital Marathon is equally representative of marathoning in the two years, 1979 and 1981. The two studies give no support for the proposition that marathoning is coming to have increased participation by females, the married, older persons, and those lower in education and income. The one exception is the somewhat greater participation by older males in 1981, but we have interpreted this as due to the "aging" of older runners. Moreover, when we replicated some of our analyses considering only those 1981 respondents who had been running regularly for less than three years we found that this group had similarly high levels of income and education. Thus, those marathoners who have begun lately look very much like those who have been in the sport for a while.

Perhaps we should not expect much change, though, over such a short time span. Or should we? We are often reminded that running and marathoning are undergoing rather rapid changes in increased popularity. This is no doubt correct, with the figures on the increased participation in the National Capital Marathon being but one indication. However, changes in the numbers involved appear not to have affected the mix of types of people who were running, at least in the short period that we were able to consider.

The results also clearly show that the marathoners were, and are now, involved in other sports, including some team sports quite unlike marathoning. There is no evidence to suggest that marathoners are narrow specialists in the one sport. Comparative data for the general population would be required to test this proposition conclusively, however. It is not surprising that track and field were most frequently mentioned as sports participated in at school, because of the similarity to marathoning. The popular team sports in the marathoners' backgrounds were fundamentally different from marathoning, though. However, these sports are the most popular school and community sports in Canada generally. So, perhaps it is not surprising that men and women who are active now enjoyed these sports when they were active earlier in life. The popularity of cross-country skiing as a current sport among marathoners is also understandable, since it is probably the closest alternative to running for those who live in snow-bound areas during the winter months. The other most popular sports, squash, tennis and golf, which have experienced great popularity recently are also activities of the higher social classes, requiring substantial financial outlays for club membership. As we have shown, most marathoners are quite economically advantaged. The frequent hockey backgrounds and current hockey activity of the marathoners are understandable, given the prominence of this game in Canadian culture.

The analyses presented here provide only a step towards understanding the recent popularity of marathoning. Further research should be directed toward understanding the recruitment process for marathoning. This research could be profitably begun with in-depth comparisons of samples of marathoners, those less intensely involved in running, others involved in sports, and those not involved in sports. It should also prove useful for us to monitor regularly the social status characteristics of marathoners, and changes, if any, in these.

NOTES

1. This paper presents a replication and extension of analyses in an earlier paper based on the first of the two surveys reported on here (Curtis and McTeer, 1981). We gratefully acknowledge that Wilfrid Laurier University and the University of Waterloo provided computing and other support for our two surveys and sets of analyses. We also acknowledge with thanks that the race organizing committee for the National Capital Marathon facilitated our research. Helpful comments were provided by Barbara Brown, Barry McPherson, and Harry Crockett.

REFERENCES

Carmack, M.A. and R. Martens
1979 "Measuring commitment to running: a survey of runners' attitudes and mental states." Journal of Sport Psychology 1:25-42.

Curtis, J. and W. McTeer
1981 "Toward a Sociology of Marathoning." Journal of Sport Behavior 4(2); 67-81.

Glasser, W.
1976 Positive Addiction. New York: Harper and Row.

Henderson, J.
1976 The Long Run Solution. Mountain View, Ca.: World Publications.

Kostrubala, T.
1977 The Joy of Running. New York: Simon and Schuster.

Sachs, M. and D. Pargman
1979   "Running addiction: a depth interview examination." Journal
       of Sport Behavior 2:143-155.

Statistics Canada
1971   Methodology of the Canadian Labor Force Survey. Ottawa:
       Statistics Canada, Publication No. 71-526.

Thomas, E.
1980   Canadian Marathon Annual. Ottawa:

White, P.G.
1980   Sport Participation Among Anglophones and Francophones
       in Canada. Unpublished Master's thesis, University of Waterloo.